Eyes of a Monster

In memory of Anthony Vito Milano (1961-1987), who always wanted to be famous.

Table of Contents

Prologue

There are men who walk among us, whose charm and charisma is legendary. Such men prey on the weak, the vulnerable, the broken and the emotionally tortured. Using their charms, they beguile the innocent and the naive for their own personal gratification. These ultimate persuaders, these social predators, are capable of anything when it comes to getting whatever it is that they want and whatever ends they seek to achieve. They are the Svengalis, the Don Juans who pride themselves in being career heartbreakers who ruin countless women's lives, leaving shattered dreams and permanently devastated victims in their wake. They are also the calculating, unfeeling cold-blooded killers who rail at the injustice of their own demise while thinking nothing of precipitating the demise of others. Able to be the consummate charmers, their eyes often mask the depth of their debauchery and deceit. Occasionally, their masks slip. The eyes are the window to the soul. Sooner or later, their eyes reveal their true nature, previously so artfully concealed. But for a brief moment frozen in time, we see them for whom and what they are. We see the blackness of their souls. We know we have looked into the eyes of a monster. On the night of December 14th, 1987 a young and promising artist from Bucks County, Pennsylvania looked into the eyes of a monster. He didn't live to tell about it. Nine years later, I looked into the eyes of that same monster. My life had been changed forever.

Chapter 1

"And the raven, never flitting, still is sitting, still is sitting on the pallid bust of Pallas just above my chamber door; And his eyes have all the seeming of a demon that is dreaming, And the lamp light o'er him streaming throws his shadow on the floor; And my soul from out that shadow that lies floating on the floor shall be lifted - nevermore." ~ Edgar Allen Poe (*The Raven*)

The cold mist of the early morning hours of December 15th, 1987 shrouded the woods on Ashby Avenue just off of Route US-13 in Bristol Twp. The trees bore silent witness to the most brutal murder ever to occur in Bucks County PA, whispering in acknowledgment in the cold winter night air as the mutilated, lifeless body of Anthony Milano lay under their silent gaze in the field grass, the earth beneath him drenched in blood that was being washed into the ground by the cold, steady pouring of a December rain. The most visceral, shocking murder in the annals of history in this eastern Pennsylvania community had unfolded and would rock the entire nation. People across America would become riveted to their TV screens, watching the retelling of this story on the Sally Jesse Raphael Show and Good Morning America. Anthony Milano would become the epitome of victim-hood in a gay-bashing of the most extreme nature this country would ever know. He would later become known as the "Matthew Shepard before Matthew Shepard."

Less than twenty-four hours later, a car sat abandoned and burning on Ashby Avenue just off of US Route 13. Officer Charles McGuigan of the Bristol Township police department responded to the call that came in around 11:30 PM on the evening of December 16th, 1987 about a suspicious car fire across the street from 1324

Ashby Avenue. Upon arriving at the scene, he confirmed the car to be a 1976 Chevy Nova registered to a Rose Milano. After the fire marshal arrived and extinguished the blaze, Officer McGuigan investigated the wooded area nearby and discovered the grisly sight of a nearly decapitated man with multiple gaping slash wounds to his throat, his left eye partially open in sightless reproachfulness. His face was swollen and bruised, marred with multiple cuts and lacerations. His arms were pinned underneath his back. It was a sight that would haunt Officer McGuigan for the rest of his life. The victim's wallet lay nearby with money still in it. Under his body lay a pack of Kool cigarettes. The pack of Kools didn't belong to him. He had a pack of Salem's in his shirt pocket. The pack of Kools was gathered and tagged as evidence. Since the pack was wet, the probability of getting fingerprints from it was low. The victim was identified as twenty-six year old Anthony Milano, son of Rose and Vito Milano of Levittown PA, who had reported him missing earlier that morning after he failed to call or come home.

Officer McGuigan recognized him as one of three patrons with whom he had briefly spoken the previous evening in the parking lot of the Edgely Inn where he had been dispatched to investigate a stolen car complaint. Except for the murderer and Jimmy Phillips, the young bartender and part-owner of the Edgely Inn, Officer McGuigan was the last person to see Anthony Milano alive. From what he could tell, it seemed as if the young man hadn't stood a chance against his assailants. It was also troubling because there was no apparent motive. Robbery was ruled out because Anthony's wallet still lay nearby with all of its contents intact and the car was set on fire instead of merely taken. The fire marshal ruled the fire was intentionally set – an act of arson.

Anthony Milano's parents would have to be notified. Their son was no longer missing. Officer McGuigan dreaded making this call. This would be the absolute worst Christmas imaginable for the Milanos, to learn their son had been the victim of a senseless, brutal murder without any reasonable explanation.

Anthony Milano was the only son of Vito and Rose Milano. Vito and Rose believed in the American system of hard work and education for getting ahead in life. Vito came to America in 1959 without a nickel in his pocket after meeting Rose in Bari, Italy when she and her parents were visiting her parents' birthplace in the old country.

After many years of working hard, he opened up his own business as a barber. He and Rose finally had their first born child - a boy whom they named Anthony Vito Milano, and eighteen months later they had their second child, a daughter whom they named Annamarie. The Milanos spent their lives building their children's futures, saving for their daughter's college education fund and building a fund for their son's tuition at the prestigious Philadelphia Art Institute. Anthony's talent as an artist became evident when he was a small child. Rose and Vito proudly encouraged and nurtured their son's natural creative abilities.

He was an intelligent, incredibly shy and sensitive mild-mannered boy with allergies and a creative flair. Exceptionally bright, he earned good grades in school and was a happy child. However, when Anthony reached his teen years, his laughter and smiles slowly were replaced with sadness and tears. High school years were hard for Anthony because he was a very gentle, mild young man who lacked athletic abilities and did not look overly masculine. He frequently had to be excused from gym class due to his allergies. This earned him ridicule by a gym teacher who jeered, *"Everyone head out to the field to play ball, while we leave Anthony inside to take care of the dishes"*. The gym teacher threw the ball hard at Anthony, hitting him in the stomach, taunting him in front of the entire class by sing-songing, *"What's the matter, Anthony? Is the ball too heavy for you?"*

Taunts from the gym teacher elicited snickers from Anthony's classmates, encouraging them to bully and ostracize him. After that incident he was never the same. His grades, which were always excellent, began to suffer as did his social life with classmates. Rose and Vito's young son would frequently come home from school and hole himself up in his room, playing his records loudly so that no one would hear him crying. Teen years are difficult for everybody, but they are especially hard for the youth who doesn't fit in. His unpleasant high school experiences of being teased and bullied were the saddest years of his short life. He decided to postpone going to college at the Philadelphia Art Institute because of his painful high school experiences.

In 1987 Anthony was just starting out at age twenty-six to pursue his career dreams as a commercial artist after completing a four year art degree curriculum in only three years. Life was so full of promise except for one major factor: his struggle with his own sexuality. He knew from the teachings of his family's church that homosexuality was a sin. It was not until he reached his mid twenties that he began to come to terms with his sexual orientation and was beginning to face his life as an independent young man.

News of Anthony's murder felled a frail Rose Milano. She sank into a heartbreaking depression from which she would never recover. Why had this happened to her gentle, thoughtful son who had never harmed anyone? She was so proud of her son who, as a small child, was featured as a wonder tot in *Philadelphia Daily News* for being able to read seventy-five words per minute. Rose Milano would eventually succumb to the grief over the loss of her son: she died of a broken heart in 1993. In a tragic way, it is merciful that Rose Milano did not live to see the day nineteen years later when one of her son's killers would be awarded a new trial by federal district court —and thus have to relive all the emotional carnage and the details of her son's murder for a second time.

Anthony did not have a malicious bone in his body and could never hurt a fly. He was a sensitive soul who was quiet and somewhat withdrawn and shy. He always sought to please others and avoided any potential for confrontation at all costs. One of his closest friends, a plump and good-hearted middle-aged lady, Orpah Newswanger from his Mennonite Bible study class, fondly recalled him as considerate and thoughtful to others' needs and feelings. Most of Anthony's friends were older women from his church who had children his age. They often admonished their own sons to be more thoughtful and considerate like Anthony. He gravitated towards those who didn't tease him, many who felt like social pariahs themselves due to weight problems or extreme shyness.

"He saw me as a whole person and treated me as a human being instead of just looking at me and only seeing a fat lady," one older woman from his church would later recall. She weighed close to six hundred pounds. Anthony would often sit with them over coffee, lending a sympathetic ear to their concerns and cheering them up. Orpah Newswanger was his most trusted confidante, except for his sister Annamarie to whom he first confessed his agonizing secret about his homosexuality. He sought Annamarie's advice in coping with it, and deciding whether or not to "come out" to his parents whom he did not wish to disappoint. Only his sister knew of his agonizing secret.

Many of the middle-aged women in the bible study class from his Mennonite church guessed about his sexual orientation but they refrained from ever mentioning it. To bring such a delicate matter up would be impolite and Anthony was their friend. To hurt his feelings or embarrass him in any way would have been unthinkable.

Anthony's body was examined by Bucks County pathologist, Dr. Raafat Ahmad. The official cause of death was listed as aspiration in his own blood. His delicate, finely sculpted face was cut, bruised and swollen. His teeth had been punched or kicked in. The base of his skull was fractured from trauma, possibly caused from being struck with a blunt object. His brain had swelled. He had three cerebral hemorrhages. His larynx and thyroid had been cut out. His throat had been hacked to shreds in frenzied slashes too numerous to count. All that was left of his neck was a jagged, gaping hole. His throat was cut to the spinal cord severing the C-5 and C-6 vertebrae. It was as if a great white shark had taken a bite out of him.

Whoever had attacked him nearly cut his head completely off. Death was a slow lingering. The forensic pathologist determined that it took Anthony Milano ten to fifteen minutes to die by drowning in his own blood. Official time of death was listed to have occurred between 3:15 AM and 3:30 AM on December 15th, 1987. Anthony was only five foot six and weighed one hundred fifty pounds. Whoever attacked him was an assailant against whom he never stood a chance. His last moments spent struggling for his life were filled with terror as he died an agonizing, torturous death — alone in the cold December rain and mud in a desolate field in the Venice-Ashby area of Bristol, unable to cry out for help.

Even if Anthony's throat would not have been slashed, the severe beating that fractured the base of his skull causing his brain to swell would have killed him; or left him in a permanent vegetative state. Had he lived, he would have never regained any semblance of a normal independent life. His gentle dark sloe gin eyes that saw the beauty in the world he portrayed through his drawings would never see again. The last sight this young artist's eyes beheld were the deadpan eyes of a psychopath with no value for human life — a monster who murdered him in cold blood just ten days before Christmas.

Bristol Township police officers took turns staying with the body and securing the crime scene until daybreak when Anthony's body could be photographed and removed for pathology examination. Officer McGuigan and two fellow policemen immediately recognized Anthony Milano as one of the patrons questioned less than twenty-four hours ago while at the Edgely Inn during the investigation of the stolen car complaint. Officers McGuigan and Newsinski also distinctly remembered Frank Chester and Rick Laird — the two menacing ruffians seated near Anthony at the bar.

When McGuigan and Newsinski went to the Edgely Inn at 1:30 AM on December 15th, 1987 to question the patrons as part of their investigation about a stolen car reported as being in the Edgely Inn's parking lot, Rick Laird immediately got surly and belligerent when asked politely by McGuigan to produce some ID. Laird was not singled out: everyone was being asked for their ID. It was a routine investigation and everyone else in the tavern at the time politely cooperated — except this hulking brute who rudely responded, "Fuck you. Why don't you go do your fuckin' job and leave us alone?" Although McGuigan had two other patrolmen with him for back up, the potential for an ugly physical confrontation with Rick Laird was a situation McGuigan wanted to avoid if possible. A scruffy-looking kid in a football jersey standing between Rick and the police officer intervened, "Yo Rick, relax dude. They're just doin' their job." Rick backed down, "We're not doin' nothin'. We're just havin' a couple of beers." Rick dropped his piercing glare from McGuigan's eyes. He gave his name as Rick Laird and his address as being across the street from the bar in the Ambassador Arms apartment complex on Haines Mill Road.

The smaller, scruffy kid in the football jersey who was trying to be a peacemaker calming his friend down was Frank Chester. He stated he didn't have a driver's license on him but lived up the road on Lovett Avenue in Tullytown and the bar kept an LCB form on file with his information on it should the police wish to see it.

Meanwhile, the clean-cut small man seated with Rick Laird and Rick's buddy Frank Chester had politely complied without question, showing McGuigan his drivers' license. The officers studied Anthony Milano's drivers' license. He looked so different from these other two men with whom he was sitting. He certainly wasn't antagonistic, foul mouthed or uncooperative like Rick Laird. A good kid. No criminal record, not even any outstanding tickets. McGuigan was still finishing his police report in his patrol car an hour later in the parking lot in front of the Edgely Inn when Rick Laird, Frank Chester and Anthony Milano left. He remembered seeing Anthony getting into the driver's seat of the Chevy Nova while the bigger and rougher looking of the two men got in the car to ride shotgun, his buddy climbing into the back seat. Anthony, clean-cut, wearing a black jacket over a stylish button-down shirt and pinstripe designer jeans letting the slattern, large, bearded, tattooed leather jacket-clad biker-type man and his smaller, scruffy-looking disheveled buddy into the Chevy Nova and driving off into oblivion on the cold rainy night, was a strange sight. "Talk about a rose between two thorns," Officer Newsinski remarked to McGuigan as they watched the trio pile into the black 1976 Chevy Nova after the Edgely Inn closed at 2:30 AM on that fateful night.

It was obvious to the casual observer that Anthony was a different caliber of man than the two who got into his car with him. What an odd looking threesome, McGuigan thought to himself. Pulling out a copy of his notes recalling the questioning and identification of the decedent and the other two men in his company at the Edgely Inn, Officer Charles McGuigan already had two immediate suspects. The last persons known to have seen Anthony Vito Milano alive were the two men seen climbing into Milano's black 1976 Chevy Nova. They were 24 year old Richard Roland Laird who lived in the Ambassador Arms apartment complex on Haines Mill Road in Bristol and 19 year old Frank Robert Chester of Lovett Avenue in Tullytown, both which are part of Bristol Township.

Chapter 2

"For in that sleep of death what dreams may come, when we have shuffled off this mortal coil, must give us pause." ~ William Shakespeare (*Hamlet*)

District Attorney Alan Rubenstein was at home in bed when he was roused from his sleep by Bucks County Chief Detective Frank Dykes to head up the investigation into this grisly and apparently motiveless murder. Alan Rubenstein had been a prosecutor for sixteen years for Bucks County, Pennsylvania. Extremely meticulous, known for his attention to detail, he was a man who took the responsibilities of his job as a prosecutor very seriously. He had a rule for protocol to be followed in any homicide: that he receives a call immediately, regardless of the time of day or night.

"Boss, we have a murder", Detective Dykes relayed the gruesome details of the murder and the condition of the victim's body to Alan Rubenstein on the phone. Fully awake, sitting up and lighting a cigarette, Rubenstein sat horrified as his chief detective told him of the macabre murder scene. It seemed to the district attorney like a cross between Edgar Allen Poe's *Fall of the House of Usher* and an *X-files* episode. In his distinguished career as a district attorney in Pennsylvania's wealthiest county, he had never encountered a homicide as brutal and senseless as this one.

A killing over money, a jealous rage, drugs or car theft can be rationalized. You can understand — but not condone — someone getting shot in the head when robbery, drugs or dispatching a romantic rival is the motive. But Anthony Milano was not killed for his car. Nor was he killed over an apparent drug deal gone sour. Further checking into the victim's background revealed that he had no prior criminal record, not even any traffic tickets. He was not relieved of any of his personal possessions, not even his watch or the contents of his wallet amounting to $10.50. That ruled out robbery as the motive.

Furthermore, he was not killed by a simple quick act such as a shooting. He was viciously beaten, kicked, punched, bludgeoned, and slashed repeatedly with a knife. His throat was completely gone as if hacked out in a crazed frenzy. His car, which was deliberately set on fire, was not stolen. The car fire was intentionally started, possibly to cover up clues about the homicide that might identify the perpetrators. This was an act of lunacy, utterly psychopathic. Jack the Ripper himself would have been impressed, having found his fiendish style nearly outdone. Rubenstein wanted to ensure the guilty parties would be made to answer for this. He gave Detective Dykes the thumbs up to do whatever it would take to bring in Rick Laird and Frank Chester. No stones were to be left unturned. He wanted to ensure very "i" was dotted, and every "t" was crossed.

Within less than one week, Bristol police would get a series of mysterious calls from "friends" who asked what they should do if they knew certain things about the night of the murder. It became clear at that point to Alan Rubenstein that one of the killers was a talker due to all these anonymous calls from these "friends".

Armed with the stolen car police report from patrolman Charles McGuigan documenting the names and addresses of Frank Chester and Rick Laird, the last known persons seen with the decedent, Alan Rubenstein had probable cause to bring Frank Chester and Rick Laird in for questioning. Rubenstein had a statement from a bartender and a police report showing that the victim left the bar with both Chester and Laird. Rubenstein believed that if he gave the "talker" enough rope, the killers would hang themselves. He collaborated with Detective Dykes to accomplish just that. His plan would be to wait for the killer or the killer's friends to talk again. The challenge for the investigation and the prosecution would be to crack the "Croydon Code", an unofficial code of silence.

This Croydon Code was a tactic employed by Bristol Township's working class people when dealing with any level of authority, especially law enforcement personnel. Croydon is a rough blue-collar, tight-knit community near Levittown and Philadelphia. One of the *mores* of Croydon was that you just don't talk to the police. You don't know anything if asked. And you never trust anyone in a suit - period. Due to so much class bias in our society, which carries over into the criminal justice system, it is not surprising to see an "*us versus them*" attitude among working class people, especially among young adults. One need not be a genius to see that our prisons house far more members of the lower classes than the upper ones. This is not because the poor are more predisposed to committing crimes. Rather it is because they have more difficulty extricating themselves once entangled in the system because good legal representation doesn't come cheap. For those in the lower income brackets, access to legal help is non-existent.

Much of this distrust of authority by lower socioeconomic status people stems from prevalent classism that is deeply ingrained throughout all levels of our society. Poverty profiling in hiring practices is not uncommon. Those who become police officers tend to come from middle class families with an "in" for a job with the municipality. Members of the middle class also tend to have a strong value and respect for authority. The same holds true for those who become probation and parole agents. The upper classes, which arguably include the upper-middle class professionals with advanced college degrees, tend to look down on the uneducated and write them off as those whose opinions don't count. Such condescending arrogance bleeds through polite veneers. Class bigotry held by many in the ranks of the diploma'd elite is not unnoticed by the lower classes, most of whom find a college education to be financially out of reach.

Young people are not stupid. By the time they reach junior high and high school, they know where they stand in the socioeconomic pecking order. Snooted, excluded and always to blame for everything, kids from the lower socioeconomic classes begin to internalize resentment and develop apathy at tender ages. All they really have are their fragile egos, which they fiercely guard by demanding respect. Therefore, it should be no surprise that young males from the lower socioeconomic groups are overprotective of their masculinity and are far less comfortable with anything they perceive as an affront, challenge or assault to their manhood. Prime examples of potential threats to working class males' masculinity is the effeminate male, the homosexual, and women's liberation.

While none of this excuses the level of homophobia that culminated in the cruel slaying of a young man who was perceived to be gay, it sheds some light on the origins of such attitudes. It may help to give us a better understanding as to what we can do in our communities to prevent future occurrences of the kind of brutality that was meted out to Anthony Milano, and later to Matthew Shepard. Having some understanding of this complex social group thinking regarding classism can also help law enforcement personnel overcome barriers such as the "Croydon Code" in their stalwart efforts in making our communities safer places to be.

Meanwhile, until the killers or their friends and associates talked again, the investigators would talk with Jimmy Phillips, the young bartender at the Edgely Inn who closed up on December 15th, 1987 — the late night/early morning of the murder. Except for the two prime suspects, Rick Laird and Frank Chester, Officer Charles McGuigan and Jimmy Phillips may have been the only people to have seen the victim alive before his killers ruthlessly dispatched him and left him to die in a desolate wooded lot in the crime-ridden drug infested poorer region known as the Venice-Ashby projects. There was also the distinct possibility that the victim had been attacked by someone other than Chester and Laird. The illicit economy is brimming with cutthroats, and the Venice Ashby projects were a breeding ground for that. It was possible that whomever the trio tried to meet on Ashby Avenue was the culprit. This alternative possibility would make Chester and Laird witnesses. But it was unlikely. Two fearless toughs like Chester and Laird would not simply stand by while someone else killed Milano – unless they were in on it.

Detective Dykes and Alan Rubenstein were correct in their initial assessment of Chester and Laird as prime suspects wanted for the questioning in Anthony Milano's murder. Upon speaking with Jimmy Phillips and other patrons of the bar where all three men were last seen together alive, Rubenstein began putting the missing pieces of the puzzle together. There *was* indeed a motive for this murder. Bristol police and Detective Frank Dykes had their suspects, and the motive for the crime: the victim was thought to have possibly been homosexual and as such, met his demise due to foul play by a couple of gay-bashing bigots. The pieces began to fit as the story unfolded.

The story actually began in a predominantly blue-collar working-class community in southeastern Pennsylvania with a couple of men struggling to defend their machismo and sexuality in a macabre drunken male bonding ritual, and a third man struggling to come to terms with his sexual identity. This is not merely another gruesome tale of murder; it is also a story of men. Three men who were striving to come to terms with who they were, trying to find their place in society, and in the world.

It is also a story about a personal journey: A journey that was undertaken in the quest for social justice. It is a story about coming to terms with truths too uncomfortable to face.

It ends not with this murder nor the subsequent conviction and sentence, but with a plethora of unanswered questions for us all as we try to comprehend what could possibly cause some of those who walk among us to become monsters in the first place. Monsters do not dwell in the recesses of our imagination. They walk among us, cold and calculating, bereft of any sympathy or compassion for another human being.

It is through the retelling of the events on the evening of December 14th, 1987 by witnesses as stated in police reports and news articles, given in the original trial testimony from May of 1988, recounted to me in interviews, and subsequently in testimony given during Rick Laird's February 2007 retrial, that the murder of Anthony Milano unfolds. It is also through my own personal involvement in the case during the appeal phase, and my own experiences surrounding it.

Chapter 3

"It is the high esteem we naturally have for violence, force. It is what makes us effective, men whose judgment impinges on others, on the world." ~ Jack Henry Abbott (murderer, author of *In the Belly of the Beast*)

The Edgely Inn was a thriving tavern nestled along route US-13 in Bristol Township between Bristol, Tullytown and Levittown - small blue-collar working-class Bucks County communities. Above the door was a sign, "The Edgely Inn Motto: *He who drinks and drinks with grace is always welcome in this place. He who drinks more than his share isn't welcome anywhere.*"

Known for reasonably priced good food and drinks, the Edgely Inn was a favorite watering hole for local residents. Jimmy Phillips was a quiet, sensible young man who worked to keep this small business that his father built up to be a successful tavern many years ago. When the local television news station splattered the gory details on the six o'clock news of the murder of Anthony Milano, the quiet young man who had just been in the other night for a beer and a sandwich after a Bible study class, Jimmy Phillips was shaken. His heart sank into his stomach as he sensed that the murderer was one of the men who had been in his bar with the victim. Jimmy had had an awful premonition that the two men who left with Anthony after pushing him for a ride home were up to no good. Years of working as a bartender had honed Jimmy's ability to read people pretty well. Rick Laird and Frank Chester, two local young toughs, had been in his bar before.

Frank was a fairly congenial and likeable kid who never caused trouble, at least not as long as he was alone. While Frank had never really been a serious troublemaker, it was Frank's sidekick Rick Laird that concerned Jimmy. Rick was a hulking, solid figure built like a football line backer who stood six feet four inches tall and weighed about two hundred forty pounds. His unkempt beard and shoulder length hair gave him a look somewhat like a psychopathic version of Grizzly Adams. He was also an aggressive bully who had frequently become boisterous and confrontational if he woke up on the wrong side of bed that day or if he simply didn't like your looks.

On the evening of Monday, December 14th, 1987 Jimmy Phillips, Jr. got to work at his father's bar later than usual. A neighboring bar was hosting a shuffleboard tournament and Jimmy's team was short a member. Although he knew that he should be relieving the day shift bartender who only worked part time, Jimmy figured it wouldn't do any harm to fill in for the absent shuffleboard team member next door. After all it was a Monday night and Monday nights are usually dead because people have to get up early the next day to go to work, so he did not expect the Edgely Inn to be busy. He was not on duty when Rick Laird and Frank Chester, accompanied by Rick's fiancée Barbara Anne Parr, her nine year old son David, and Frank's pretty seventeen year old friend Gale Gardner arrived at the Edgely Inn. Nor was Jimmy present when the other bartender allowed nine year old David to be served several shots of Wild Turkey, which is illegal since minors cannot be served in bars according to Pennsylvania state law. The fact that a bartender allowed underage people, including a nine year old child to be served alcohol in the

Edgely Inn later figured prominently in a *dram shop liability*[1] action against the tavern's owners.

Barbara Anne Parr, an attractive and petite young woman with light brown shoulder length hair, began arguing with Rick over his giving her nine year old little boy, David, shots of alcohol. This was something she definitely didn't approve of. Formerly Barbara Anne Kessler, she and Rick had known each other since they were thirteen years old. They even lived in the same neighborhood in Levittown, PA. But their world was far from innocent and carefree, even as tender adolescents.

Levittown was a blue-collar steel mill and factory town near the Pennsylvania-New Jersey border along the Delaware River. It was a planned suburban community comprised of small, meticulously landscaped lawns and Cape Cod homes built by a man named William Levitt, often referred to as the "Henry Ford of housing", during the 1950's, a period when the American middle class had been at its most prosperous and largest in numbers throughout American history. Levittown was the epitome of affordable home ownership. It symbolized the Americana of suburbia and backyard barbeques to many who sought a little slice of the pie with their hard-earned factory paychecks.

When the factories began to close in the late 1970's and early 1980's and the jobs vanished due to NAFTA and GATT and disappeared into the mists of globalism, an underground economy took root. A notorious outlaw motorcycle gang known as The Breed infiltrated and plagued the neighborhood where Barbara Anne and Rick grew up. The Breed ran one of the biggest methamphetamine rings in southeastern Pennsylvania.

---

[1] *Dram shop liability* : refers to the body of laws governing the liability of taverns, liquor stores, and other commercial establishments that serve alcoholic beverages.

Methamphetamine, commonly known as “meth” or “speed”, was often thought of as the poor man’s cocaine. Gradually, crime infested the small and formerly peaceful suburban town.

By the time Barbara Anne was fifteen years old, she was pregnant with a child from a relationship that only lasted about five months. Then George Parr, the president of The Breed and just released from federal prison on drug charges, claimed Barbara Anne for his own. George Parr was twenty-two years older than she. During the five years that she was the wife of George Parr, Barbara Anne was a princess in a world where the princes rode Harley Davidsons and the princesses knew their place.

When Barbara Anne divorced George Parr, she met Rick Laird again. He had been dating her sister, Kim. At first, she thought Rick was a little too loud and obnoxious for her. She was a young struggling single mother who wanted a better life for herself and her small child than the world of drugs, brawls and arrests which disproportionately plague the poorer working class communities that suffer significant job losses. But Rick was persistent. And he was very charismatic. He finally won Barbara Anne over and she fell deeply in love with him. He could have schooled Rasputin in the art of seduction. When Rick ended up back in prison on a parole violation, he began romancing Barbara Anne in earnest and thus they began their relationship with letters back and forth through the prison inmate mail system. In one of his letters to Barbara Anne, he announced his intentions to care for her and her little boy whom he would accept and raise as his own. Barbara Anne broke the news to her sister Kim, who had begun dating someone else.

When Rick was released from prison, he and Barbara Anne got an apartment together. That was in 1985, almost two years before the night of Milano’s murder. Meanwhile, Rick was still legally married at that time to his estranged first wife, JoAnn Laird (née Walters). JoAnn was the mother of two young children by Rick and she was adamantly refusing to sign the divorce papers. Rick Laird sure had a way with women. Now two years later, he finally had Barbara Anne: the woman he had always wanted, the woman who was having his baby. But what did he want to do on this rainy Monday night a week or so before Christmas? He wanted to go out and get drunk, carousing around in the bars with Barbara Anne's newly single cousin, Frank Chester, instead of staying at home with her.

Rick was impossible to talk to when he drank, so Barbara Anne Parr simply took her little son David, who was now beginning to get sick from the liquor, and left for the apartment she shared with Rick. She headed across the street towards the Ambassador Arms apartment complex with her son and Frank's friend, Gale Gardner. Barbara Anne was seven and a half months pregnant with Rick's baby and was under doctor's advice to be on complete bed rest due to a very difficult pregnancy. The last thing she needed was the added stress of an argument with her man, especially when he had been drinking all afternoon.

She knew Rick had a troubled past with a penchant for fighting as well as drug and alcohol abuse, and that he had had more than just one run-in with the law. He certainly was no angel in most people's eyes. But when he was with her and her nine year old son David, Rick seemed so happy and contented. Rick took little David to Great Adventure, the shopping malls and to Halloween hay rides. Rick even helped him with his homework, too. David began calling the gruff biker who was now in his mother's life "Dad". When there were parent-teacher conferences at little David's school, it was Rick Laird, clad in his black leather jacket and biker boots who attended; taking a sincere interest in the child's education.

Barbara Anne thought that as long as Rick was not being influenced by the party animal crowd, he was wonderful to her and to her little boy. Her theory was that as long as Rick wasn't out with his buddy - her cousin - Frank Chester, and rest of the partying crowd, Rick would be content to stay at home with her enjoying a simple and tranquil domestic life, the life she thought Rick really wanted. But Rick wasn't interested in being a tranquil homebody tonight. He had already had more than he should have had to drink and was becoming an obnoxious bully. Now her little boy wasn't at home doing homework. Instead he was sick from drinking shots of Wild Turkey.

Rick was in one of his loud, argumentative moods and Jimmy just wished Frank would get Rick to just leave. Throughout the evening, as Rick and Frank got progressively inebriated between shooting games of billiards, Rick called another patron with whom he played pool "pussy" and "faggot" as he got sore when the other man was winning at the game. Rick yelled for all the patrons in the bar to hear, that if his opponent kept winning at the pool table, he would "ram a pool stick up his ass and turn him into a Popsicle". He got so rowdy that he bounced a billiard ball off of the pool table. Jimmy thought about asking Rick and Frank to leave because other patrons were clearly beginning to get uncomfortable, but he hesitated. Jimmy was not any sort of tough guy. He wasn't afraid to stand up for himself, but he didn't particularly relish the prospect of a serious physical confrontation with someone as formidable as Rick Laird.

Jimmy was small, like Anthony Milano, weighing only around one hundred fifty pounds. He stood at only about five foot six compared to Rick's six foot four and a half. Rick outweighed him by close to ninety pounds. He didn't want to invite a confrontational situation when it would soon be closing time anyway. Then he would be rid of this Neanderthal who had the manners of swine and the disposition of a moose in rutting season. Rick's appearance matched his demeanor with his leather jacket and unkempt beard that matched his wild-looking shoulder length chestnut brown hair. As the evening progressed, the other patrons gradually began leaving the Edgely Inn. It had been one of those nights.

It was around 11:30 PM when the petite, quiet, unassuming and clean-cut Anthony Milano arrived at the bar for a beer and a cheesesteak after his Bible study class at Orpah Newswanger's home. Rick nudged Frank, looking across the bar in Anthony's direction and snickered. In addition to sporting a neatly groomed mustache and stylish haircut, Anthony appeared effeminate because he was slender and small and had a smooth looking face with a picture-perfect smile.

He was suspected of being gay by the two young sloppily dressed toughs who occupied the two bar stools at the end of the bar near the entrance. Anthony went to the other side of the bar and sat down to order a beer and a cheese steak. After putting up with Rick Laird all evening, Jimmy wished more of his customers could be like Anthony who was always quiet, kept to himself, ordering a sandwich with a beer, minding his own business as he ate and drank, and tipping well when finished.

Rick and Frank giggled between themselves as they shared their third pitcher of beer. "Merry Christmas!" Rick yelled at Anthony from across the bar. Anthony meekly replied in kind, "Merry Christmas" while trying to avoid making eye contact with the huge, rough-looking bearded biker type guy and his scraggly-looking sidekick in the football jersey. "What did ya say?" Rick shouted menacingly at the much smaller quiet man. Anthony repeated his 'Merry Christmas' greeting a little louder than he said it the first time. Anthony could feel the piercing stare of the huge man's eyes burning holes through him. There was no well-intentioned holiday wishes or friendly spark of merriment in Rick's eyes as he fixed a steely, unwavering stare on Anthony, "If you mean that you'll come over here and buy us a drink."

Rick and Frank were already drunk from an entire day of partying, beginning with a couple cases of beer they previously consumed while at Frank's new apartment and were working on their third pitcher of beer at the bar. The last thing either of those two men needed was another drink. Rick ordered first, "I'll have a shot of vodka", then Frank ordered his drink, "Jack Daniels", and then Anthony ordered a shot of Sambuca for himself. Frank and Rick exchanged glances with raised eyebrows as if to say, *'What's that? A pussy's drink?'* Anthony, sensing the tension and the need to justify his choice of drink added, almost apologetically, "It's licorice. My family toasts with it on holidays." Anthony got up to go to the restroom. Rick turned to Frank and said "I hate fuckin' faggots!" loudly enough for Jimmy the bartender and another patron - a regular, to hear from the other side of the room where Jimmy was restocking the beer coolers.

After Anthony returned from the bathroom, Rick decided he wanted to have some fun with him. "Let's do another shot," Rick ordered, in a dictatorial tone as he poured Anthony a beer from the pitcher he had been sharing with his friend Frank. Anthony had finished his cheese steak and beer and the first shot and did not particularly wish to drink anymore, at least not with the likes of Rick Laird. He declined quietly, "I don't want another shot." But Rick would have none of it. He wanted to have some fun bullying this smaller man he had pegged for a queer. "Set 'em up!", Rick demanded of the bartender. Jimmy looked hesitant for a second, having just heard Anthony say he didn't want any more shots. Rick grew impatient and growled "I said *'Set 'em up'*!" while fixing an unwavering, threatening stare on Jimmy Phillips.

Jimmy reluctantly refilled the three shot glasses and waited for Rick to pay for the drinks. But Rick just glared at him in a stare-down until Anthony meekly pulled out his wallet and offered to pay for the second round of shots.

Suddenly two Bristol Township policemen entered the bar. Officer McGuigan and Officer Newsinski were doing a routine investigation on a stolen car reported to have been seen in the parking lot outside. The officers asked to see everyone's ID and asked which car they drove. There were four patrons in the bar and three of them sat together: Rick, Frank and Anthony. Rick cursed at Officer McGuigan and got belligerent, challenging him in a stare-down duel of the wills. After his friend Frank placated him and calmed him down, he told Officer McGuigan his name and address and reiterated that he had done nothing wrong and just wanted to drink his beer and be left alone. Meanwhile, Anthony politely complied with the request for ID without saying a word. After satisfying themselves that no one in the Edgely Inn was connected to the stolen car, the officers went back outside to finish filling out their police reports in their patrol car. Except for Rick Laird, the large loudmouth biker, everything had gone pretty smoothly.

After the police went back outside, Rick yelled as Anthony got up to go to the bathroom again, "You'll give us a ride home, right?" Frank, looking somewhat bewildered at his friend, wondered what Rick was up to now, "We don't need a ride; we're just going right across the street to your place." Rick silenced Frank with a malevolent glare, growling at his friend, "Why should we *walk*, Frank, when we can get a *ride*?" Anthony was a little confused. He had just heard Rick tell the police that he lived right across the street in the apartments in the Ambassador Arms complex on Haines Mill Road. Why would he need a ride when it was less than a two minute walk? Did he just lie to the police and give a phony address? Or was it that he wanted a ride somewhere else first, then back to his apartment?

Jimmy was cleaning up and finishing the stocking of the last beer cooler when he was suddenly startled by the resounding crash of a shot glass on the floor just behind him. "What the *fuck* is your problem?" he spun around, confronting Rick. After a few seconds of silence, Rick apologized, "Listen, I didn't mean to do that, but I am just sick and tired of those people trying to infiltrate us", motioning towards the general direction of the restroom where Anthony had gone. Jimmy knew Rick was referring to homosexuals, specifically to Anthony Milano. He was at a loss for words. Did Anthony even know how much this creepy guy the size of a line backer hated him just for possibly being a homosexual, something that was never actually confirmed in the first place? If Rick was determined to pick a fight with Anthony Milano, this nice quiet young man would never stand a chance.

This whole scenario was really starting to bug the hell out of Jimmy. It made no sense to him that Rick Laird would want someone representative of something he obviously despised to buy him drinks and then want to get into his car to go for a ride – especially when Rick lived practically across the street. Jimmy Phillips sensed foul play. He decided to take the first opportunity he could to discreetly warn Anthony that these two guys were clearly up to no good.

Suddenly, Rick got up as the jukebox began playing a slow song and grabbed Frank by the arm, "Get up. I wanna dance." Frank sheepishly hesitated, but his companion fixed him with a steely look that brooked no opposition. So Frank got up at Rick's sharp command and began slow dancing with him just as Anthony was coming out of the bathroom.

Anthony watched the pair dancing and laughing. Frank, no longer embarrassed by the spectacle he made of himself by slow dancing with his much larger, very macho buddy Rick, was giggling like a schoolgirl. He was a strikingly handsome young man, built only slightly bigger than Anthony.

Like Anthony Milano, Frank Chester was also Italian. Like Anthony, Frank was also raised in a Christian home. Frank was also just beginning to get his life together to find his place in the world. However, *unlike* Anthony, Frank Chester was troubled tonight over his fiancé getting an abortion, dumping him, and returning the engagement ring he had scraped to buy for her.

Anthony must have noticed Frank's good looks. Even in a disheveled state and dressed in a sloppy football jersey, Frank Chester was a very good looking young man. His lean, sinewy build was supported on his five foot eleven inch frame: he was as perfectly proportioned as Michelangelo's *David*. He moved with the grace and agility of a cat. He was definitely a heart-throb and had a smile that could break your heart. A healthy crop of dark brown hair framed his handsome face. His brown eyes sparkled mischievously and his award-winning smile, which left many a young girl dreamy-eyed, was completely disarming. He could have been a male model or maybe even a movie star like Nicholas Cage or Lorenzo Lamas. He was a very likeable kid (when he wanted to be) who had just turned twenty. He was just beginning to straighten out after his troubled youth of constantly running away after his parents divorced.

Frank's mother, Elaine Holley, said that the trouble with Frank began when he was ten years old, almost immediately after his dad left the family. The struggling divorcee with two older daughters and one older son lost control over young Frank's behavior rapidly. Having called every social service agency listed in the phone book trying to get help for her youngest child, Elaine was frustrated at every turn. Her youngest child Frank had literally gone from being an angelic-faced altar boy at Sacred Heart Church one day to being brought home by the local police the next. But apparently, no one would help her unless Frank got into trouble with the law. As a single mother with three other teenagers to raise alone, Elaine couldn't seem to get any preventive help for her youngest child anywhere. Her older children helped out with the bills and helped put food on the table with their part-time after school jobs. Meanwhile Frank ran away from home repeatedly and committed petty crimes, and soon found himself caught in the revolving door of juvenile delinquent centers. Just like he ran away from home, he ran away from those places for troubled youths, too. During one of his escapades, he had even hopped aboard a freight train and fallen off, getting a concussion. He was lucky he didn't lose any limbs or his life! Things went from bad to worse. When Elaine remarried, Frank, who had already been stealing from both his parents, began stealing from his new stepfather as well. He was also constantly getting into fights, as if beatings were a normal past-time. He was clearly a very troubled teen with a lot of serious anger issues.

Finally, Frank Chester ended up court-ordered to Glen Mills Reform School, which had an open campus. Surprisingly, Frank didn't run away. A teacher at Glen Mills mentored the troubled young lad and took him under his wing. Frank did well at Glen Mills and excelled on all the sports teams. He took a serious interest in the martial arts and learned karate, which definitely improved his self-esteem and confidence. He earned the trusted and privileged position of working at the snack bar. He was known by all the staff as friendly, likeable and basically an all-around good kid. A positive male role model like this teacher was the best influence that had come along in Frank's life up to that point in time. This teacher also explained to Mrs. Holley what the real problem with Frank was.

Frank acted up and ran away from home because every time he did so, Elaine would call his father. It was the immature young Frankie's subconscious belief that if he acted up and ran away often enough, eventually his father would come back. At Glen Mills Frank began to improve and show signs of growing up to be a responsible young man who dreamed of one day becoming a teacher or maybe even a counselor just like the mentor he worshiped, so that he could help other troubled kids in similar situations.

When Frank returned home from Glen Mills, he was beginning to show promise as a socially conscious young man. Just a year before the murder, he proudly escorted his Bristol beauty, Colleen Ingram, to her senior prom. He was holding a steady job as the night time cashier at the De Grande Diner in Bristol along Route US-13 and he never made any mistakes in handling the cash drawer. He had begun making plans for his future: marriage to Colleen Ingram, the pretty blonde who worked as a shampoo girl in his mother's beauty salon. Elaine helped to fix her son and Colleen up. They hit it off from day one. They made such a cute young couple. He wanted a family and a home of his own - a slice of the American Dream. He would soon be starting a new and well-paying job at the same company his older brother worked at. He would be dealing with pollution control and the clean-up of hazardous spills and industrial pollutants. He had passed all the prerequisite courses and training for the job and was ready to begin his new career.

Having grown into a charming and very handsome young man, Frank Robert Chester was becoming quite the eligible bachelor, but he had his heart set on one girl whom he planned to marry. Frank had just moved into his first apartment and was starting out life on his own as an independent young man with all the bright hopes, dreams and aspirations the future seemed to hold for him.

Then he met twenty-four year old Richard Roland Laird, his cousin and Barbara Anne's rough and tumble boyfriend – the father of her unborn baby. Had he not formed this toxic friendship with Rick, no one knows how Frank's life might have turned out. Unfortunately, fate would lead Frank Chester down a different path. It was a path that no mother ever wants her son to tread.

Now Frank was drunk and slow dancing with his macho loudmouthed buddy, feeling rather foolish. While Frank was feeling foolish, Jimmy was feeling apprehensive. Jimmy knew Rick and Frank were making fun of Anthony. He was unsure as to what he should do. Jimmy wondered if Anthony knew the full situation. It was after last call: hopefully they would leave any minute now.

Anthony watched the pair of drunken dancing men carefully, not sure what to make of it. "You *are* gonna give us a ride home, right?" Rick barked from across the room to Anthony as the mild-mannered artist collected his change off of the bar. Jimmy saw he had the perfect moment and seized the opportunity to warn Anthony.

He was at the other end of the bar, finishing with the coolers. From where he was, Rick and Frank couldn't see or hear him from where they were over by the jukebox. "Tony, come here a minute. I want to talk to you. Those guys are up to no good. They're just looking to cause trouble. Get your stuff and get outta here - NOW!" Anthony hesitated for a moment. Throughout his teenage years he had often let others push him around, coercing him into giving them rides home from school, giving into them to avoid trouble – it was better than getting a beating, or worse. Anthony stood quietly as he thought for a minute about what Jimmy Phillips just told him. He stood still while weighing his options. If he didn't agree to give Rick and Frank a ride home, they might get nasty — just like the tougher, more macho kids in his high school class used to do when they would coerce him into giving them rides. "I'll just give them a ride home. I don't want any trouble," Anthony whispered quietly to the concerned bartender.

"Just leave. I'll make sure they stay here. You just leave. Please Tony, just go. Go now!" Jimmy urged. Anthony hesitated for a second, but seeing the concern in Jimmy's eyes he figured the bartender was right and he should make a quick exit.

Unfortunately, the second that Anthony hesitated was just one second too long. As Anthony turned around to retrieve his coat to leave, he found himself almost bumping into the massive chest of Rick Laird.

"You ready to drive us home?" Rick said, almost as if to accuse Anthony of trying to leave without him and his buddy Frank. There was very little Anthony could do now to escape. Regretfully, Jimmy Phillips watched, helpless to alter the course of events as the trio walked out of his tavern together. Anthony, Rick and Frank got into Anthony's car, but not before Frank approached McGuigan who was still sitting in his patrol car finishing his report on the stolen car complaint. Frank politely asked the policeman for his permission to leave. Officer McGuigan smiled at Frank who had earlier played the peacemaker during the questioning of the bar patrons, specifically Rick Laird, and nodded that they could go. But McGuigan scrutinized the larger man who was previously surly with him and who was now climbing into Anthony's car.

What transpired afterwards from the time the men left the Edgely Inn together until the darkest hour before dawn when Anthony lay bleeding and struggling for his life in a wooded lot on Ashby Avenue is known for certain only by Rick Laird, Frank Chester and Anthony Milano. Rick Laird would later point the finger at his pal Frank Chester, and Frank Chester would point the finger at Rick Laird. Anthony Milano would never be able to look his attacker in the eyes again or point his finger at anyone.

However, Bucks County District Attorney Alan Rubenstein *would* point the finger - and he would do so at both Richard Roland Laird, Jr. and Frank Robert Chester. He surmised that the two blue-collar hard-drinking hoods singled out their victim because they thought he was gay and that they both harbored a deeply fierce hatred for homosexuals.

Frank Chester and Rick Laird were part of the "Pep Boys crowd" as the working-class of Pennsylvania's wealthy Bucks County are frequently referred to by the more affluent, professional crowd. Many sociological theories steeped in classism purport that members of the lesser educated and lower income working class crowd tend to be more racist, sexist and homophobic than members of the middle and upper classes. The 1970's sitcom "*All In The Family*" illustrated and reinforced such stereotypes with Archie Bunker. However, Archie Bunker was not predisposed to criminal activities, nor was he violent. The middle and upper classes often lay claim to better breeding, more intelligence, and higher educational attainment. They present an image of having more tolerance and acceptance of non-mainstream individuals.

The incomprehensible violence behind this hate crime was evident by the vicious frenzy in which Anthony Milano was murdered. Lack of tolerance and extreme hatred for homosexuals manifested itself in this tragedy in which one young man's life was violently cut short and the lives of two other men would be wasted, while their families' lives would be forever torn asunder.

The working class communities of nearby Levittown, Fairless Hills and Croydon now have a tolerance promotion program in many public schools in hopes that teaching tolerance for homosexuals will prevent such prejudice from escalating into more gay-bashing fatalities such as those of Anthony Milano and later, Matthew Shepard. Extreme gay-bashing stems from hatred and prejudice. Hatred and prejudice are the bastard children of fear, resentment, insecurity, and anger. In both the cases of Anthony Milano and subsequently Matthew Shepard (a young gay college student), the killers were angry, aggressive lower income working class white males who fiercely sought to protect or defend their masculinity. It is difficult to tolerate something one views as a direct assault to one's sense of self and security. This makes you wonder if teaching tolerance alone will really suffice to prevent future tragedies, or if we should teach respect while also addressing the insecurities that drive the engine of prejudice and hatred.

We see a similar lack of tolerance or acceptance of the lower classes often exhibited by those higher up on the socioeconomic ladder – the very same people claiming to be more sophisticated and enlightened than the lower class. The middle and upper classes claim to be tolerant of racial minorities, women, homosexuals and eccentric intellectuals. Yet when it comes to extending any tolerance for the poor and working classes, there is no tolerance to be found — let alone respect.

Belonging to a social class is not merely an objective fact; it is generally accompanied by a perception of class identity. Social class is not merely a personal attribute, but also a contextual variable used to characterize an entire group of people. The shared culture of a particular class influences people's attitudes and lifestyles.

It is therefore my opinion, that in order for tolerance programs to work, the root causes of intolerance must first be acknowledged and addressed. The root causes, I believe, lie in the classism that is interwoven in our alleged classless society. It seems that it would be far more socially productive to address the roots of classism in our communities. It is pervasive classism, which we like to pretend doesn't exist in our society; that fosters the insecurity, apathy, resentment, anger and distrust among those on the lower socioeconomic rungs.

Insecurity and resentment makes the perfect breeding ground for hatred, intolerance and prejudice to fester. It is not simply the material comforts and luxuries of the well-to-do that engender resentment from the have-nots; it is the perception that those in the top socio-economic ranks want to dominate everybody else beneath them. It is the dominant classes who set the trends. They get to decide the norms, mores and social customs; what is "normal" versus what is not. It is the dominant classes whose values are thrust upon everyone else – including but not limited to the privilege of changing the rules in midstream. It is *this* that the lower classes resent above all else.

Chapter 4

"The police shall never catch me because I have been too clever for them." ~ Zodiac (November 9th, 1969 letter to the *San Francisco Chronicle*)

It was the darkest hour before dawn with cold rain pouring in a steady rhythm on this dismal December morning. Around 4:00 AM December 15th, 1987, Rick Laird and Frank Chester were running as if the hounds of hell were in pursuit. But neither the sweat nor the cold December rain would wash away the blood on Rick's clothes. Anthony lay dead among the four foot tall weeds in a wooded lot across the street from Tommy Main's house at 1324 Ashby Avenue. Tommy Main was reputed to be one of Bristol's meth dealers. Rick wanted to get some meth. But Rick never made it to Tommy Main's and instead was fleeing a murder scene with Frank Chester. They ran nearly a mile in the dark to Lakeview Manor Apartments where Richard Griscavage shared an apartment with Pete Carpinona and Christine Bogarde and their newborn baby.

Rich Griscavage, Pete Carpinona and Pete's eighteen year old fiancée Christine Bogarde were all friends of Frank's. Frank had hoped he could outrun Rick and lose him, but Rick was right on his tail. Running up two flights of stairs to his friends' apartment at Lakeview Manor, Frank pounded loudly on the door to Apartment E-5 with his fists, "Yo! Open up, man!" The commotion startled Rich Griscavage from a sound sleep on the warm sofa where he had been hunkered down in a pile of blankets like a bear in hibernation. Rubbing his eyes and barely awake, he shuffled from his comfortable couch across the living room and opened the door for his panic-stricken friend, "Yo, what's going on?" Breathless and excited, Frank rushed in and tried to explain what happened, "We got in a fight and the dude is dead …" Rick silenced Frank with a vicious stare, snapping, "Shut the fuck up, Frank!" Rick entered the apartment on Frank's heels. Rich Griscavage noticed that Rick didn't have a shirt on: he was wearing only his black leather biker jacket, boots and jeans. On a cold rainy winter night, it seemed odd that the huge burly and belligerent man would be bare-chested beneath his biker jacket. Then Griscavage noticed blood on Rick's pants. He was fully awake now and was still standing there in the living room staring at the blood on Rick's clothes when Rick Laird tossed his leather jacket to him as if he were merely the butler. Rick casually strolled over to the kitchen sink and began washing his hands and arms. Still holding the jacket, Rich demanded of his friend Frank, "What the hell is going on here?" Frank began to try to relay what had just transpired to his pal Rich Griscavage, " Something fucked up happened - " and once again he was abruptly cut off and shut down by Rick Laird who fixed Frank with a malevolent glare and growled menacingly, "Shut up!"

By this time, Rich's roommates, Pete and Christine were also awakened by the racket. Pete ventured down the hall toward the kitchen as his fiancée Christine, a thin wisp of a girl clad in her nightgown, followed right behind him. Christine looked at the big man with the tattoos and nipple ring whom she didn't know standing in her kitchen. "Get back in the fuckin' bedroom. This ain't no place for a woman!" Rick rudely ordered her. Christine Bogarde thought to herself, *'the nerve some people have.....talk to ME like that in MY own home!'* as she turned around and walked back to her bedroom. Pete didn't know what this guy's problem was but he had just about had enough, "Get him the hell out of here!" he told Rich Griscavage, motioning to Rick Laird. This was his and Christine's home - not Rick Laird's place. "Yeah, gimme a ride home," Rick demanded.

Rich Griscavage fumbled about the sofa looking for his keys while getting his coat and two motorcycle helmets so he could take Rick Laird home and get him out of Pete and Christine's apartment. It was not the best time to have to go for a motorcycle ride, he thought while grabbing a spare helmet, noticing that it was pouring rain and was very dark and dismal outside. Rick accepted the helmet, put it on, and donned his leather jacket as he followed Griscavage down the stairs. The two men climbed onto the motorcycle and drove off to Rick Laird's apartment.

Now that Laird was gone, Pete Carpinona sat down next to his troubled and shaken friend and asked him again what had happened. Frank blubbered that he and Rick had met some guy named Tony at the bar and Rick asked him for a ride home and got into a fight with him along the way. Rick cut Tony's throat. Tony ended up dead. He ran here, with Rick hot on his tail. He was still telling Pete what happened when Rich Griscavage returned. "I can't believe that fucking asshole did this," Frank sat shaking his head, "He's ruining my fuckin' life."

After he finished pouring out the whole story to Pete and Rich Griscavage, Frank asked Rich to take him on his motorcycle over to Rick Laird's apartment. He had left a female friend, Gale Gardner, there earlier. Frank apologetically explained to Rich and Pete that he felt responsible for Gale's safety and thus had to return to Laird's apartment. Gale was only seventeen and pregnant, her boyfriend was in jail. Frank was good friends with Gale, having previously dated her sister Gretchen before Colleen. During his volatile relationship with Gretchen, he had often talked with Gale when he needed a sympathetic ear. Now Gale was not in exactly the best situation: car broken down, no money, and over an hour's drive away from her place in Philadelphia. Given Rick's frame of mind, there was no telling what he would do next. He couldn't just leave Gale alone there when she had only just met Barbara Anne earlier that night and didn't know Rick from a can of paint. Having his buddy Rich Griscavage drive him back to Rick's may not have been the wisest choice for Frank to make, but he was just a dumb kid. He made the choice he made for reasons only he knew. That choice would later come back to haunt him.

Meanwhile, back at Rick Laird's apartment, Barbara Anne was crying. Rick had just come home. As he entered the apartment, he woke up Gale, who was camped out on the sofa. "Where's Frank?" Gale asked the huge man whom she barely knew. "Shut up and go back to sleep," came the inconsiderate reply. Rick went down the hall and into the bedroom and passed out, but not before Barbara Anne sat up in bed and questioned him. She wanted some answers. He had left her home pretty much neglected and ignored all night. She was seven and a half months pregnant. Rick should have been home with her, not out carousing all night with her cousin Frank. She was worried about Rick, but she was also angry and hurt. "What, were you out getting laid?" she demanded as Rick undressed for bed, ignoring her. "Yeah, I was out getting laid," Rick mumbled nonchalantly as he rolled over to go to sleep. He was not about to tell Barbara Anne what had really happened. Barbara Anne left the bedroom and sat down in the living room crying.

She, little David, and Gale had left Frank and Rick at the Edgely Inn at around 11:00 PM, about a half hour before Anthony showed up there for his beer and sandwich. She felt bad for Gale, whom Frank had just introduced to her that evening. Gale was pregnant and her man was in jail and, from what Barbara Anne understood, she was also without a ride to get back home to

Philadelphia — over an hour away. She told Gale that she'd be welcome to sleep on the living room couch until Frank and Rick returned from the bar. Around midnight – and hour after leaving Rick and Frank at the bar, she and Gale and little David were still awake and watching a movie when the telephone rang. It was Rick. Barbara Anne had asked him if he needed a ride home and he said 'No'. With a complicated pregnancy, she did not need this emotional stress. She was still in tears when the doorbell rang. It was her cousin Frank with his friend Rich Griscavage. Griscavage stayed only a moment and then left. He had to get up in less than two hours and go to work.

"Where's Rick?" Frank asked his favorite cousin, whose unborn nephew was expected to be his godchild. Barbara Anne told him Rick had gone to bed and passed out. "Get him up!" Frank urged. Now Barbara Anne had taken all she was going to take. She blew up at Frank and told him to wake Rick up himself. Picking up the first thing she could lay her hands on, she hurled a motorcycle helmet at him, screaming and crying, "Dammit Frank! Every time you two go out, you get in trouble!"

Barbara Anne did not yet fully know or grasp the gravity of the situation. She thought Rick had been out cheating on her with some thinner, non-pregnant chick due to her own huge pregnant belly. She got up and walked over to the door and retrieved Rick's muddy boots, taking them into the kitchen. "I don't control his mind, Barbara Anne. I don't stop Rick from doing what he does!" Frank tried to defend himself to his cousin, but she didn't want to hear it. Had Frank not called earlier the previous day and bugged her and Rick about coming over to see his new apartment, his very first apartment, Rick would not have been out all night doing God only knows what with God only knows whom. He would have been at home paying attention to her.

Frank walked into the bedroom to wake Rick while Barbara Anne put her boyfriend's dirty boots in the sink under the running faucet. Frank started shouting, "Get the fuck up!" Rick rolled over and mumbled something about needing to be left alone to sleep. Frank persisted, nudging Rick, "What are you gonna do? Lay here until the cops come?" Frank kept trying to rouse Rick who merely looked at him through narrowed eyes and replied, "Frank, you better get the fuck outta here, man. You're ruinin' my fuckin' life," rolling over to go back to sleep again. There was nothing Frank could do except go back out to the living room and sit there with his friend Gale who was wide awake by now and looking very confused. She knew that something serious had gone down that night, but she had no idea it was as serious as murder.

In the kitchen, Barbara Anne, who had just stopped crying, was thoroughly scrubbing off Rick's boots in the sink, carefully getting all the mud and debris from out of the tracks on the soles. Frank sat up awake with his friend Gale: Neither got any sleep. He slowly explained over the course of several hours what had transpired earlier. However, given his protective machismo – or chauvinist tendencies – Frank had a much harder time explaining what had happened to a friend who wasn't "one of the guys."

At around 10:00 AM, Gale and Frank, both still awake, heard Barbara Anne stirring in the bedroom. Rick woke up to make a telephone call to his brother Mark Laird, who lived in nearby Bensalem. "Things got a little crazy last night; I have to talk to you. Just wait till I get there, I'll talk to you in person." Rick hung up the phone and collected the clothes he had worn the night before, stuffing them into a trash bag. Barbara Anne, still not fully knowing everything, was upset at seeing this. She and Rick were so desperately poor. They had a baby on the way. Where the hell did he think they were going to get the money to buy him another leather jacket, pair of engineer boots, and jeans? They didn't have enough income to keep the lights on and the rent paid! Passing by the kitchen counter, she noticed his key ring had blood on it.

It was his special key ring that said "DAD". It had been given to him for a Father's Day gift from little David. It wasn't anything terribly important or expensive, but in the eyes of a child it was a priceless treasure of incalculable sentimental value. It meant a lot to little David to see Rick carry it everyplace he went. And Barbara Anne knew it. She began to put the pieces together. Rick had not been in any regular, run of the mill bar room brawl last night. Whatever had gone down, it was very serious.

"C'mon Frank", Rick said, as Barbara Anne and little David got into their coats preparing to leave. The five of them - Rick, Barbara Anne, Frank, Gale and little David all piled into Rick's Pontiac. He would drop Frank and Gale off at Frank's apartment, and then head over to Bensalem to meet his younger brother Mark for lunch at a pizza shop.

While en route to Frank's apartment, Barbara Anne noticed something dangling from the rear view mirror that wasn't there before. It was a crystal prism in the shape of a multi-faceted orb. When the sunlight struck it, rays of various colors scattered everywhere. "Where did that come from?" Barbara Anne asked. Frank told her it came from a car belonging to some guy named Tony Milano whom he and Rick met last night at the bar.

Rick pulled a utility knife out of his pocket. It is the kind of knife with a one inch razor sharp retractable blade that is often used by carpenters, electricians and plasterers for scoring drywall or cutting out small holes in walls for mounting electrical outlet boxes. He pressed the button sliding the deadly blade out and turned around to face Frank, "No evidence, no crime," he said as he retracted the blade, snapping the knife shut again. Frank and

Gale sat in the back seat, brooding in silence for the remainder of the ride back to Frank's apartment. The whole previous evening and the sequence of events that transpired just seemed too surreal to Frank. Gale stared aimlessly out of the window, wishing she were anyplace else but in the back seat of Rick Laird's Pontiac. She knew she was riding with a madman.

After dropping Frank and Gale off, Rick and Barbara Anne headed towards Bensalem. On the way, he tossed the utility knife out of the car window off a bridge into the Neshaminy Creek. Once he and Barbara Anne arrived at the pizza shop to meet Mark, Rick climbed out of the car and placed the trash bag containing his boots, leather jacket and his key ring - the Father's Day gift from little David - into a dumpster behind the pizza shop. Barbara Anne didn't ask any questions. She didn't need the scenario of the previous evening drawn out for her in crayon.

Meanwhile back at Frank Chester's apartment, Gale pressed Frank to level with her about the night before. She knew Frank very well from the days he dated her sister Gretchen and she was used to seeing him get a little wired and upset, but this entire morning from the time Rick woke her up by coming in at 4:30 AM had been insane. None of it made any sense to her. Sitting down on the couch with her friend, she said, "Now tell me what happened last night, Frank." He recounted the events from when Anthony Milano came into the bar, telling her his version of the truth. He told her how Rick bugged Anthony for a ride even though his apartment was right across the street because Rick wanted to go get another pack of cigarettes and buy some drugs from Tommy Main before going home. Frank explained how they all left the Edgely Inn together and how and when they got to where Tommy Main lived on Ashby Avenue, all hell broke loose.

Gale sat patiently and listened as Frank told her how Anthony tried to flee after they stopped at the 7-11 where Rick wanted to use the pay phone and buy cigarettes. This was the golden opportunity for Anthony to make a quick escape, since both Rick and Frank were out of the car. Oddly, Anthony waited until Frank got back in the car before trying to take off. Anthony, sensing danger and in a state of panic, hit the gas too hard and stalled the engine when he threw his car into reverse in an attempt to leave Rick there. Rick heard the commotion from the payphone and slammed the phone receiver down, hard. Running toward the stalled car, he jumped in and began slapping Anthony around while Anthony cried and pleaded to go home. What Frank did *not* explain was his own lack of intervention during the entire forty-five minute hell ride. Nor did he explain why he stopped to grab the six-pack of beer when he decided to get out of the car to investigate the beating he claimed he saw Rick inflicting on Anthony.

Frank told Gale that Rick marched Anthony into the woods along Ashby Avenue across the street from the projects, where Rick launched into a vicious frenzy, culminating in the near-decapitation of the mild mannered artist. Frank described how Anthony's blood squirted out from his throat and the horrible, gurgling noises it made as Anthony lay there dying. He kept shaking his head in disbelief as he recounted the sequence of events that he had found himself in the middle of. It all seemed just too surreal, like he had been transported into some macabre episode of Rod Serling's *Night Gallery*.

Gale looked accusingly at Frank and solemnly asked him if he had hurt Anthony, too. He told her that all he did was shove Anthony out of Rick's way, to try to stop the fight from escalating because Rick was uncontrollable. First Frank said he knocked Anthony out of harm's way, then he changed his story and said he knocked him unconscious, then he hastily replied that no, Anthony was not unconscious.

It could have been because of the lack of sleep combined with the excitement from last night that Frank didn't quite have his story completely straight. Or maybe he was not telling the whole truth. Or perhaps Frank — being a twenty year old dumb kid — was terrified and in shock at what transpired. No one will ever know. The fact that Frank had these discrepancies in his story would later be used against him by District Attorney Rubenstein whose experienced prosecution skills were honed to a razor sharp ability.

Shortly after telling Gale of the prior evening's adventure from hell, Rich Griscavage showed up. He was concerned for Frank and confused. He wanted to know about the blood-splashed psychopath Rick Laird who had been with Frank, and whom he had given a ride home on his motorcycle in the wee hours of this morning. "Tell me what happened, Frank", Rich urged his friend. "Some faggot came walking into the bar and Rick kept on fucking with him," Frank answered. He told Rich Griscavage that he personally did nothing to participate in the fracas and that all he did was "kick Anthony a little." Now this was a different story than the one he previously told to Gale Gardner, where he claimed that he merely shoved Anthony to knock him out of Rick's way.

Later, Pete Carpinona showed up and so did Allen Hilton. Throughout the day more friends of Frank's showed up; all young inexperienced kids, and all of them asking questions and offering suggestions and advice for their troubled friend. They debated whether Frank should leave town or go to the police. Frank kept saying he was worried about Anthony's car. "My fingerprints are in it," he told his friends. At one point during the discussion, Pete told the group he was going out for more cigarettes. Frank asked him to drive by the Venice-Ashby projects and see if the car was still there. Then the phone rang. Frank nervously answered, "Yo, what's up?" When he hung up, he told his friends that it was Rick Laird who called and that Rick and his brother Mark Laird were going to take care of Anthony's car by blowing it up.

At one point, the group tossed about ideas as to how to get rid of the body. One friend suggested burying it in the mountains. Another suggested Frank dump it in a lake. A third said, "Take it to the Poconos." Frank asked Allen Hilton, who was twenty-three and the oldest one in the group, if *he'd* drive the body to the Poconos. Allen Hilton jumped up, responding, "Fuck no! You want my advice? If you didn't do the slashing, you should just go to the cops and come clean with all this."

Then a guy named Mike DeWitt, who had a brand new red Chevy Beretta showed up. Frank asked, "Hey Mike, can I borrow your car?" Mike replied warily, "What for?" to which Frank answered, "I got a dead deer to take care of." Mike eyed everyone in Frank's living room suspiciously. "Sorry Frank, no way," he told Frank and turned around and walked out the door. Whatever was going on, Mike DeWitt sensed that it was something he wanted no part of. "Wait! Can you give me a ride home?" Gale asked and jumped up, running through the door after Mike. Then Pete said he had to leave too, because he had to go pick up a Christmas tree. Gradually, one by one, all of Frank Chester's friends left Frank's apartment by nightfall to go about their lives.

The next morning, Wednesday December 16th 1987, after Officer McGuigan's chilling discovery of Anthony Milano's body, Rose Milano and her daughter Annamarie received that dreaded telephone call from Bristol police department. An hour or so later, Bristol police officers were escorting Rose and Annamarie to Vito Milano's barbershop. Instinctively Vito knew the worst when he saw the police physically helping his distraught wife and daughter towards the door of the barbershop. He knew that his son was dead. "No! No! My boy....my boy," Vito cried as he crumbled to his knees, his frail body racked from sobbing in anguish. This just could not be happening. Not to his family. Not to his only son whom he and his wife had recently proudly presented with a check for a thousand dollars as a college graduation gift which he was planning to use as a security deposit for a studio apartment in the trendy arts district of Philadelphia's Rittenhouse Square.

While the autopsy on Anthony Milano was being performed that same afternoon, Rick Laird and Barbara Anne were going about their Christmas shopping as if nothing happened. They stopped at some of the lower scale department stores like K-Mart's and finally an Army & Navy store. They didn't have much money, but they were able to buy little David some cheap ninja toys and army shirts for his Christmas presents.

Within twenty-four hours after the discovery of Anthony Milano's body, Rubenstein knew he had ample probable cause to arrest both Frank Robert Chester and Richard Roland Laird, Jr. But Rubenstein wanted to make sure he had everything he needed because this would be a death penalty case and death penalty cases are not built on probable cause alone. He took the biggest gamble in his entire legal career and on December 18th, he began to put his plan into action. He would let Frank talk. He was the suspect who talked to friends, who in turn gave anonymous tips to the police. Rubenstein wanted to let Frank have enough rope to hang himself and his accomplice, too. It was a very high-stakes gamble, but it was a chance Rubenstein felt compelled to take if he was going to ensure that the charges of first degree capital murder would stick.

Chapter 5

"There are truths which are not for all men, nor for all times."
~ Voltaire

On December 18th 1987 roughly forty-eight hours after the murder, Frank Chester was stopped by a patrol car while he was driving down Route 13. "You Frank Chester?" the officer approached the car and asked. The color drained from Frank's face. He was suddenly very scared. Frank was shaking. He nodded his head and replied, "What did I do?" The cop answered benignly, smiling at Frank in a friendly tone, "Aw nothin' Frank. Just a matter of some outstanding traffic tickets is all. Why don't you come down to headquarters and we'll get it all straightened out." Frank, feeling relieved replied politely, "Yes sir."

He was sure the reason he was initially stopped was for questioning in the murder of Anthony Milano and for that brief moment his heart jumped up into his throat. Frank breathed a sigh of relief as he followed the police officer to the Bristol police station. He was only being pulled over for some outstanding tickets. The officer went over some of the outstanding tickets in question with Frank. As it turned out, they had all been paid except for one, which Frank promptly paid.

When Frank was getting ready to leave the Bristol Township police precinct, another police officer stopped him and said, "Listen, by the way, we're investigating a murder. A kid left with his throat slashed out near Venice-Ashby. You don't know anything about it, do you Frank?" Frank Chester hastily responded, "No, just what I read in the papers." The officer paused and paced around the room a little, "Just read about it, huh Frank?" Frank was afraid now. He tried to justify himself answering, "Well, it's in all the papers." The cop persisted and prodded further, "Right. Well, you see Frank, we have a little problem. There's this bartender out at the Edgely Inn says you were with the guy that night."

"Yeah, well I saw him", said Frank. "You saw him...." the cop replied, looking skeptically at the tall, lean murder suspect in his presence. "Yeah. I went to the Edgely Inn, had a couple of beers and left. When I left, he was still sitting at the bar...with Rick Laird," Frank lied. Then the chief detective of Bucks County, Frank Dykes walked into the room. Detective Dykes was personally chosen by Alan Rubenstein to lead this investigation. He was a tall, well-dressed, clean-shaven man with stylishly short light auburn hair. His smile was very disarming. The distinguished, intelligent detective looked more like a banker or a stockbroker than a homicide investigator. He said to his murder suspect, "Frank, that's not gonna work, either. We have a cop, see, who says he saw you leave with Anthony Milano."

By the end of the conversation, Frank Chester had changed his story several times. His last story went something like this: He did leave the bar with Anthony Milano, but had Anthony dropped him off alone first. He claimed he didn't come forward sooner because he was terrified of Rick Laird, especially after he read what Laird seemed to have done to that kid and since Laird knew where to find him if it got out that he had talked to the police. He emphatically reiterated to Detective Dykes that he was in mortal fear of Rick Laird. He adamantly insisted to Dykes that this was the whole truth.

Detective Dykes responded to the nervous young man, telling him, "We can understand that Frank. But we need you to help us out. Why don't you come in tomorrow and take a polygraph test to clear your name in all this, and maybe answer a few more questions for us." Frank gratefully accepted Detective

Dykes' offer and said, "Anything I can do to help." As per Alan Rubenstein's instructions, Detective Dykes shook hands with Frank Chester and sent him home.

Regardless of the reason for this prevarication on Frank Chester's part, these inconsistencies in his conversation with the police as well as with his friend Gale Gardner previously; later proved to be his undoing. Frank Chester had dug himself into a hole. This is precisely what Alan Rubenstein was counting on. No court or jury in the land would believe a suspect whose credibility was marred by inconsistencies. Those inconsistencies would make Frank Chester look like a cover-up artist and a liar. The idea that it took a lot of guts for Frank to violate the Croydon Code, and that - in and of itself - was an extremely traumatic thing to do, would not be appreciated or understood by either the authorities or a jury. So far, Rubenstein's plan was working. For this to be a capital case that would stick, stronger, and hopefully irrefutable, evidence was needed. Rubenstein wasn't about to bring a stick to a gunfight.

Meanwhile, later that same evening, Frank told his friends that the cops were on his side. He was helping the cops out. They were after Rick Laird, and not him. Frank was lulled into a false sense of security.

The next morning Detective Dykes picked Frank up at his apartment and brought him to the Bristol Township police headquarters for Frank to take a polygraph test. Common practice when giving polygraphs is to recite the questions in advance to the person before they submit to the polygraph. Frank was asked if he was present when the murder actually transpired. Frank got nervous and began to have second thoughts about following through with the polygraph test. "I'm not so sure I want to do this," Frank told Detective Dykes who was standing patiently by, observing that Frank was growing anxious and looking worried.

"All right, Frank," the detective replied, "But let's go over this again."

Frank admitted he had not been entirely truthful the day before when he told Detective Dykes that he had been dropped off first. Frank's new version went something like this: He remained in the car for the entire time with both Rick Laird and Anthony Milano. They drove around for about forty-five minutes. Anthony kept begging Rick to let him go home. But instead Rick slapped Anthony around in the car and made him take the three of them over near the projects on Ashby Avenue. Rick and Anthony got out and walked into the woods together to "take a piss". Through the shadows and the tall grasses, Frank could see that they began fighting. Frank claimed he climbed out of the back seat of the car and got out to see what was going on when Rick Laird, covered in blood, ran out of the woods. Frank said he began running, in fear of his own life, and tried to lose Rick, but couldn't do so.

Detective Dykes politely thanked him for his time and cooperation; shook his hand, advising him not to worry and sending him home again. Detective Dykes assured Frank that he could return home and go about his business, provided he agreed to return later that same evening and make a wiretapped telephone call to Rick Laird. He then added one condition. He told Frank that he was not to have any contact whatsoever with Rick Laird until they made the wiretapped phone call. Frank eagerly agreed.

While Frank Chester tried to mentally prepare himself for incriminating his buddy Rick, Barbara Anne was hanging up the Christmas stockings over the ornamental fireplace mantle in her living room and began decorating her small and modest Christmas tree. Meanwhile, Rose and Vito Milano were picking out a casket for their son who would not be with them decorating their Christmas tree or opening up his presents on Christmas morning or enjoying a warm family Christmas dinner. Alan Rubenstein dressed for a holiday dinner party, leaving instructions for his detectives to call him after the wiretapped call had been completed.

The appointed time for the wiretapped phone call came and went. Frank Chester failed to show up. Detective Dykes began wondering if Frank Chester had caught onto their plan to arrest him as well as Rick Laird. He began thinking that Frank Chester, fearing arrest, decided to vanish. Alan Rubenstein was worried about this, too. But those concerns were short lived. The next morning, Sunday December 20th, 1987, Detective Dykes got a phone call from Frank Chester who apologized profusely for standing up his date with the detectives. "Colleen and I got in a fight," Frank said, apologetically.

At 2:00 PM that same afternoon, Frank sat surrounded by patrolmen in the presence of Detective Dykes and surveillance expert Detective Potts. They were all waiting and looking on anxiously as Frank dialed Rick Laird's number. The detectives told Frank that all he had to do was get Rick Laird to admit to the murder. But what they did not tell Frank was that he would still have to find a way to clear his own name. They watched eagerly as Frank dialed the phone. This would prove to be interesting. Rick answered the phone.

Rick: "Yo, what's up?"

Frank: "Yo."

Rick: "What's up?"

Frank: "So what's, what's, what are we gonna do? What's goin' on?"

Rick: "Huh?"

Frank: "What's goin' on?"

Rick: "Nothin' man."

Frank: "A lot of people coming around asking me questions about you and me in the bar."

Rick: "So?"

Frank: "So..."

Rick: "What's up with that? There ain't nothin' up with that."

Frank: "No, but, you know, if the cops come to me and wanna talk to me, what am I gonna say?"

Rick: "What do you mean, what are you gonna say? Nothing. You just say, yeah, we got fucking wrecked and came to my place and passed out."

Frank: "Yeah."

Rick: "Did they talk to you yet?"

Frank: "No."

Rick: "Oh, well, what the fuck, Frank. You got me shittin' my pants, dude."

Frank: "Why?"

Rick: "I thought you said the cops questioned you and shit."

Frank: "No."

Rick: "No? I thought that's what you said last night."

Frank: "I didn't talk to you last night."

Rick: "Yes you did."

Frank: "No, I didn't."

Rick: "The fuck you didn't, Frank."

Frank: "I was with Colleen."

Rick: "Frank, you called me last night."

Frank: "No, I didn't."

Rick: "Yes you did, dude."

For a brief moment of silence between Frank Chester and Rick Laird, Detective Potts and Detective Dykes exchanged curious glances. Detective Dykes had previously told Frank to refrain from having any contact with Rick Laird until it was time to do the recorded call. Had Frank lied about this, too? He made a gentlemen's agreement, seemingly in earnest. Had he gone back on his word? What else was he lying about regarding his role in this homicide? Then Rick resumed speaking to Frank.

Rick: "I'm gonna fucking hide out until this blows over."

Frank: "Why? Do you think it will?"

Rick: "Yeah, eventually it will have to go into a dead case."

Frank: "Are you sure?"

Rick: "Yeah...the statute of limitations is something like seven years."

Frank: "...That has nothing to do with it when something, you know, something like that."

Rick: "I know, but there's no evidence, Frank, you know?"

Frank: "Yeah..."

Rick: "We didn't do nothing, you know?"

Frank: "Yeah."

Frank: "So what are you gonna do, just hang out there?"

Rick: "No, we're getting ready to go out."

Frank: "Where are you going?"

Rick: "I don't know, somewhere. Christmas shopping or something....What are you gonna do?"

Frank: "I don't know. Like, what am I supposed to do if they come up to me and, and, you know, 'cause you can't, you, if they do tell you to take a polygraph test, you can't, you know, pass them things."

Rick: "With downs." [Rick suggested Frank try to get some downs from a doctor to help him relax]

Rick: "You gonna be able to do this or not?"

Frank: "I don't know...you know I've never been in this kind of shit before...I'm scared."

Rick: "Yeah."

Frank: "Cause that's, what can they do to you, what can they do to you for that?"

Rick: "Kill you."

Frank: "They can kill you?"

Rick: "Lethal injection...or put you in jail for fucking life. Which would you rather have?"

Frank: "Nothing, I didn't do nothing."

Rick: "Me neither. Just go away for awhile, man."

Frank: "I can't leave."

Rick: "Why?"

Frank: "Cause it's Christmas..."

Rick: "So what?"

Frank: "...You know what I mean, my family and shit."

Rick: "You just be cool, man. Like the motherfucker gave us a ride here and that was it. We came in and passed the fuck out."

Frank: "Yeah."

Rick: "Can you handle that?"

Frank: "Yeah."

Rick: "I hope so, Frank, man."

Frank: "So do I."

Rick: "What do you mean, so do you?"

Rick: "You know, if they ask what you're nervous about, say what the fuck do you think? You're trying to pin a fucking homicide on me, you know?"

Frank: "Yeah."

Rick: "You know? I ain't no fucking murderer, you gotta be fucking crazy."

Frank: "All right, so what are you gonna do? Go shopping?"

Rick: "You got me a paranoid fucking wreck, man, you know? I don't want nobody try pinning no fucking homicide on me either, you know?"

Frank: "Yeah, all right, how long you gonna be [shopping]?"

Rick: "Just get your shit together and stick to it, all you gotta do is stick to your guns...No evidence, no case, you hear me?"

After saying their goodbyes, Frank ended the call. The recorded call lasted for fourteen minutes, but to Frank Chester, it was the longest and most intense fourteen minutes of his life at that point. It was a small slice of time, but it was a moment that would be forever frozen in infamy. His life had just taken a turn for the worst. His whole world as he knew it was changed forever. It changed the moment he got into Anthony Milano's car with Rick Laird.

On Monday, December 21st, 1987, Alan Rubenstein was gathering his legal papers in anticipation of a busy week. Statistically, more violent crimes occur during the holidays than other times of the year. There would be a crunch to adjudicate the caseload because of the upcoming long holiday with New Years right around the corner. While Rubenstein was stealing a moment to collect his thoughts, his secretary buzzed him. Frank Chester and Colleen Ingram were outside his office, asking to speak with him. Initially, the district attorney thought his secretary was teasing him.

Alan Rubenstein had listened to the wiretapped telephone conversation between Chester and Laird several times. He knew that the conversation did not go favorably for Frank. Here Frank was, out to prove that Rick Laird and Rick Laird alone murdered the young artist, yet Rick Laird said several times throughout the conversation that he had nothing to do with it.

What was even worse was the fact that all Frank could manage to say was "Yeah, all right." Frank, who claimed he was an innocent bystander, didn't react with indignation, surprise or outrage. If Frank were truly innocent, he should have responded to Laird during that phone call with something along the lines of "What do you mean? You're the one who cut him up!" or "You're a liar, you killed him." Instead it was just "Yeah, all right." Things weren't looking real good at this point for Frank Chester. But the most sickening part of it all was Frank Chester and Rick Laird's cold, callous attitude of indifference throughout the telephone conversation regarding the man they had murdered.

They referred to Anthony Milano as "the motherfucker" and "the dude". Then they went on to talk casually about going Christmas shopping, having less concern for Anthony Milano than if he had been road-kill.

Frank entered Rubesntein's office with Colleen anxiously holding onto his arm. Looking up from his desk at the young man, Rubenstein politely offered him a cigarette. Frank shook his head and politely declined, "I got some, thanks." Trying to keep the meeting casual so Frank would feel comfortable and at ease, Rubenstein smiled, indicating Frank could sit and said, "So, what's on your mind?" Frank said he just wanted to talk. Slowly, he gave Rubenstein more details, mentioning that he knew karate and was a kick-boxer. He also told Rubenstein there was a girl named Gale Gardner who was at Rick Laird's the night of the murder who could testify to such things as the blood on Rick's clothes when he came home, the "No evidence, no crime" remark Rick made in the car and Rick's disposal of the bloody clothes. Frank finally asked Rubenstein what he thought of the wiretapped phone conversation.

The district attorney coolly replied, "It was OK, Frank. But we need you to make one more." Frank Chester grew apprehensive. Trembling, he replied, "Yeah. OK, sure." Rubenstein escorted Frank and Colleen to the door, shook Frank's hand like a gentleman, and told Frank to go home and wait for Detective Dykes to call him to set it up. By sundown that same evening, Frank Chester had disappeared.

Chapter 6

"Every unpunished murder takes away something from the security of every man's life." ~ Daniel Webster

On the evening of December 21st, Rose and Vito Milano quietly dressed for their son's viewing. The suit they had chosen for Anthony to be laid out in was the same blue suit they had bought him for his graduation from the Philadelphia Art Institute just two months prior to his death. They never dreamed in a million years that they would be burying their son in that suit. For that matter, they never dreamed they would bury their child at all. Your children are supposed to live well into adulthood, bless you with grandchildren to dote on, and eventually bury you.

When they painfully selected Anthony's burial clothes and finally decided on his graduation suit, a white shirt and his new tie, the undertaker quietly laid it aside. He had known the Milanos for many years. He was one of Vito's regular barbershop customers. He was at a loss for words. His friend's grief weighed on him like a millstone. He didn't have the heart to tell Vito and Rose that it would take a miracle to rebuild their son's neck with plaster of paris skillfully enough to cover the evidence of the violent destruction. He told the Milanos it was a good choice for a suit and then quietly went to work to make Anthony as handsome as he was in life.

Anthony's coffin was placed amidst flowers and pictures from his scrapbook. Ironically, he had just completed the scrapbook the last day of his life. There were pictures of him smiling with his sister Annamarie. His portfolio from the Philadelphia Art Institute was placed on a table. It had been voted best in his class. Next to his art school portfolio was the graduation picture of Anthony smiling, proudly holding his degree, and wearing his blue suit - the suit that now served as his burial shroud.

For the twenty-eight years that Vito and Rose Milano had been married, Rose had never seen her stoic husband cry. Now the tears coursed silently down his face. His frail, thin body shook as he struggled with his grief. Mourners somberly lined up in the freezing December air to pay their respects. Many were from the Mennonite Church, which Vito and Rose both belonged to, having left Catholicism for the Mennonite faith when Anthony was fifteen years old and a sophomore in high school.

Mennonites refrain from alcohol and drugs and refuse to bear arms. Mennonites are excused from military service as conscientious objectors and cannot become policemen. Mennonites strictly adhere to the bible as the literal word of God in all matters, including homosexuality. Oddly, Mennonites oppose capital punishment in general, even though there are several biblical passages that call for it. They also disregard *kashrut*, which are the kosher dietary laws Jews try to adhere to and which are enumerated in the book of Leviticus. They are a peace-loving people who take the commandment "Love thy neighbor" very seriously and thus, like the Amish, they rally in mutual aid and support for one another in times of need. Mennonites lead such devout lives that, among the stricter orders, they even refrain from driving and refuse to collect social security. They drive so rarely and carefully that they are permitted to have their own self-insuring program for automobiles that costs a mere $12.00 per month.

Vito asked those who mourned with his family to pray that the police capture those responsible for his son's murder. In a few days, the heartbroken Milanos would read in the newspapers that Anthony was gay and as such, was the victim of a slashing because of his homosexuality. Anthony's homosexuality has never been absolutely proven one way or the other and his orientation is mere speculation, sadly fueled by the publicity surrounding the murder as well as his effeminate appearance. Vito refused to believe his only son was gay. All that mattered was that his only son, the promising young artist whom he was so proud of, lay dead before him. This would be the last time he'd ever see his son.

On December 22nd at 11:00 AM, Anthony Vito Milano was laid to rest in Rosedale Memorial Park Cemetery in Levittown. A picture of Anthony was inserted into the brass and marble plate that marked his grave. Underneath the photograph the inscription read "Anthony V. Milano 1961-1987 We will always love you." Vito, Rose and their daughter Annamarie bade farewell to Anthony as his casket was lowered into the ground. Never again would Annamarie see her brother's smiling face or hear him laugh with joy as he often had when they went out to trendy nightclubs together. Never again would Rose hear Anthony's thoughtful, concerned voice asking if he might pick up anything at the store for her on his way home. Never again would he come into his father's barbershop for a haircut, after which Vito would beam, proudly telling other customers, *"That's my son."*

While Anthony Milano was being interred, several Bristol police officers stood poised with their guns drawn outside the door of Room 32 of The Falls Motel in Falls Township. The Falls Motel was a seedy roadside stop, reminiscent of your garden variety flea-bag pit stops frequented by drunks and whores. *"Open up! Police!"* Upon entering, police found Rick Laird and Barbara Anne in one bed, Mark Laird and Mark's girlfriend Lisa in the other bed and Barbara Anne's little boy David using two chairs pushed together as his bed. One officer pointed his pistol directly in Rick's face while a second officer, brandishing a shotgun, tore the blankets off of Rick, yelling, *"Don't move!"*. Barbara Anne let out a blood curdling scream. Little David began to cry, hiding in a corner, terrified of all those armed men in the tiny room who looked like they wanted to kill the man he thought of as his dad. The officers hauled Rick out of the bed and handcuffed him while they Mirandized him: "You're under arrest for the murder of Anthony Milano. You have the right to remain silent. Anything you say can and will be used against you in a court of law. You have the right to an attorney. If you cannot afford an attorney, one will be appointed for you by the court." Rick craned his neck toward his pregnant woman as he was being led out in his long johns and sneakers and yelled, "I love ya' baby!"

When Rick arrived at the Bristol Township police headquarters, Detective Dykes was ready for him. He strolled confidently over to Rick, staring intensely into his eyes, "First of all, there's a couple of things we oughta get straight. The death penalty in this state is carried out by electrocution, not lethal injection. The other thing is there is no statute of limitations on a homicide charge. Do you know what I'm saying?" Rick glared at the formidable Detective Dykes and responded, "Yeah, I *really* know what you're saying."

Dykes wasted no time in dispensing with the pretense of civility. Getting directly to the point, he said, "Then you know why you're here. So where's Frank Chester?" Determined to maintain his machismo, Rick sneered back, "I'm no rat. Are two rats better than one?" The Croydon Code kicked in, in high gear. "When was the last time you spoke to him?", Detective Dykes fired back, his face flushed red in a mixture of anger and disgust for this punk with more tattoos than brains who had utterly destroyed another human being's life.

Rick sneered at the detective, "Don't you know?" confirming that he had picked up the hint that his calls with Frank Chester had been intercepted by police.

"Listen, you're the one in the cell right now. You better start thinking about your own problems," Dykes said. As Rick was led to the other side of the room by the uniformed officers for his fingerprinting and mug shot, he retorted: "I am. You're trying to pin a homicide on me."

"Yeah. I've heard that before, too," replied the detective as the other officers finished processing and booking Rick Laird.

"Yeah, I already figured that out," Rick snarled.

"You know Rick, you really should have taken off somewhere good instead of just running to the Falls Motel," Dykes goaded Rick, hoping to elicit an incriminating statement.

"Yeah, I know but," Rick said, as he gestured by rubbing his thumb and fingers together, implying that his lack of money was the reason he didn't get any farther than the border of Bristol and Falls Township.

Looking at a fellow detective and back at Rick, smirking and half-heartedly laughing, Detective Dykes said, "You know Rick, this was the dumbest homicide we ever saw." And Detective Dykes was right. It *was* a dumb homicide. Not merely in the sense that the killers made no attempt to conceal the victim's body afterward, but also in the sense that they knew a Bristol Township police officer had seen the three men all leave the bar together in the victim's car just hours earlier. Did they really think they wouldn't get caught? But the ultimate stupidity of the crime is this: No matter how deeply you might despise another person, you don't have to assault them. You don't have to kill them. You can choose to disassociate from that person entirely. The world is certainly a big enough place to avoid those whom are objects of your contempt. There was absolutely no reason for sadistically beating someone to a bloody pulp and then butcher them. In reality, is there ever really such a thing as a "smart homicide"?

Meanwhile, Frank Chester's whereabouts were still unknown and he remained at large. Alan Rubenstein suspected that Frank didn't go very far because his attorneys called twice over the next few days trying to arrange Frank's surrender in exchange for a deal. Rubenstein wished Frank's attorneys a 'Merry Christmas' and hung up. Rubenstein later said during an interview, "The only deal I was willing to offer Frank Chester was AC current or DC current."

It was December 30th when Alan Rubenstein got a call from a Bristol attorney who was friendly with Frank Chester's family. Frank was ready to turn himself in. Two Bucks County detectives were patiently waiting at the attorney's office when Frank Chester, sober and shame-faced, walked in with his stepfather at his side. He bowed his head in silence as the charges on the arrest warrant were read against him: First degree murder, kidnapping, criminal conspiracy and a host of minor charges. Then he was handcuffed and taken to the police headquarters where his buddy Rick had been taken just a little over a week before.

Detective Dykes was waiting for Frank. He said, "So Frank, is there anything you would like to add to your previous statement?"

Frank responded, "The last story I told you *was* the truth."

"Well we have information that's different from your last "truthful" statement, Frank," Dykes retorted.

As he was booked, Frank Chester replied, "Well maybe I didn't tell you *all* of the truth."

Thus, as the New Year ushered in 1988, Anthony Milano's killers sat behind bars. The relationship between the two men between the two men cooled significantly: at one time they had been close enough to get tattoos together, share a minor assault charge together, drink and shoot pool together. Frank had even been asked by Rick to be godfather to Rick's unborn baby. Now they ceased all communications with each other as each built his defense by blaming the murder exclusively on the other. However, both men admitted being present at the scene of the crime. Both bore witness to the actual murder, which would prove to be the downfall for the both Richard Laird and Frank Chester.

Chapter 7

"Whosoever sheddeth a man's blood, by man shall his blood be shed." ~ Genesis 9:6 (the Bible)

The trial for the two men charged in the slaying of Anthony Milano began on May 15th, 1988. Newspaper journalists and television news crews swooped in with a vengeance and converged on the tiny Bucks County Courthouse in the center of Doylestown. Everyone was going to be watching the outcome of *this* trial. It was the first trial in the history of American jurisprudence of its kind: a homophobic-induced hate-crime in which the prosecution would try both men together. The judge denied the severance of their cases which would have granted them separate trials. The prosecution sought the death penalty against both men.

Doylestown is the county seat for Bucks County. It is a quaint, semi-rural historic small town community nestled among the rolling green hillsides and fertile farmlands of eastern Pennsylvania, equidistant between Allentown and Philadelphia. With an abundance of three hundred year old stone farmhouses and gracious Victorian mansions, Doylestown exuded an aura of old money. Specialty clothing stores, pastry shops and eateries and a Starbucks Coffee shop lined Main Street within a block of the courthouse. Parking near the courthouse was limited and scarce.

After *voire dire* - the selection of the jury - the trial began on a sunny May morning in 1988. Judge Beister presided over the trial. The courtroom was jam packed with representatives of the media as well as friends and family members of both Rick Laird and Frank Chester. Also in attendance were eager young law clerks apprenticing in the district attorney's office. Other up and coming lawyers serving clerkships for local criminal defense law firms were present to observe the trial as well.

There was also a large crowd of gay rights activists from Philadelphia led by spokesperson Rita Addessa who had come in support of the Milanos and also just in silent protest. And of course, there were also your garden variety collection of curious onlookers from the public at large. Cameras flashed and onlookers watched as a sheriff escorted Frank Chester into the courtroom, cleanly shaven and dressed in a new charcoal colored suit with his head bowed. Two larger sheriffs escorted Rick Laird. Rick shamelessly grinned at the cameras like a movie star attending the Academy Awards ceremony. Rick wore a dark blue suit with his hair styled and beard neatly trimmed.

Alan Rubenstein was short in stature, but a Redwood Giant in the legal community. He projected a formidable presence in the courtroom. He delivered his opening argument in the case of *The Commonwealth vs. Richard Laird and Frank Chester* like a powerful thunder clap. The courtroom was packed, leaving some in attendance having to stand. Everyone's eyes were on Rubenstein, mesmerized by every word of his opening statement to the court.

Rubenstein paced back and forth in front of the jury box, addressing the jurors, "You will hear testimony in this courtroom that what we found was horrifying. The unspeakable. Horror in the form of a young boy, a young man, who had his throat slashed. Not once, not twice, but more times than you can count. *More times than you can count*. Anthony Milano was beaten, *violently*. He had a skull fracture. He was hit. He was kicked. He was stomped. He had a brain hemorrhage. His brain was swelling in his head."

Rubenstein paused momentarily to let his words sink in. Locking eyes with each juror, Rubenstein resumed making the statement on behalf of the commonwealth. "Now you may say to yourself, *'What was the reason for this? Was it a robbery?'* No... *'Did they take his ring, his watch and his clothes and his car? Of course not. There had to be a reason. Why would someone do that to another human being? There must have been some provocation.'* No, you won't hear that. But there *was* a reason. Because on the last day Anthony Milano was alive, he had the misfortune to walk into the Edgely Inn. And he meets Richard Laird, who sits here and Frank Chester, who sits here. He has nothing in common with them. He doesn't know them. He's there to get a sandwich and a couple of beers before going home." Rubenstein paused briefly again.

He resumed speaking slowly and deliberately, "But they don't *like* him. They didn't like his clothes. They didn't like his *style*. They didn't like the way he looked. They thought — *they thought* — he was a homosexual. And because of that, they killed him." Rubenstein let those words fall like a ton of bricks.

Then, pivoting on his heels and glaring at Rick Laird and Frank Chester before turning to look at the jury, he continued, "But the key words in this trial are not that they didn't like the way he was dressed, that they didn't like the way he was talking. The key thing isn't even that he was or may have been a homosexual. The key word is that he *was*. He is no more. He's dead. He was butchered...They did it!" He dramatically spun around and pointed at Rick Laird and Frank Chester, emphasizing those last three words as the jury sat transfixed.

Vito and Rose Milano and their daughter Annamarie sat in the gallery, weeping and holding onto each other for support. Vito had a heart condition. Although five months had passed since their only son's death, they were still as grief-stricken and heartsick as they were on that awful day a week before Christmas when the police, choking back tears, approached them with their hats in their hands, informing them of Anthony's demise.

Rick Laird and Frank Chester were flanked by their attorneys. Frank was obviously trying very hard to refrain from looking at Rick. His attorney, Tom Edwards, had given him strict orders not to look at Rick Laird. Not even one glance. Throughout most of the proceedings, Frank Chester sat with his head bowed in silent shame.

But Rick looked at Frank throughout the trial without blinking his eyes even once. There was a soulless look about Rick's cold, deadpan stare that had Rick's attorney Ron Elgart very concerned. Attorney Elgart was from the largest and most highly reputed criminal defense law firm in Bucks County: Fink, Fink & Associates. This was Ron Elgart's first murder case. In fact, it was the twenty-eight year old lawyer's first capital trial. It was a very high profile media event as well.

Elgart had seriously considered having his client wear a pair of eyeglasses to minimize the effects of his penetrating, cold stare. That look was the last thing he wanted the jury to see. Rick's eyes were just indescribably cold. Instead, he ended up placing Rick with his face away from the jury and instead, facing his former buddy Frank as if to convey to the jury that Rick was saying *'look what you got me into, man.'*

However, the young, inexperienced attorney failed to anticipate that Rick would stare down everyone else in the courtroom as well. Rick Laird's new, stylish look really transformed him into an extremely handsome man, but his behavior completely subtracted from his new good looks.

Rick leered at the women in the press row, ridiculed the gay rights activists and snickered at the male news cameramen. He periodically rolled his eyes and looked nonchalantly around the room as if he were bored. His occasional glances at the clock situated high up on the north wall of the courtroom conveyed the sense that he had better things to do with his time. His demeanor reflected the attitude that "the system" had no right to force him to be there. In his mind, he hadn't done anything wrong. He sneered at the entire court as if this was all a joke.

Rick had been in and out of prison since he was nineteen. His record included everything from assault charges to drugs to the time he stole somebody's boat "just for the hell of it". His mother Joyce Kessler also had a colorful history and a criminal record as well. Although she had remarried to a state trooper after divorcing Richard Roland Laird, Sr., that didn't stop her from playing the role of a modern day Ma Barker. She had just pled guilty in March 1987 to 12 counts of embezzlement and forgery that were filed against her by her employer. The employer told police that she stole the money for her sons. Out of the 339 checks she forged, 97 were payable to Richard Laird.

By the end of the first day, Rubenstein paraded twenty-five witnesses for the commonwealth into the court to take the witness stand. He called up all of Frank Chester's friends, including Allen Hilton and Gale Gardner, Dr. Ahmad the pathologist, Officer McGuigan, Jimmy Phillips, Yolanda Thompson and even Nancy Frey who had witnessed the defendants' quarrelsome behavior and anti-gay comments in the bar. Dr. Ahmad demonstrated Milano's injuries by use of an artists' easel with oversized white paper on which she drew with red marker every cut, laceration and bruise. The easel's oversized white paper was awash in red ink by the time she was finished.

By the end of the first day, the emotions in the courtroom had grown intense. The gay rights activists saw the murder of Anthony Milano as the ultimate form of censorship - a permanent silencing. The slaying of the closeted young artist from Levittown was the manifestation of their worst nightmares and deepest fears. There was no love lost between the activists and defendants. The activists had witnessed and personally experienced various degrees of gay-bashing in their own lives, including criminal assaults.

Emotions were so tense on both sides that everyone was searched for weapons before entering the courtroom. While that may be common practice now in a post-9/11 society, in 1988 things were far different. Courthouses, airports and various other public places were not littered with metal detectors and x-ray machines for the scrutinizing of personal belongings. Good guys, like district attorneys, could be smokers without being criminalized for their use of tobacco. America was a freer society then, and that included the Bucks County Courthouse.

For Rick Laird, the animosity between the gay rights activists and himself was mutual. He was heard to remark to one of the constables that "those gay-lib people are fuckin' nuts." He even requested that his estranged wife JoAnn be moved to another row so "she wouldn't catch anything from the homos" that could be passed onto his kids. Attorney Elgart considered fitting Rick with a bullet-proof vest.

One of the regular spectators was Colleen Ingram, Frank Chester's sweetheart. She attended every day, clutching the prom photo of her and Frank, and sat with Frank's mother and sisters, looking crushed. She couldn't help but begin to second guess herself. Would Frank not be in the predicament he was in now if she had not upset him by returning his engagement ring? What if she and Frank never had a tiff and broke up, would he have been anywhere but the Edgely Inn that fateful night with Rick Laird? These alternative scenarios played over and over in her mind.

Frank's mother seemed to age practically overnight as the trial progressed. Elaine asked herself silently over and over in her mind, where she had gone wrong as a mother. Just when it began to look like Frank was finally getting his act together, this happened.

Then there were Rick Laird's women, on whom his influence was legendary. JoAnn and her mother sat with Rick's kids, periodically checking on them to see if they were ok. She had just recently signed the divorce papers and changed her last name from Laird back to her maiden name of Walters. The children also had their last names changed and had changed schools due to the negative attention they were getting from other children and their parents because of Rick's arrest for murder. The older of the two, although only in second grade, was well aware of what was going on.

Barbara Anne with the eleven week old infant son she just had by Rick had to sit apart from JoAnn, however. The jealous animosity between those two women was poorly concealed. JoAnn had put up with a lot from Rick ever since she had gotten pregnant from him. When the two women ended up in the same elevator, they emerged screaming "Fuck you" at each other and engaged in a shoving match, even though Barbara Anne was holding Rick's newborn baby in her arms.

For all that Rick had put Jo Ann through, she still loved him. He was her first true love. Rick had met JoAnn Walters at the Levittown Rollerama skating rink when he was thirteen and she was fourteen. Rick was too young, too immature and too wild for responsible married life when he had gotten JoAnn pregnant with his first child, a boy they called little Ricky. They had two kids together. It's not so easy to stop loving someone with that history there. Their marriage only lasted a few years and it was an abusive one. They were just too young.

Even JoAnn's tough-looking, tough-talking brother, Mike Walters, was there in support of Rick. Mike Walters walked with a cane that had a solid brass serpent coiled on the top. Throughout the first day of the trial, he muttered obscenities and anti-gay epithets about the activists with Rita Addessa. Oddly, by the last day of the trial, he and Rita ended up chatting amicably over coffee in the snack bar of the courthouse. Speaking in a low tone to keep others from overhearing their conversation he told her, "Look, I don't mind men in dresses. I know a few dykes and homos myself. But don't tell anyone I said that. My friends wouldn't understand."

"Sure, sure. I understand," Addessa assured him. She told the tough looking young man what her role was as a gay rights activist. She explained briefly that she was there to support the victim's family but also that by making her appearance; she was making a statement against the death penalty for Anthony Milano's killers as well. She believed that an eye for an eye solves nothing, but teaching tolerance goes a long way.

"Yeah but what I'm saying is that if anything happens to me or my kids because I told you I had gay friends, are you gonna support *me*?" Walters said. Addessa assured him once more that she not only understood but also supported the friends and loved ones of those who are gay. That is what supporters of gay rights do. Gay rights activists support equal rights and equal justice for everyone, and that included macho young men like Mike Walters and his family.

Furthermore, she was concerned that a death verdict would serve to breed more resentment in the straight community because of the special status of "hate crime" that the prosecutor was going for, which she felt others might resent and see as getting special treatment. And that would be unfair since any violent, senseless, unprovoked murder is technically a hate crime. Addessa was a staunch opponent of the death penalty, as was Mike Walters. It was in their shared belief about capital punishment that these two dissimilar souls found common ground and formed a bond.

One by one, Rubenstein called Allen Hilton, Gale Gardner, Richard Griscavage, Pete Carpinona and Christine Bogarde to the stand. They each testified to the actions and words of Chester and Laird after the killing. They laid out everything from Gale Gardner seeing Rick snap the utility knife open and shut while saying "no evidence, no crime" in the car, to Pete Carpinona's recollection of the bloody clothes. They recounted the discussion in Chester's living room about needing a car to "take care of a dead deer" and Chester's worrying that his fingerprints were in Anthony Milano's car.

Hearing her brother referred to as a "dead deer" and then how Frank Chester's teenaged friends suggested ways he could dispose of Anthony's body to cover up the murder was too much for Annamarie. Where did people like that come from anyway, she wondered. What kind of people can sit there and talk like that about someone who was murdered? What if it was their brother, their son? What kind of values and morals did their parents teach them? The whole sordid affair was sickening. Rose and Vito Milano were not taking it very well, either. The jurors listened to every word as the events of December 15th, 1987 were retold in vivid, painful detail.

After each of the teens stepped down from the witness stand, Rubenstein grew more confident that his case against Laird and Chester was a slam-dunk. One of the major factors that really sealed the fate of the two men was Laird's demeanor under cross-examination. Another was the defense tactics employed by the counsel for both of the accused.

From the beginning, both men told their attorneys that the other man did it. Pleading guilty was not an option, especially for Rick Laird who adamantly insisted he had done nothing wrong. In hindsight, Elgart should have insisted his client agree to a diminished capacity claim, even though such a claim means admitting to a degree of criminal liability.

Ron Elgart had to build his client's defense on the premise that Rick Laird was only guilty of merely trying to protect his friend, Frank Chester. Laird's smug coolness about going Christmas shopping was proof that he wasn't guilty and that he only tried to help Frank cover his own ass so his friend wouldn't go to prison or worse, be executed for capital murder. Elgart tried to paint a mental picture for the jury of what happened in the woods that night. He tried to show that this frenzied killing had to have had a tremendous amount of rage behind it. "You're holding a short knife. So your fingers are right in the blood and you're slashing and dragging this knife through the throat. You can hear the sounds of blood gushing and the trachea breaking. You're being sprayed by blood, and you're eye to eye, face to face with the victim. There was just a huge amount of anger involved here." Elgart contended that such rage had to come from Chester, not Laird.

Meanwhile, Chester's lawyer built his client's defense on the premise that the police knew he was innocent because if it were otherwise, they would not have repeatedly let him go home after successive questioning. If Frank Chester were truly guilty of this unspeakable crime, why let him go after the very first time they had him in the Bristol police headquarters? Now if Frank Chester truly was guilty, why would he go to the police? Why would he go seek advice from his young, inexperienced teenaged friends? Why would he risk being suspected by police because of talking about what he saw that night in the woods while Rick Laird unfeelingly went about his Christmas shopping? Furthermore, every witness for the prosecution came in courtesy of Frank Chester. Edwards' tactic was to present Frank Chester as a stupid, mixed-up young kid who was terrified of Rick Laird, the real killer.

On the morning of May 18th, after the prosecution rested its case, Frank Chester took the witness stand. "The defense calls Frank Chester."

This time Frank Chester added a few more pieces to what he previously claimed happened once the three men left the bar together. He added details of what happened in the car that he had not previously mentioned to the police. He recounted the forty-five minute terror ride with Anthony driving, himself in the back seat with the unopened six-pack of beer, and Laird riding shotgun while ordering Anthony through every turn and stop and slapping him around as he pled to go home. Chester added that he got into the car expecting to be dropped off at Laird's apartment even though it was practically across the street from the bar. He added that Laird wanted to drive around first.

They made three stops before ending up on Ashby Avenue. The first was at a 7-11 where Rick Laird wanted to make a phone call and went into the store to buy cigarettes with Frank while Anthony waited in the car. Anthony, presumably sensing a chance to escape, tried to back out of the lot. However, it probably seemed odd to the jury that Anthony waited for Chester to get back in his car before attempting to leave. Chester continued, claiming that Anthony hit the gas pedal hard enough to stall the car, probably in a state of panic in his desperation to get the hell away from Rick Laird. Then Laird, hearing and seeing the stalling car and realizing it was an attempt to leave him behind, furiously slammed down the phone receiver, ran back to the car and began beating Anthony up.

Chester claimed they made two more stops. The first stop was for drugs because Laird was looking for speed. The second stop was to "take a piss". He claimed all three men got out to "take a piss", yet according to the coroner's report and Dr. Ahmad's testimony, Anthony Milano died with a full bladder. It was another inconsistency in a in a tangled web of inconsistencies in Chester's story of what happened.

According to the route Chester testified that they took, they rode around for about six miles total. They also passed several all-night diners, gas stations, and even Anthony Milano's home and his Mennonite Church.

Neither the defense nor the prosecution could come up with an explanation as to why Anthony didn't do something to try to escape, such as leaning on the horn and flashing his headlights. Could it be that Anthony wasn't the only one behind the wheel the entire time?

In one of Chester's earlier stories to the police he placed Laird behind the wheel for some of the time, taking over after the first stop at the convenience store. Since Anthony's keys were never found, it is plausible that Chester did tell the truth when he testified that Laird drove for a portion of the ride. That would also explain why, once arriving at Ashby Avenue, Anthony got out of the car in a dark, isolated area with Laird instead of taking off the minute Laird stepped out of the car. If Laird was the driver and refused to give Anthony his car keys back, Anthony could not have simply gunned the accelerator and driven away.

Edwards asked his client what happened after the three of them arrived at Ashby Avenue. Chester began by reciting what he told Detective Dykes before his arrest. He said they stopped there because Rick Laird wanted to go to Tommy Main's house across the street at 1324 Ashby Avenue to buy some meth. He and Anthony got out on the passenger side while Laird climbed out of the drivers' side closest to the woods.

"I had the six-pack with me. I got out and started walking towards the house when I saw that Rick and Tony weren't there. They were walking towards the woods together," Chester stated. "Rick had one arm around Tony and punched him squarely in the face with the other arm." Chester claimed he saw this from the rear and then he ran over and knocked Anthony to the ground. Frank Chester's eyes darted nervously from the jury box to his attorney, his hands folded neatly in his lap as he spoke.

"Why did you push Anthony Milano?" asked Edwards.

Chester: "Well, look at the size of Rick...."

Edwards: "Did you want to stop a fight?"

Chester: "Yeah, you could say that. I didn't want to see the kid get beat up there for no reason."

Edwards: "So you pushed Milano out of the way?"

Chester: "Yes sir."

Edwards: "Then what happened?"

Chester: "I said to Rick, 'Let's get out of here'. And then Rick said, 'Fuck that', and jumped on him."

Edwards: "Then what happened?"

Chester: "...I thought he was hitting him, you know what I mean? Because when you're on top, you can hit something like this."

Frank Chester described how Rick knelt on the victim pinning his arms beneath him and made the motions with his hands, showing how the victim can be slapped in the face, sweeping his arm moving back and forth to demonstrate the hitting. Continuing with his testimony, Frank Chester gulped hard as if the words stuck in his throat, "When I walked, when I went over there, he was doing....the thing."

Edwards: "What was he doing?"

Chester: "Slashing his throat."

Edwards: "What did you do?"

Chester: "I froze. I never seen anything like that. Even on TV."

Edwards: "Then what happened?"

Chester: "Well I was just, like, standing there. Then Rick looked up at me. I turned around and ran."

Next it was Rubenstein's turn to cross-examine. Chester described the blood squirting up from Anthony Milano's throat and the gurgling noises he heard when Rick was cutting him.

Rubenstein: "You were afraid of Rick Laird, correct?"

Chester: "Yes. I mean, I wouldn't want to have to fight him."

Rubenstein: "Me neither."

Edwards: "*Objection!*"

Judge Beister: "Sustained."

Rubenstein: "After you saw Rick making these motions back and forth with his hands, did that scare you?"

Chester: "Yeah."

Rubenstein: "Were you worried?"

Chester: "I was in shock..."

Rubenstein: "Never saw that before?"

Chester: "No."

Rubenstein: "Kind of stuff they won't show on TV?"

Chester: "No, they don't."

Rubenstein: "Pretty horrible, wasn't it?"

Chester: "Yes."

Rubenstein: "Scared as you were of Richard Laird, you went back to his apartment that night, didn't you?"

Rubenstein let the irony in that statement weigh on the minds of the jury. Frank Chester was at a loss for words. Rubenstein knew that Chester's claim of fear would be far less credible because of the fact that Chester returned voluntarily to the apartment of the man he now claimed to have been in mortal fear of. It just didn't make sense for Chester to have done that if he was an innocent man. Especially when, according to Rich Griscavage's testimony about giving each man a ride home on his motorcycle separately, Chester could have gone anywhere else but back to Laird's. Anyplace else other than a savage killer's home would certainly have been a safer place for someone who was a potential witness to a brutal crime. Being an innocent bystander to a horrible murder makes you a potential target simply for being able to come back and point the finger at the perpetrator.

This reasoning was not lost on the jury or anyone else witnessing the trial. Turning the court's attention to Chester's relationship with Laird and their behavior in the bar, Rubestein briefly asked about the slow dancing incident. Chester, visibly embarrassed, squirmed and fidgeted in the chair. When Jimmy Phillips testified for the commonwealth, one of the things he testified to was the manner in which Rick Laird and Frank Chester ridiculed the victim in the bar by slow dancing in front of him. If Chester and Laird killed Milano because they thought he was gay, Rubenstein needed to prove the defendants' hatred for gays led up to the murder. One way to achieve that was to depict either one or both men as insecure in their masculinity by being flustered over questions about things like the slow dancing.

Rubenstein said sarcastically: "Now, this dancing or not dancing, you weren't dancing cheek to cheek with Laird, were you?"

Chester: "No, sir!"

Rubenstein: "Then how did this happen, this thing that people have described as dancing which you say was not. Can you tell us about that?"

Chester: "How it happened? If I'm saying it didn't? If it did, I don't remember it."

Rubenstein: "In other words, you're not saying that you didn't dance with Laird, just that you don't recall?"

Chester: "I'm saying to my recollection."

Rubenstein: “Let me ask you this question: Do you usually make it a habit to dance with other guys, and I don’t mean that as a joke, Mr. Chester, but do you usually make it a habit?”

Chester: “No, sir!”

Rubenstein: “So if you *did* that, you would probably remember that, right?”

Chester was silent.

Rubenstein was satisfied that he proved another inconsistency in Chester’s testimony and diminishing his credibility. Frank Chester was able to remember in vivid detail everything else concerning the night in question. He recalled every stop and every turn during the car ride. He remembered everything that was said and done. Yet he couldn’t remember slow dancing with another man. Either he was lying under oath about what he claimed to remember, or he was so insecure with his own sexuality that he would have a reason to participate in a fatal gay-bashing. Thus, Frank Robert Chester was pinned squarely between the horns of dilemma, where Rubenstein wanted him.

Rubenstein returned to questions about the specifics of the murder. Tilting the easel on which Dr. Ahmad depicted the victim’s wounds towards the witness stand, Rubenstein began discussing Milano’s injuries.

Rubentstein: “You mentioned that you saw Rick Laird punch him in the face *once*, right?”

Chester: “Yes.”

Rubenstein: “Then all of a sudden, Rick’s on top of him, right?”

Chester: “Yes.”

Rubenstein: “Are you sure about that?”

Chester: “Positive.”

Rubenstein: “One punch in the face?”

Chester: “Yeah. Bang.”

Rubenstein: “Bang, right in the face. That’s it? That’s all you saw?”

Chester: “Like I said....that’s what I seen.”

“Ok. Who did *this* injury, this bang to the head, do you remember *that*?” Rubenstein slapped the easel with his open palm, thwack.

“How about this bang to the head here?” Rubenstein slapped the easel again.

Chester: “No.”

Rubenstein pointed another spot, slapping the canvas again, “How about the bang to the chin?”

Chester: “No.”

Rubenstein: “You *heard* the pathologist’s testimony, right?”

Chester: “Yes.”

Rubenstein: “Wasn’t Rick Laird, was it?”

Elgart hoped that the inconsistencies in Frank Chester’s testimony might prove his client’s innocence. Elgart’s strategy was to show that Chester’s testimony conflicted with the physical evidence and that other things were never explained, either. One example was in Chester’s claim that Rick Laird was the one who jumped on the victim. Since Laird outweighed the victim by close to ninety pounds, there should be post mortem tissue damage corresponding with someone that heavy jumping Milano and kneeling on him while cutting him up. Yet, according to Dr. Ahmad's testimony, there was no trace of that sort of damage. There was nothing to show that someone as heavy as Laird pinned Milano to the ground. Another missing piece to the puzzle was that Chester never explained how the victim ended up more than thirty feet into the woods when there was no evidence of Milano being dragged. Why would Milano, who was scared enough of Rick Laird to try to escape while at the 7-11, get out of the car and walk with Laird into a dark, isolated area as Chester claimed? It just didn't add up. It was patently obvious that Chester had not told the whole truth and nothing but the truth on the witness stand.

The tape recorded telephone conversation and the testimony from others depicting Laird as a homophobic bully was still damning. But if the only concrete thing going against Laird was the testimony of Frank Chester and nothing else, Elgart's chances of winning his case for his client would be greater. But realistically he really had a no-win situation on his hands regarding this case — especially after Dr. Ahmad's testimony scientifically describing the multitude and severity of the victim's injuries. The carnage was graphically portrayed by the sea of red ink on the easel depicting the slash wounds of the victim. The young friends of Frank Chester testified how Laird appeared and acted following the murder. Using Chester's inconsistent testimony as the only real evidence against Rick Laird was a long shot, but it was the only shot Elgart had.

Ultimately, it was Rick Laird's courtroom behavior that sealed his fate. Everyone in the court had waited for both Chester and Laird to take the stand and hear what they had to say. Having heard Frank Chester's version as well as testimony from Chester's lovers and friends, everyone's eyes were on Rick Laird as he strutted like a peacock past the jury box to take the witness stand.

The minute Elgart put Rick Laird on the witness stand he regretted his decision. When he opened by asking his client what the weather was like on the night in question, Laird played the tough guy, laughing and saying, "Kinda shitty." The jurors were completely put off from the start by his arrogant swagger and longshoreman's vocabulary. Jurors and spectators gasped in shock at Laird's callous disregard for the formalities of the courtroom. As Elgart tried to lead Laird through the events of December 15th 1987, Laird's testimony became increasingly obnoxious, laden with expletives. When asked if he had ever called Anthony Milano a faggot, Laird grinned, exclaiming as if proud of himself, "Sure. I call lots of people faggot."

Laird swore there were no stops between the Edgely Inn and Ashby Avenue. There was no terror ride that he knew of. No, he didn't threaten Milano. No, he didn't lay a hand on Milano. Yes, he rode in the passenger seat. No, he didn't need a ride home - he lived across the street, it was Chester who needed the ride. Amazingly, Elgart, Edwards, nor Rubenstein ever tried to establish why Laird would accept a ride that he didn't need from a man he admittedly derided as a homosexual.

Both defendants swore under oath to tell the truth, the whole truth and nothing but the truth so help them both under God. Yet, for both accounts to be *completely* truthful, one would have to surmise that Anthony Milano drove somewhere he didn't want to go of his own volition, got out of his nice warm car and walked into the cold dark woods, then slapped himself silly, fractured his own skull and then viciously cut his own throat. If the jury bought that, then everyone could put on their ruby slippers, dance down the Yellow Brick Road and live happily ever after.

Directing the court's attention to the murder itself, Elgart asked, "What happened when you pulled up on Ashby Avenue?"

Laird: "I got out my side there and started walking towards the houses."

Elgart: "What happens next?"

Laird: "Well, I heard [Frank] yell, 'Yo, over here!'....I turned around. I started walking towards him. I heard a punching and a smacking, that's what it sounded like."

Elgart: "Noises?"

Laird: "Yeah."

Elgart: "Voices?"

Laird: "Just grunts."

Elgart: "What happened when you went towards the noise?"

Laird: "I started, you know, I got up towards it, and I seen him rolling around on the ground......they were rumbling, you know? And I says, 'Yo, Frank! What the fuck you doin', man?' "

Elgart: "And what happened next?"

Laird: "Well, [Frank] jumped up, you know? And [Anthony] started to get up, and he was all wobbling, you know? And he grabbed onto my jacket..."

Elgart: "What happened next?'

Laird: "I heard noise coming [from] behind me."

Elgart: "And then what?"

Laird: "And then Tony's eyes got *real big*, man. And I started getting sprayed with all this hot shit, you know? And I heard this fucking noise like water going down the drain."

From that point on, his testimony was similar to Chester's, except the roles were reversed. Laird said he got scared and ran. Chester caught up to him, and from there on, all he did was try to protect his buddy from the possibility of being arrested and charged with a capital crime.

Laird said that everything he did, including discarding the utility knife and his own bloody clothes and advising Chester to just take off and leave town for a spell were all part of his extreme attempts to protect his friend. He admitted to telling Chester to shut up in front of Rich Griscavage, Pete Carpinona and Christine Bogarde. He didn't want to see his pal sent away for life. That's why he even went as far as telling Chester that he [Laird] was thinking of leaving town and laying low, hoping everything would all blow over and that his buddy could beat the murder rap. At one point, Laird stopped in mid-sentence and glared at Frank Chester from the witness stand pointing an accusing finger and blurted out, " I loved you like a brother, dude, and you *fucked* me, you know that?!"

For a brief moment, you could have heard a pin drop in the courtroom. Judge Beister looked on, shocked by this outburst. The lawyers looked down at their briefcases, their shoes, anywhere but the jurors' faces. While no attorney expects to be able to win every case, Ron Elgart certainly was not expecting his client to blatantly sink his own ship, when he was on trial for his life either. The jury sat in shocked silence. Rubenstein stood still and was silent. He was confident that he had won his case without needing to revisit the specifics of the murder. He was certain he would not need to demonstrate which defendant specifically did the slashing.

The key to Rubenstein's ability to win this case rested on his ability to prove conspiracy. Under the Pennsylvania Criminal Code, conspiracy requires only that the actions of both were used to achieve a common goal. In this case, that goal was the murder of Anthony Milano and subsequent cover up of the crime. Covering up a crime and aiding a felon are crimes by themselves: Obstruction of Justice and Accessory After the Fact.

Rubenstein began cross-examining Laird by revisiting the wiretapped telephone conversation between him and Frank Chester. No need to revisit what happened in the woods. He began by leading Laird through his relationship with Frank Chester, trying to let Rick Laird respond as if everything were "normal".

Rubenstein: "You had an OK relationship with Frank Chester for a couple years?"

Laird: "Yeah."

Rubenstein: "So you can't figure out any other reason why he is saying that you carved up Anthony Milano?"

Laird: "Any other reason?"

Rubenstein: "You can't think of any reason why he would say that, would you?"

Laird: "I can't think of any? Look where I'm sitting! He's trying to get the fuck out of this and what he did."

Rubenstein moved onto the wiretapped telephone call. He knew this was the crux to sealing the fate of both defendants.

Rubenstein: "Now when you spoke to Frank Chester on the phone, you didn't know that he was making the call for the police, did you?"

Laird: "No."

Rubenstein: "You remember you said to him in that phone conversation: 'Nothing, you just say yeah, we were there drinking,' right? You remember saying that?"

Laird: "Yeah."

Rubenstein: "And 'we got fucking wrecked and came to my house and passed out,' right?"

Laird: "That's right."

Rubenstein: "That's what you told Frank to say to the police, right?"

Laird: "I was trying to help him cover up, man."

Rubenstein: "That's what you told Frank Chester to say to the police, right?"

Laird: "Yeah."

Rubenstein: "That wasn't true, right?"

Laird: "That's right."

Rubenstein: "So, you were giving Frank lies to tell the police?"

Laird: "I loved the kid, man."

Rubenstein: "Not anymore though, right?"

Laird: "I forgiven him in my heart."

Rubenstein: “You said to him: ‘Oh, well, what the fuck, Frank, you got me shitting my pants dude.’ Why were you shitting your pants? What were you worried about?”

Laird: “What do *you* think?”

Rubenstein: “You tell me.”

Laird: “Look where I’m sitting, all right. Well look where I’m sitting. What do you think I was shitting my pants about?”

Rubenstein: “And Chester said, ‘Look, you know I was there talking to everybody in the bar and they know that the dude was sitting next to me,’ he was referring to Anthony Milano, wasn’t he?”

Laird: “Yes.”

Rubenstein: “Now you mentioned to Frank that you were going to hide until this blows over, right?”

Laird: “That’s correct.”

Rubenstein: “Well, what were you worried about? You didn’t kill him, did you?”

Laird: “No, I didn’t. I was trying to give, to put an idea in his head to get the hell out of here.”

Rubenstein: “So, you were trying to be a good Samaritan with him and get him to go, right?”

Laird: “If you want to put it that way, sir.”

Rubenstein: “You told him that the statute of limitations on murder was seven years, right?”

Laird: “Uh huh.”

Rubenstein: "And you figured if he could hide out for seven years, he would have this rap beat?"

Laird: "I told him that."

Rubenstein: "You told him this case would go into a dead case file, right?"

Laird: "That's what I told him."

Rubenstein: "All he had to do was hide out for seven years, dead case file, it's over and people just forget about this murder, right?"

Laird grew visibly agitated on the witness stand. His answers, while devoid of four letter words and gutter slang, did not conceal the venom in his tone.

Laird: "I was trying to keep him calm, sir."

Rubenstein, satisfied his witness was in the hot seat and caught in his own lies, pressed on. Pacing before the witness stand and the jury box, he continued. "Police wouldn't go after it. Seven years pass by like Milano was never there, right? That's what you told him?", snapping his fingers, "Right?" Laird responded by looking brazenly at the jury as he snapped his fingers: "Just like that."

Rubenstein couldn't help but notice that the jury was completely on his side now. What they had seen on the witness stand was a man whom, even if he was not the slasher, had no regard for the human life of the victim which was snuffed out "just like that", snap. Laird's cold indifference towards the victim, a life that could be forgotten with the snap of a finger, spoke volumes about his character. Rubenstein may not have smiled outwardly owing to the serious mood, but inwardly he glowed from the warmth he felt inside from his victory. He continued.

Rubenstein: "Just like that. You told him, 'there is no evidence, Frank', right?"

Laird: "That's what I said, sir."

Rubenstein: "No evidence. What did you mean by that, Mr. Laird?"

Laird: "It's self-explanatory."

Rubenstein: "You tell me. You're the one answering the questions."

Laird: "No evidence."

Rubenstein: "What's that mean?"

Laird: "No clothes, no nothing, no evidence."

Rubenstein: "No body?"

Laird: "I wouldn't know about that."

Rubenstein: "Well, did you think Mr. Milano was still alive when you said that or did you know he was dead?"

Laird: "The papers told me he was dead."

Rubenstein: "But other than that, you didn't know that, did you?"

Laird: "No."

Rubenstein: "Did you think maybe he just got up from Ashby Avenue, walked home and resumed his life?"

Laird: “That’s not funny.”

Rubenstein snapped: “You’re damn right it’s not funny. In fact, you knew just how unfunny it was that you said:

[Frank] ‘What can they do to you? What can they do to you for that?’

[Rick] ‘They can kill you.’

[Frank] ‘They can kill you?’

[Rick] ‘Lethal injection.’

Remember, you said that?”

Laird: “Yeah, I remember.”

Rubenstein: “You knew it was a pretty serious case, right?”

Laird: “Yes, sir.”

Rubenstein: “What did you mean by that? The death penalty?”

Laird: “Yes, sir.”

Rubenstein: “You figured that’s what Frank would get, right?”

Laird: “Yes, sir.”

Rubenstein elaborated more on the wiretapped phone call to drive the point home that there was proof of a conspiracy between the defendants. He forged ahead.

Rubenstein: “Then you said to him, ‘Or they can put you in fucking jail for life, which would you rather have?’ What did you mean by that, Mr. Laird?”

Laird: "I meant they could put you in fucking jail for life."

Rubenstein walked Rick Laird through the rest of the wiretapped phone conversation to make it was clear that both men were collaborating. Both acted in concert together to avoid arrest. Rubenstein also knew that this solidly middle-class jury did not relate well to hoodlums from the lower class, which is exactly how Rick Laird presented himself throughout most of his testimony. Playing the class card, Rubenstein directed Rick Laird's attention to the portion of the conversation where he used crude street slang in connection with the identity of Anthony Milano.

Rubenstein: "Now, let me ask you this question. I'm referring to page 15 in the end of the conversation. You said to him [Frank]: 'Just be cool, man. Like the motherfucker gave us a ride here and that was it. We came in and passed the fuck out.' Who was the motherfucker you were referring to?"

Laird: "That's street talk for Anthony Milano."

Seeking to emphasize Rick Laird's lack of couth and callous disregard for the victim, Rubenstein repeated the question.

Rubenstein: "Who was the motherfucker?"

Laird: "I just answered your question."

Rubenstein: "Who was it?"

Laird: "That's street talk for Anthony Milano, all right?"

Rubenstein turned, facing Judge Beister: "No further questions, Your Honor."

The prosecution rested. Neither Tom Edwards nor Ron Elgart had any further questions for either defendant. Judge Beister called Rubenstein, Edwards and Elgart up to the bench for a sidebar to ask about the time they thought their closing arguments would take. Judge Beister wanted to ensure each would have adequate time for finishing closing arguments once they had begun. He also needed time to instruct the jury. He preferred that Elgart go first but Elgart demurred, indicating he wished Edwards to go first instead. Edwards was agreeable to that arrangement. The order of presentation was a mere formality and it really would not have affected the outcome of this trial.

Chapter 8

"Justice does not descend from its own pinnacle."
~ Dante Alighieri (*Purgatorio*, VI, 37)

Tom Edwards prepared his closing argument well. However, given the troubling aspects of his client's inconsistencies in the police reports and on the witness stand he was somewhat worried. After witnessing the spectacle Rick Laird made of himself on the witness stand, compared to his client who was clearly the better behaved and more socially skilled of the two, Edwards still had hope that his client would be found not guilty. As agreed by Ron Elgart and approved by Judge Beister, Edwards went first.

"Your Honor, Mr. Elgart, Mr. Rubenstein, ladies and gentlemen of the jury, when we began this case I asked that you put on your glasses of life's experience and to evaluate the evidence from the witness stand through those glasses. To make your decision to what to believe, what seems rational, what makes the most sense to you. I hope you've done that. As you were instructed, the Commonwealth has the burden of proving beyond a reasonable doubt. Now, beyond reasonable doubt is a difficult concept. So I like to try and use an analogy."

" Let us suppose that you have a son, or a daughter, a grandchild, a little brother, niece or nephew and that child wants to go ice skating. So you bundle up that little child and you take them out to the lake. You look out at the lake. There are other children skating on the lake. Seems great. You walk down to the edge of the lake. You look down and you see a crack. You think to yourself, is it safe for my little one to go out on that ice with that crack? You may decide yes and you may decide no. If you decide yes, then you don't have reasonable doubt. It's fine. If you decide no, I respectfully submit to you that would be a reasonable doubt."

"Using that analogy, let's look at this case. And I am only concerned with this case against Frank Chester. At the beginning, before my evidence was presented, Mr. Rubenstein told you, gave you an outline of what the Commonwealth would attempt to prove and he used such words as grievous beating, and if I'm not exactly right it's your recollection what was said: unspeakable crime, etc. And he told you that the Commonwealth will prove that Anthony Milano went through a horrible beating, not only slashes but also stomped on. I believe you can all remember that." Edwards paused for a moment.

"When we had Dr. Rafaat Ahmad on the stand and describing the injuries to Mr. Milano, terrible injuries, there was no stomping. There were no marks on the upper chest, on the legs, on the extremities. Mr. Rubenstein told you defensive wounds," Edwards continued, indicating by holding up his hands before the jury. "There were two marks on the right hand. There was no brutal beating, there was a murder. A murder."

"Dr. Ahmad told us that yes, there were three places on the head where Mr. Milano was hit and I asked specifically could that be from a punch; and she said, ' yes, a hard punch'. There were two on one side and one on the chin and one on the other side. Four marks. I asked if these two could be from the same blow. Yes, they could be. So we've got three, possibly four. There is no other beating."

Perhaps splitting hairs over semantics regarding the definition of the term beating is where Tom Edwards failed to convince the jury. One will never know conclusively. The fact remains that had Anthony Milano only suffered those four blows and no slashing, he would have been a vegetable for the rest of life if he had survived. There was also the fact that Frank Chester willingly accepted a ride on the back of his buddy's motorcycle back to Rick Laird's apartment. Are these the actions of an innocent man? Regardless of how poor one's judgment may be, regardless of how impaired it may be due to the influence of alcohol or drugs, we all have an inborn sense of self-preservation. What man would feel safe in the company of another man who had just meted out a fatal attack on another human being? Unless he was in on it, or perhaps was the attacker himself, there seems to be no reasonable explanation. Of course, this is merely speculative. It's easy to play armchair psychologist when you are not the one who was in the midst of it all. Still, one can't help but wonder.

Mr. Edwards continued, brilliantly using his cracks in the ice metaphor in his closing statements. His argument was well constructed, showing off all the skills of an accomplished trial litigator. But no matter how well a lawyer may be able to effectively argue, the visible results of the crime overpower all else and there is no way to erase gruesome visual images from the minds of a jury.

"Mr. Rubenstein also told you in his opening statement that you would hear the words: well, it's only a dead fag. You remember that? And I asked you in my opening, I said listen for it. Did you hear it? I didn't hear it. We heard the tapes. It wasn't there. I respectfully submit to you that the only person that has ever called Anthony Milano a 'dead fag' was Alan Rubenstein. That's not part of the evidence."

"Let's look to what was presented from the witness stand. We have numerous people who came up to testify as to what happened. Jimmy Phillips, the bartender: He said both Frank

Chester and Mr. Laird were in the bar and recounted various things that happened. The police officers coming in, Frank trying to be the peacemaker. When the police officers come to the stand to testify, yes, Frank Chester tried to be a peacemaker, tried to keep Mr. Laird calm. You have Jolanda and Nancy Frey, and Nancy Frey says, 'Frank came up and said if this guy is bothering you, I'll stop it.' Looking out for a friend, not that he was looking for a fight with this guy. Never had any words with this other guy............I also pointed out that if the police officers believed that Frank Chester was this dangerous criminal, and you have heard testimony now that, yes, they did have him on the 18th, they let him go. That's a crack. They had him on the 19th, they let him go. That's another crack. They had him on the 20th. Go back home, Frank. Go back to your family. Go back to your neighborhood. Go back to my neighborhood. Go wherever you want. That's another crack. And they had him on the 21st. He met with people such as the District Attorney himself, Chief of Detectives Gourley, and these other competent police officers, but they did not believe that Frank Chester would go out and kill or harm. They believed Frank Chester was telling them the true story."

"Now Frank Chester...when he heard on the 22nd that he was charged with first degree murder, he got scared. He got nervous. He got upset. He laid low. Did he go to Iowa or Idaho or wherever? No, he didn't. But what he did was call different attorneys, tried to get someone to tell him, you know, what he should do. Remember, Frank Chester is only 20 years old. And finally on the 30th, what does he do? He surrendered. No one had to go out with guns drawn to find Frank Chester. He finally got the correct advice. And he surrendered himself as has been testified from here."

"After the alleged crime, Frank Chester ran back to friends and he was getting counsel as I would from friends. How many times do we do that? You ask your friends, '*what would you do?*' How many times did we say, gosh darn it if I had called my accountant or whatever, I would have done it right. Well, he doesn't have our experience. And his friends are talking about....well, you could do this, or you could do that and maybe this and maybe that. Realize that his friends are trying to be helpful but they didn't see this grisly murder. They didn't see what actually happened. They weren't as shocked as Frank was. Frank was confused. And from his testimony and the testimony of others, he wasn't in the room for much of the time that much of this was going on. I respectfully submit that they were trying to be honest."

"They are trying to tell what they remember the facts to be: Did he push him, did he kick him? Frank Chester says, '*I tried to push him out of the way*'. He also testified he's the kind of guy that when a man's down, he's down, that's it. End of it. Guy was down, he says, c'mon, let's go. That's the way Frank Chester sees things. Maybe other people don't see it that way." Looking between the jury and Rick Laird, Edwards gestured towards Laird, "Obviously, some people don't."

"You heard the testimony of Allen Hilton, as an example. Allen Hilton said, 'Well Frank told me that he kicked him.' When I asked him, I said, 'Well Mr. Hilton, you said that it was punched.' Well, punched, kicked, what's the difference? A big difference to me. He also testified, '...the way Frank told me is that they got out of the car and Frank kicked him.'..... Well let's look at the facts as we understand them. The car was on the road. The body was found 50 yards into the woods..........Maybe Allen wasn't exactly right. Allen also testified that: 'Well, Frank said that he was covered with blood from head to toe.'......But people like Gale Gardner said: 'No, I didn't see any blood.' So maybe Mr. Hilton was a little wrong on that, too.....Let's remember one other thing. Every witness that came in was the result of what Frank Chester told the police....He was scared. Talks to one police officer, Detective McDonough. He talks to Detective McAteer. He talked to Detective Dykes and slowly over this four day period he feels, 'I can be the most honest with Detective Dykes', that was his testimony....And what happens at the end of this? The police officer he can trust, couldn't trust him. Turned right around with murder in the first degree. They charged him with every crime that they charged the other defendant, and I respectfully submit that at that point, Mr. Chester was baffled, confused. That's why he went away for a few days.'

Edwards continued, referencing the wiretapped call. "Now, if an individual is innocent of a crime and he says, 'Ok..I'll call him. I'll talk to him,' I think that should tell us something because if I had done something and I call someone on the telephone and I know it's being taped, I don't know what that other individual is saying. That other individual could say, *hey Frank, what are you worried about. It's your fault. You're the one that cut him. You're the one that pushed him. You're the one that hit him*. The other end of that phone could have said anything. But he's so sure that he's right, that he's innocent, he knew that wasn't going to come out on the other end of the phone.....He makes the call because he knows he didn't do anything. And he knew that would come out through the telephone conversation."

"I respect that Frank Chester was in the wrong place at the wrong time. I respectfully submit to you that Frank Chester saw something. He was appalled by it. He was shocked by it. And being the young inexperienced man he didn't know how to handle it. I respectfully submit to you that Frank Chester did nothing except be there. I believe there are a number of cracks in the light of the Commonwealth's evidence, so many cracks that if you have a loved one that wants to go out on that lake, you have to put them in a rowboat. I respectfully submit that Frank Chester is innocent. That the Commonwealth has not met any burden of proof in this case and I hope and pray that you will come back with the only decision, the only verdict that you can for Frank Chester and that is not guilty. Thank you."

Next it was Ron Elgart's turn to deliver his closing argument to the jury. He had a feeling of dread in the pit of his stomach. He knew that his client was not the embodiment of innocence, or even a likeable person. He knew the jury would recall his colorful language, his outburst against Frank Chester while on the witness stand. And he knew that they'd been alienated by Laird's description of the victim bleeding to death. All he could do was hope for the best. He had been given a sow's ear and he had done everything possible to turn it into a silk purse. The weight of the world seemed to rest on the young attorney's shoulders. Despicable or not, loveable or not, his client was a human being whose life was at stake. He decided to use the tactic of pointing out Chester's inconsistencies to convince the jury that there existed reasonable doubt regarding the guilt of Rick Laird. It was a one in a million shot.

Elgart began his closing statement. "Frank, to be frank, definition being to be straightforward, candid, truthful. Momma named that boy wrong. In the beginning of this trial I followed up on Mr. Edwards' opening. He asked what would an innocent man do. And now we heard what Frank Chester does."

"The Commonwealth's case rests on whether you believe in the gospel according to Frank Chester and I submit you can't....All we had in this courtroom was the latest revised edition of the gospel according to Chester. You had to buy his gospel. He told his buddy Pete Carpinona, what did he tell us? I heard three versions. You heard Griscavage, Carpinona and Allen Hilton. All good, close friends of Frank Chester. People he relied upon, people he called around him in his time of need. From that, you might think he's a good guy. Maybe he is. You just have to judge him by the quality of his friends, the ones who wouldn't go to the police. The ones who knew of a grisly murder and didn't report it. They told you what Frank told them. And they told you each statement and every revision. The gospel according to Chester does not hold up in this courtroom. All we got from this chair, from Frank Chester sitting here, was the latest. Lord knows if we would have another chance to get Frank Chester up there again, what would he come up with this time? If he hadn't taken off and laid low after the warrants were put out, what would the latest edition of the gospel according to Chester say? We compare them to the question Mr. Edwards asked in his opening, 'What does an innocent man say?' "

"It was not a good night for Frank Chester that Monday night. Girlfriend had an abortion. She didn't want to see him anymore. He was upset. He was depressed. He sold his car and was involved in a major rumble Saturday night. Some guys came to see him Sunday night. They're armed with hockey sticks to take care of him and it's just Frank there. And Monday night he's still thinking about it. Who has a reason to carry a knife?"

"He calls Rick Laird over and tells Rick about it. He was concerned about retaliation.....He goes into the bar that night...and offered to beat up a guy who was showing baby pictures. He was willing to beat up a guy who was showing a picture of his daughter to a lady. He was a guy with problems. He was angry and he was a guy who was armed."

"Frank Chester time after time in this case says Rick Laird did it. Rick Laird killed him. Let's look at how the evidence supports Chester."

"Richard Laird didn't have a problem with his neighbors or guys looking for him. You heard about the autopsy. Frank Chester tells people....that the murder was committed in such a way that Rick Laird jumped on Milano, that he just comes out of nowhere and jumps on the body, pinning the shoulders to the ground with his knees and starts hacking away. You can take a look at the size of Richard Laird. He's a big fellow. He jumps on you, you're going to know it."

"Mr. Rubenstein was very specific about abrasions and cuts and you remember the testimony. There is no bruising, none. There is no indication whatsoever that...the way Milano was put to the ground ever occurred. No bruising on the body....None of the physical evidence shown here supports anything this person has told you."

"Remember Chester's testimony. Laird pinned him to the ground, knees on shoulders and started hacking away. Compare it to the testimony of the medical examiner. When I asked her what happens when the trachea, the windpipe is cut, the blood that is forming is going to shower out. What happens when the throat is severed, the carotid artery is cut, blood goes several feet into the air."

"Richard Laird had long hair and a long beard that night. If he was in the position as Chester describes it, he would have been dyed red like Eric the Red. He would have been crimson red and you don't have to read Macbeth to know that blood doesn't come out that easy. You heard that Richard Laird was washing his hands, yes; but he never washed his face. When they ran from the murder scene and got to Griscavage's apartment, was there any mention of Richard Laird being dyed red the way he would have been had he committed the murder the way Frank Chester said? The gospel of Chester doesn't add up."

"The gospel according to Chester. Which version should we look at now? The one that he told you about where he shoved him [Milano] after he took the two six-packs and heaved them and then went to the rescue, by pushing Anthony Milano to the ground? Frank says he bought two six-packs. You heard Mr. Phillips say only one six-pack was sold. Yet, nobody has found these six-packs. It doesn't add up."

"He shoved Anthony Milano. Now that's what he told us today. Previous occasion, it was he kicked Anthony Milano. He's punched Anthony Milano. He's been unconscious. He hasn't been unconscious. He's been knocked out. He hasn't been knocked out. He went back in the woods. He didn't go back in the woods. He went in the car with Milano. He didn't get in the car with Milano. The gospel according to Chester."

"We deal with two different kinds of things in this case. We first deal with the murder. Who murdered Anthony Milano? The evidence clearly shows in this case that Richard Laird did not kill Anthony Milano. The proof doesn't hold up."

"What does an innocent man say when he's accused of murder? He gives the truth. One truth, one indivisible truth. Now, we've never heard that out of the mouth of Frank Chester. There was one bright light that came into this courtroom and it came in that telephone conversation that they set up. Frank gets on the phone. We have a conversation. Frank is going to prove his innocence, and how does he do that?"

“Richard Laird says, F that, I didn’t kill nobody, man. I ain’t got it in me to kill somebody, you know; and what is Chester’s response? What is the response when you’re an innocent man and you’re fighting back? Frank should have said: That’s a lie. You killed him. Or, that’s not true, or something to that effect. He didn’t do it. Frank Chester didn’t come back at Richard Laird. He didn’t contradict him. That’s the clearest thing here. Richard Laird doesn’t know he’s being taped. He thinks he’s talking to his buddy who he’s helping out and Frank Chester doesn’t reply. That’s against everything that we know about human nature.”

“Now the DA doesn’t believe and he charges Frank Chester, drags him in here. That’s still based on the statements of Frank Chester. Do you believe Frank Chester and which gospel do you believe? Clearly the murder was committed by Frank Chester who, for whatever reason in the world, did it. ”

“Now, you may not like Richard Laird. You may not invite him over to your place for coffee after this is over. Richard Laird appeared no different on this stand than he probably did that night. He is foul mouthed. He is obnoxious. He lacks the social graces, as one would say. But he told you the best way he could what this is all about and it’s about friendship. Richard Laird stands no differently in this case than Richard Griscavage, or Pete Carpinona or any of the other people.”

“There’s a charge of conspiracy here. It’s a nice thing for the prosecution. They can say, well we don’t have to prove who actually killed Anthony Milano. We can just say conspiracy even though the other individual did it. Conspiracy links you and you’re just as guilty as him and I don’t have to prove who actually did it. I got a conspiracy. It’s real easy, but he still has to prove it. As an example, you’re 14 people. Mr. Hawkins, maybe you’ve just had it with juror 11. You just lost it. You stand up and punch him in the nose. Now, everybody else knew about it. But does that make you guilty of conspiracy? The answer is no. It does not, and that's exactly what we have here. "

"Remember there was a statement that Frank was with Peter, that they were driving and saw the car fire and that Frank really didn't pay it any attention. That's nonsense. Frank would have paid real close attention to that. His fingerprints were in the car. He was worried about that and he expressed it to all his friends time and time again. Frank Chester blew up that car. He set it on fire. Frank Chester asked his buddy about the dead deer. Remember that sick piece of evidence? 'Can I borrow your car, I got a dead deer to take care of.' Frank Chester was real worried about it and no one here can account to where Frank Chester was that night. Frank Chester blew up that car on his own after everybody left that place. Let me take it [Milano's body] up to the Poconos and bury it up there."

"Notice that Richard Laird isn't involved in any of these discussions. He's going home. He's with his girlfriend. He's with their baby. They're staying in their apartment while Frank Chester avoids arrest. Richard Laird is arrested on December 22nd and where, oh where is Frank? Frank is out consulting legal help. He's making appointments. And they don't get him until December 30th when he finally gives up and comes on in."

"We have friendship here and we've seen the kind of friendship that people have shown Frank Chester. Griscavage seems like a nice enough kid. He has a criminal record now. He had to spend time in jail. He had to testify in this mess of a trial because of his friendship with Frank Chester."

"Pete Carpinona. Another good friend. Another guy who wouldn't squeal until it was all out, knew everything. Carpinona seems like decent kid but because of his friendship with Frank Chester he wouldn't say a word. Chris Bogarde, Carpinona's girlfriend. She wouldn't say a word either. Allen Hilton, who really seemed to care about Frank, stood by Frank too. And Richard Laird, who lives with Frank Chester's cousin, who has known him for three years, cares about Frank. He tells the police, 'I'm no rat.' Richard Laird is guilty in this case, but not of the charges that have been brought against him. He's just as guilty as Richard Griscavage of hindering apprehension. He's guilty of destroying evidence. He is guilty of withholding evidence. Richard Laird did not commit the murder of Anthony Milano and the only conspiracy that existed was in the mind of Frank Chester."

"It was the Commonwealth's burden of proof in this case. Their burden alone. Did they prove Richard Laird guilty of the murder of Anthony Milano? Of conspiracy to murder Anthony Milano, beyond reasonable doubt? They did not. All they showed us was a lot of stuff from Frank Chester, from Frank Chester's friends; and that doesn't add up to anything. The evidence in this case shows nothing more than a friendship and that is not a conspiracy. Richard Laird spoke bluntly. He spoke obscenely, I beg your forgiveness."

" 'F that. I didn't kill nobody, man. I ain't got it in me to kill somebody, you know.' That's what this case is about. I ask you to find Richard Laird not guilty based on that evidence, that lack of evidence. I ask you to return a verdict of not guilty. Thank you."

Ron Elgart sincerely hoped for the best, but his heart was heavy with trepidation about what seemed to be an inevitable outcome.

It is customary for the DA to close last in every courtroom throughout all sixty-seven counties in Pennsylvania. Since the prosecution has the biggest challenge to meet, the burden of proof, and the least amount of latitude within which to do so, the prosecution gets the last word. Alan Rubenstein made sure his last speech before deliberations would leave a lasting and profound effect on the jury. Conspiracy is a very tricky animal and very difficult to prove. And that is where the key to this entire case lay. He wanted to impress upon this jury the importance of not getting caught up in who said what, who did the hitting and who did the cutting. He spent the entire duration from the time the investigation began until the trial commenced waiting for this moment. This was indeed, Alan Rubenstein's day in the sun.

Rubenstein began by reminding the jury that they were selected because he had faith in their ability to discern the difference between fact and fiction, between lies and truth, and between guilt and innocence. He told them he was confident in their ability to understand the instructions from the court under the laws of Pennsylvania and how to properly apply that knowledge in rendering a verdict. Rubenstein's closing argument in this case was brilliant, perhaps the most compelling ever in his history of trials as a prosecutor.

"We've heard some talk about he did it; no, *he* did it. Ladies and gentlemen, under the law of Pennsylvania there is a charge of conspiracy but it is not, as was suggested, conjured up when you just want to lump everything together. Quite the contrary."

"The court will tell you that when two or more individuals agree by their actions and their deeds, not just their words, but work together for a common purpose, a crime, that it doesn't make a difference who did what as long as both want to accomplish the same end. Don't get caught up in who plunged the knife, who hit where and who hit first. It doesn't make a difference. It doesn't make a difference under the law and more importantly, it doesn't make a difference under the facts."

"This case is not about anything other than someone is dead and two persons are charged with the murder. And we know that the only two persons there with Anthony Milano were Richard Laird and Frank Chester. No one else. It's not a suicide. It's a homicide. It's not an accidental death. It's a killing. It's not a happenstance. It's a murder."

"We are not here in this courtroom to determine if maybe Frank Chester is a better fellow than Richard Laird, or if Richard Laird is a better guy than Frank Chester. That's not what this is all about. We're here because someone is dead. Someone is dead and he's never coming back. And that is tragic but it wasn't something that had to be. It wasn't something that would have occurred anyway. It was something that occurred because two people, and the only two people in the world it could have been, wanted to accomplish that purpose. How did they do it?"

"Well if you listen to Frank Chester, he saw Richard Laird take one shot at him, but I would ask you to look at the evidence. Is that what we see here? There's multiple bruises. Doesn't that sound to you like it took more than one person to do that?"

"It's the versions of the defendants that one guy did it. He did it, no *he* did it. Does that make sense to you, the fact finders of this case, the ones who do justice, or does it make sense that they both did it? Maybe one hit him and another one hurt him and one punched or kicked him and the other cut him, and ladies and gentlemen, it doesn't make a difference who held the knife. What did they want to do? They wanted to kill him. And at that, they are resounding successes."

“I’m not going to minimize what happened to Anthony Milano. How can we? Maybe a brain hemorrhage, maybe blunt trauma, maybe a smack on the side of the head, two bangs in the lip, a hit on the chin, a flattening of the brain. What do you think? Do you think it happened by one person doing it or do you think it happened with two? No one has said it might have been somebody else. Everybody puts them there. They both put themselves there. And the reason we’re here is because one of them didn’t come back and they left him [Milano] there.”

“They didn’t take his wallet. They didn’t take his money. Didn’t take his car. Didn’t take his watch. They took only one thing, they took his life. How did they take his life? I need not go into detail about what you heard from Dr. Ahmad or those pictures, but this was not an accidental killing. This wasn’t luck of the draw. So many slashes that they couldn’t be counted. An intentional killing.”

“The defense is right. The commonwealth is seeking a conviction of murder in the first degree and the reason is very, very simple, because it is. In Pennsylvania, first degree murder is a homicide that is deliberate, that is willful, that is intentional and done with malice. And you will hear from the court that a person who uses a deadly weapon on a vital part of the body has the requisite intention or requisite malice to take human life, and that’s what happened here.”

“You might understand, you might be able to justify, you might be able to reason through the things that happen in this world. You can’t justify this at all.”

“You heard testimony that Anthony Milano went into this bar and he didn’t bother anybody. He’s five foot six. He’s 150 pounds. He went in. He got a beer and a sandwich and he was in the wrong spot. Don't we know it now. Shouldn't have gone in there. And he meets these two, Richard Laird and Frank Chester and whatever they did in there, whatever they had in their minds, whatever intentions they had were manifested out in a lot in the woods on Ashby Avenue."

"Does it make sense that one person did this, or did two people do it? And ask yourselves this question ladies and gentlemen, could this have been accomplished by only one? He didn't even have a chance to fight back. Didn't have a chance to fight him off, and you think Frank Chester is telling the truth when he says: 'Nah, I didn't kick him. I just pushed him.' What a good Samaritan!"

"Do you think what he has in his mind is trying to save Anthony Milano's life? For two guys who were interested in helping Anthony Milano out, they certainly did a lousy job because they left him swallowing his own blood in the field."

"This is a nightmare, a nightmare come to life. A horrifying killing. We're not here because Frank Chester and Richard Laird may have been friends. We're not here because they want to point the finger at each other. We're here because together with the coldness of heart that's hard to believe, and with an evil intention of mind that we just can't comprehend, and with ice water running through their veins and a coldness of disposition, they treated him like a cheap piece of tenderloin and carved him up. And that is why we're here. We are here because a man was murdered for no reason. We are here because they did it. And I ask you to so find. Let's look at the evidence."

"They come back, not one at a time, but together to Pete Carpinona's apartment. Frank Chester doesn't say, 'I had nothing to do with this.' He got in a fight and the dude is dead. And

Richard Laird doesn't say at that point, 'Hey you killed him, not me - you have the knife.' No. They get back and you heard the exchange: 'Shut the F up.' Frank Chester says, 'You ruined my life.' Richard Laird says, 'You ruined my life.' No. They ruined Anthony Milano's life. That's why we're here."

"They're in the apartment, Blood not on one but on both. Think of that conversation on the tape. What does that tell you? Just get out of town, man. This will blow over. They'll put it in a dead case file. Seven years. Richard Laird snaps his fingers, just like that. That's what they think of human life. Just like that."

"Why get rid of the car? Well if the fingerprints of one were in it, the fingerprints of both were in it. It's in their common interest to do it. It doesn't make any difference who did it."

"And if one is so concerned about being convicted or being charged with a murder he didn't commit, why not go to the police? These guys are out there helping each other out. These guys are out there trying to make sure the other doesn't talk. These two are out there trying to make sure the other doesn't spill his guts to the police because they know what they have done. And over the last few days, now you know, too."

"Kidnapping. Doesn't require somebody taken at gun point or knife point or be held for ransom. It requires that a person be taken a substantial distance away for a substantial period of time with the intent to commit bodily harm on that person, or the intent to terrorize that person. The court will tell you that. Isn't that what happened here? Didn't they take him, oh under the nicest of pretenses, to a place where he didn't want to be? Didn't they take him into the woods, and didn't they intend to terrorize him? You can bet he was terrorized. Didn't they intend to commit bodily harm, the ultimate bodily harm?"

"Believe Richard Laird. Had nothing to do with this. Believe Frank Chester. Had nothing to do with this. If you listen to their stories long enough, it's almost as if they don't know a thing about this, but each and every one of you know that only two people were there with Anthony Milano and that only two leave. And everything they do, everything they say when they leave is inconsistent with their innocence, and shows their guilt. Their statements, their actions and their deeds outside of this courtroom."

"Think about the evidence. Does it show an intentional killing, a deliberate killing? Because if it does, if you can find that they, together, wanted to accomplish the purpose of taking his life, you can stop. And in good conscious under the law and the facts say first degree murder because that's what this is, nothing less. An intentional, deliberate willful, cold-hearted, cold-blooded killing of another human being who had just as much a right to live as any of us, and they took it from him for no reason. For no reason."

"The commonwealth doesn't have to prove a motive. Can you think of one? They took his life for the worst reason of all. None. That's why we're here."

"Ladies and gentlemen, sometimes these trials are difficult. It's tough to listen to the testimony. Each and every one of you, twelve individuals who didn't know each other two weeks ago, who maybe don't have that much in common, we ask of you to be of one mind, one heart and one soul. We ask you to evaluate and look at the facts and come back with a verdict. And I would suggest to you that for what they did, for how they did it and for why they did it, there can be only one verdict."

"There is a bill outstanding for the life of Anthony Milano. There is a debt to be paid. The bill has a balance. The balance has their names on it and it says to both, first degree murder. Thank you."

Rubenstein knew he had already won the jury over. Twelve solemn faces listened intently to every word; their eyes followed his every step as he paced to and fro while he delivered his final argument. They knew what they had to do.

Chapter 9

"Justice is a terrible but necessary thing." ~ Jessamyn West

Friday, May 20th, 1988. It was a tense, quiet moment in the courtroom. Everyone was waiting to hear the jury's verdict. Finally, at around 11:20 AM the jury returned its collective, unanimous verdict. All twelve members of the jury convicted Frank Chester and Richard Laird as guilty of murder in the first degree, kidnapping, and conspiracy. The courtroom suddenly came to life with the buzz and chatter from among the spectators.

Elaine Holley and Rose Milano both bowed their heads and cried. Elaine was heartbroken in the face of having her youngest child forever torn from her and Rose crying from relief that her beloved child's killers were found guilty. Barbara Anne Parr broke down, sobbing hysterically in the face of being left alone with two children to raise, having her man — her baby's father — taken away from her and her children when she and their newborn son needed Rick the most. Colleen Ingram, Frank's love, swooned and was caught by a sympathetic guard.

Rick Laird was escorted from the courtroom amidst the bright lights of the TV cameras past Barbara Anne who was still crying and holding their baby. A TV reporter called out to Laird above the din, "Any comment on the verdict?" which was met with a prompt shout of "Fuck you!" from Rick Laird. Inclining his head toward his woman and their baby that he saw for the very first time, Rick shouted above the noisy crowd, "I love ya' babe!". A short distance away, JoAnn was being interviewed by another TV news crew. Mascara and tears running down her cheeks, she said between sobs, "I love him. I'll always love him."

Anthony Milano and his family were not the only victims of this crime. The families of the men convicted of crimes are often the most forgotten victims and rarely get any sympathy or support at all.

Later that afternoon, after the lunchtime recess, the women in the defendants' lives took the stand to plead for the lives of Frank Chester and Rick Laird. Elaine Holley as Chester's mother took the stand, trembling with shock and grief. Barely able to hold back her tears, she pleaded for mercy for her son. "I don't want you to take my son's life." After Elaine stepped down, Frank Chester's sisters took the stand and repeated more of the same. Colleen Ingram poignantly begged for Frank's life to be spared, "I love him with all my heart. Please let him live."

Barbara Anne Parr, clad in a light blue suit, took the stand for Rick Laird. "I love Richard very much. He's a wonderful person. We all love him...and we all need him." As if on cue, Ron Elgart left the courtroom and immediately returned with Barbara Anne's baby, her baby by Rick, born while he was incarcerated awaiting trial. Elgart approached the witness stand and handed Barbara Anne the three month old Nicholas Laird. Rick burst into tears. Elgart's last hope was that the jury would feel sorry for the young mother who was facing having to raise her baby all alone in poverty, and that she would someday have to explain to the child what happened to his father. The sympathy ploy was not lost on all those who were present.

Thirty hours later, the jury decided the penalty. Their decision of life versus death took far longer for them to reach than the actual verdict of guilt. They unanimously decided to sentence both men to death.

Deciding whether to sentence a person to death is not a decision reached lightly. Death is final and, even where prescribed by the law of the land; playing God in such matters is fraught with a lot of conscience-wringing agony and soul searching. Deciding whether someone should be executed is no small matter. Perhaps that is what separates the majority of people from the murderers that walk among us. On hearing the jury's vote for execution, Frank Chester silently bowed his head as if praying. Rick Laird said, "Shit."

After the arrest and trial, Barbara Anne was forced to move back in with her mother. Rick was the breadwinner, the economic provider. With two little ones and few prospects for a good job Barbara Anne couldn't afford an apartment on her own with an infant and a ten year old child. When she was interviewed in late November of 1988 by journalist Lisa DePaulo from *Philadelphia Magazine* who documented this case in a two part article titled *Killing Anthony*, Barbara Anne had just found an apartment she could afford on her welfare check, her sole source of income.

Trying to start out all over again, she applied for financial aid and began taking courses at Bucks County Community College. She planned on majoring in psychology to try to build a career. She had lost her man and her favorite cousin. It was a hard blow. As with most female-headed families of convicted felons, her prison visits tapered off. Keeping a used car in mechanically sound enough condition to withstand the ten hour round trip to the prison in addition to the cost of traveling was simply too much for her. In Pennsylvania, it is not uncommon for prison inmates to be moved to subsequent prisons that are increasingly farther from home, farther from their families.

JoAnn Laird reverted back to her maiden name, Walters. She changed the children's last names and enrolled them in a different school where no one knew who they were, or of their shame in having “that murderer” for a father.

Elaine Holley still believes her Frankie was telling the truth and was not a willing party to the murder. Visiting her youngest in prison left her emotionally crushed beyond her ability to cope. Colleen Ingram eventually got on with her life, but it was not easy. When someone you love is whisked away from you out of your life so abruptly, you don’t just forget how much you loved that person, and you never stop missing them. The women in both Frank’s and Rick’s lives are without a doubt the forgotten victims in this tragedy.

Chapter 10

"Guilt soon learns to lie." ~ Mary Elizabeth Braddon

It was 1996, eight years after the murder of Anthony Milano and the dual conviction and sentencing of Frank Chester and Richard Laird. Chester and Laird were shut safely away on Pennsylvania's death row. They spent twenty-three hours a day locked down in their 9' x 9' reinforced concrete cells, getting out for one hour for exercise and one hour for law library time. Every second of those designated two hour periods outside of their cells was spent in shackles and leg irons under the accompaniment of heavily armed guards. Their days were spent formulating their appeals and waiting for mail.

For everyone else, life moved on. Little did I know that my life's journey would intersect with the path of Rick Laird. I lived in Allentown in the heart of Lehigh County Pennsylvania, an hour's drive northwest of the Levittown-Bristol area of Bucks County.

In order to understand how I could have been so easily become duped by a manipulative homicidal psychopath and his equally manipulative brother, it is necessary to first understand where I was at during that point in my life. It is necessary to see what I saw through my eyes from my life's experience; how I viewed the world, my situation, and those around me. In 1996, I was not the content and confident person I am today. I had minimal to zero economic security.

When anyone finds that they are saddled with more than what they feel they can handle, it alters their ability to find peace of mind. Those lenses through which I viewed life, people, and situations back then were clouded and distorted, largely because of the personal history of social injustice, hardship, isolation and utter abandonment I had experienced as a desperately poor woman with physical and learning disabilities. After my car accident, I found that those whom I thought were my friends were gradually pulling away from me until I was utterly abandoned. It was as if my misfortune was contagious and could somehow contaminate them.

1996 was six years after my car accident. I had just recently regained the ability to walk unaided and without use of a walker. The accident which forever changed my life occurred on May 14th, 1990 exactly ten days before my twenty-fourth birthday. One day I was competing in martial arts tournaments, earning over $30,000 a year as a union plasterer and investing in real estate, the next I was unable to walk or earn any money at all. An elderly lady without auto insurance ran a red light broad siding me in my 1978 Dodge Ram Charger 4X4 while I was driving to work after a six month winter lay-off.

The impact dislodged the rear of my truck and left me with my lower back broken in four places and both knees smashed. I never fully healed and recovered, even to this day as I write this book sixteen years later.

While surgery was an option, there were inherent risks and I was told that the best I could hope for would be regaining 70% of my pre-disability health and capabilities. I would never regain 100% of my mobility, strength and stamina. It would be a miracle if I could even walk again.

I would never again be able to work in any job that required standing for long periods of time or any repetitive lifting. That not only ruled out returning to my well-paying union construction job, but also precluded me from working even at minimum wage cashier jobs at fast food restaurants or as a retail sales clerk in a video store. I found that even such minimum wage jobs without health benefits refused to accommodate a disabled job applicant with something as simple as permission to sit while ringing up sales on a cash register. Pennsylvania, like most states, is an "Employment At Will" state, which basically means an employer may refuse to hire you or may fire you for any reason or no reason at all, without having to provide any justification. So much for the Americans with Disabilities Act requiring employers to accommodate the disabled worker or preventing unlawful discrimination in hiring and firing practices!

The Americans with Disabilities Act (ADA) requires that employers who have more than 50 employees adapt their workplaces to accommodate disabled job applicants and employees as long as the costs to do so are “reasonable”; which is subject to vague interpretation under the law. Disabled job seekers are, in theory, not supposed to be denied jobs for which being non-disabled is a bona fide occupational quota (BFOQ). For example, someone who cannot stand for long periods of time can still operate a cash register sitting down as well as those who are able to stand all day, thus are supposed to be afforded equal opportunity employment.

In academic environments, the ADA requires that students with learning disabilities be afforded the reasonable accommodation of extended time in order to complete exams. Another reasonable accommodation is permission to tape record lectures if the student’s disability makes note-taking prohibitive. Thus, it was not until the passage of the ADA that learning disabled students were afforded the equal opportunity to attend college. However, laws cannot dictate a change in attitudes. The barriers to full participation in schools and jobs were, and still are, extremely high. Employers hide behind “At-Will” statutes in order to get away with discriminating against job applicants with disabilities, even against those whose disabilities are minor and very easy to accommodate.

Professors and college administrators must often be forced to accommodate the learning disabled (who are otherwise academically worthy) in classrooms. It is not unusual for the dyslexic student in need of extended time for tests or permission to record lectures to spend more time in the college campus ADA Coordinator's office fighting for their rights to such reasonable accommodations than getting to learn and participate in their classes. The non-disabled population in general resists the law and begrudges the disabled (and any other marginalized group) any leveling of the playing field. Those in mainstream society often complain, unfairly accusing the disabled of getting special treatment. The loudest complainers are, not surprisingly, those who have always enjoyed middle class and able-bodied privilege. Relatively few disabled people are able to overcome such obstacles in order to get college educations and secure meaningful jobs even now as I write this book.

After my savings completely ran out and my properties were sold at a steep loss, I was forced to turn to the government agencies that are supposed to help those desperately in need. I was frustrated at every turn and got no help at all. I did not have enough work credits paid into social security to qualify for social security disability, but I was not deemed "disabled enough" to qualify for a meager SSI check of $530 per month either. Welfare wouldn't help me because I didn't have children. Having no family who could help me or support me, I was totally screwed.

The bureaucrats at the social security office sent me to Pennsylvania Office of Vocational Rehabilitation (PA OVR). PA OVR is a state agency affiliated with PA Career Link, previously known as "the unemployment office". PA OVR is the agency charged with helping the disabled retrain and reenter the job market in new careers after a disability renders someone unable to work in any job for which they are suited by previous education or experience. The "experts", the educated professionals trained specifically in the training and job placement needs of the disabled, told me I needed to go to college for a degree in math and computer science in order to reenter the workforce and get their help with being placed in a new career, earning almost what I previously earned as a union construction worker. They ignored the fact that I was functionally illiterate due to having dyslexia: I graduated high school in 1985 with a 4th grade reading and math competency level. I could not believe this OVR vocational rehabilitation counselor was insisting I go to college!

I had been in special education classes since 7th grade. I was basically pushed through high school. If I couldn't learn and be successful in junior high and high school, how could I possibly be expected to learn and be successful in a post-secondary academic environment? When I raised these questions to the OVR counselor, my valid concerns were met with empty clichés. The sum total of the OVR professional's expertise was summed up with responses along the lines of, "Having a learning disability is no excuse. You can't use that as a crutch. You'll just have to work a little harder and it may take you a little longer than someone without a learning disability in order to get the education and marketable skills needed to reenter the workforce."

I asked this "expert" just how I could possibly be considered a desirable job candidate by any prospective employer when "taking a little longer and working a little harder" at getting this education and "new marketable skills" meant several more years out of the job market on top of the six years I was already out of the workforce. Trying to get an education, even if the outcome was ultimately successful, I would be out of the workforce for another several years in addition to the time I had already been out of the loop since my accident. My legitimate concerns were met with, "Don't be so negative. You have to have a positive attitude. We can't help you unless you help yourself by trying hard enough instead of being too lazy or a quitter." Jesus H. Christ! What planet were these sanctimonious crackpots from?

Meanwhile these "experts" had no clue as to how I was supposed to be able to support myself and survive without any help from family while "taking a little longer and working a little harder" at getting any type of education since I had no money or means of earning any money in the interim. Nor did these "experts" have any back up plan for me if I couldn't succeed in getting the education they recommended.

I struggled to overcome my illiteracy with endless hours of hard work and with help from volunteers at the local literacy center. I could not have tried any harder. Finally, things got unbelievably bad because of my lack of ability to earn a living and the denial of any economic help and support. I was forced to beg for help from the local food banks and soup kitchens. At any given time, either my gas, electric or phone was shut off for lack of income to pay the bills. Although I qualified for help from LIHEAP Energy Assistance, it was only a small annual amount that covered one month's worth of either the gas bill or the electric bill, but not both. For the remaining eleven months of the year, I was out of luck as to paying the bills and keeping these most basic life sustaining utilities from being shut off. I needed help desperately and there was simply none to be had anywhere, even from private charities.

In total desperation I applied for help from welfare because I needed medical and dental care and was unable to afford it on my own. I couldn't get any care at all. I had no income. I couldn't even afford to eat without the free hot meals served at the soup kitchen. I was denied any help with my medical and dental needs from welfare. I didn't qualify because I was a single adult without any kids. When I lucked out in getting the part-time job at the Hilton, I found I would be eligible for health and dental benefits after a year of service. Since I had been without health and dental care for the past six years, the chance to get care after a year on the job was a blessing, even though the job only paid $7 an hour. Plus I would also get the perk of a daily hot meal prepared by the hotel chefs free of charge.

It was getting hired at the Hilton that indirectly brought me into the death sentence appeal of Rick Laird. Sometimes for reasons unknown and unexplained, our paths in life are crossed by people whom we would never expect to meet in other circumstances. Such was the case when I came to know Mark Laird, Rick Laird's brother. I met Mark Laird at my job at the Hilton. He was a fellow maintenance mechanic and he was my age. He was very tall and he towered over me. He had close-cropped raven hair with a finely groomed mustache to match and the charming dark-eyed look of a gypsy. He was a strapping man with generous rippling muscles, but even though he was not bad looking, he definitely was not my type. He seemed to be so wrapped up in himself that he didn't need anyone else. Everything was always all about him.

He was a strutting braggart, thinking himself to be a real Casanova: a legend in his own mind. Anyone that self-absorbed didn't have room in their selfish little world for others, or time for others' needs. He was a narcissist. Besides, my own plate was more than full with my own problems and as experience had taught me, I was totally on my own in coping with them. I had learned the hard way how life is for those lacking family support and unable to count on anyone else for anything in emergencies. I had learned the hard way how little one can depend on the government agencies and private charities that supposedly do so much for the disabled, the poor and disadvantaged.

I was twenty-eight years old and struggling to pick up the pieces of my own ruined life. I had no knowledge of Mark Laird's criminal past, nor did I know anything about the murder of Anthony Milano or that one of the convicted killers was Mark's brother Rick. I had never heard anything of this high profile case before. This was before there was an Internet-ready computer in almost every home bringing the instant on-demand news and information into our living rooms from the far corners of the world. Although there was cable TV, television was a luxury I couldn't afford. I had no income from the time of my accident in May of 1991 until getting hired part time at the hotel in November of 2005.

Orphaned since the age of thirteen, I had no family, no one at all to care about my well being. I had no support network at all, none whatsoever. In addition, I had been marginalized throughout high school because of a learning disability. I had to cope with all that in addition to the shock, grief, denial, and bitterness that I felt when my entire world and everything in it was torn asunder in the blink of an eye by a horrific accident.

A significant portion of my attitude, thoughts and feelings back then were influenced by several years of grinding poverty, the helplessness and despair that accompanied it, callous mistreatment by others and a seemingly infinite series of disappointments. What should have been the happiest years of my life were the saddest. While friends dated, got married, had kids, bought their first homes and progressed in their careers, I was begging and scraping for daily bread. I had to fight for the right to access buildings and get helped with minimal accommodations just so I could do the most rudimentary things that others took for granted. I was struggling to overcome a severe learning disability without any support or help just to get to the point where I'd be able to attend community college. I had to endure cruel treatment and ridicule from inconsiderate rude kids in my classes and elitist professors who felt that older learners, especially those with learning disabilities, didn't belong in college or have a right to get an education. I had to navigate this difficult path alone.

My learning disability was not my only hardship in the classroom. I didn't fit in very well when everyone else in my college classes was right out of high school and were eleven to twelve years younger than me. Added to that of course, was the social pressure from the fact that learning came so much easier and faster for my younger classmates than it did for me. Plus, there was the "digital divide" – I was not computer savvy back then. I had no knowledge of how to use a computer. Being able to use a computer was expected as requisite background. Professors did not understand that older learners coming from blue-collar backgrounds would need a lot of extra help just to overcome the steep learning curve that accompanies mastery of computer use. The younger students couldn't be bothered with taking any of their time to help an older student for whom learning how to use a computer was a daunting task.

I had been out of high school for twelve years. Even when I was in high school, I certainly wasn't in the college prep track. Since my dyslexia required me to put in an additional eight to ten hours of studying and struggling to absorb the material and complete assignments each day outside of class, I also lacked the luxury of any sort of social life. Keeping up with current affairs is hard to do when you're isolated, marginalized and over burdened with problems - poverty being chief among them.

My views were also fueled and nurtured to some degree by the liberal politics in the university environment where the popular thought is that everyone - even the most vicious of criminals - is a victim. I certainly was no criminal but I definitely felt like a victim. Perhaps I was feeling sorry for myself, but at least I had good reason for it.

Getting hired at the hotel was the first thing in several years that had gone right for me. The daily meals were a Godsend for which I was profoundly grateful. Although the meals were not kosher and often comprised of *treif* (forbidden foods under kosher dietary laws), embracing my Jewish heritage by keeping kosher was the last thing on my mind: I had bigger fish to fry. I had to worry about making it through college despite a learning disability, poverty, and rotting teeth with no way to get dental care. I was hoping to successfully graduate college and get a chance in a new career that paid something comparable to what I earned prior to becoming disabled. I dreamed of being able to support myself and have a life once again.

My job at the Hilton paid a third of what I previously made, but due to my physical disabilities, it was something I could do that didn't require the heavy lifting and constant standing that working in construction does. My plastering background was what got me in the door: None of the other maintenance mechanics were able to do intricate plaster cornish restoration.

One day in January of 1996, shortly after New Year's, the snow began to fall and didn't stop. We got hit with a blizzard, a nor'easter, which dumped enough snow across the state to warrant then-governor Tom Ridge shutting down all roads and travel statewide. Drifts were five to six feet deep and even reached as high as ten feet in some areas. The hotel was at full occupancy, all of its two hundred thirty-four rooms were filled with anxious guests worried about being stranded indefinitely due to the storm.

Out of the entire department of maintenance mechanics, only Mark Laird and I lived within walking distance from the hotel. The other maintenance mechanics, including our boss Bruce "Stumpy" Achey, lived in the suburbs and had to drive in order to come to work. Driving was impossible due to inclement weather, impassible roads and a standing statewide emergency cease-travel order from the governor's office. No other maintenance mechanics except Mark Laird and I could make it in to the hotel to ensure smooth running operations and calm stranded guests. Mark and I were required to work double ten hour shifts and spend the night on the premises. On the plus side, we were paid triple time for hazard pay.

My tiny row home was snowed in. The drifts reached one story high. I had to roll out onto a drift from my second floor window just to get out of my house. Although I only lived four blocks away from the hotel, it took me over two hours to get in that day as I floundered on foot through the snow, traversing ten foot high drifts that completely buried cars and trucks everywhere. The blizzard of January 1996 was definitely a memorable event.

It was during our meal break on that snowbound evening at the hotel that Mark Laird dropped the bomb on me. I was tired and hungry. Tucked into a plate of filet mignon and lobster tail, I was not predisposed for making small talk. I was just too hungry and the food tasted too good. Mark spoke first, hesitating, "Hey, uh Jacqueline, can you, uh, you know, use that math and physics stuff you're studying in college for things like crime scene investigations?" I nodded absent-mindedly, my mouth full of lobster and drawn butter. I looked up at Mark from across Stumpy's desk in the maintenance office, which was little more than a glorified boiler room located in the hotel's lower level. "Yeah. Most of forensic pathology is based on physics. Why do you ask?" I was surprised at his sudden interest in academics. He was usually more preoccupied with his sexual prowess, flexing his well-defined huge biceps and washboard abs while preening in front of a mirror than interested in Newton's Laws of Motion.

Mark demurred, looking nervously about as if he was afraid of being overheard. "Well, you see.... it's my brother. He's on death row for a crime he didn't commit. He was framed. I don't know how to help my brother prove it. I don't know nothin' about that stuff. My family can't afford to pay for experts to do this for us."

I was stunned. My fork with a piece of filet on it was suspended in my hand in a freeze-frame moment. I couldn't believe what I was hearing. Maybe I misunderstood. I was tired and going into my second shift. I asked him to repeat what he had just told me, and he did. He fidgeted anxiously, thinking I would somehow judge him because of this.

I was intrigued. I always had a penchant for true crime stories and this was an actual case. My interest piqued, I asked more questions. "How did your brother get framed? What was he convicted of that he would get the death penalty? How can a forensics type of investigation help your brother?" Mark poured out some of the story, but conveniently left out the fact that it was a brutal, calculated, Jack the Ripper style slashing instead of something along the lines of self-defense. He also omitted other facts I would discover later.

Mark's version of the story was as follows: Rick had been set up by a manipulative, back-stabbing friend (Frank Chester) who was the real killer in a barroom related murder while an over-zealous, power hungry DA saw that his career could be catapulted as a result of getting a guilty verdict. According to Mark Laird, it was just another story of a slimy, glory hound yuppie lawyer whose success and career would be built on blood money. And it was a story that was believable.

Mark's story spurred me into undertaking a mission of social justice, or so I thought. At that point in my life, I was cynical and jaded due to my own personal experiences. I did not need much convincing to believe that the system was broken. The social services system had certainly failed me as a disabled woman without any family support when I desperately needed help and a hand up, so it was not a far stretch to assume that the criminal justice system was no less broken.

It all seemed so very believable. There is certainly no shortage of greedy people who will stop at nothing to further their own agendas of power, their career ambitions and accumulation of wealth by any means necessary, even if it means utterly destroying and sacrificing others less fortunate along the way. Trial-fixing is not an unknown phenomenon in the Philadelphia area. What real chance does someone with no money have when wrongly accused of a capital crime? Almost none.

It had been only four years earlier, September of 1992, that Dr. Jay C. Smith was acquitted and walked from death row on appeal before the PA State Supreme Court in a case precedent which expanded the double jeopardy law in Pennsylvania, precluding retrial in the event of prosecutorial misconduct and trial-fixing. Dr. Jay C. Smith was the former principal of Upper Merion High School in Philadelphia's wealthy Main Line area. He was wrongfully convicted in connection with the 1979 murder of English teacher Susan Reinert and her two children. The children's bodies had never been found. The crime and subsequent trials and convictions of Dr. Smith and fellow English teacher William Sydney Bradfield were the talk of the town. When Smith's conviction was overturned and his death sentence vacated, everybody knew about it. Every Pennsylvania college campus buzzed with excitement at the news and the tale of prosecutorial misconduct and illegal evidence suppression. Newspaper headlines in bold print read, *"Jay Walks!"*

Dr. Smith's conviction was grossly flawed on several grounds. First, he was charged with the murders of Susan Reinert and her two children Karen and Michael, largely based on hearsay from William Bradfield and Bradfield's lovers and friends. Smith had no motive for killing Susan Reinert, but William Sydney Bradfield had every reason in the world: Bradfield taught English at the same high school as Reinert and they had a stormy love affair. Bradfield was listed as Susan Reinert's intended husband in her will naming him as executor of her estate and sole beneficiary on $750,000 worth of life insurance policies. Reinert had taken out those life insurance policies a mere few months before her death.

Second, while Bradfield spent months constructing what he thought would be the perfect alibi, telling friends and colleagues that Smith was planning to kill Susan Reinert, not one of these people ever told her about it so she could take measures to protect herself. No one reported any of this to the police, either. Then coincidently on the weekend that Bradfield plans a trip to Cape May with colleagues and friends Sue Meyers and Vince Valaitis, Susan Reinert mysteriously ends up murdered. Susan Reinert's battered and nude body was found in the hatchback of her car, but her children's bodies were never found, not even as of the writing of this book, twenty-one years later. Reinert's body was worth $7,500 per pound to William Sydney Bradfield, but you can't collect on a life insurance policy unless you have a body. The children's bodies weren't worth anything. They were probably killed because they were witnesses to their mother's murder. It was assumed they were with their mother when she was killed because the last person to see Reinert and her kids alive two days before the discovery of the body was an elderly neighbor who testified that she saw Susan Reinert and her kids leave the house together in Reinert's little Plymouth Horizon. They knew the killer and could identify him, thus had to be eliminated as potential witnesses. While merely circumstantial, that bit of evidence is no small matter.

Third, the prosecution withheld critical forensic evidence from defense counsel at Smith's trial. Part of this forensic evidence came from the sticky rubber "lifters" the forensic pathologist used to swab the feet and in between the toes of the victim during the pathology examination. Quartz was found on the lifters. Quartz is sand. The sand on these lifters was critical: It showed that Reinert was murdered at the shore where Bradfield and several of Bradfield's friends were, but not Smith.

Sand is not indigenous to the environment around Dr. Smith's home in the Main Line or anywhere in downtown Philadelphia. But sand is consistent with a "coastal plane environment" - like the beach at Cape May. Bradfield and friends were at Cape May. The other piece of forensic evidence was a "lost" report from one of the PA State Police forensics team members who noted a post-mortem lividity imprint on Reinert's body. The fact that this report was "lost" throughout Smith's trial was damning and a huge black eye for the prosecution, especially since the same DA, Rick Guida, had just convicted Bradfield for the murder of Susan Reinert and the disappearance and possible murder of her two children. Smith was not charged and brought to trial until after Bradfield's conviction. Bradfield was sentenced to life without parole, which just goes to show how capricious the death penalty is.

A post-mortem lividity mark shows where a body comes into physical contact with another object after death when the blood begins to settle. Now this post-mortem lividity imprint on Susan Reinert's body was an exact match with the front seat area and handbrake of a VW Bug. Bradfield's car was a VW Bug. In sum, Smith's trial was rigged in 1986.

In 1992 a junkman named Mark Anthony Hughs who ran his ad "Cash For Your Trash" in the local paper was called by Trooper Jack Holtz to remove boxes and other unwanted items from Holtz's attic. The evidence regarding the Smith case was in a cardboard box that was among the pile of boxes Holtz wanted removed. Holtz was present when the junkman removed the boxes and left. Holtz got his attic cleaned out and the junkman got some treasures he could re-sell in his second-hand goods store. Everybody was happy. Once Mark Hughs got back to his store where he unloaded the goods, he found the box marked "EVIDENCE". The happy-go-lucky junkman found the evidence of the "lost" report about the post-mortem lividity imprint on Reinert's body and other notes regarding the rubber lifters with sand on them in a box that he looked in hoping to find a gas grill or something else which he could sell at his second-hand store. When he saw that the box instead contained correspondence and evidence from a murder case, he knew he was onto something hot. It is not common practice for the police to keep evidence in cardboard boxes in the attics of their homes. Such evidence is normally kept under lock and key in an evidence room at police headquarters. Mr. Hughs immediately tracked down Attorney William Costopoulos who represented Smith and turned the box over to him.

Pennsylvania State Attorney General Paul Yatron had to get involved with an internal investigation of the Philadelphia district attorney's office because of the misconduct. In a fatal error in judgment, Yatron directed Deputy Assistant Attorney General Skip Ebert to take charge of the case and gave Ebert his marching orders: Uphold the position maintaining that the Philadelphia DA had done nothing wrong and that Smith's conviction and death sentence should be upheld. Even if the Philadelphia district attorney's office knew nothing about the concealment of the lifters, the fact remained that the end result was that a man on trial for his life did not get a fair trial.

The integrity of the criminal justice system was breached and the public's trust was shattered. Had Smith's defense counsel known about the existence of the lifters and the report detailing the post-mortem lividity imprint on the victim's body during the initial trial in 1986, the outcome probably would have been quite different. In sum, due to this intentional and illegal withholding and concealment of critical forensic evidence by the Philadelphia DA and Pennsylvania State Police trooper Jack Holtz, Dr. Jay C. Smith was convicted and sentenced to death for a capital crime that he didn't commit. Smith spent seven years languishing on Pennsylvania's death row as a result. Although he was finally freed on appeal due to the dedication and diligence of his loyal attorney, there is no way for him to get those seven years of his life back. There truly is no adequate compensation for that.

But the result was case precedent: The expansion of the double jeopardy clause in the state of Pennsylvania, whereby the prosecution is prohibited from retrying someone charged with a crime in the event of gross prosecutorial misconduct. Normally when a defendant is deemed to have been denied a fair trial, the remedy is a new trial. However, given the egregious misconduct by the investigators and prosecution in Smith's case, the PA Supreme Court decided that the only adequate legal remedy was for Smith's conviction and sentence to be overturned and permanently vacated with no possibility of being retried again. Trooper Holtz and former DA Rick Guida were implicated in engineering the outcome of the trial by intentionally concealing critical forensic evidence from the defense.

Unlike the majority of death row inmates, Dr. Smith did not come from poverty nor was he uneducated: He had a PhD in education. If this gross miscarriage of justice could happen to an upper-middle class white male, a distinguished high school principal from Philadelphia's affluent Maine Line, a man who had been a Lt. Colonel in the military and who had very generous economic resources at his command, it could happen to anyone.

The formerly distinguished district attorney, Rick Guida, who had been implicated along with Jack Holtz in rigging the Smith trial, suffered a tragic blow from which he would never fully recover. It compounded his indictment for trafficking cocaine and using his position of power and privilege to do so. Rick Guida was charged with corrupting his office - the Office of the District Attorney.

US Attorney General Gordon Zubrod, described as a Marine who walked and talked like an officer and a gentleman, prosecuted Rick Guida. Gordon Zubrod was not impressed with what he construed as an attempt by the moneyed elites of Philadelphia to play the class card by seeking special privileges and buying favors. Zubrod believed that extending leniency to a DA gone bad would be accepting a two-tiered justice system with double standards and two sets of rules: one set for privileged white male professional elites and another for poor and disadvantaged inner city classes. Rick Guida was relieved of his position as DA, sanctioned by the Bar Association, and sentenced to eleven months in jail. It was a disgraceful end to what would have been an illustrious career for Rick Guida.

However, Guida did get a fair trial, which is far more than what Jack Holtz, possibly in collusion with Guida, gave Dr. Jay Smith. The reason: alleged payment for "character depiction" from ex-cop turned crime writer Joseph Wambaugh for his book deal, a best-selling book that depended on a verdict of guilt. That book was *Echoes in the Darkness*.

Wambaugh's book, which was made into a made-for-TV movie featuring Stockard Channing as Susan Reinert, Eric Roberts as William Bradfield, Treat Williams as DA Rick Guida, and Robert Loggia as Dr. Jay Smith. Another writer, Loretta Schwartz-Nobel, also wrote about the Reinert case. Her book was *Engaged to Murder.* I also have the book *Principal Suspect* written by Attorney William Costopoulos which was written and published after Dr. Smith's acquittal on appeal.

Smith was fortunate in that as he had an excellent attorney who believed in him. Smith had much better legal representation than the average defendant charged with a capital offense. I doubted that Mark Laird's brother had been as fortunate.

Given scandal of Jay C. Smith's wrongful conviction, it was not unreasonable for me to believe Mark Laird's claim of trial-fixing in the railroading of his brother. It was believable because most people assume that anyone arrested by the police must be guilty. Additionally, members of the underclass are highly over-represented among the prison rolls. That is why the penitentiary system is often referred to as the largest public housing project for America's poor. After all, nobody cares about the "undeserving poor" who come from dysfunctional families and disadvantaged backgrounds. Locking the poor up and throwing away the key without real concern as to actual guilt is a convenient way for the well-off to ensure the poor are kept out of their neighborhoods, out of sight and out of mind.

The fact that those with "invisible" disabilities such as the mentally ill and those with cognitive impairments are overwhelmingly poor corresponds to an extraordinarily high percentage of death row inmates being mentally disabled and poor. Unfortunately, there is very little public sympathy for them. Nobody with the power to serve justice had any sympathy for Ricky Ray Rector, an indigent and mentally retarded man executed for murder, whose guilt was highly questionable. Rector lacked sufficient cognitive ability to grasp the concept of death. When he was served his last meal right before his execution, he requested permission from the prison guards on duty that he be allowed to "save his dessert for later" thinking he would be returned to his cell. Ricky Ray Rector was incapable of understanding that he would be leaving that cell for the last time, never to return. The poor, the disabled, and the elderly are easily expendable in America. Particularly those with "invisible" disabilities.

If you are from the lower socioeconomic classes and you stand accused of a crime, you are disposable because as someone who is poor you are automatically beneath contempt. You are treated as if you simply don't count by everyone else in society: the comfortable middle class, the successful professionals and the affluent. They would prefer to lock up all the poor, the mentally ill, the disabled and the cognitively impaired and throw away the key as if they never existed rather than see one dime of their precious money go to support social programs that help ensure the poor get a fair fighting chance to get a grub stake in life.

Anyone disputing this need only to look at all the job placement and subsidized employment programs targeted specifically to the socially and economically disadvantaged which were totally eliminated under former president Ronald Reagan. Social safety net cuts were followed by the subsequent slashing of federal student aid in the Gramm-Rudman Bill under the leadership of the elder Bush president, and then finally the Welfare Reform Act of 1996 under former president Clinton.

Of course, during this same time period that social programs for the poor were being gutted we saw a burgeoning prison population commensurate with the increase in arrests and convictions for drug-related offenses as disadvantaged people turned to the underground economy in an effort to make enough money to be able to live. No surprise there. With a shrinking pie of fewer opportunities and less jobs to go around for everyone, this is a logical sequence of events. Not surprisingly, the compassionate conservative response was to enact draconian measures such as the "Three Strikes Law" whereby someone convicted of such a minor third offense such as shoplifting a pair of pants got automatically sentenced to prison for the remainder of their life.

The system cannot be trusted. That is what the saturnine and bitter part of me believed back then. To some extent, I still believe that: the statistics and blatant classism in our society speak for themselves. Under a system of competitive capitalism dependent upon inequality and exploitation flowing from the unfairness of discrimination based on age, sex, race, and ethnicity, there are winners and there are losers. In a perfect world your socioeconomic background would be of no importance since everyone would be competing for jobs under the same fair conditions. But we know there are marked differences in the social circumstances of classes, of men and women, people of different races and ethnic groups, of the old and the young and of the disabled and non-disabled. Not everybody starts with an equal footing. Some have a significant head start in the race for social prizes. But those who are the losers do not deserve to remain permanently stuck at the bottom with nothing, forever on the outside looking in.

But the winners, members of the upper classes, generally hold that their position of privilege is their just reward for living right and making all the right choices. Luck has absolutely nothing to do with it. Neither does unearned privilege. They lived righteous, moral lives and got everything they have through hard work and honesty. If you are poor, if you are at the bottom, it must be solely your own fault and as such, you are not deserving of any help or support to be able to get back on your feet in the battle to survive and make it. The tough love of compassionate conservativism with the admonition to pull yourself up by your bootstraps even if you have no boots is the only help you deserve.

If you're poor because of health problems, a disability or any form of job discrimination and you are consequently suffering without adequate food, shelter, clothing, medical and dental care, you are expected to just shut up and suffer quietly, out of sight and out of mind. Nobody else wants to hear it. They don't want to know about it. They have theirs, too bad for you if you never got yours. They simply wish to pretend that you, your needs and your problems don't exist and don't count. They have more important things to pay attention to: shopping for $400 Prada shoes, baby-sitting their 401(k)'s on their $3,000 Dell computers from the comfort of their McMansion estates, tucked neatly away from the rest of the world while hidden in their exclusive gated communities. If the poor are unable to cope, oh well: *Are there no prisons? Are there no workhouses?*

The harsh reality is that there is a lot of job discrimination. Health problems limit opportunities, and massive jobs off-shoring resulting in fewer opportunities to go around for everyone. This means more exclusion, preventing people from getting an equal chance to survive in a Serengeti economy. It is social Darwinism at its worst. This is a more fundamental root cause of poverty, crime, injustice and social unrest than anything else.

Poverty and crime are intertwined. However, what is true of the part is not necessarily true of the whole. Serial killers Ted Bundy, Sam Berkowitz (the "Son of Sam"), and John Wayne Gacy all came from the middle class and were definitely not underprivileged. They murdered simply because it excited them. None of them had any sympathy for their victims, whose final moments were undoubtedly filled with sheer terror. Michael Skakel, murderer of Martha Moxley in the exclusive Belle Haven region of Greenwich, CT on October 31st, 1975 is another case in point. Both victim and killer hailed from the elite ruling class, enjoying sheltered and privileged lives. They were both members of America's royalty.

The killer, Michael Skakel, was from one of the most powerful, politically connected and wealthy families in the entire nation. His father was steel tycoon Rushton Skakel, brother-in-law of late Senator Robert F. Kennedy and late president John F. Kennedy. Michael was the middle son in a large, decidedly unruly brood whose collective criminal antics were always winked at by local authorities. Since the death of their mother Anne Reynolds Skakel, the Skakel kids were unsupervised and undisciplined while their father Rushton spent most of his time out of state running the family empire: Great Lakes Carbon.

Rushton relied on live-in hired help such as the gardener and housekeeper and a long line of well-paid tutors, but none of them could bring Rushton's feral progeny under control. The Skakel boys did what they pleased, when they pleased - obligation, morality and convention be damned. Their father's money could always be counted on to discreetly take care of any damages caused by the havoc they wrought. By all accounts from those who knew the Skakels intimately, Michael was the most troubled, uncontrollable and dangerous one of the entire Skakel clan.

Although Michael Skakel evaded investigation and prosecution for over twenty years due to his family's wealth and political influence, he was recently brought to justice. On June 7th, 2003, Michael Skakel was found guilty for the bludgeoning death of his neighbor and friend Martha Moxley and sentenced twenty years to life.

Skakel had bashed her head in repeatedly with a Toney-Penna golf club until it broke, finally ramming the shaft of the broken six-iron through her throat less than one hundred yards from her front door on her family's property on a cool Halloween night in 1975. Classism, lack of culpability or social injustice could not be used to explain that depravity. They were both only fifteen years old with brighter futures laying ahead of them than most other kids in America could ever hope to have.

What is really an affront to me personally in this case is the fact that Michael Skakel resorted to falling back on his dyslexia during his trial in an attempt to get leniency from the courts for beating his friend to death. Coming from one of the wealthiest families in America, Michael Skakel had the benefit of unlimited resources at his disposal to help him cope with his learning disability.

He had access to the aid and support that the average dyslexic does not: live-in tutors with the highest credentials, cutting edge assistive computer technology, high priced private boarding schools and exclusive private colleges known for their accommodation of learning disabled students. He had family ties to ensure his gainful employment and minimize the negative effects a learning disability had on his quality of life. If only I had had it so good!

While heinous murders know no class bounds and cannot be ascribed to poverty and social injustice, lesser crimes such as drug peddling, theft and prostitution would be greatly reduced if more opportunities and help for the poor were in place. As brilliantly illustrated by Holly Sklar in her book *Raising the Floor*, much can - and should - be done to improve our society from the bottom up. A living wage and guaranteed income support would set a minimum standard in which a human being in a civilized society should be expected to live. Making healthcare accessible for all and eliminating the barrier of classism to good jobs would alleviate much of the anger and resentment from those at the bottom.

Universities, the last bastion of liberal thought and the cradles of future leadership, embrace that position. Reading the Greek tragedies like *Oedipus Rex* and constructing math proofs in the fashion of Euclid were not all that I was learning in college. Once I became a confident reader, a whole new world was opened to my dyslexic mind. I was also getting a healthy dose of political propaganda at college. By the time I reached my sophomore year, I had overdosed on the Kool Aid — believing our criminal justice system to be nothing more than an extension of colonial imperialism used to keep the "unwashed masses" in line.

One example of politically liberal thought that permeates academia is the widely held view that most convicted felons are victims of an unfair, cruel and selfish system that discarded them unjustly. They were merely misunderstood children who needed hugs, not handcuffs. After all, it wasn't their fault that society was penalizing them for failing to succeed in a world where the deck was stacked against them from the start.

However, prisons are also full of men who all swear they're innocent victims of a system gone awry. To hear them tell their stories, you would think that nobody ever died of unnatural causes such as murder. No one is ever raped and no one is ever robbed because the perpetrators are all innocent.

Therefore, with all these innocent men, there should be no such thing as crimes. Without any crimes there should be no need for any municipality to maintain police departments and prisons. Everyone would be able to leave their front doors wide open when not at home or when in bed sleeping. Obviously, this is not the case. Poor or not, disadvantaged or not, misunderstood or not, there is no excuse for causing harm to others in society. Self defense is the only justification for deliberately injuring or killing another. I found myself in a sort of mental tug-of-war over the two conflicting opinions about the justice system. It is unjustly biased in favor of those with money, yet nobody goes to prison without having done something. I could only guess what it was that Mark's brother could have done to be convicted in spite of being innocent, as Mark clearly claimed he was.

I was intrigued by what Mark told me. I wanted to find out the truth. If Mark Laird's brother had indeed been a victim of the criminal justice system, simply used as a convenient scapegoat by a DA facing re-election that year, who hoped to ride into office on the blood of an innocent man, that would be the ultimate miscarriage of justice. The trial-fixing in the infamous Smith case was still fresh in my mind. It was not difficult for me to give Mark the benefit of the doubt about his story. I contacted Rick Laird on death row at SCI-Pittsburgh by writing him my first letter in January, 1996 and introducing myself. I agreed to help Mark and his brother.

Chapter 11

"It takes two to speak the truth - one to speak and the other to hear". ~ Henry David Thoreau

After the snow emergency was lifted, I returned home after having spent over twenty-four hours at the hotel. While the room had been comfortable and equipped with a television set, it wasn't home. No one likes to live at their place of employment, unless perhaps they are the owner.

I enjoyed a scrumptious breakfast fit for a lumberjack before taking my leave. Three eggs over light, hash browns with melted cheddar cheese, an 8 oz rib-eye steak and a plate heaped with thick slices of warm golden brown toast with a generous assortment of jellies and jams arrived on a cart, complete with a carafe of piping hot coffee, fresh cream and pitcher of cranberry juice. I sat down to one of the best breakfasts I had enjoyed in a long time. Those chefs at the Hilton Hotel certainly took care of the maintenance department staff.

While enjoying the hot food, I looked out of the window at the white blanket that had covered the Lehigh Valley. My mind drifted back to the previous evening's discussion with Mark in the maintenance shop over our dinner break. I saw a chance to make a difference. I saw an opportunity to do something directly involved with the criminal justice system and actually help someone obviously in dire need of assistance.

Ever since I was a small child, I dreamt of becoming a lawyer like *Perry Mason*. Of course, the ability to afford to go into $120,000 additional student loan debt for law school after completing my undergraduate degree on student loans and Pell

Grants just wasn't in the cards for me. I was already approaching thirty and no longer a young kid with all the time in the world to get a chance for fulfillment, happiness and a bright future.

Wealthy kids who don't have learning disabilities and whose parents can afford to defray the costs of their education and living expenses while in school have the opportunities to pursue their dreams. They can choose their futures, pursue their goals and follow their own star. Well-heeled mid-life professionals deciding on law for a second profession and who have had the good fortune of enjoying many years in stable and solid careers where they have gained wealth and acquired assets can afford to do so as well.

Not so for older students who are poor and disabled. Definitely not so for those lacking help and support from family, and those who must worry about making it through another day without access to health and dental care.

I had no choice but to settle for community college and a state university and try for a bachelor degree program that would enable me to reenter the job market full time in a career that paid a living wage. Maybe after getting my undergraduate student loans paid down, perhaps then I could afford to go back for the *juris doctorate* and take the bar exam. It was a dream that I clung to, but my hold on that dream was tenuous. I would never see twenty-five again. I had to start out all over with nothing while I faced my rapidly approaching thirties and had not even obtained my bachelors degree yet. I had begun to wonder if I ever would be able to do so.

With the extreme difficulties I faced on a daily basis of being accommodated for my learning disability in college, I was not very optimistic that I would ever be able to graduate, no matter how hard I tried. I also had the very real obstacle of poverty to contend with: one substantial illness, one abscessed tooth or one costly car repair for which I lacked the health insurance and money to solve, would leave me unable to get to Kutztown University twenty-six miles away for my classes. Since most people are too wrapped up in themselves and their own little worlds, trying to get help with rides on a regular basis from other commuting students was also a slim to zero chance. It's everybody for themselves, survival of the fittest - like life in the Serengeti Plain in Africa.

Nobody ever seems to have time to help somebody less fortunate who is in dire straits. Most people assume that everybody has family to help them in a time of need. They think that if you are an orphan and disabled, that there is "all this help out there" if you are really down on your luck. How wrong they are.

If there truly was all this help out there for the genuinely needy, there wouldn't be any poor people suffering without basic human needs. Nobody would ever die in residential fires from unsafe alternative heating methods after their gas was shut off in the winter for unpaid bills. Nobody would be walking around in tattered clothes and missing half their teeth. No senior citizens would find themselves choosing between getting prescription drugs and paying their rent or property taxes, skipping medicine doses at peril to their health and lives. Nobody would be seen huddled in doorways and under bridges in piles of filthy rags struggling to stay warm and dry outside in the elements. The welfare offices would be closed permanently. And all these charities, along with every single soup kitchen, homeless shelter and the Salvation Army would be as extinct as the dinosaurs because they wouldn't be needed.

It had been a hard enough battle for me just to get PA OVR to help me with paying for the $1,500 diagnostic test that I needed to qualify for the reasonable accommodations I was entitled to in an academic and employment setting under the Americans with Disabilities Act of 1990. The fight for something that I as a disabled American needed and was entitled to was a three and a half year excursion of begging and pleading with the OVR bureaucrats for help. Eventually I had to resort to appealing OVR's refusal of help to the state CAP program. Only then did I finally get helped with the payment for my learning disability diagnosis and documentation.

I was no stranger to social injustice. Once, in a letter to my senator addressing the shameful treatment of the learning disabled and lack of help, I actually referred to the Americans with Disabilities Act as the Americans who have been Discarded Act. "Discarded" is exactly how poor adults with disabilities are treated with all this non-help and lack of accommodation that is out there, civil rights laws notwithstanding.

I had lost my faith in the system a long time ago after I became physically disabled and had to rely on PA OVR and all these other agencies that are supposed to help you if you truly need it, but don't help you at all. Since the system obviously doesn't work for disabled law-abiding citizens who are down on their luck, I certainly had no reason whatsoever to believe that the criminal justice system worked any better. I was so jaded and discouraged that I found it easier to believe a convicted psychopathic criminal rather than anyone representative of mainstream society.

Turning my thoughts back to Rick Laird, I hashed out in my mind all the possible reasons for his being scapegoated and railroaded by the DA, as Mark had claimed. Fumbling for the hotel stationary usually kept in the drawer of one of the end tables next to the bed, I thought up lots of questions I would have to ask Rick. I also had to give some thought as to how I would even approach Rick. He didn't know me from a can of paint.

From everything I had ever heard or known about Bucks County, including my impressions from the times I had driven through it, I knew it was the wealthiest county in the state. A district attorney in Bucks County was certainly better paid than a district attorney in one of the poorer, rural Appalachian counties in the central or western part of the state. So I ruled out money as motivation. I began listing the questions that I wanted to ask in the order that they entered my mind, which was racing at 900 miles an hour over all the possibilities and scenarios:

1.Did the DA have a personal grudge against you? If so, why?

2. Did you have prior run-ins with the law and the courts, earning yourself the label of being a persistent thorn in everybody's sides?

3. Was the DA friendly with the murder victim's family?

4. Did the DA and the victim's family belong to the same country club and play golf together?

5. If the co-defendant who worked in legion with the DA to frame you also got the same conviction and sentence, what did he gain by framing you?

6. Did you know the victim before the murder?

7. Was your co-defendant a jealous romantic rival?

8. Was there any longstanding family feud between your family and the victim's family, or the co-defendant's family?

9. Why did this murder case merit capital status when the vast majority of other murder cases don't?

10. Were you on drugs at the time? If so, what kind and how much?

11. Do you have any type of disability or learning difficulty?

12. Did you graduate from high school?

I was certain Mark's brother wouldn't even write back. Why should he when I just blew in out of nowhere asking all sorts of personally invasive questions. Especially the final question about having a learning problem.

Most people with learning disabilities are often too ashamed to admit they have this handicap. Given the fact that the disabled in general are treated as second-class citizens, this reticence is no small wonder. Those with learning disabilities have been subjected to a life of seemingly never-ending failure, scorn and ridicule beginning in early childhood. By the time they reach high school, they have a solid history of being discarded by teachers and treated with disdain and contempt by their peers. As children with learning disabilities grow up into adulthood, the learning disabilities do not disappear. In adulthood, those with learning disabilities face bleak prospects for having any decent future. The visual and auditory processing deficits that impede the ability to succeed academically are the same deficits that impede the ability to read social cues and body language. It is the latter which impacts someone's employability the most.

Prior to the onslaught of factory automation, computers, and the Internet ushering in the new global economy, learning disabled adults could get decent paying jobs with health benefits and pensions working in factories, steel mills, textile plants and foundries. They could enjoy full acceptance and participation in society and live the American Dream. Now, learning disabled adults are discarded and consistently left out of the "new economy", getting little to no sympathy, help or support from anyone else. The bachelors degree of today is the same sort of gatekeeper to jobs that the high school diploma was thirty years ago. If those of us with learning disabilities are "too dumb" to be able to fit in and adapt to the workplace demands of the "new economy", that's our tough luck and somehow our own fault.

I seriously considered leaving that last question about learning difficulties out of my letter to Rick Laird as I trudged home in the snow.

Chapter 12

"Justice is always violent to the party offending, for every man is innocent in his own eyes." ~ Daniel Dafoe

Arriving home, I had to enter in the same fashion in which I had left the day before on my way to the hotel. My fingers were painfully cold as I struggled to jimmy the window open so I could get inside. Climbing through my second floor window, I tumbled onto the floor.

Mini-Stain, a pretty calico stray cat who had recently adopted me as her pet human, yawned and stretched lazily on my bed. For the past twenty-four hours, she had to make do with Purina instead of stealing food from my dish because I had been at the hotel instead of at home for my meals. She was as bad as she was cute: Always making off with food from my plate which she would scoop from the plate onto the floor with her paws. Sometimes she would not wait for the food to be cooked. Her favorite trick would be absconding at lightning speed with a piece of raw chicken less than a minute after the pack had been opened and before I could get it into the oven. I didn't mind sharing my food as a special treat with her, but I definitely minded the idea of her paws on my plate: these were the same paws she used to scratch around in her litter box. Unlike people, cats do not wash their paws with anti-bacterial soap after going to the bathroom.

Struggling to get out of my heavy coat and boots, I relaxed briefly on the moleskin divan next to the window. It was Friday and I was looking forward to sleeping in over the weekend and not leaving the pile of comforters on my bed for anything except coffee, hearty soup and plenty of hot chocolate. After a few minutes of thawing out, I felt rejuvenated and made a beeline for the coffee pot: I needed my caffeine fix to concentrate on my letter to Rick Laird. Once settled in for the evening, I racked my brain for the right words, the right things to say. Before I knew it, I had nodded off to sleep. I finally finished my letter by Sunday night. In it, I told Rick that I was writing him at Mark's request. I told him that I thought the entire system was broken and the reasons why. I closed the letter asking him to write back.

Time flew and Monday morning came too quickly. I had an early morning chemistry class that would be over by noon and then I had the rest of the day to sleep, study, and do my lab reports.

Dr. Gauntlet was not your typical chemistry professor. He was a good-natured, bespectacled fifty-something year old man who wore a tie-dyed lab coat. That day, we were doing a hydration experiment. I had really hoped we would be tie-dyeing our lab aprons instead. His lectures were never boring and he always tried to make the class fun. It was fascinating to learn that carbon was a building block of life and that the most electronegative element was fluorine. Fluorine is a member of the halide class and is always trying to "lose" a valence electron in an attempt to acquire noble gas structure, sort of like molecular snob appeal.

After class, I stopped by the campus computer lab. The computers had Internet access. Curious about Rick Laird's case, I typed his name into the search bar to see if anything would come up in a search. Nothing came back, probably because court records were not yet entered into computer data bases.

Three days later, I got my first letter from Rick in the mail. A business sized white envelope addressed to me with Rick's inmate return mail number lay on the floor inside my front door where I accidently stepped on it as I returned from work. I grabbed it and opened it before taking my coat off to sit down.

January 18th, 1996

Jacqueline:

Hello! This is Rick, Mark's brother. I received your letter. Thank you for writing. Please bear with my spelling and grammar, they are not what they should be....You sound like a very intelligent and interesting woman. That guy Gary you were dating, what a knucklehead. From what my brother tells me, you are a very attractive woman so don't let some childish knucklehead get to you.....Ha! Very Mark! Turd indeed...Between you and I, I will tell ya' a little secret. We, Mark and I, come from a rough world where terms of endearment, nice ones, are looked upon as a weakness. Hence, the rougher, more crude terms of endearment. When I was in Huntingdon State Prison, Mark came to see me for a visit, we were joking back and forth and whatnot and he said to me, oh fuck you, and I knew he meant I love you. See what I'm saying?

Yes, I am on death row. It is this Friday, eight long years. I am glad to hear you are against the death penalty....Sometime, if you like, I'll tell you the story. I will say this, I am in the process of fighting this mess legally, what a headache. But God willing, things will improve. Again Jacqueline, thank you for writing. I realize my response in no way does justice to your letter, but know that I both enjoyed reading your letter as well as writing back to you...Until I hear from you again,

God Bless,

Rick - Luke 2:4-14

I was disappointed that Rick had not answered any of my questions. How could I investigate his case if he wouldn't tell me anything that I needed to know? What really struck me was the reference to the New Testament he wrote next to his signature. I guess when one is faced with the depressing certainty of never leaving prison except feet first in a pine box; one tends to rely heavily on religion. He was a born-again Christian. I am a Jew, although a very secular and unobservant one.

I wrote him again. This time instead of launching right into interrogation mode, I tried to make it a little more personal. I told Rick about Mini-Stain and her chicken-pilfering antics. I told him that the very first thing I read after overcoming illiteracy was the entire IRS Tax Code and that I had found one hundred and twenty-seven contradictions in it. I also enlightened him as to my opinionated views on politics.

Rick answered in more detail in his response to my second letter. It was now the second week of February and I finally received his reply in the mail:

Jacqueline *Feb. 7th, 1996*

Hello, how are you? I just received your letter and am very glad to hear from you. I had thought you had decided not to write back to me....Hold on, room service just brought my dinner.

Okay where was I? Oh yes, please my friend, what I say to you, I say so trusting that you will hold it in complete confidence. You know, that little piece I shared with you, I have never told that to anyone else.

You have cats? Tell me about them. I like cats, in fact I have a tattoo of a cat. And you mentioned research, if you like, I would enjoy hearing about that also.....Your offer of your expertise and of those you know is very generous and I greatly appreciate it, concerning my legal case. I will keep all of that in mind. For now, I have a set court date. It is February 29th of this year. We will be going and arguing my case.

You are of a scientific mind so I shall enclose a piece of our new evidence for your review. This new evidence is material that my trial attorney failed to uncover and use at my trial. To understand the full impact of this material one must understand the law as it is applied to degrees of homicide.

For instance, in order to have First Degree Homicide one must be able to commit premeditated murder, calculate what one is about to do, etc. For Second Degree Homicide, basically it is a murder which occurs in the commencement of a felony (Note: Prosecutors will also apply this to First Degree). Third Degree Homicide covers all other avenues of murder, those lacking ability to form specific intent, etc. Now, see the enclosed piece of evidence and respond with your thoughts.

We will have Dr. Spikes at the upcoming hearing to testify along with another expert witness. We are pursuing "26 issues" and God willing I will see relief from at least one of those issues. Needless to say I am quite excited about the upcoming hearing, God willing...It is about time for the evening news so I will put that on, and I must write to another person yet so I will close this letter to you. I apologize that it is so short. The next will be better. Hope to hear from you soon, I enjoy your company very much. Take care and God Bless.

Rick

The "enclosed piece of evidence" turned out to be a copy of a police report and a toxicology report prepared by Dr. Spikes - the one Rick referenced in his letter. According to the police report, the victim, twenty-six year old Anthony Vito Milano, died when his throat was repeatedly slashed.

In the toxicology report, Rick Laird was listed as having a blood alcohol level of 0.46! I had to re-read it to make sure I wasn't having a dyslexic moment because 0.46 is damn near enough to be fatal, or at least render him unable to control his bodily functions. If Rick Laird had 0.46 alcohol content, how the hell could he have possibly been found guilty of first degree murder which requires premeditation? How could anyone with 0.46 blood alcohol content premeditate anything when they would be almost a vegetable?

I was convinced he had to be innocent. His letters exuded seemingly genuine warmth unbecoming of a brutal slasher. The concept that someone could be capable of slicing someone's throat one day and then be a warm, caring human being the next was a thought that turned my brain. I did not want to believe that both a caring man and a psycho killer could coexist inside the same mind.

There were still many other details about the crime that he was not telling me. But at this point I believed he was innocent because I felt I had to. Part of it was the fact that I did not wish to believe in monsters. Part of me was very desperate to believe that pure evil simply could not exist outside of Christian mythology, B-rated horror movies, ancient superstitions and old wives' tales.

There was a more compelling reason that I wanted to believe this man was innocent instead of a psychopathic killer. The reason was that the criminal justice system had a long established track record of dog and pony shows where lawyers were determined to get their own way: The truth was far less important than some high-powered prosecutor getting to collect his gold star and ride off into the sunset like a hero. A classic example is the flimsy fabrication of evidence that resulted in the conviction and execution of Ethel and Julius Rosenberg for espionage during the height of McCarthyism and the "Red Scare" during the Cold War era. The disgusting sham of the Rosenberg trial will always be an embarrassing stain on American jurisprudence.

I needed to get to the bottom of things regarding Rick Laird's case. In order to do so I needed all the facts. I had only two facts concerning his case thus far: A toxicology report and a police report. And that was no small matter. I wondered what the remaining twenty-five issues Rick had that his attorney would be pursuing since Rick had not gone into detail about them in his letter. I wondered if there had been a clerical error in that toxicology report. I decided it would be wise to confer with my best friend and mentor Dr. Fred Wilson Weiler whom I affectionately called "Doc". He was someone whose judgment and discretion I trusted.

Doc Weiler was sixty-eight years old and a semi-retired part-time professor who taught basic physics at Lehigh County Community College. It was in the capacity of being a student in his class that I initially made his acquaintance. He recognized that I had talent in applied math courses like physics and he mentored me. He understood my dyslexia and encouraged me to not give up. It was under his encouragement that I minored in physics. We had a lot of other things in common, too. Like me, he was fascinated with trying to solve the mystery of Jack the Ripper's true identity and was a confirmed Ripperologist. In fact, he once traveled to Great Britain specifically to visit Scotland Yard and seek access to the Ripper crime scene documents not open to the public, using a bogus investigator pass and ID. He loved cats and preferred their company over that of most people. He had two huge male tabby cats named Zodiac and Romeny Rye - meaning “gypsy gentleman”. He had a strong belief in correcting social injustices wherever possible and he loved true crime books. He drove with a severe lead foot and was a recluse; both traits I shared to some degree.

His doctorate was in mathematics. When Fred Wilson Weiler was a graduate student, he studied under legendary algebraic topologist legendary algebraic topologist Marshall Hall. After graduating from Muhlenberg College, an exclusive private college in Allentown’s wealthy west end, he began his graduate studies at the University of Pennsylvania, a prestigious Ivy League school in Philadelphia.

Although he excelled academically at the University of Pennsylvania, he found the elitist old money environment stifling. He switched to Ohio State University where he felt more socially comfortable cavorting with a mostly middle class student population that enjoyed beer and pizza and that took their school’s football games seriously. In fact, Doc Weiler often told me that any university that didn’t give a damn about their football team wasn’t a school where he wanted to be. Knowing that I could care less about any sports, especially football, Doc Weiler justified his football addiction by claiming that the boorish sport had a lot of mathematics in it. That’s what I loved about my friend Doc Weiler: he had a unique style.

After earning his PhD he built a successful career over the next two decades in the math departments of the College of William and Mary in Virginia and later at the University of St. Francis De Sales. Doc Weiler had taken a hiatus from academia for over a decade after the death of his beloved wife Jeanie on Christmas Eve of 1972 at the young age of forty after a long and debilitating heart condition caused by a childhood bout of rheumatic fever which permanently weakened her heart. After Jeanie died he was inconsolable. Jeanie was the love of his life, his soul mate, and there had never been another.

A mere couple of months after the death of his wife, tragedy struck another hard blow in Doc Weiler's life. He had just completed the renovation of an old barn on his property which he converted into a climate-controlled library to safely store his entire collection of books, many of which were extremely rare and irreplaceable. The final stages were complete except for the final turn-on for the new and separate electrical service at the transformer by the electric company, PP&L. Less than twenty-four hours after PP&L turned the power on, an electrical fire which was determined to have originated with a problem at the transformer's line hook-up broke out in the library. Within a matter of minutes, the blaze engulfed the barn consuming all its literary contents: thousands of precious and rare books which Doc had spent his lifetime acquiring.

He sued the utility company but due to the extreme technical nature of the basis for his negligence suit, the jury was simply too confused to be able to follow and piece together all the evidence. Had the jury been solely comprised of mathematicians and physicists, the outcome would have been quite different. He got nothing, except the money his homeowner's policy was obligated to pay under the terms and limits of his policy. The payment from the insurance company represented only a very small fraction of the actual monetary value for his book collection.

At the time of Jeanie's death and the freak fire that destroyed his second true love, Doc held the chair of the math department at the University of St. Francis DeSales on the border of Lehigh and Bucks counties in eastern Pennsylvania. An upcoming math professor who had not yet earned his PhD eyed Doc Weiler's position of department chair with greed and ambition. Doc Weiler just didn't have the stomach for defending his title and position at St. Francis after his personal tragedies so he simply resigned and never once looked back. It was an unceremonious end to his career after he had contributed so much to that institution of higher learning.

Doc was in his forties when he found himself in transition. Although the ivory towers of academia purport to adhere to the liberal ideals of workplace diversity, age discrimination is alive and well. Doc Weiler found to his dismay that his job search turned from months into years. He finally was hired as a part-time adjunct professor in the physics department at Lehigh County Community College, for an insulting fraction of his previous earnings.

Doc Weiler was the most easy-going person I had ever known. In fact, he was so eager to be agreeable that even when a colleague was wrong, Doc Weiler would let the other person prevail just to avoid conflict. How could anyone have difficulty working with someone like Doc Weiler? What was even more distressing was the fact that someone would be so desperately greedy that they would seek to ruin Doc Weiler's career just to further their own agenda when Doc Weiler never did anything to hurt anybody. He was the most non-confrontational person I had ever known. He was just too nice, to a fault.

Unfortunately, nice people often finish last. Academia, like corporate America, is loaded with office politics. Fitting in, being willing to play the game, knowing the right people and being socially accepted among your fellow professors carries more weight than academic contributions and whether or not your students actually become inspired, learn anything, or succeed in your classes. Merit counts for nothing.

Fishing my phone out from the sofa cushions, I dialed Doc Weiler's number. "Ahem....mmm. Hello?" my friend's familiar voice answered. I dove right into the reason for my call.

"Doc, I know this is kind of short notice, but I have a true crime situation happening right now that you're probably going to want to sink your teeth into. This guy, Rick Laird, is on death row for murdering some guy named Anthony Milano. Now Mark Laird, Rick Laird's brother, is a coworker of mine at the Hilton in the maintenance department. He asked me to investigate this, claiming that Rick had been framed. So I wrote Rick and Rick sends me this toxicology report. The problem is that if this toxicology report is correct, there's no way in hell that I can see this guy being guilty of capital murder because according to the data he would have been a vegetable, or dead. His blood alcohol level is listed here as 0.46. Something isn't right."

After a long pause, I thought my geriatric friend had dozed off while on the phone (which he had been known to do on occasion) even with his TV set blaring in the background. "Hello? Doc, are you still there?"

"Yes, I'm awake," he yawned into the other end of the phone. "Do you have the toxicology report handy?"

I told him that I did and a police report as well. Doc Weiler told me to bring them both over to his house immediately.

It was bitter cold outside so I decided to take a thermos full of fresh coffee along. Doc left his outside lights on for me so I could see to walk up the path to the front door without tripping over anything. My friend greeted me in his favorite maroon colored sweat pants and sweatshirt. In the den we heard a loud crash and commotion. A pile of Doc's books had hit the floor and the culprit was perched high up on a bookshelf. Apparently, Romeny Rye didn't want a bath from Lara, Doc's Siberian Huskie who took it on her own authority to groom the cats that she decided to adopt as puppies. Zodiac was only slightly less resentful of this maternal canine smothering and slobbering.

Unphased by the ruckus, Doc sat down at the long hand-carved wooden table in the den and invited me to sit, too. He briefly read the police report. Looking over the entire toxicology report in deep thought, Doc was silent. I was eager to hear his conclusion and opinion on the matter. After a long and thoughtful pause Doc looked over the table at me and said, "We are going to need more information regarding this case. If you can get the trial transcripts or anything from the Bucks County coroner, we'll have more to go on. There may be other factors that would account for such a high blood alcohol content that would not completely incapacitate Rick Laird, but without seeing everything else we won't know for sure."

I racked my brain for what else could possibly account for such an anomaly. "Doc, I don't know what you think of this possible explanation but is it possible that Rick Laird could have counter-acted the effects of such high blood alcohol levels by using drugs that would have had the opposite effect, like maybe cocaine?"

Doc, looking very reserved, reached for his favorite snack, a chocolate doughnut, and chose his words carefully. "Anything is possible. He also could have built up an unusually high tolerance for alcohol over years of heavy drinking. But let me tell you this, even if Laird killed this guy in a fit of drunken rage, he did so by slicing his throat, according to the police report. Now, that's a pretty horrible way to kill someone and anyone who does that really does deserve the death penalty, in my opinion. You don't cut someone's throat with a knife with the intent of only hurting them or punching out their lights. Be careful in this, don't get roped into something potentially harmful to you just for trying to be a good egg, OK?"

Doc made a photocopy of the report and after finishing my coffee I got up to go home. Doc had an early morning vet appointment for Lara and I had a calculus exam first thing in the morning. I helped Doc pick up the stack of physical chemistry books that Romeny Rye previously knocked down during his escapade with Lara's unsolicited grooming attempt. Doc handed me a new book, *The Diary of Jack the Ripper*, saying thoughtfully, "Oh, here, before I forget. I meant to give this to you this past Monday at our last Ripperology meeting. I already have two copies." It was the diary of a cotton merchant named James Maybrick whom, by his own claims and in his own handwriting, admitted to being Jack the Ripper. I was chomping at the bit to immerse myself in the book. Doc was also trying to tell me something else in giving me the book. He was trying to tell me that there really are monsters that walk among us, evil incarnate like Jack the Ripper.

I had my doubts about Rick Laird's guilt initially because if someone that intoxicated should be an incoherent vegetable, it did not seem feasible that he would have been able to maintain the balance and coordination required to physically engage in a fatal dispute. I thought about what Mark Laird had told me about this friend of Rick's, Frank Chester. Mark insisted that Frank Chester framed Rick in hopes of getting away with murder. I wondered if this crime could have paralleled something like the murder of Dr. Robinson in Mark Twain's fictional classic *Tom Sawyer*.

In *Tom Sawyer* the loveable town drunk Muff Potter was knocked out cold with a shovel by Injun Joe while Injun Joe murdered Dr. Robinson in the graveyard. Injun Joe placed the weapon in Muff Potter's hand and claimed that Muff Potter did it. Muff Potter had no proof that he didn't do it and the only witnesses were Tom and Tom's pal Huck Finn whose presence in the graveyard had gone unnoticed by the three men. Fearing the murderous Injun Joe, Tom and Huck swore a blood pact of secrecy, agreeing to remain silent about what they saw. It was Tom Sawyer's sudden outburst in the courthouse while Injun Joe lied under oath on the witness stand that freed Muff Potter but raised the ire of Injun Joe. The story of course culminated in a deadly cat and mouse pursuit in McDougal's Cave where Injun Joe tried to kill Tom Sawyer and Tom's sweetheart Becky Thatcher. Could Laird have been wrongfully convicted because of being a Muff Potter to Chester's Injun Joe?

Tom Sawyer is a classical work of fiction where everything worked out to a happy ending for everybody, but in real life things often don't work out the way they're supposed to. Truth and justice do not always prevail: in fact that rarely happens unless you have plenty of resources and money. If no one else actually saw the murder, who would come to the rescue of someone wrongfully convicted sitting on death row by coming forward with the truth? What bothered me even more was the possibility that someone else could have witnessed the Milano murder, but unlike the ne'er do well hero in Mark Twain's classic, had remained silent because self-preservation overrode the impulse and desire to do the right thing.

Another possible scenario was that Rick had been present but due to being so drunk he might have had no way of foreseeing that his buddy Frank would end up in a fight resulting in the death of Anthony Milano. That was a very believable situation. It certainly was preferable to believe that than believe that either or both men intended to murder another human being in cold blood. But there was a gnawing voice in the depths of my soul and in the back of my mind saying that Anthony Milano's murder at the hands of Rick Laird and Frank Chester was simply not an accident resulting from a drunken brawl.

A few days after visiting Doc, I contacted the Bucks County courthouse to inquire about getting a copy of the trial transcripts. Each trial transcript is prepared individually by the court reporter who works as a contracted service provider for the county and as such, the county cannot regulate their fees. The fees are determined by each reporter. I contacted the one for the Laird and Chester case and found out that the cost was one dollar per page and there were well over a thousand pages. The cost would have been about $1400 - money that I didn't have and had no way to come up with. I discreetly brought up the matter to Mark Laird while at work. Mark didn't have (or wish to spend) that kind of money.

I asked about the possibility of his mother helping out since I remembered him telling me that she was retired and married to a retired state cop. While they were not wealthy, they certainly weren't dirt poor and scraping to get by from one week to the next either. Surely she could afford to help defray some of these costs if she wanted her older son's life spared from an unjust execution. Mark knew I was poor. He also knew how I was suffering from teeth rotting out of my head that I couldn't do anything about until I became eligible for health benefits at the Hilton. He knew I was definitely poor beyond a doubt. But he claimed neither he nor his mother could help defray the costs. Yeah, right.

For the wife of a retired state cop who supposedly had absolutely no money, Rick's mother certainly lived in a much better house than I could ever hope to afford, barring getting lucky on the lottery and winning the Powerball jackpot prize. The reason I knew she wasn't as poor as Mark claimed was because Mark had shown me recent pictures of her home and their family Christmas holiday celebrations complete with a table set with a feast fit for royalty less than a month ago. I spent the winter holidays eating in a soup kitchen. Now *that* is being poor!

When I had commented at that time on how nice the house was I made an off-handed statement about how high the mortgage payments must be. Mark told me their house had been paid off for several years. Compared to me, they were rich! Her home was easily worth upwards of $200,000 and was located in a solidly middle to upper-middle class suburb. I lived in a run-down sliver of a row home that had been converted into a flat in the 1940's which was located in an overcrowded inner city ghetto...and I was lucky to have *that*. I certainly didn't have the means to put on a swanky holiday spread. I couldn't even afford oil for my small menorah and a small corned beef brisket to celebrate Chanukah!

Nothing annoys me more than people who cry poverty with two loaves of bread under their arms. In the case of Mark Laird and his mother Joyce, it was more like crying poverty with the whole damn bakery under their arms plus the deli and wine shop, too. Joyce Laird Kessler may not have had a million dollar 401(k) to live on, but she certainly had something. She wasn't reduced to scrubbing toilets for minimum wage in her golden years just to be able to afford her Medicare co-pays and a few meager frozen TV dinners on sale at Wal-Mart. Retired PA State Troopers get decent pensions.

If it were my child on death row for a crime he or she didn't commit, I would sell every last thing I owned and downsize to a smaller, far more humble home if that's what it took to see justice done. I guess greed and mammon worship were Laird family values. Living it up came before saving the life of one of their own.

Now it was standard practice in Pennsylvania at the time Rick Laird and Frank Chester were convicted that capital prisoners would receive one free copy of his or her trial transcript. The utmost care has to be taken regarding these materials because if the prisoner should trust the wrong person with their transcripts another copy would not be made available free of charge for an appellate attorney to use in helping the inmate proceed through the appeals process. Trial transcripts are like the "Schindler's List" for those on death row. They are the only hope and thread potentially connecting to the literal life saver of a sentence commutation, full pardon, clemency, or legal remedy and relief on appeal of the original conviction and sentence.

While scraping up $1,000 or more may be a daunting prospect for someone on the outside, it is an impossible task for a prisoner on death row. Prisoners on death row are not permitted jailhouse jobs with which to earn any money and must rely solely on friends and family to put money on their books for them so they may buy things like toothpaste, shampoo and a bathrobe. They are isolated from the prisoners in the prison's general population. Even those inmates in the prison's general population don't get minimum wage for their prison jobs. The top pay rate for a prison job in 1996 was around $0.25 an hour. If I couldn't scrape together $1400 to pay the court reporter fees for a copy of Rick's trial transcripts on my $7 an hour job, there was no way an indigent prisoner on death row could do so.

Helping a prisoner on death row is fraught with difficulties and barriers: Money, time and even a lack of cooperation from the prisoner himself if he does not trust you. In order for me to help

Rick Laird, he would have to help himself: he would have to cooperate by in sending me his trial transcripts. If Rick would not trust me enough to send me his only trial transcript copy, there would be nothing else I could do to help him with his case.

In order for my friend Doc Weiler to be able to help, he needed a copy of those transcripts and any medical reports pertinent to Rick's background. A forensics report would definitely be needed as well. I wrote Rick and asked him if there was anything else that could be material to his appeal that he could send me, such as a pre-trial neuro-psych evaluation or anything along the lines of the forensic pathology reports. I also told him about my friend Doc Weiler and let him know that he was also helping with the case.

In my letter, I told him about my involvement with the volunteer organization known as the Learning Disabilities Association of PA - Lehigh Valley Chapter (LDA). That very same organization had helped me to fight for my "reasonable accommodations" in college. LDA volunteers also helped me assert a formal complaint against PA OVR in order to compel that agency to help me with paying for the neuro-psych test required to render me eligible for reasonable accommodations in the classroom.

In my own struggle to understand and cope with dyslexia, I learned how to be an advocate for myself and eventually for others. Eventually I got on the board of LDA. In between semesters at the community college, I served as a volunteer by escorting parents of learning disabled children to intimidating school meetings regarding their children's unmet needs, helping them fight discrimination when they were denied the Free and Appropriate Public Education (FAPE) they are entitled to under Public Law 94.

I knew from attending the LDA advocacy conferences that teens and adults with learning disabilities were at higher risk for incarceration and that it was not necessarily due to actual guilt in the commission of a crime. Learning disabilities increase a child's risk of adjudication by 220%, especially among those who also suffer from Attention Deficit Hyperactivity Disorder, commonly known as ADHD. In fact, the relationship between ADHD and antisocial behavior is so strong that some consider ADHD to be a predisposing risk factor.

Frequently, a learning disabled teen or adult finds themselves scapegoated by unscrupulous "friends" who commit crimes and then let the blame fall squarely on the person with the cognitive impairment. Adults and teens with learning impairments make convenient targets because many are far less socially savvy than others. They also tend to be too trusting of others, often with disastrous consequences.

One need not be a clinical psychologist to make the obvious connection between academic failure and social failure. Excellent references can be found in the *Last One Picked, First One Picked On: The Social Implications of Learning Disabilities* workshop by foremost expert on learning disabilities, Rick Lavoie. Among the teen and young adult population with learning disabilities, desperate attempts to fit in is a factor in delinquent behavior. Endless failures in school accompanied by ridicule, humiliation, and ostracism by peers put learning disabled youth at a much higher risk for making the wrong friends and getting involved with the wrong people in their desperation to find comraderie and acceptance. While adolescence is always a difficult time for kids, it is a far more difficult and frustrating period for those with learning disabilities.

Youth and adults with ADHD are more likely to be arrested and convicted than their non-disabled peers for the exact same offenses. This may be because those with learning disabilities lack the cognitive and language skills to avoid detection, conceal intent, and respond properly to questions and warnings by the police. It is well known that the demeanor of the arrestee is an extremely important factor in determining whether an arrest will actually be made during routine encounters with the police.

Difficulty in maintaining consistency while trying to explain a sequence of events also results in higher conviction rates among the learning disabled. If someone can't keep their story straight even though they are innocent, the authorities and the courts take it as a sign of dishonesty and guilt. Inability to "read" body language, extreme frustration causing impulsiveness, and social skills deficits translate to inability to behave properly in court in front of a judge. The same cognitive impairment that makes reading print difficult can also make reading social cues difficult. Mastery of nonverbal communication is a key factor in the interpersonal skills necessary for success in the workplace as well as success in forming lasting bonds in personal relationships.

Learning disabled adults are also less likely to have prestigious careers with autonomy, or even just a plain vanilla job that pays a living wage in which they can succeed. In fact, studies compiled by the National Coalition for the Learning Disabled (NCLD) show that only 51% of adults with learning disabilities are gainfully employed permanently on a full time basis for a consecutive twelve month period in any given year. Sadly, the talents, gifts and potential social contributions of the learning disabled population tend to go underutilized and countless precious resources are wasted as a result.

Jobs held by adults with learning disabilities are usually menial and low-paying with no medical or retirement benefits and no job security. So it should be no surprise that many learning disabled adults are unable to afford adequate legal representation if they do get entangled in the criminal justice system.

I had hoped struggling to overcome dyslexia to earn my bachelors degree; I would become a success story instead of another failure statistic. I hoped that by being a part of an organization committed to advocating for the learning disabled, I would be able to make a difference in society. I recalled reading somewhere that inmates with learning disabilities make up 85% of the prison population. There was a good chance that Rick Laird was learning disabled and possibly easy to target and frame for this murder. A week later, I received Rick's five page handwritten response in the mail.

February 20th, 1996

Jacqueline,

I received your letter today, it made for a pleasant surprise. And again, feel free to write about anything at all Jacqueline, good or bad. All of your input on my legal situation is very welcome. First off, the toxicologist's report is basically new testimony of my drinking on the night in question. It was not exploited by my attorney at trial. His failure to gather and marshal evidence of my intoxication is inexcusable and we will be raising that at this hearing. My trial attorney just basically stood still and watched as I got slapped with a sentence of death. I, needless to say, was very ignorant of the law and justice system or I would not have stood by and allowed this to happen without saying something.

And again, we have had a psychiatric evaluation done and the psy. has determined also that the amount of alcohol I had to drink that night left me with no cognitive ability. I could not have planned or carried out a plan to kill another person.....There are several areas where my trial counsel was ineffective which we will be attempting to prove. In all we are arguing, of those 26 many are claims of ineffective assistance of trial counsel. Today I managed to get my attorney's secretary on the phone, according to her all is still on for the 29th and everything is going well, rounding up witnesses, etc. I then called a family member and they told me that the attorney has them getting some clothing together for me for court.....You see, I expected that the district attorney would be postponing to have the Commonwealth's experts go to work on the same thing our experts did, but then again the Commonwealth uses the same lab where Dr. Spikes works out of so.....Anyway I would very much like to get this process moving. I am so tired of just sitting waiting out postponements.

And my past, yes it is a bit rough and there are many areas of it that I am not proud of and that is about to be splattered all over an open court, embarrassing...Before I found Christ, I would not have cared what was said in that courtroom, but now....I am ashamed of my past.

Your 5 points are very interesting and <u>I tell you this, in one of them the truth lies</u>. Anyone who drinks the amount of alcohol I did on that night would not recall anything that happened when - and if - they woke the next morning.

The learning disabilities argument you put forth is all very interesting and may prove useful, however the psy. who tested me concluded nothing of that sort. He judged me "normal" overall, whatever that means? Believe this, if I were a rich man I would have the tests you mentioned performed. I would explore and investigate every avenue, but unfortunately I am indigent. But God willing we have enough as it is. That, as I mentioned briefly to you in my last letter is one of the major flaws in our system, wealthy vs indigent defendants.

Man! What was I just saying earlier in this letter? I just received a message from the Sgt., said my attorney called and wants me to get in touch with him tomorrow morning around 9:00 AM. That hearing for the 29th has been postponed. You cannot imagine how depressing that is to me. I'll have to check tomorrow and see exactly what the postponement is for, but I know this - it wasn't asked for by me, so........

Anyway, as I was about to say before the interruption, you being a board member of the learning disabilities advocacy group for PA and helping the people you do is all a very good thing. I am proud to know someone who does such.

What, or rather how, do the degrees of L.D. vary? I ask for a reason, my line of concentration has been shattered........I keep getting interrupted here so I had better finish this letter up....I have a book waiting for me, too. I lent my TV to one of the guys for a couple of days, his TV blew up on him recently and he is in the process of getting a new set, so for me it is a bunch of reading and writing, and radio for the next couple of days.

What do you do with your free time? I know you enjoy shopping for new shoes, what else do you enjoy? I have many such questions. Guess I'll save them for later though, wouldn't want to bore ya too much here. Take care. God Bless.

Rick

PS: I am enclosing some material you may find interesting.

PPS: If there is anything that I can do for you, just ask. If it is within my power I will do it. *R.*

Chapter 13

"It is often easier to fight for one's principles than live up to them." ~ Adlai Stevenson

The pieces of the puzzle now began to fall together, or so I thought. The material Rick had enclosed with his letter to me was a copy of his court-ordered neuro-psych report that was performed prior to his trial by Dr. Joseph S. Silverman.

Silverman worked on behalf of the Commonwealth, so the report was not without some bias against Rick. While forensics, which is based on chemistry, physics, mathematics and anatomy, is founded on more concrete sciences, psychology is not. Psychology is not just based on empirical evidence and studies, but also on a lot of theories, maybes and guesswork. As such, a psychological evaluation can easily be biased depending on who is doing the report. A psychiatrist working on behalf of the prosecution for the Commonwealth is not going to go out of his way to list anything that may later prove useful to the defense. Nor will he take the extra time to see if the subject has ADHD instead of antisocial personality disorder: two completely different conditions but with many identical traits.

According to the DSM IV (the American psychiatric diagnostics manual), the symptoms of ADHD and antisocial personality disorder are frighteningly similar. There is only one small difference: someone who has antisocial personality disorder feels no sympathy for their victim or remorse for the harm caused. Someone with ADHD does not intend to cause harm, and generally feels bad when it is brought to their attention that they have done so. Also, someone with ADHD usually has acted out on a sudden unsuppressed urge of extreme frustration without forethought or malice. But a psychiatrist working on the side of the prosecution is not going to trouble himself to make such a distinction. Juries tend to pity a defendant with potential claim for diminished capacity due to ADHD, but they tend not to have much sympathy for a cold-blooded psychopath incapable of shame or remorse.

I did not have the background to fully absorb all the psychiatric jargon in the report, nor did I have the desire to grapple with the entire report. It would have taken me far longer to do so than what I realistically had the time to spend on it. I looked for key terms and phrases that might be indicative of a learning disability.

Two sentences that stood out in Dr. Silverman's evaluation of Rick Laird were: "*subject seems to admit having derived benefit from a criminal lifestyle, has aggressive tendencies, clearly displays signs of having antisocial personality disorder...Possible Attention Deficits during childhood and during adulthood to some extent as well.*"

Antisocial personality disorder is the fancy technological term meaning "sociopath". I inwardly railed against what I felt at that time to be a biased report, writing off Dr. Silverman as a stooge for an ambitious and publicity-craving district attorney who had his own agenda. Silverman's report left a foul taste in my mouth as I bitterly reminisced over my own dealings with those claiming to be "experts". My perception was skewed and as such, I didn't see the red flags concerning Rick Laird's guilt that I may have otherwise seen. Instead, I saw it as higher ranking members in society using the criminal justice system as a means to dispose of the "unworthy" person who was a convenient scapegoat because of his ADHD.

I had written Rick requesting his trial transcripts, explaining that my friend Doc Weiler would assist with his appeal. In the interim, a friendly but short letter from Rick arrived. It was dated February 16th, 1996. Somehow, it must have crossed with my letter in the outgoing mail in the prison inmate mail system. It was a response to my earlier letter in which I had shared a little bit about my personal life. I had sent him a photocopy of some of my college class notes as well as a picture of my neighbor, Carl "Blackie" Ebert, taken a year earlier. Blackie was holding one of my cats, Putt-Putt - so named for his purring which sounded uncannily like the hum of a Harley Davidson V-twin engine.

Putt-Putt was a sweet, loveable gray and black cat with white feet who followed me everywhere, even into the bathroom. I was heartbroken when I came home from college classes one day and found him laying on the floor dead for no apparent reason. After consulting with a vet, I learned Putt-Putt had a urinary tract infection which, unlike for people, is fatal for cats.

I also sent a picture of me and two old friends: Ed Neri and Ed's girlfriend "Minute", taken in front of Keiper's Pharmacy on 7th Street in Allentown. We had been clowning around and me being the flirt that I am, I was wearing a hot pink denim mini-skirt with matching stiletto heels. I wanted Rick to see me as a person and thus trust me, not simply view me as some condescending and impersonal egg-head who was scrutinizing his case the way a scientist studies bacteria in a petri dish.

Jacqueline *February 16th, 1996*

Hello, I received your letter today. It is very good to hear from you. Let me start off by saying you are a very attractive woman! Thank you for the pictures, may I keep them? Blackie looks a lot like someone I knew years ago. The kid came from one of the richer families, had a huge house. He was a roughtie guy, a rock - n - roller, always talkin' about playin' his guitar, loud and bold personality but one of the nicest people I ever knew. He claimed that before George Thorogood and "the Delaware Destroyers" became famous they used to practice at his family's home. And ya' know what? I believe him. Funny what kind of memories a photo will bring to mind. Ron Wheeler is his name.

I see you wear glasses, let's see what else I can see in this photo....you smoke, very unhealthy habit. I quit several years ago and feel much healthier for it. You have beautiful hair, and your eyes are, blue?...I have no pic of myself or I'd send one. Let me briefly describe myself so you get a general idea: 6'2", around 235 lbs, brown hair to my shoulders parted in the middle, I wear a beard and keep it fairly neat. I used to enjoy the wild look. Brown eyes. I try to keep in half decent shape, but under these conditions it is hard. I sit in a cell for 22 hours a day, the other 2 hours I am in an area not much bigger than the cell......

Interesting talk on the legal system. Recently I was watching a program on TV of a group of lawyers discussing our legal system and they all agreed that the world thinks our legal system is a joke because our system can be manipulated and twisted by the rich and the indigent don't stand a chance. Lady Justice may be blind, but she can sure smell which side the money is on. Capital punishment is very ugly and has no place, in my opinion, in society. The very ugliness of it all is one of the reasons executions in this country are carried out at nighttime, under the cloak of darkness.

Thank you for offering advice on my legal situation......... For instance what you said about having a learning disability and the intoxication, it being a threefold effect, I did not know this.......Listen, this is all very interesting. Therefore would you be interested in calling my attorney and giving him this info? If so, it must be done soon. I have a scheduled court date - the 29th of this month. If so here is his name and number:

Michael S. Goodwin (215) 345-8088.

You told me you were going to go buy yourself new shoes to cheer yourself up. What kind did you get? For years after I was sent here I used to dream about a good pair of boots. That's all I used to wear. Strange to dream about such, huh?

You're 28 ½ years old, when is your birth date? I asked a fellow rowman for his map so I could see exactly where Allentown is.....

I would very much enjoy a visit from you, however your description of a "go-cart" leaves much to be desired. I would hate to think of you breaking down half way across state. I must also tell you that I am not permitted "regular" visits such as the regular inmate receives. My capital status entitles me to visits from 8:00 AM to 3:00 PM. Glass separates the visitor and myself and we must speak through a telephone.

Now if your go-cart is dependable, and after hearing the conditions under which we must visit and you still wish to visit, I'll put you on my official visitor's list. One cannot get in to visit a prisoner without being on the official visitors' list. If you wish to bring Mark that would be great, but since he must also be approved for the list and he is an ex-con, that may prove difficult.

I have reviewed the photocopies from your notebook. I now have a headache! Ha Ha Ha! For instance, what does the symbol "∫" stand for as in ∫∫∫x∂ Cx? I could go on as I am always interested in learning. I hope I'm not boring you and I further hope that I do not seem too scatter-brained here jumping from subject to subject.....I will close for now. Take care and God Bless.

<u>Rick</u>

I was curious about the part where Rick mentioned Mark having a criminal record. As it turned out, Rick's brother Mark had an extensive criminal record. He had been arrested and convicted of running one of the largest meth rings in southeastern PA. Mark bragged to me, as well as to everyone who would listen, that his bail had been set higher than that of the rogue Central American dictator-turned-thug General Noriega, whom our CIA had the dubious honor of capturing. What a lifetime achievement to be proud of! Just the kind of guy I'd want to entrust with guest room keys, computer pass codes, and access to the hotel safe.

I had not known about this meth ring conviction when Mark initially asked me to help him with his brother. I found out when I asked him what he served prison time for that he wouldn't be allowed to visit his own condemned brother. When Mark told me about it, you would think he had just won recognition as a National Merit Scholar by the way he acted so proud of it.

He told me that he got paroled after serving only part of a reduced sentence because of a deal that he made with the district attorney where he had turned states' evidence by testifying against the president of the Breed motorcycle club and others who were higher up in the meth distribution ring whom were all sentenced to an average of sixty years or more under the RICO Act. One of those whom he testified against to save his own skin was his common-law wife — the mother of his children — whom he blamed for his criminal activities in his bid for leniency. From what I had learned about the case, his wife was also learning disabled. What a stand-up guy! He took the concept of "women and children first" to a whole new level.

He told me that The Breed had put a hit contract out on him with a generous price on his head for his complicity with the Commonwealth in taking down the largest methamphetamine ring in the state. Perhaps he thought this would impress women and get him laid out of sympathy. When he told me that he made enemies because of his testimony, I was unsympathetic. Any man who lets the mother of his children take the fall for his crime gets no sympathy from me. He could find his sympathy in the dictionary: between "shit" and "syphilis." Men abrogating self-responsibility by blaming women for everything is as old as the shell game in Genesis, in the fabled story of the "original sin."

Mark explained he was living at the half-way center for convicts in transition between prison and full parole. This half-way center was housed in the former H. Leh & Co department store building, located only three blocks from the Hilton Hotel on Allentown's Hamilton Mall. H. Leh & Co had been one of Allentown's oldest department stores before massive factory closings and "white flight" to the suburbs left a pocket of poverty and urban decay behind.

Local real estate mogul Abraham Atieyah bought that venerable building and leased it to the state for the housing of felons in transition between the state penitentiary and parole. The center was supervised by only a couple of guards. Escapes made by felons merely walking out and never returning were not an uncommon occurrence. Mark Laird was one of over two hundred ex-convicts living at this center. Their offenses ranged from murder to child molestation to minor drug offenses. Mark told me that his felony status is how he got hired full-time at the Hilton Hotel in the maintenance department.

In Pennsylvania, employers receive generous tax credits for hiring convicted felons. In fact, the tax incentive for hiring felons is far greater than any incentive for hiring any other class of economically disadvantaged people. In Pennsylvania, felons have better job opportunities because of these employer tax incentives than poor women: middle-aged displaced homemakers who have been out of the workforce for many years who lack recent references, poor single mothers, or disabled women who had to retrain in order to reenter the job market. Apparently crime pays in some ways. But Mark couldn't visit Rick, according to Rick's letter. That was the price of being a felon that Mark had to pay.

The other oddity in Rick's letter was his disapproval of my smoking, telling me how he quit smoking out of concern for his health. He felt duty-bound to admonish me to do likewise. The Commonwealth of Pennsylvania was going to put him to death by lethal injection but he was going to make sure he died with smoke-free lungs. Only a little less than a week after requesting Rick's trial transcripts, another letter came in the mail from Rick.

February 28th, 1996

Jacqueline:

Received your letter, very glad to hear from you. However, first we must address a subject. Mark sent me a letter, said you are giving him a rough time, etc. Mentioned that you had asked him to assist you in obtaining a copy of my trial transcripts. He then went on to request that I do not supply you with a copy of my transcripts. He did not explain himself on this subject....I am so pissed at my brother's letter that I have not bothered to write him back yet. And I have a few more choice words for my brother....

Now, the official visit form will be placed in tomorrow's internal mail. Should hear something back on it before too long.

That was some adventure that you undertook on 2-18-96! Woman, had you have asked I would have told you that those people listed on that police report were and are no friends of mine! I am very touched that you undertook that investigation, you cannot imagine how very much that means to me. Okay, I am going to try to respond to you as I receive it from your letter.

My T.T., you mentioned fine-tooth combing them for testimony, note T.T. = trial transcripts from now one. You mentioned going over "expert testimony", etc. Jacqueline, I had no expert testimony at my trial, NONE! I insisted that my present counsel, Goodwin, obtain experts on toxicology and psychology once he was appointed to represent me. So you will find none in my T.T. The only thing you will have to work with is testimony from the prosecution witnesses who saw me drinking, how much they saw and one pros. witness in a police report stated that she saw me "stagger into my bedroom". This was at the end of that night. My trial counsel did not use this info at trial, and I am insisting that Goodwin also use this evidence at the hearing.

Can you work with only that info, if reviewed from my T.T.? And I supplied a copy of the police report. That is what Dr. Spikes used, aside from the police report, to reach his conclusion. Also something I must mention, a report or paper cannot be submitted and stand on its own, it will have to be backed up by testimony by an "expert witness".

Al Hilton, saw the inconsistencies did ya? He was not on the stand very long, more used for theatrics by the prosecution than anything else. I'll tell you something, you are one very special woman. Can you imagine my surprise when I read about this undertaking of yours?

What did the bartender say to you? That guy is nothing more than a punk also. I am glad you did not get hurt Jacqueline. You got guts, woman.

I tried to call Goodwin this morning, apparently he was not in. What he told you about me driving that night upon leaving the bar is dead wrong, and as I mentioned, I was observed to stagger. I was going to let that guy have it (Goodwin). Did Goodwin treat you well? What was the outcome of your meeting? I only have about a hundred questions for the both of you.....

Okay, I read the literature you enclosed on ADD. I sent in a slip here at the prison and am going to request to see the psychologist, ask if she is board certified to give the test, if so will she do it and give me the results, etc. Now, I doubt that she will be able to do this because she works for the Commonwealth, but maybe she can offer a referral. I have several symptoms of ADD and I am very interested to see if we can develop a case history to present here as evidence. I just do not know if we have enough time here.

You are a woman with great depth and much love. I truly wish I were out there Jacqueline, I truly do. I'd love you deeper than you could possibly imagine. Love you like you truly deserve to be loved, completely, fully and forever............

I will be getting the T.T. to you as soon as I can. Please, as I have mentioned, this is all very personal material, please treat it as such. I am going to go through the volumes and send you the relevant volumes. Jacqueline, these are the only copies I have. Please make a copy of all and return my set ASAP. They are my only lifeline to these court proceedings....

Love,

Rick

Upon reading the very first paragraph of Rick's letter, I initially tossed it into the wastebasket without reading the rest of it. I was fuming mad. According to Rick, Mark's letter to him urged him to refrain from cooperating with efforts to help him. I resented that immensely. The truth was I felt ill-used. I was made a laughing stock for agreeing to help someone with only a few facts to go on, and someone who seemed to be of increasingly questionable innocence.

I had not sought out Richard Laird or intruded uninvited into his life and legal quagmire. It was Mark Laird who approached me, playing me for a sucker to get my help - free of charge - to aid in his brother's problem. I seriously considered walking away from Rick Laird's case right then and there. I should have walked away the minute Mark Laird opened up his mouth begging for my help. This wasn't my mess. I didn't put Rick in prison and I owed him nothing.

If Mark was miffed at my legitimate and reasonable request for some reimbursement or cost-covering contribution to get document copies, he should not have asked someone financially worse off than himself and his mother to help with his brother's capital case. I had not received one red cent to cover postage or photocopying costs. I didn't ask for a nickel of the smaller costs and Mark didn't offer, although he must have known what was involved. I also did not receive one dime in reimbursement for my gas and tolls costs to go running all over Bucks County tracking down the witnesses who had given police report statements. All I had asked for was a contribution towards what I could not reasonably afford on my own. Coughing up $1400 for trial transcripts was not something I could afford, and those transcripts were needed in order to help Rick.

I was also infuriated because merely getting involved in Rick's case put me potentially in harm's way by forcing me into a hostile environment to do some old-fashioned investigating. All this meant nothing to an ingrate like Mark Laird. He did not care that I could have gotten hurt by asking questions in trying to get facts to work from, poking around where I was clearly not welcome and an outsider. This sort of potential danger is one of the reasons why private investigators charge hefty fees for their time and efforts - which Mark Laird implicitly asked of me for free.

One of the least hostile people I interviewed while driving all over Bucks County was Jimmy Phillips, Jr. However, he was far from friendly. Just the mention of the name Richard Laird got me threatening dagger eyes from several male regulars at the Edgely Inn, including Jimmy Phillips, who happened to be tending bar when I entered this place on February 18th 1996. I was outnumbered and out of my element.

After filling my gas tank and paying for the turnpike tolls, I didn't even have enough money to order a sandwich. But it would have been rude for me to go in like Sgt. Joe Friday with tons of questions without buying something. I ordered a cranberry juice since I was not a drinker. When I told Jimmy that Mark Laird engaged my help with Rick's appeal, Jimmy shook his head, "You're helping the wrong guy."

Jimmy was uncomfortable having to recount the night of the crime. He and his family were in the midst of an ongoing lawsuit filed by the Milano family under *Dram Shop* liability for the murder of Anthony Milano. I could fully appreciate his position. He had done nothing wrong the night of the murder. Yet, for merely serving alcohol to the men who committed the murder after they left his bar, he and his family faced a lawsuit and financial ruin as a result.

Despite the hardship posed to me, I never once complained to Mark about the potential threat to my own safety. I simply rolled up my sleeves and did what I had to do. Mark had *solicited* my help and involvement. Yet he whined behind my back to Rick about my asking him if he could assist with some of the costs connected with getting trial transcripts. I was poor. I couldn't afford to undertake the costs entailed in a death penalty appeal.

Brooding over this insult, I thought about whether I should find some way to gracefully bow out. But I had already promised Rick in writing that I would I help if I had what I needed, and further committed my best friend's help as well. My other difficulties in the matter were the principles I firmly held with regard to helping someone else with a learning disability, someone who might possibly have been unjustly sentenced to death due to society's marginalization of those with "invisible" disabilities.

Picking up Rick's letter where I had tossed it in disgust moments earlier, I finished reading it. That was my fatal mistake. The end of the letter really got to me where Rick talked about how much I deserved to be loved, how special I was, and how I needed and deserved someone in my life, someone who would stand by me until my dying day. There is nothing that means more to someone like me, someone with no one and whose life had been anything but happy, than to hear something like this. Finding love and commitment instead of marginalization, isolation, and abandonment was the single most important thing in the world to me.

Yet finding it eluded me: nobody wanted to love, cherish and commit to a poor disabled woman with no family, no money and few - if any - prospects for ever having a good income to bring value into a marriage that would support a middle class lifestyle. I hoped for that unconditional love and commitment ever since I was an orphaned thirteen year old girl, whom nobody wanted, valued or cared about. But my hopes had gradually dissipated. After I was abandoned at age one and a half by my mother, after I was orphaned at thirteen and had to fend for myself out on the streets after my grandmother died, after an accident that left me unable to support myself at twenty-four, after I was unable to get any help from "all these agencies", after all of my friends except Doc bailed on me; and after all I got from men was used and discarded after being strung along on maybes, false hopes and empty promises of love and security, I stopped acknowledging God. I figured that God, if He truly existed, had abandoned me too. All I had left was anger, resentment and bitterness; and a loneliness that cried out for consoling and a desperate need to be valued.

The last part of Rick's letter struck a chord deep inside me. Surely he had a heart and was not the monster, not the psychopathic killer bereft of compassion and remorse that others thought he was. If he could care about a disabled woman who obviously was not one of society's successful winners, if he could love the orphan whom society discarded years ago, he certainly could not be a remorseless homicidal maniac without a conscience.

My anger at Mark's lies and insults melted away. All my suspicions and my thoughts of walking away from the entire mess dissolved. I was bound and compelled, by forces unexplained except in the equations of love and compassion, to help Rick Laird seek justice.

Juggling a college class schedule and my part-time job, it took me a few days to draft a well-thought-out response to Rick's letter. I set the story straight regarding his brother Mark. I had not given Mark a hard time about anything. I merely stated the facts: Mark is the one who asked me to help; he had solicited my involvement - not the other way around. And while I was happy to help where possible, providing that help would not be easy and with all it entailed it was certainly no walk in the park. The very least I deserved was consideration and respect.

I had been physically threatened. I had been stonewalled. I had spent money I couldn't afford on travel costs to traipse all over Bucks County trying to investigate everything since I lacked the transcripts for Doc and myself to go on. I had also taken time away from my own needs in getting through my class material in order to drive the two hours round trip to New Britain to meet with Rick's court-appointed appellate lawyer, Michael Goodwin. And going to *that* appointment was no treat for me.

Attorney Goodwin's office was in a converted 250 year old stone house on the main road through New Britain. A lone electric candle light graced each one of the house's window sills. The interior of the office was wall-to-wall books, accented by a real fireplace with antique mallard duck decoys adorning the mantle. The wall behind Goodwin's solid cherry executive desk was covered with impressive college diplomas and law school degrees. I could only imagine what it would be like to have a life like that with a successful and meaningful career.

From the start, my encounter with Michael Goodwin was adversarial. Goodwin rudely rebuffed me when I met with him. His arrogance surfaced beneath a polite veneer, tersely speaking to me as if I was some insignificant little peasant serf who dared to enter the presence of the manor lord. Apparently, since I had no standing or social position and was not one of the diplomaed elites with a PhD, MD or an Esq behind my name, anything I had to offer on a case didn't count. That is the first impression Michael Goodwin made on me. And first impressions are lasting ones.

It did not matter to Goodwin that I had a wealth of life experience and hands-on education as a learning disabilities advocate. It didn't matter that I had already done all the leg work in lining up experts willing to document Rick's ADHD and testify to his diminished capacity. He was completely uninterested in everything I had thus far compiled regarding the solid foundation for a diminished capacity claim as it pertained to Rick's claim of ineffective trial counsel. He just would not listen to anything I had to say. He indicated in so many words that it was his opinion that Richard Laird was too intelligent to have ADHD or brain damage.

I was just a "nobody" without a college degree and a prestigious high-powered career, a fancy office and an impressive job title. Michael Goodwin had his own agenda. Exerting any energy to objectively review someone else's hard work and efforts in trying to help his condemned client wasn't part of it. After all, he was the rich, successful lawyer who knew it all. Anyone less educated than him couldn't possibly know anything, so his time was too important to take a minute to recognize that somebody else might actually know something, too.

Maybe I was too harsh about Michael Goodwin. Maybe he really is a nice guy instead of the condescending snob he came across as. Maybe he was just having a bad day. Maybe he had to go for a colonoscopy instead of getting to hit the greens at the country club. Maybe he ran out of Viagra the night before and lost out on scoring a hot date. Who knows and who cares? I'm just not that forgiving.

In order to help Rick, I needed a copy of the trial transcripts but I had no way of coming up with $1400 to pay for it and they don't give them out free of charge. I told Rick in my reply that I had no way of paying for these trial transcripts out of my own pocket when I was desperately poor, far poorer than anyone in his family. The cost of the transcripts exceeded my entire month's income, for crying out loud! If he and Mark felt that I was giving them a hard time, they wouldn't know what a hard time was if it bit them in their asses.

I also reminded Rick that I had just been brought into his case and his entire situation whereas his brother had been involved for the past eight years. Mark was better suited to help as someone with inside knowledge and as someone from the lower Bucks County region who knew his way around. Yet what help had Mark provided that was material to Rick's appeal during these past eight years? None that I was aware of, except maybe the occasional chump change he put on Rick's prison account to keep him in a steady supply of prison commissary goodies, postage and stationary. Unknown to me at the time that I was drafting my letter, Rick had already sent a portion of his transcripts to me and they were en route via certified mail. I closed my letter to Rick and received the following reply a couple of days later:

March 2nd, 1996

Jacqueline,

Received your letter. I have not received the certified mail return receipt back yet for the trial transcripts. Did I explain what I sent? I believe I did...that those volumes contained the relevant testimony on the alcohol subject. Those were volumes 6,7 & 8, volumes 1-5 you missed very little, all voir dire and opening arguments, I believe. What you have there is the rest of the guilt/innocence phase of the trial. Disgustingly little for a capital trial, don't you agree?

I hope you read the letters I send in the correct order, too. Listen, I am going to tell you something. You are correct, there are people I have known much longer than you that could assist me, but you, I do not know how to explain this properly, are a total surprise, a God send, with each letter I receive I feel closer to you. You have taken it upon yourself to assist me and you have done more for me than anyone else in the short time you have been involved! I know of no way to thank you enough, Jacqueline. I can tell you this: I thank God in my prayers for you.

I do have some friends & family assisting in certain areas, don't get me wrong there. For instance a friend (ex-sister-in-law) is assisting in rounding up character witnesses. A family member has put together a nice set of clothes for court, etc., that sort of thing, but you have jumped in this pool with both feet! But it is not only that which draws me so close to you. You are intelligent, warm, caring, understanding, God-fearing, beautiful to the eyes and so many other things a man looks for in a woman. And I must rate that for a man to find two or three of the good qualities that you possess in a woman, he would be exceedingly fortunate. You have so many...

Okay, you mentioned my "26 issues" in this letter and the last one also. I combed through the transcripts several years ago & found them. I raised them in my pro se PCRA brief that I filed almost 3 years ago. Since then I continued to research and came up with an additional 10 issues I insisted that my present attorney raise. He has <u>not</u> come up with one issue on his own. I can prove everything I say if need be. I insisted that he petition for experts, *etc. As I said I did my pro se brief about 3 years ago and am just getting into court now. But I am a better litigator today, so you see I do know a little something about criminal law.*

I am still trying to get tested for ADHD. I sent another slip to the psy here. I did write to that address on the literature you sent. But I came across something else, too. On the psychiatric report I have, listen to this:

"Possible attention deficit during childhood and in fact, during adulthood to some extent as well."

When I first read this I took it to mean that I was not given enough attention during childhood and possibly adulthood as well. I found the statement a little strange. However, after reading the material you enclosed, I went back and re-read the psych report and that jumped off the page at me. I then called my mother and asked if I was hyperactive as a child. She tells me "Yes"! In fact, when I was in the 4th grade, a teacher called her in and asked if she would consider placing me on Ritalin. Does this sound like ADD or what? Request for Ritalin was denied by my mom. Now I really feel this is worthwhile here. It needs to be gathered together and incorporated into my appeal. However, I am having one hard time of getting a hold of my attorney. I have tried calling his office every day this week. I left messages w/ his sexretary, I mean secretary. I told of ADD & said I must speak w/ him. Last I heard, a letter from him is on its way to me.............

Yes, I believe the attorney is trying to duck out of anymore work...Yes, we will get this testing done pro bono, someone is going to offer that assistance. Either the psy here or the place I wrote to, or you will find someone...Time is running out though. I figure it must all be finished at least one week before the scheduled court date and submitted to the court through my attorney, in accordance with the rules of court : "in a timely fashion". This way if the prosecutor wishes to respond he will have a week to do so & can't kick up a fuss too loudly. The attorney will have to cooperate if we are to have it ready to go & I instruct him to file it...The psych report...it is very confidential, please return it, you will see mention of my childhood, etc. The doctor will be testifying at the hearing....

Yes, trial attorney (Elgart) did investigate witnesses, but not all witnesses, an issue I have raised. He failed to interview and call to the stand the first bartender, hence neglected useful info about alcohol, demeanor, etc.

Your testimony will be welcome as our official L.D. Advocate...Combine that and the fact that you are intelligent & the effect you will have on the judge should prove very interesting.....

Okay, something you should know about the mail room here at the prison. There are times when it misdirects mail, etc. A letter has been sent to me & returned to the person who sent it, marked "Inmate Released" on a couple of occasions. So if anything like that happens, you will know it's the mail room's fault & no fault of mine.

You say you are dyslexic. Have you overcome the disorder, trained your brain? Can you read my handwriting OK? If not I will try to neaten it up for you.

Elton John! Are you familiar with "Tiny Dancer"? He is one of my favorites. CCR is top shelf...I enjoy music, even classical, don't laugh, Mozart, Valverdi, Bach - just to name a few. Have you ever been to the symphony? To me it was a truly moving experience. Then again I can be a real corn ball at times....

I feel as though I am forgetting something. Did I forget to address a point in your letter? If so, forgive me for I care about everything you have to say. Everything from how you feel to your opinion offered on a subject....

I guess I will close this one up. I can't seem to get my mind off a certain subject right now. If I continue on here I am liable to heat up this letter with flames of passion....So until later, then...God Bless and know that I hold you near and dear.

Love,

Rick

Rick's suspicion that Attorney Goodwin was doing less than he was duty-bound for his client was not without just cause. Court-appointed lawyers, with rare exception, tend to do the bare minimum for indigent clients, regardless whether it is adequate representation or not. Court-appointed lawyers are not paid well for the cases to which they are assigned. They usually do not receive reimbursement for all of their costs such as getting expert witnesses in connection with their work while representing an indigent defendant. But when a lawyer enjoys the benefits of wealth and a successful career as a result of being enriched by the community in which they live and practice, it is wrong to balk at giving back by failing to give one's best in legal representation of those without money, those considered to be the least among us. Privilege does not come without duty, obligation and responsibility.

Goodwin rubbing me the wrong way merely fueled my determination to help Rick. I was blinded by resentment of his elitist attitude and beguiled by Rick's uncanny knack for saying all the right words at precisely the right time in my life. In retrospect, the truth is that it was a damn shame that the only man who made me feel good about myself, who had warm and kind words of encouragement, who made me feel like I was somebody with a lot to offer, was a manipulative psychopathic killer on Pennsylvania's death row.

Aside from my friend Doc Weiler, Rick Laird was the first person since my accident, who didn't judge me. Rick didn't belittle me for being a dummy asking "stupid questions", like the inconsiderate kids in my college classes did. He didn't ridicule me for requesting or needing accommodations as someone with a disability. He didn't talk down to me the way the condescending caseworkers did at the social security office, PA OVR, and the welfare office. He didn't put me down for not having been successful in a career compared to most others my age who were well on their way to the American Dream of buying nice houses, raising children, accumulating retirement wealth and enjoying prosperity.

Eligible bachelors with good jobs who had some economic stability and bright futures treated me like I wasn't worthy of a commitment because I was poor. As such, I would just be a drain on their wallets since I obviously couldn't support myself or contribute anything of monetary value to a marriage and a family. Marrying a disabled pauper with no social standing like me would simply cramp their style.

Rick didn't make me feel like I was too unimportant to take up any of his time. Since my accident, he was the only person who had actually asked me what I thought and how I felt about anything. If he was incapable of truly, genuinely caring about my hopes, dreams and aspirations he did a damn good job of pretending. How could I not want to help him? How could I despise him and see him as a monster?

Chapter 14

"There is a point at which even justice does injury." *~ Sophocles*

The urgency to get Rick's trial transcripts photocopied and returned weighed heavily on my shoulders. Time was of the essence and I couldn't let grass grow underneath my feet. I also had to move like the north wind in getting a prospective back up attorney for Rick since it was patently obvious that Michael Goodwin wasn't going to do anything to pursue the diminished capacity/ADHD issue.

The challenge that lay before me was threefold. First, I had to find a lawyer knowledgeable in death penalty appeals. Second, I had to find one who would take the utmost care in proceeding with Rick's appeal with the understanding that he or she would be representing someone who couldn't pay for legal help. And finally, I had to find this lawyer ASAP because the Post Conviction Relief Act appeal hearing date was approaching fast.

I also had to contact psychologists and psychiatrists on Rick's behalf for his neuro-psych tests and bring them on board, too. I was only one person. The whole task was overwhelming. And around doing all this, I had to have enough time to get through my college studies.

What didn't make matters any easier was that Rick Laird, like most prison inmates, didn't understand just how difficult it is to have to do everything on the outside to help an inmate on top of just trying to live. I had other things to do in my life too, such as study for exams, go to work, sleep, and eat once in awhile. I didn't have office equipment at my disposal so photocopying his stuff to truck all over creation to lawyers and learning disabilities specialists took time. Plus it costs time and money to go out somewhere to use a copy machine. And when you're dealing with hundreds of pages, it's quite a significant amount of money for a college student with only a part time job and student aid.

The following letter came from Rick, dated a mere two days after his last lengthy epistle:

March 4th, 1996

Jacqueline,

Just a note to bring you up to speed. I spoke with the psychiatrist today. First off they are unable to test us for court purposes, etc. However, she and I did go into a detailed conversation on my case history. Head trauma, alcohol, etc all came into play. She gave the opinion that "Neuro Psychological Testing" should be done on me. Said this will turn up among possible learning disabilities also whether or not I have "Organic Brain Damage". Ever hear of it? Said organic brain damage combined with alcohol would prove very useful.

I got my hands on Dr. Michael Moran's name and address and number. In fact, my letter to him just went out. Was told he may do this for me pro bono, that I should have someone call and hound him on my behalf. Are you interested in doing this? I know of no one else that would be as effective. If you decide to do this, here is the info:

Michael Moran, PhD

Lawyers Building

Pittsburgh, PA 15219

tel: (412) 281-1320

Whatever you decide, please let me know. If you do in fact call, let me know all said. Oh, if you do call, when speaking with him have him refer to my letter of 3/4/96, letter and reports. They should reach him a day before you receive this note as he is here in Pittsburgh.

Well, no letter from the attorney, no receipt from the certified mail I sent you (transcripts). And I am still waiting on responses to the last couple of letters I sent you so I will keep this note brief. Will write more when I hear from you. Take care, God Bless.

Rick

I had not fully realized just how time consuming it would be to try and help Rick when I initially agreed to Mark's plea for assistance. However, I was never one to backpedal and run when the going gets tough. I felt obligated since I already committed to helping this man and felt I couldn't bail ship at this stage. A person's word is their bond.

However, I was also a little annoyed. Thus far, in the span of less than one week, I had been hit with five letters the length of short stories with demands for help needed yesterday. I am not lazy and have never been a slacker, but a person can only move so fast to get things done! I had only received the partial volume of trial transcripts the day before this letter had arrived. Even at a nickel per page to copy all the transcript pages, it cost me $70, which was a princely sum for me on my income. It wasn't just the money, either. Standing there photocopying upwards of seven hundred pages took hours.

Of course, Mark couldn't be bothered with taking any time to do any of this for his brother. He claimed he didn't have any time. He had previously evidenced by his letter complaining to Rick that I supposedly gave him a hard time regarding help with any aspect of his brother's appeal. Mark was a pre-release convict who only had to go to work and report back to the center. He didn't have college classes in his schedule. Yet his time was more important than mine.

What Rick had no way of knowing was that while he was waiting for the return receipt from the certified mail of his trial transcripts, I had already begun working to locate a different lawyer for him as he had requested in his letters. At this point, whether Rick was innocent or guilty was not the only issue: possible breach in the integrity of the justice system was also a big issue with me.

It was his appointed counsel's duty to pursue all appropriate venues for representation of the client. Especially where the client is on death row with minimal time to get appellate motions filed introducing the appropriate evidence in accordance with the rules of the court. I doubted that Rick was completely innocent, but I also doubted that he was completely guilty. I also felt very strongly that if the integrity of the criminal justice system could be breached with impunity when dealing with the dregs of society, the justice system could not be trusted even for those who are unequivocally innocent.

I was also troubled by the death penalty in and of itself. It is no secret that the death penalty is capriciously applied. It is a well known fact that the amount of wealth and resources possessed by a defendant charged with a heinous crime has more bearing on the outcome of the verdict and sentencing than the nature of the crime itself. Also, court proceedings are well known to be something of a popularity contest: If the jurors are alienated by the defendant's attorney or if they don't like the defendant's image, the defendant could receive a death sentence for the exact same crime committed by someone else who gets a far lighter sentence. A case in point is demonstrated by that of an Amish man named Ed Gingrich.

Ed Gingrich had a history of cruelty and violence toward his young wife, Katie (Shetler) Gingrich. He also had a history of mental health issues for which he refused to take medication, believing the medicine to be poison in his state of paranoia. He killed Katie by beating her to death with his fists and stomping on her head in the kitchen of their small farmhouse near Mill Village in Erie County Pennsylvania on the evening of March 18th, 1993. Without any warning at all, Ed viciously attacked his wife yelling, "Is this how you want it to be, Katie!". He slammed her face with his fists, breaking her nose and knocking her senseless to the floor as she was washing dishes in the kitchen sink. She lay unconscious and unable to get up while Ed went out onto the rear porch and put his boots on, after which he came back inside and stomped on her head until her skull was crushed and her brains splattered on the floor while their children stood there in shock frozen with fear. He did this in order to "get the devil to come out of her".

He lashed out because he was angry with Katie for telling him that she and the children would be attending the wedding festivities of Noah and Lovina Stutzman without him and that he had to stay behind at home. Ed had been acting unpredictable and weird all day until he lay down complaining of headaches. Before that, he lay on his bed spitting upwards onto the ceiling. The last thing Katie wanted was Ed making a scene at the party and ruining everybody else's time, especially for the bride and groom. She felt that in his state of mind, he was too sick to attend the Stutzman wedding party. This infuriated Ed. Of course since the Amish do not have electricity or telephones in their homes, Katie couldn't call the police for help when he first struck her – even if she were not knocked unconscious.

After Katie was dead, he undressed her and proceeded to disembowel her by gutting her like a deer with a kitchen knife, placing all of her organs in a bloody heap next to her nude body on the floor. He did all of this in front of their small children, the youngest who was only three. Had Ed Gingrich not been Amish, he probably would have been charged with capital murder and sentenced to death. Instead, his ultimate conviction and sentence was five years. Not a bad deal for beating your wife to death and then carving her up in front of the kids.

Katie Gingrich's slaying was just as brutal and sickening as that of Anthony Milano, if not more so, but people have difficulty believing the Amish can commit heinous crimes because the Amish, as a general rule, lead such pious and God-fearing lives and are a non-violent people. Conversely, people also have difficulty believing a tattooed, loud and foul-mouthed Neanderthal-type man with a history of crime and drug abuse could possibly be innocent. How a defendant presents himself in front of a jury matters a lot.

Ed Gingrich's attorney, Don Lewis, presented his quiet, Amish client as an object of pity before the jury. He called upon Dr. Lisa Morrow who examined Gingrich and who testified that Ed Gingrich's mental illness was exacerbated by his exposure to Gunk fumes (Gunk is a brand of carburetor cleaner) and a bad bout of anxiety. Dr. Morrow said Gingrich was mad at his wife because she told him he couldn't go to the Stutzmans' wedding party. Dr. Morrow claimed that as a result of inhaling the Gunk fumes while he puttered in his workshop, Gingrich went around the bend and killed his wife without realizing what he had done. Attorney Don Lewis asserted that Ed Gingrich had suffered diminished capacity due to pre-existing mental problems and improper use of Gunk in a non-ventilated work shop.

The non-Amish jury bought the "Gunk Defense" hook, line and sinker. The fact that Ed Gingrich knew what he was doing and whom he was doing it to when he yelled, "Is this how you want things to be, Katie?" while he pulverized her head in front of their three small children who cried and looked on frozen with fear apparently escaped the jurors' reasoning. The fact that immediately after murdering and disemboweling his wife, Gingrich dressed the children in their coats and took them by the hand as he walked up to a state police patrol car on Sturgis Road and said to the trooper, "I am the bad man you're looking for" also escaped the jurors' reasoning. The significance of those chilling statements as proof that Ed Gingrich was fully aware of what he did and as such, the proof of intent to kill existed, was obviously also lost on the jury. Diminished capacity by reason of Gunk ruled the day.

Ed Gingrich's jury certainly cut him a lot more slack than the jury that convicted Rick Laird. Unlike Ed Gingrich, Rick Laird was not a likeable defendant, someone easy to pity and forgive. In his Amish garb and with his quiet demeanor, Ed Gingrich made a better impression in a courtroom than the rough-speaking, tattooed Richard Laird did. The end result was that Ed Gingrich was found guilty of third degree manslaughter and sentenced to a mere five years, most of which was served in North Warren Mental Hospital for the criminally insane. When he was released he went to Indiana to live in a community for "troubled" Amish. It was hardly a fitting sentence for someone who beat his wife to death, undressed her battered corpse, and then disemboweled her in front of her terrified children.

Richard Laird on the other hand, was convicted of first degree murder and given the ultimate punishment - capital punishment - which requires that he forfeit his own life at an appointed date and time set by the governor of Pennsylvania when he signed Rick's death warrant.

Maybe it's because the life of a woman counts for so much less in the public mind than the life of a man. Maybe it's because juries are more willing to excuse men for the abuse and murder of wives and women in general than when the victims are male. Maybe it's just that juries are less tolerant of diminished capacity claims when the apparent motive is based on bigotry, regardless if the victim is a man or a woman. Or maybe there exists a different justice system for a devout and God-fearing homicidal maniac than for a crass motorcycle hood from the lower class.

However, despite the sickening cruelty of Anthony Milano's murder, there was a nagging pang in my conscience about the death penalty. In rushing to execute murderers, in our relishing in the death of another human being, however judiciously deserved, do we not as a civilized society become monsters similar to those whom we seek to be protected from? Do we not sink to the same depravity when we collectively cheapen the life of another and play God in deciding who we discard and who we do not? It is hard to argue that psychopathic killers have enough social contribution to offer to outweigh their deeds against humanity. But it is equally hard to justify the rational taking of human life outside of self-defense.

While mulling over the question of Laird's guilt or innocence and my own feelings toward the death penalty, I read the transcripts Rick sent, photocopied them, and sent his originals back just as I said I would.

Since time was very pressing, the first thing I had to do was help Rick get his Organic Brain Damage and ADHD documented and incorporated into his appeal. If Rick indeed was the one who killed Anthony Milano, or helped to kill Anthony Milano, there was a big difference between intent and lack of intent to do so because of diminished mental capacity.

I contacted fellow board members of the Learning Disabilities Association (LDA) to see if they knew of any psychologist or psychiatrist affiliated with our network who would be willing to do a pro bono evaluation with a formal diagnosis for Rick. It was a hard sell, an impossible task. My inquiry was met with considerable resistance… And that was not without sound reason.

Convicted killers on death row are not a popular group. The potential for negative publicity for the entire LDA organization was high if it was perceived as being a soft-on-crime group who wanted to push an agenda for excusing the violation of laws by reason of a learning disability. It was difficult enough just trying to fight for the civil rights of ordinary learning disabled children and teens who were being denied an education and who were being harassed and picked on with the tacit approval of teachers and school administrators.

In the wider scope, LDA even had parents of "normal" kids as adversaries because they felt their children shouldn't have to slow down in the classroom just so those children who couldn't cut it were given a chance to catch up. Some such parents even went so far as to refer to learning disabled children as "nuts who didn't know how to act right". Of course, with that prejudice and intolerance from the parents of the other children, it was no surprise that their kids picked up on the idea that it was perfectly okay to bully and tease the child for whom learning was difficult. Serving as an advocate for parents of learning disabled children and hearing the horror stories from these worn-out parents brought back a host of unhappy childhood memories for me as I remembered not having any friends and being pushed around for having been in special education classes as a “slow” learner.

The general political climate also gave the sense that any organizations or individuals, who were helping convicted criminals, whether their convictions were just or not, were being “coddlers of criminals”. That was a very unpopular label to be slapped with in mid-1990's America. Another problem was the fact that most psychologists and psychiatrists don’t usually do any sort of *pro bono* work.

I studied the photocopies of Rick’s partial set of trial transcripts. I wasn’t sure what to think. His testimony and his recorded wiretapped phone call with Frank Chester was damning evidence. Yet the prosecution’s witness, Dr. Ahmad, stated there was no evidence that Anthony Milano was tackled to the ground in the slaying. If Rick had supplied me with the complete set of trial transcripts, including those volumes he claimed in one of his earlier letters were “unimportant”, maybe some of the confusion would have been dispelled. But the inarguable fact was that Rick was not merely present at the scene when the murder occurred, but was aware of the murder occurring and afterwards aware of the need to conceal or dispose of evidence. What was even more compelling was that he recalled such detail about Anthony’s bleeding to death in his courtroom testimony, referring to the victim’s blood as “hot shit” that sprayed on him.

It was also clear that Rick had not lifted a finger to stop the murder from happening, if indeed Frank Chester had been the killer. Rick was certainly big and intimidating enough to have done *something* to help Anthony. I didn’t know what to think or what to believe. None of it made any sense at all to me.

But one thing did stand out, and it leapt out at me from the pages of testimony in the transcripts: it was Frank Chester's obvious craftiness. Despite his testimony claiming that Laird was solely responsible for this murder, Frank Chester invested considerable time and effort going behind Rick's back to friends and the police claiming Rick killed Anthony. While Chester was contacting detectives and so on, he was still calling Rick to see what Rick was going to do next. Chester also invested significant effort in asking his friends for help to get rid of the evidence that Milano had been murdered, including making the victim's body disappear.

There was courtroom testimony about a conversation in Chester's apartment shortly after the murder between Frank Chester and his friends Allen Hilton, Pete Carpinona and Mike DeWitt about making Anthony's body disappear. They talked about Chester possibly burying it in the Pocono Mountains or dumping it in a lake because Chester feared he would be arrested for being present at the time and place of the murder. Pete Carpinona and Allen Hilton testified that Chester asked Mike DeWitt if he could borrow his new car because he "had a dead deer to take care of". That "dead deer" was Anthony Milano. It seemed to me that Frank Chester was too crafty and sneaky for his own good and he had been caught up in his own tangled web during the trial.

Chester's duplicity also made Rick the perfect fall guy, although I never knew for sure and still don't know today just which one of them really intended to harm Anthony Milano. Was Mark Laird telling the truth about his brother being railroaded? I took the photocopied transcripts with me to confer with my mentor and friend, Doc Weiler. I called Doc to make sure he was awake and available.

He had not yet eaten his dinner and suggested he treat at a local diner known for their excellent broiled stuffed flounder and salad bar. While I spoke with Doc on the phone, Mini-Stain jumped three feet from the top of my book case onto my lap, rubbing up against my cheek and the phone receiver affectionately as if to say, "Don't forget to feed me before leaving". Doc told me he would thoroughly read and absorb better on a full stomach. I concurred wholeheartedly. I would drive to his house then we would take his car, meaning Doc would be driving. Now that was the scary part. Nonetheless, I was happy for the thoughtful treat and time with my best friend. I just hoped he wouldn't blow through too many stop signs on the way to and from dinner.

When Doc carefully read over the report from Dr. Silverman and the trial transcripts, he looked confused. This was not a good sign. If Doc was confused and didn't understand, would I ever be able to understand it myself sufficiently in order to plead Rick's case to prospective lawyers who specifically handle death penalty appeals?

Trying to be discreet, the waitress and other patrons pretended not to hear our ghoulish dinner table conversation about a grisly murder. Before our food arrived, it did not escape my notice that an older lady clucked in disapproval of our conversation as she got up to pay her bill and leave. Oh well, she shouldn't eavesdrop on others' conversations if what she heard might offend her. She was lucky we were not having our Monday night Ripperology meetings there at the diner, going over Scotland Yard reports and studying the gruesome tin-type photos of the remains of Mary Jeannette Kelly - Jack the Ripper's final and most horribly mutilated victim. Doc, oblivious to the woman's display of sharp disapproval of our conversation, was in deep thought about what he had just read.

Doc's source of confusion upon reading the report and transcripts was the same as mine. According to Rick's testimony, he certainly didn't seem too brain damaged, learning disabled and alcohol-impaired to begin implementing a cover up plan immediately after the murder. He knew enough and was self-aware enough to tell Chester to "Shut up!" in reference to Chester's blurting out that a murder occurred after they reached Pete Carpinona's apartment. Rick had enough cognitive ability to wash up; ridding his hands and arms of the evidence of the victim's blood in Carpinona's kitchen sink.

Rick also was cognizant enough to dispose of the weapon and clothes he was wearing less than twenty-four hours after the murder. If he could plan enough to do that wasn't it arguable that he could form intent to kill in the first place?

Doc also brought up another valid point to consider. He spoke while peering intensely through his horn-rimmed eyeglasses at the transcripts. "Just because Rick Laird may have all of these problems, the learning disabilities, the ADHD, the organic brain damage and the history of being abused as a child, these do not rule out the possibility that he is a psychopath independent of these issues, and a cold-blooded killer. There is no way you can excuse that with arguments about brain damage and ADHD."

As we drove back to Doc's house after our meal, I silently pondered everything he had said concerning the excuse versus intent theory regarding Rick Laird. Doc certainly had a very valid point, and it was one that also crossed my mind more than once. However, I wasn't as sure about things as Doc was. I believed Rick's psychotic behavior and sociopathy could be inexplicably linked to his other problems. Blunt trauma to the head causing organic brain damage can indeed alter behaviors and personalities. A prime example is the infamous case of Phinneas Gage.

Phinneas Gage was a railroad foreman in 1848 Vermont. He sustained brain damage when a metal rod skewered his head. As a result of the damage to the orbital frontal area of his brain, he lost the capacity to feel regret regarding the outcome of his behavior and choices, i.e., he had diminished moral capacity.

As the story goes, Gage received major damage to the middle parts of the frontal lobes when an iron bar he was using to tamp an explosive charge had blown up and shot through his eye-socket and out of the top of his head. Gage never lost consciousness and seemed to physically recover within days, but he was never the same person. Prior to the accident, he was an intelligent person, a capable and efficient worker, an excellent manager, a responsible family man and an upstanding citizen. His life afterward was a different story altogether.

While Phinneas Gage retained his general intelligence after the accident, damage to his frontal cortex resulted in him becoming unreliable, capricious, socially inappropriate, and amoral. He lost his job and family. He remained unaware of his problem. We have since learned that victims of this form of brain damage often have difficulty regulating their behavior or abiding by norms of socially acceptable or moral behavior. Such individuals may violate social conventions, laws, ethical standards, the rules of courtesy and lose regard for the well-being of others. Fundamentally that is what the definition of antisocial personality disorder is: Someone incapable of feeling remorse and regret for their actions toward others.

I didn't feel Rick's history of ADHD and learning problems was being used as an excuse or a crutch to the extent that Doc thought. It certainly wasn't any more of an excuse than Ed Gingrich's "Gunk defense". I also believed that Rick's blood alcohol content of 0.46 per the toxicology report was reason enough to suffice for diminished capacity, if he in fact did kill

Anthony Milano. But I was not totally convinced that he did. It was also a matter of principle to me, a matter of justice, a matter of fairness and equality under the law. The whole thing reeked of class bias to me.

If Ed Gingrich got a slap on the wrist for brutally killing his wife whom he admittedly never loved, by reason of diminished capacity from Gunk fumes, then Richard Laird deserved to have the mitigating circumstances of his diminished capacity by reason of brain damage, ADHD and a blood alcohol content of 0.46 considered in his appeal if indeed he truly was guilty in the first place. Perhaps he truly was guilty under a diminished capacity, and thus deserved to have his sentence commuted from execution to spending the remainder of his life in a maximum security facility for the criminally insane.

However, I was not even sure if Rick was truly guilty. The possibility that he might have been innocent gnawed at me. But I had a gut feeling that if I came flat out and asked him if he did anything at all to contribute to Milano's demise, Rick would simply freeze up and break off all communication with me. The other thing that bothered me was there had been years of tell-tale signs that Rick had problems and yet nobody intervened.

According to the copies of Rick's reports and what his own mother confirmed, Rick had experienced problems since he was a child due to brain damage. The brain damage resulted from a combination of beatings, ADHD and also from a skull fracture incurred by a fall from a moving car. ADHD is a chemical imbalance and neurological impairment that is genetically inherited at birth. Blunt trauma to the head from a skull fracture results in brain tissue damage. The combination of ADHD at birth and damage from injuries to the head long after birth can have lifelong implications. Unlike other cells in the human body, brain cells do not regenerate. Once the brain sustains an injury and is damaged, that's it.

Over the next couple of days, I wrote to Dr. Moran as Rick had asked me to, but I didn't stop there. I also contacted a high-powered criminal defense lawyer from Easton Pennsylvania's Northampton County. This attorney had an established reputation for taking up cases for the underdog and winning. His name was Gary Asteak. I wrote Attorney Asteak a brief letter describing Rick's situation, stressing the importance of Rick's case history and the fact that neither Rick's trial counsel nor his present court-appointed counsel had investigated Rick's mental disabilities thoroughly. Neither Ron Elgart nor Michael Goodwin had brought up these problems as mitigating factors in Rick's behavior in connection with the crime, or as a defense against premeditated murder under diminished capacity.

I stressed that Rick Laird had untreated ADHD as well as organic brain injury from a skull fracture, and that these impairments were compounded by an inordinately high amount of alcohol consumption on the night of the crime. I also stressed that while Rick might be very literate now, it was after eight years on death row with nothing else to do but endeavor to overcome the learning disabilities and other mental handicaps he had in 1987.

What was most troubling was that Rick never got any help for his problems at any point in his childhood. Even though teachers knew he had problems and documented them, specifically acknowledging his ADHD, he got no help. When Rick first began getting into trouble with the law as a juvenile offender, no one in the juvenile justice system took any action to help him so that he could have turned his life around. They knew of his ADHD, learning disabilities, organic brain damage and the child abuse that he suffered. They knew that all of these things were factors in

Rick's inability to function correctly in society. All of these "experts" with all of the resources at their disposal failed to intervene in Rick Laird's life when they had every opportunity to do so, before it was too late.

Should someone have to end up convicted of murder and sent to death row before they find out they have problems and get any treatment? Where is the justice in that? How much would society have benefited if Rick Laird had received the diagnosis, treatment and possible assistance with special skills training and job placement, if any single one of all those experts had done their jobs? If Rick had gotten real and tangible help, including counseling and support for his disabilities and help in coping with being a survivor of extreme abuse while he was still a kid, maybe - just maybe - Anthony Milano would be alive today because Rick Laird would have had a chance for a life outside of unresolved emotional problems, drugs, drinking, poverty and crime. Intervention is not a one hundred percent guaranteed solution but we will never know now if it might have made a difference for Rick – or for Anthony Milano.

I was sick to my stomach. I was thoroughly disgusted at the thought of what could have been, what should have been, and what might have been had Rick Laird not been failed miserably by his family and by society from the time he was a child. What did all these child welfare workers, all these juvenile caseworkers, do all day except shuffle papers, maintain files and pretend to work while they passed the buck? For jobs like that, you don't need a college degree. Apparently, fitting in with the office clique, goldbricking and slacking suffice as qualifications for those jobs. Anyone with a sincere desire to make a difference in the lives of disadvantaged people, anyone with an ounce of intelligence and ambition, and anyone who truly needs and deserves a chance for a good job in a government agency with job security and benefits need not apply.

Maybe I seem bitter, but maybe I have a right to be. I was acutely aware based on my own dealings with social security bureaucrats and OVR "experts" that are always handy with lip service that helps no one. They apparently don't care because they still get theirs, regardless of the outcome in the lives of others – the people they are supposed to help. And I resented and mistrusted the entire system because of that. While OVR is not the same state agency as Office of Children & Youth or Juvenile Probation, the common denominator is that they are all state agencies run by bureaucrats who suffer little to no consequences for failing miserably to help those they are paid to help. Regardless of the end results in the lives of all the real people behind their statistics and their case files, these state workers still get to collect a middle-class paycheck with job security and benefits that ensure them comfortable lives. They have no vested interest in the outcomes.

However, I should not have been surprised by the fact that caseworkers view their "clients" as disposable and as such, not lose sleep over whether or not their clients' lives end up in the toilet from lack of help. We live in a disposable society. Everything from overpriced new cars and overpriced new homes are designed with planned obsolescence in mind. People who are unable to fit in and conform are denied a fair chance to succeed. They are excluded and marginalized. Rarely is any thought given to the question of their ability to conform versus their unwillingness to conform. If we either can't or won't conform, we are discarded like broken misfit toys. From the moment we are born someone slaps disposable diapers on our disposable asses. Yet when we all eventually take that final journey alone and unaccompanied, a multi-billion dollar market for serving the bereaved lays in waiting with air-tight, waterproof coffins and embalming fluid to keep our corpses from becoming disposable. The irony of *that* should give everyone something to think about.

Disposable people with disposable lives are kept from being disposable compost in death.

While I was stewing in my anger over what appeared to me to be the senseless waste of the lives of both Anthony Milano and Rick Laird, the phone rang. It was Rick calling collect from prison. He sounded so youthful and boyish over the phone. And he sounded so very harmless.

"It's so good to hear your voice. You sound as beautiful as you look. I got you approved on my official visitors' list. Are ya' coming out to see me this weekend?"

I didn't want Rick to feel I was back-pedaling, but I had to be honest. I told him, "No Rick, I can't. I'm flat broke after photocopying your stuff because it cost $70, and that was using the cheapest copy machine in town. So I'll have to wait till I get paid again before I'll have the gas money to drive all the way out to Pittsburgh, plus I'm going to need money to get a hotel room and something to eat, too. I'll have to see what my next paycheck looks like."

I could feel the weight of his disappointment through the telephone in his momentary silence. In the background, I could hear other inmates yelling and cursing as well as the clanging of bars. I felt bad that Rick was disappointed but what else could I do? I couldn't pull money out of thin air, for God's sake! I broke the silence by telling him all I was doing on my end. Hopefully, he could appreciate it and understand.

I told him about writing Attorney Gary Asteak and told him that I had set up an appointment for the following week to meet with Asteak regarding the appeal. I told him we would discuss what options might be available to an indigent capital prisoner who had compelling new evidence but who also had an uninterested court-appointed attorney. Rick replied, telling me that he had already lodged a formal written complaint about Michael Goodwin to the courts, and he asked me if I would type it up for him since handwritten correspondence of that nature is typically not accepted by the courts. I told him I would do it if he sent me his handwritten letter of complaint.

The call was under ten minutes – the time limit on inmate phone calls – and ended amicably. I told him I had a physics exam to study for, so over the next couple of days I would be indisposed. He said that he understood.

In the meantime, another letter had arrived from Rick. Since he was unaware of all I was doing on my end in trying to help him, I half expected it to be laced with impatience, chastising me for not doing enough quickly enough or making me feel guilty for not being able to visit this past weekend as he had hoped I would. For a moment I stood in the hallway, just staring at the envelope as it lay on the floor. I wasn't sure if I really wanted to open it.

Mini-Stain circled between my feet, rubbing against my ankles and meowing affectionately. I wondered what she would say if cats could speak, and what she would think of all this. Mini-Stain's world was devoid of worrying about bills, about utilities being shut off, about passing difficult college classes, and about hopes for securing a good job after struggling through it all. Oblivious to the dilemmas I faced, Mini-Stain only wanted love.

Doc Weiler often told me that animals have more common sense than most people. He also said that the only living creatures that were capable of giving unconditional love and acceptance dogs and cats. I believe he was right. They certainly are more loving and loyal than most people I have known and are a hell of a lot less judgmental. Mini-Stain was always affectionate and accepting, and always quick to forgive my faults.

People on the other hand, can be manipulative, selfish, intolerant and downright ignorant. Too many people behave like petty tyrants and lord their social privileges over others – just like a clique of bossy, spoiled brats who exclude other children from the games on the schoolyard playground.

Mini-Stain sat upright on the mail, her tail curled neatly over her feet. She looked up at me and meowed. Stooping over and petting her, I decided I had two choices: ignore Rick's letter and not see this through even though I had given my word, or be brave and open it. I would never know what was in that letter unless I opened it and read it. And so I did.

March 10th 1996

Jacqueline,

Received your letter, good to hear from you. You have been on my approved visitors' list all week now. I expected to hear back from you by mid week at the latest on one of the pieces of mail that I sent you. I see that the trial transcripts did not get delivered until 3/5/96 and that's ridiculous. It coast me a small fortune to send those certified mail, small fortune according to prison standards, and then it took them 5 days to reach you, pissed me off. Anyway it's for the best that you did not stop out this weekend. It's a snowy mess all over the place. Listen, if and when you do decide to stop out this way always call here in advance and check:

#1. That I am still here, and;

#2. That I am permitted visits (I get in any kind of trouble, visits are taken away)

#3. Always get the name of the staff member you speak with.

I was not a regular at the Edgely Inn. In fact I was only in there a couple of times at the most. The people who referred to me as scum, a bat-wielding whatever, do not know me from a can of paint. People can talk shit behind someone else's back, it's quite another thing when a man is standing there looking another in the eyes.... Edgely's is a sports bar, not exactly my type of scene back then, just happened to be close to the house, I guess.

I can see that you read the trial transcripts. Yes, trial counsel was a waste. Did an ineffective job all around.

Spoke with my attorney yesterday. The PCRA hearing has been postponed for awhile yet. We are having an Evidentiary Hearing on April 1st, that will be the jury issue, a newer issue where a sheriff allegedly influenced the jury.

Take a wild guess what the judge has done with my PCRA?! He consolidated it with Chester's! I am so pissed I can hardly see straight. That is the reason for the delay there. ......Since it is consolidated now, the entire PCRA process will be consolidated and I will have to wait on any delay he may cause. There may be some adverse ruling the court sees in his case and try to apply it me - co-defendant - etc. Lovely, isn't it.

You asked about Frank Chester. He was what you would call an in-law. That is why I looked out for him, understand?

The photos of my hometown...That diner, I used to go in there quite often, Sunday mornings for breakfast. Been a long time since I have seen anything of the home town, thank you again. These photos mean a lot to me Jacqueline, more so than I think you know. They help me to feel alive, give me warmth, remind me that there is still a world out there. You're good people, don't ever let anyone tell you different.

This doesn't seem to be much of a letter, bear with me, a lot of crap going on around here lately.

Do you have any children, and if so how many? I have a couple myself. Don't get to see too much of them, for obvious reasons. Let's see, what else am I forgetting....

How are things with you lately? What's new? I guess I'll get this one in the mail to ya'. Take care and God bless. Looking forward to seeing you in person.

Love,

Rick

Chapter 15

"The sword is ever suspended." ~ Voltaire

The consolidation of Laird's and Chester's appeal from this point forward was very bad news for the both of them. If the appointed appellate attorney for one of them loused up the petition for his respective client or alienated the Commonwealth Superior Court judge, the other appellant was automatically affected by his petition for relief being denied. If the appellate judge was in a bad mood that day and felt like throwing the book at everybody, both Chester and Laird would be screwed. There were too many variables, too many chances for things to go wrong during the appeals process. It was an ill wind that blew no one any good.

The consolidation effectively made the appeals of Chester and Laird into Siamese twins from a legal standpoint: The outcome of one man's appeal would affect whether the other could raise similar issues. Furthermore, if the respective attorneys filing petitions on their clients' behalf failed to communicate in depth with each other regarding who would raise which issue and how, the probability for procedural error was magnified. There was too much risk that human error could cause the appeal for either man to be denied. And that meant Chester and Laird would both be moved another step closer to the execution gurney. This was a very serious problem. The ultimate crime would be if one of the men actually was innocent and ended up getting executed because an appeal issue raised by the other man got rejected.

As of today I do not understand why Judge Beister ruled to consolidate Chester and Laird's appeals during the Post Conviction Relief Act (PCRA) appellate processes. What could possibly be the point in doing that?

Not only is the death penalty dependent on the luck of the draw, but the appeal process itself is structured such that it is next to impossible to win legal remedy, regardless of the merit of evidence upon which an appeal motion is filed. In Rick's case, his claim for relief fell under §9543 (a)(2)(ii) of the Pennsylvania PCRA: "That the conviction or sentence resulted from one or more of the following.....ineffective assistance of counsel which, in the circumstances of the particular case, so undermined the truth-determining process that no reliable application of guilt or innocence could have taken place."

If anyone could help with a complicated death penalty appeal, it was Gary Asteak. But would he do so for free, given that Rick was already represented by court-appointed counsel? Moreover, would Attorney Asteak want to deal with this morass of a consolidated PCRA appeal? That quagmire required a whole separate legal argument, accompanied by a paper storm of petitions and motions. What a mess. It seemed to me that there was one, and only one, purpose for the consolidation of Laird and Chester's PCRA appeals: to make it impossible for either man, regardless of evidence, to obtain legal remedy sparing either of them from execution, no matter what. This case was definitely one that only the most highly skilled criminal defense lawyer could maneuver in successfully. Gary Asteak was such an attorney. I sincerely hoped that he would agree to take Rick's case.

I first made Attorney Ateak's acquaintance before I was injured and taken out of the workforce in my accident. I did some moonlighting during a lay-off period by doing restorative plaster repair work in one of the rooms in his impressive house in the old-moneyed neighborhood in Easton known as College Hill for its proximity to Lafayette College. He had always impressed me as very intelligent and he and his wife were gracious hosts to guests. It was through being invited to stay there for dinner occasionally that I broadened and educated my palate to include foods I previously would never have tried.

He was impressed that I had expressed a sincere interest in the study of law. Despite my dyslexia and lack of education at that point in my life, he told me I should not give up on the idea of college and eventually law school. He felt that my ability to debate would make me a force to be reckoned with in any courtroom. It was not just my ability to debate effectively, but also my firm sense of what is right and what is fair: My desire to pursue justice to the ends of the Earth. In other words, I wouldn't take any shit and I would fight to the death for my client if that client and the principle at stake were right.

Those words, words which rekindled my long-forgotten childhood hopes of becoming a lawyer, replayed in my mind over and over three years later when the OVR vocational counselor insisted that I go for a degree in math/computer science. I will regret until my dying day letting the self-proclaimed "experts", coerce me into walking away from my dream when I was vulnerable and in need of real help rather than lip service.

You only get to go around once in life. No matter what any sanctimonious condescending know-it-all says, never ever go against your gut instinct or let anyone steal your dreams. I should have listened to Attorney Asteak instead. I should have mustered the courage to tell the "vocational rehabilitation specialist" from PA OVR to go shit in his hat.

No one has the right to steal your dream. Especially if they're not willing to step up to the plate and be the ones to pick up the pieces if things don't work out after you do everything they say, jump through all their hoops, and follow their program guidelines to the letter.

Gary Asteak would have made it big no matter where he chose to live and practice law, yet he chose to remain in Easton, PA - a small city flanking the Delaware River on the New Jersey-Pennsylvania border. He was a highly successful trial litigator and he knew his way around the criminal courts. Some say he would have affected the same end result for O.J. Simpson all by himself without the rest of O.J.'s "dream team". He was, all by himself, a one-man dream team for anyone retaining him. His fees reflected that accordingly. If you had enough money and you got into trouble with the law, Gary Asteak was the lawyer you wanted to represent you.

He was a slender man in his early forties who didn't look a day over thirty. He loved wearing brightly colored hand-painted silk ties and blue suede shoes to accentuate his courtroom attire. His long and wavy chestnut hair, always worn in a ponytail, matched mischievous brown eyes that sparkled when he flashed his famous award-winning smile. He looked a lot like a young version of pop culture icon Frank Zappa. That was his style and it worked very well for him.

In the courtroom, he was a formidable adversary and a magician in the eyes of those who retained him. One incident I will always remember involved a highly controversial capital murder case. The victim was an eleven year old girl who had been kidnapped, raped and killed. The accused was a black man with a long criminal history. In his cross-examination of the prosecution's key witness - a man suffering from schizophrenia - he attacked the witness's credibility mercilessly. But he did so in the most polite and disarming manner.

First, he asked the witness what medical conditions required his taking Thorazine and Lithium. When the witness answered, "schizophrenia and bipolar disorder", Asteak responded with, "Now for the benefit of the court, which one of you is testifying today?" with a poker face. Spectators burst out laughing and several jurors covered their mouths in an attempt to conceal their amusement. Even the judge smiled as he banged his gavel to restore order to the court. The witness was visibly shaken and his credibility damaged as a result. He had been made to look like an unreliable mental patient whose testimony couldn't be taken seriously. Attorney Asteak's hot-dog courtroom antics matched his wardrobe. That's what you really had to admire about him: he had a lot of style. He won that case for his client, just as he had won most of his cases.

Attorney Asteak's office was in the historic district of downtown Easton. It was a three story Victorian style row home. The ornately carved trim was six inches wide. It recalled a bygone era when craftsmanship of this caliber produced by artisan tradesmen was the rule rather than the exception. Narrow, winding stairs led from the reception area to his cherry paneled office with solid cherry built-in bookcases containing antique leather-bound books covering subjects ranging from ancient history to law. He knew it must have been a highly unusual and complicated legal matter which prompted an appointment from me to meet with him. I never got into trouble with the law and never needed a lawyer for anything outside of a standard real estate transaction other than my attempt to sue that uninsured driver who ruined my life.

Smiling and cordially inviting me to sit down in one of the burgundy leather chairs across from his desk, he asked what he could do for me. I didn't know where to begin. It was all so overwhelming. I poured out the whole story, and didn't stop to take a breath. In essence, I said:

"Gary, it's not for me. It's for a co-worker's brother who is currently on death row. This co-worker claims that his brother -

Richard Laird - had been framed. I am not totally convinced that this is *not* the case, although there is some damning evidence including a wiretapped phone call between Mr. Laird and his co-defendant Frank Chester. At the original trial back in 1988, eight years ago, Laird's attorney Ron Elgart put him on the stand where he made one hell of a spectacle of himself, and not in a good way. He and his co-defendant were found guilty and sentenced to death. They were tried together, represented by different attorneys with each claiming the other was the only guilty party. This appeal requires the skill and experience of a lawyer who knows what he's doing because Judge Beister of Bucks County consolidated both men's PCRA appeals. Laird has solid grounds for a claim of ineffective assistance of trial counsel because his trial lawyer failed to go with a diminished capacity claim from the start."

Gary Asteak listened intently. He asked me about the nature of the possible diminished capacity claim that the trial counsel erred egregiously in failing to pursue. I continued:

"Rick Laird has organic brain damage, untreated ADHD which he self-medicated using small amounts of meth. He also had an estimated 0.46 blood alcohol level the night of the murder. His present counsel is court-appointed and apparently not in the least bit interested in bringing any of this evidence up. According to Laird, his current counsel is not putting together any effective motions for severance to separate his appeal from that of Frank Chester."

Attorney Asteak leaned forward on his desk, his hands folded neatly under his chin and intently listened. After I laid everything out, he leaned back in his chair and searched for the right words. Looking me in the eye, he asked, "Did Laird actually commit the crime?"

"I don't know. I… you know… I just don't know. I know this guy's no angel. But as far as having the capability to form intent, the *mens rea*, or the mental ability to commit the *actus reus* - planning the killing with intent to kill, I have doubts," I answered shaking my head. I ran my Muff Potter-Injun Joe theory by him.

I continued, "But the sticking point with me is that everyone, including someone charged with a heinous murder, deserves a fair trial. But Rick Laird didn't get a fair trial because his trial lawyer, fresh out of the law school chute, fell asleep at the wheel. I don't think he even tried to get the cases severed so that both defendants could be tried individually. Now the PCRA appeals are joined at the hip and his present attorney isn't doing anything about it, according to Laird. And I believe him because I met this attorney and he is one hell of an arrogant asshole. His name is Michael Goodwin and he's out of New Britain." I rolled my eyes in disgust, shaking my head.

Gary Asteak listened sympathetically. He was sincere and truly wanted to help. He said, "The problem here is three-fold. First, Laird is already represented by counsel that is court-appointed, so he would have to petition the judge to fire his appointed counsel. Second, I am currently not in a position to take a case this complex on a pro bono basis. I would have to be paid. I normally don't leave Northampton County, so there will be expenses for that. Third, although I have litigated capital cases in Northampton County's Court of Common Pleas, I have not handled PCRA complications such as this consolidation. That is an entirely separate can of worms apart from the claims of ineffective trial counsel issues. But there is an organization in Philadelphia called the Capital Defenders Association. They're really good guys and probably better equipped to handle PCRA complications in a death penalty case because death penalty appeals is all they do. In fact, that's the *only* thing they do. They represent indigent capital prisoners at no charge. I think they are your best bet."

He rifled through his desk drawer, rummaging through papers, receipts and business cards. "I believe I have their card somewhere. Ah, yes. Here you go," he smiled as he handed me the card of Attorney Robert Dunham and wished me well, "Good luck." He stood up and we shook hands.

Attorney Asteak was honest. But I was still disappointed for I knew that with representation from someone like him, Rick Laird would get a fair trial. I knew that Gary Asteak, that flashy dresser with rapier wit who was a dead ringer for Frank Zappa, was no dummy. I was grateful and appreciative of his advice and for the time he took to meet with me regarding Laird's case. I was also grateful that he pointed me in the right direction. I still had doubts: Would the sparsely funded Defenders Association help someone like Richard Laird, a man labeled as an anti-gay bigot?

Championing the cause of someone convicted of capital murder is one thing, but taking up the good fight on behalf of someone convicted of a "hate crime" is another matter. Anyone stained with the bigot brush has earned contempt from the court of public opinion. You can be the world's biggest asshole, a tyrant, or even a murderer, but heaven help you if you are labeled as a bigot. Societal consensus determines the definition of bigotry, and defines what is deemed a "hate crime" and what is not.

Those do-gooder groups like Tolerance.org that espouse a "zero tolerance" for bigotry often feel their own particular brand of bigotry is socially acceptable. They promote tolerance, acceptance, and fair treatment for select victims of bigotry, but not others. It's open season on atheists. Poor whites can be discriminated against with impunity and insulted with epithets of "trailer trash" and "red-neck" hurled at them with no social repercussions. The classist taunts and accusations of being inbred, illiterate and stupid never seem to elicit a peep of disapproval from wealthy liberal politicos or their elitist sycophants. Being deprived of equal opportunities for jobs based on socioeconomic class, and then being browbeaten for being poor and jobless fails to register in the minds of these tolerance/diversity promoting groups as a social injustice.

The bullying of smokers by rich anti-tobacco elitists, many of whom have interests in the pharmaceutical corporations profiting off of "nicotine replacement therapy", goes on without any tolerance-promoting group breathing a word against them. Rights, personal liberties and freedom of choice are expected entitlements for everyone, but often denied to smokers. The majority in society has decided that because they don't like the smell of tobacco smoke, smokers should be banned from being able to fully participate in society while being made as miserable as humanly possible through being denied jobs, homes and in some instances denied the right to smoke outside – where the rabid anti-smoking politically correct crowd forced them to go to begin with.

The self-appointed self-righteous know-it-alls are quick to whip anyone into line for failing to conform to their standard of political correctness, their standard of who is "worthy" and who is not. Championing the cause of atheists, poor whites and tobacco smokers is just as unpopular as championing the cause of capital prisoners whose murder conviction carries the "hate crime" label.

While societal consensuses (such as those which led to US Constitutional amendments supporting Civil Rights laws) say it is wrong to deny equal protection under the laws, equal opportunity for jobs, or housing and acceptance in society if one is a recognized protected class member, meting out injustice towards others whom the majority doesn't like is perfectly okay. Those "others" who are not favored are atheists, poor whites, victims of mental disabilities, and tobacco smokers. There is little problem with throwing smokers out of their jobs, assisted living centers, condominiums and rental housing if they can't/won't quit smoking. The *de facto* Jim Crow segregation of forcing frail little old ladies who smoke out into the bitter cold or pouring rain from their nursing home rooms and Bingo games to have a cigarette is socially acceptable. Why? The majority says so.

Those who are invisibly disabled, those who have weight or appearance problems, and those who are socially and economically disadvantaged can be treated like second-class citizens with impunity. The bigotry of classism is tolerated, so referring to low-income people as "uneducated" or "inbred trailer trash" is accepted and used to deny such people jobs or equal access to the justice system. Why? The reason is that the majority in society look down on those who are poor. Therefore, it is consensus (or more appropriately called: *mobocracy*) that determines which forms of bigotry, discrimination and social injustice are acceptable and which are not. It is what the majority wants, what the majority likes and what the majority determines is just, fair and equitable that rules the day. In sum, democracy is mob rule and to hell with the rights of the individual. *Carpe diem!*

Anyone doubting the abuse of power that accompanies consensus, or democracy, need only look to history at all the injustices that were meted out in the name of consensus: the persecution and murder of people like Socrates and Hypatia (first woman mathematician), the Holocaust, Apartheid, the conviction and execution of Ethel and Julius Rosenberg, the murder of Yankel Rosenbaum during the Crown Heights riots in Brooklyn NY, the beating of Reginald Denny during the Watts riots in South-Central Los Angeles, and the lynching of Leo Frank, just to name a few.

In the case of Leo Frank, he was wrongfully convicted in 1913 for the rape and murder of thirteen year old Mary Phagan, one of his employees in his pencil factory in Atlanta, GA. On April 26th 1913, Confederate Memorial Day. Mary Phagan went to the National Pencil Company to pick up her wages of $1.20. She planned to attend the Confederate Memorial Day parade with her friend, George Epps. She never made it to the parade. Her broken and battered little body was found in the basement of the pencil factory by night watchman Newt Lee the next day. Several arrests were made, including that of a sweeper, Jim Conley, who also worked at the factory.

Jim Conley, a semi-illiterate black man with a checkered past, was seen carrying little Mary Phagan's body over his shoulder across the first floor of the factory toward a trap door leading to the basement. The witness who observed this was thirteen year old Alonzo Mann, another adolescent at the factory. Conley reportedly threatened to kill little Alonzo Mann if he ever told anyone what he had seen. But Alonzo Mann did tell his mother after Leo Frank, the Jewish factory owner, was arrested under suspicion in Mary Phagan's rape and murder. Mrs. Mann advised her young son to keep quiet. Consensus among most people in the post-Reconstruction South was far less favorable to a rich Yankee Jew than towards a black man. Guilt or innocence had nothing to do with it. Finding someone easy to despise, someone that would be a convenient scapegoat and making him pay for the crime had everything to do with the sham of a trial for Leo Frank: Justice and truth be damned.

Leo Frank, a wealthy northern industrialist Jew, was the epitome of everything Southerners hated. In the eyes of poor southern whites, he represented the typical carpetbagger who preyed on economically vulnerable people with few options for climbing out of poverty. Their economic misery after their bitter defeat in the Civil War and twelve harsh years of the post-war "Reconstruction" imposed on them left them very bitter, angry and resentful. They were still angry and bitter over their defeat in the Civil War forty-eight years later in 1913. Many are still resentful to this day. It is not hard to see why.

The economic deprivation that resulted from the post-Civil War Reconstruction policies left most Southerners desperately poor and disenfranchised. Opportunists – "carpetbaggers" – from the north came down and took over their banks and businesses and took unfair advantage of the defeated people whose Confederate currency was worthless after the war. These carpetbaggers oppressed them with usury practices that make the predatory lenders of today look like Mother Theresa. As a result of the deep poverty that was caused by this, most southern families had to send their kids into the labor market in the cities. Mary Phagan was more than a young murder victim: she was a symbol of southern martyrdom; one more way in which poor Southerners were victimized by greedy northern opportunists – wealthy opportunists like Leo Frank.

Leo Frank was convicted in a kangaroo court for the rape and murder of a poor young girl who worked for meager wages in his factory and he was sentenced to death. Not because the evidence against him was compelling, but because the sentiment against what he represented was so strong. Mary Phagan was a victim twice: first, she had to forego any schooling because she had to work to help support her family out of necessity because of the harsh economic reality in the post-bellum south, and second, she was violated and murdered because she was a vulnerable little girl who couldn't defend herself.

Two years or so after Leo Frank's conviction, his death sentence was commuted to life by the governor of Georgia after he saw that the court chose to blatantly ignore compelling evidence of Frank's innocence. The result of that commutation was an angry lynch mob comprised of local "community pillars" who were also high ranking KKK members. The mob abducted Leo Frank from his prison cell and lynched him from a tree.

Frank's initial guilty verdict could not be explained except for seething hatred, anger and resentment for reasons that had nothing to do with Mary Phagan's murder. The evidence against Leo Frank was trumped up and contrived of largely circumstantial evidence. He was in his office on the top floor of the factory seeing his employees as they came in to collect their pay when Mary Phagan was accosted and murdered. That was the only link to Mary Phagan's murder – he happened to be at the factory when she was also there.

The testimony given by Jim Conley against Leo Frank in court consisted of unsubstantiated lies which included a crude hand-scrawled note found by Mary Phagan's body. Part of the note in reference to Mary's murder read, *"...and play like the night witch did it."* Conley elaborated further in court claiming that Leo Frank forced him to write that note and practically guided his hand in doing so, and claimed that he could never have written the note on his own without help because he was an illiterate black man. That was also a very plausible reason to evade suspicion. It was not a stretch of the imagination to believe that sort of claim coming from a poor black man in the Deep South because blacks had been completely disenfranchised and most were denied the opportunity to learn how to read and write.

The majority of poor southern blacks within two generations of the Civil War were unable to read or write. Laws in the slave-holding states forbade teaching blacks how to read prior to the Civil War. When the black slaves were suddenly freed by the Union army in 1865, they were thrust into their newfound freedom without the preparation and education to benefit from that freedom. Thus it would not be unreasonable for a jury to believe Jim Conley's claim of illiteracy. And because Leo Frank was the focal point for pent-up southern hostilities, the jury didn't try to weigh the testimony of Jim Conley logically. They wanted to believe Leo Frank was guilty because he was a rich Yankee Jew profiteering off of their misfortune by paying low wages to his poverty-stricken employees.

However, several years after the trial, an investigating scholar noticed a very important detail about that particular portion of the murder note referring to a "night-witch". In 1913 when Leo Frank was tried and convicted, the all-white jury thought that "night-witch" was night-watch misspelled, that Conley meant to write "night-watchman" instead of night-witch – inferring that Conley was urged by Leo Frank to set it up to frame the factory's night watchman Newt Lee for the crime. However, Leonard Dinnerstein – a prominent scholar and writer who wrote a book about the Leo Frank case – observed in collaborating with others that Jim Conley did not err in writing "night witch" for night watch: Jim Conley's spelling was deliberate! A little known curiosity about rural southern black culture of the time was that there was a superstition about a creature referred to as the "night witch" who supposedly killed children in the dark. This was not a superstition held, or even known, by most whites – especially not well-educated northern industrialist whites like Leo Frank. Therefore, Leo Frank would not have likely known about the "night-witch." He would not have dictated that murder note to Conley as Conley had claimed.

It was not bad enough for Leo Frank to be sentenced to life in prison when he was innocent. He was lynched. His name has never been officially cleared. The state of Georgia refuses to admit they made a mistake, even after Alonzo Mann finally mustered the courage to come forth in his twilight years and told the truth about what he had seen in the pencil factory as a young boy.

For sixty-nine years, Alonzo Mann carried the burden of his knowledge and the secret that he was pressured to keep. Finally, in the twilight of his life at age eighty-three on March 4th 1982, Alonzo signed a sworn affidavit asserting Leo Frank's innocence and Jim Conley's guilt. He set forth all that he saw that fateful day in 1913, including the fact that Conley threatened to kill him if he told anyone. He also stated that on May 1st 1913, five days after Mary Phagan's murder, Conley was seen rinsing out his blood-stained shirt that he had kept stashed in the basement of the factory. Mann further averred that shortly after Leo Frank's trial and lynching, his parents told him that "it would do no good to come forth after the verdict and to have done so before would have endangered all of them [the Manns] for sticking up for someone who the public viewed as a lecherous Yankee Jew." Given the violent resurgence of Ku Klux Klan activity in the wake of Mary Phagan's murder, the Mann family's concerns were not unfounded.

Alonzo Mann took a series of lie detector tests while telling his story to a group of reporters for *The Tennessean*, a major Nashville newspaper. The tests all indicated Mann was telling the truth. The revelation of this elderly man with deep religious convictions and the desire to unburden his soul caused the public to question whether or not Leo Frank had received a fair trial all those years ago. The Deep South in 1982 was certainly a different Deep South than in 1913.

Yet, as of 1983, the Georgia State Board of Pardons and Paroles disregarded Alonzo Mann's sworn affidavit in addition to pleas from three Jewish organizations for a posthumous pardon. The Board declined to pardon Leo Frank, claiming that it was impossible to determine the truth after seventy years. Eventually, after considerable outcry from the Jewish Anti-Defamation League, the Georgia State Board of Pardons and Paroles begrudgingly issued a posthumous pardon to Leo Frank on March 11th, 1986, seventy-three years after Leo Frank's trial and lynching.

But the final insult was that the pardon was based on the state's failure to protect Frank while he was in custody – which did not officially absolve him of the crime for which he was martyred. That pardon, begrudgingly granted and long overdue, was a back-handed apology for Leo Frank's wrongful death from a lack of protection during his imprisonment. An imprisonment based on a wrongful conviction that would not have been obtained if not for a strong, anti-Semitic, anti-Yankee consensus. The pardon said nothing that would clear Leo Frank's name. This is what can happen when we allow social consensus, with all its attendant prejudices and failings, to drive the legal system and determine the outcome of justice (or lack thereof) without checks and balances.

Just as with the Leo Frank case, the question today is this: Should someone whom the majority despises be denied a fair trial for the sake of appeasing the mob? Would the outcry against Richard Laird and Frank Chester have been just as great if the "hate crime" status had not been ascribed to their case? Would their sentences have been just the same if the victim had been straight? What if the victim had been a female or a homeless person? What if the victim was an abortion doctor? Does the status of a "hate crime" infer that one class or group of people has a higher value assigned to their lives than others, and are hence more deserving of justice than others? If this is the case, what does that say for the 14th Amendment of the US Constitution concerning "equal protection under the law"? What about the concept of the punishment fitting the crime, regardless of the status of the victim and perpetrator?

There are varying degrees of murder. Our legal system differentiates between three degrees of murder. Third degree murder is accidental. In an incident such as killing someone in a car accident (while driving sober), it is an unintended mistake called "vehicular homicide" that carries a more lenient penalty than first or second degree murder. Second degree murder (also called "manslaughter") is an unintentional killing that arises out of blind passion without aggravating circumstance. First degree murder is premeditated and if there are also aggravating circumstances such as kidnapping, torture, or felony assault, it's a capital offense meriting the death penalty in states that have the death penalty. Not all first degree murders are capital cases. But the ambiguity in different interpretations of "aggravating circumstances" in capital murder cases causes a problem.

We are a nation of laws. The Constitution is what differentiates the United States of America — a free constitutional republic — from fascist nations whose laws and justice systems are based on the whim of a dictatorship supported by mob consensus.

The importance of distinction between these degrees of murder was emphasized by another from letter Rick that arrived on St. Patrick's Day. It seemed to me that I must have been the only one he was writing to, judging by the length and the frequency that the letters came. I was getting letters every other day.

Jacqueline *March 17th, 1996*

Hey sexy, how are you? Received a couple of letters from you, very nice surprise. Your thoughts on how the DA used the conspiracy issue are correct. Rubenstein used conspiracy as a catch-all safety net for himself. If he could not prove who killed

Milano, then he decided he would claim that there was a conspiracy to kill Milano. That was a real dirty route for him to take. But he got his "gold star".

And yes, cognitive ability and conspiracy to commit 1st degree murder is directly on point. The lack of cognitive ability will be applied to all I was charged with and found guilty of. If one lacks cognitive ability, one cannot be found guilty of what I was. Trial counsel truly was ineffective on my behalf.

What you said about it being difficult to obtain relief in a capital case is correct. One of the grounds for relief was evidence tampering. Did I mention it in a past letter? We have that issue, in fact I have it on record. The DA admitted that he tampered with evidence in my case. This is all very strange, this issue was not properly raised on my direct appeal so I raised it here at my PCRA level. The DA saw that the jury disregarded the court's instructions concerning a photo that the court ordered cropped due to the photo's inflammatory nature. The jury removed the cropping and looked at the entire photo when deliberating. Well, the DA tried to hide that fact from everyone - court, defense; the DA re-stapled the cropping and let the trial proceed to the penalty stage. After the trial, a court staff person noticed this re-stapling and notified the court. The DA then admitted to what he had done. So this is an issue that is being properly raised now & needs to be addressed by the court.

As you can see, I have a wide range of issues that are being raised. Somewhere at some stage I will see relief. It is just a matter of waiting for the court to say, "Look, his rights were violated, we must grant relief." As I said, I believe this relief will be coming in my case. I have a better than average chance.

What you noted about the prosecution going for a sentence reduction rather than a complete overturning is correct also. At this stage, the DA will be trying to save face. I'll tell you though, I truly would like to nail him on the evidence tampering issue!

Thanks for writing to Dr. Moran on my behalf. Anyway, I too wrote him again, a follow-up letter asking for his assistance, etc. Still no word from him or the other place that I wrote and asked about ADHD.

Yes, I believe that every little bit will help. This testing hopefully will turn up something positive. We can use all the positive material we can get.

Oh, note: Ineffective Assistance of Counsel is a Constitutional rights violation.

Trial transcripts not here yet. Will let you know when I do have them back. I am being direct and to the point here because I have the feeling we will be seeing one another soon & talking about all of this. And listen, don't ever forget that what you are doing, helping me, I just don't know how to say thanks enough. You are very special to me, Jacqueline.

About Goodwin complying with our request for the testing: Know this, I have already told him that if he failed to use something on my behalf in the correct fashion, then he must step aside. So he knows that I have no problem firing his ass. He cannot not comply w/ my request to submit any test results that I ask him to submit, as long as they are not detrimental to my defense. If he tried that I would raise my voice in court.

I have also laid out a record of the hard time I have had in reaching Goodwin over the phone, by mail, etc. I wrote to the court w/ an unofficial complaint.

Your 16 points from reading the transcripts, very interesting. We must talk more on this in depth. By the way, I wrote Goodwin & instructed him to do whatever it takes to break the PCRA consolidation w/ Chester's. I am going to have to wrap this one up & get it in the mail so it reaches you by Saturday. About 10 minutes and the mail leaves the unit for the day.Have so much more to talk w/ you about, in fact I will start another letter shortly. Looking forward to seeing you. God Bless.

Love,

Rick

If Richard Laird was not the one who killed Anthony Milano, he deserved to have his conviction overturned. If he was guilty of a lesser degree of murder, he should have been convicted and sentenced accordingly. If Laird killed Milano in a blind rage rather than as part of a diabolical and sinister act of premeditation, he should definitely be remorseful. There would be only one way to tell if Laird was an evil monster with ice-water for blood. I would have to look him in the eye. I would have to go see for myself.

The more Rick wrote to me, the more I doubted that he was guilty. His letters radiated with warmth. He was the first man who ever made me feel loved and accepted. How could anyone be capable of showing such love and tenderness on one hand and yet on the other be a ruthless psychopath? I didn't understand. But back then, there were a lot of things I didn't understand. Even Doc Weiler didn't have all the answers. All I knew was that no other man ever made me feel like I was that important or treated me like someone who mattered as much as Rick Laird did.

Although I didn't see it then, I understand now how women can fall head over heels for men on death row, and even marry them. Unless you have walked a mile in someone's shoes and felt every single pinch, don't criticize and don't judge. Before passing judgment on women who marry condemned men, ask yourself, "Have I done anything to be a true friend to the friendless? Was I sensitive to the needs and feelings of someone truly disadvantaged who had nobody in the world to turn to? Did I take advantage of her because she was poor and didn't have a lot to offer, viewing her as unworthy of me except as a booty-call or whatever? Have I criticized where I should have listened, and been more understanding? Am I one of countless creeps who used, abused and devastated some poor woman who was all alone in this world, who had no one to spend the holidays with and be a part of things?"

Jacqueline *March 25th, 1996*

Hello, beautiful woman. Just a note letting you know that I received your letter and that I am thinking of you.

Yes, again I must say I enjoyed speaking with you on the telephone. I am sad to say that in order for me to call in that fashion, I must claim an emergency situation has come up.

Gary Asteak can separate the PCRA's, huh? I believe this. However I have not been slacking on my end, either. I believe I have found a way to do so, if need be. If necessary I would use this tact as a last resort. I have checked the rules of court and they state that a court may, under its discretion, join appeals that it considers to have the same or similar issues. However I have filed my PCRA, I have filed this motion, therefore I can withdraw said motion. See the ramifications of what I just said?

Now the repercussions of my doing that are three-fold. One, I will be wide open for the governor to sign my death warrant. Two, my character witnesses are lined up and have been waiting, and waiting and waiting........... No telling how much more of this delay crap they will put up with. Three, there will be a further delay, until after Chester has his PCRA hearing, also he may withdraw upon seeing me do so. This move would be a last resort tact.

You are not going to believe this. Yesterday I sat wondering if you had a middle name. I fully intended to ask you what it was, if you had one, and you do: Sarah. I like that name very, very much. My middle name, remember that I have Scottish ancestors, is Roland. My name is Richard Roland Laird. Also, I was 100% sincere in my letters to you when I said that you have all of the qualities a man looks for in a woman. I'd be proud to have you as my woman. I want you as, to be my woman.......I hope to one day call you saying: "Bring me home." See you soon and know that I do love you. God Bless

Love,

Rick

On April 6th, I was finally able to go out and visit Rick. It was a 7 ½ hour one-way drive from Allentown to Pittsburgh, but I made it in my 1987 Hyundai without mishap. The long drive was of concern to me because I was driving a nine year old used car which definitely had a higher risk of breaking down than a new car. I lacked credit and only had enough money to cover the cost of gas, tolls, one cheap meal, and one overnight hotel room stay using my Hilton employee discount. I was budgeted to the penny. I prayed I wouldn't break down because I would be stuck, totally at the mercy and goodwill of strangers. Not exactly the safest undertaking for a woman traveling alone.

It was 11:30 PM when I finally arrived at the Pittsburgh Hilton & Towers. The dining room was closed but room service was available, which suited me fine. I requested a courtesy wake-up call at 7:00 AM so I would have enough time to decide what to wear, shower, do my hair and get my directions to the prison in order. I was more tired than hungry. Somewhere between burger and beef on the room service menu, I was overcome by the soft king sized bed and fell soundly asleep. When I woke up at 7:00 AM, I rang room service for one of the Hilton's legendary breakfasts. I had a long day ahead of me and would have that same long non-stop drive all the way home after the visit. I was twenty-eight years old and had plenty of stamina and energy to endure an arduous road trip but it was still an extraordinarily long day.

The State Correctional Institution at Pittsburgh (SCI-Pitt), commonly known as "the Wall", was an intimidating place that filled me with a sense of foreboding. Its exterior was less creepy looking than some of Pennsylvania's older prisons, but the razor-wired perimeter and manned guard towers staffed with burly armed uniformed men served as a reminder that this place was no college campus.

I arrived at the prison at 8:30 AM and went through the processing that all visitors are required to go through. I took my place in a long line of women and children and waited to pass through the metal detector, the first stage of visitor processing. After making it through the metal detector and also an ionizer (a device which picks up the smallest traces of illegal drugs on eyeglasses, prosthetics and clothing), I went to the second stage.

The second stage starts by having visitors take a number, similar to those used in the deli section of a supermarket. They are then directed to a visitors' waiting area for their number to be called. As their numbers are called, they must step up to a guard station kiosk and sign in. It is at that point where the guard at that station decides which, if any, of the visitor's personal effects may be taken into the visiting area and which items must be locked in a locker rented by the prison for a fee of $10 which the visitor must pay in exact change in cash only. If a visitor either lacks the $10 or cannot get exact change to rent the locker, the visitor must then take the items in question to their car (if they drove) and leave them locked in their car. If a visitor is made to return to their car to lock up their non-permitted personal items they lose their place in the visitation queue, meaning they might not be able to visit that day: They would have to begin the entire process all over after returning from their cars. They would have go back to the end of the first line, go through the metal detectors and ionizers at the prison entrance and start all over again — which can take up to three hours, depending on how long the line is, and if there are too many visitors in front of them at that point the entire trip would have been for nothing.

Although I had called and spoken with a prison staff member regarding prison rules for visiting an inmate before embarking on my journey to visit Rick, this staff member conveniently forgot to inform me of a few crucial rules. What was worse is that some of these rules are ambiguous. They are not explained definitively beforehand so that visitors are able to comply without difficulty, and they are capriciously enforced.

First, there was the poorly defined, arbitrarily enforced dress code. Any visitor (most which are women) can be denied their visit if the guards at the visitors' processing center feel that the visitor is dressed "provocatively". Skirts above the knee by as little as a hair's breadth can be arbitrarily deemed as too short, and the visitor would have to leave and find a change of clothes to wear that would meet approval, even if it meant having to go to a nearby store to buy an outfit. A sweater or shirt judged as "too tight" could also abort a visit.

Second, anything the guards of that day happen to feel nit-picky about permitting in the inmate visiting area would require the visitor to either rent a locker (if available) or take any items in question back to their cars to be locked up there. For example, one day the guards on duty might let a visitor bring in a writing pad and a pen with them into the visiting area; the next day different guards may decide not to and as a result, the visitor would have to rent a prison locker to put those items in or take them out to their car. Many visitors do not have cars. They came to the prison by Greyhound Bus. They simply have no place to leave their "questionable" items. Without the ability to utilize a prison-approved secure location to lock up such items, they would be denied their visit. They would have to turn around and leave and head back to the Greyhound Bus terminal to wait for the earliest bus to take them back home.

Even for those fortunate enough to have a car, parking poses another problem because visitor parking is not located conveniently close to the prison; a real hardship for the physically handicapped visitor. Unfortunately, the Pennsylvania Department of Corrections doesn't care about accessibility issues or the ADA. They're not interested in making things comfortable and convenient for the friends and loved ones of inmates: As custodians of the law, they are above the law.

So visitors basically have to plan for wearing shapeless flour sacks and renting a prison locker for a non-refundable $10 fee for which no change would be made by prison staff. Checks or money orders are not accepted. The locker rental scam was for the purpose of storing any items that the guards deem "inappropriate" to the visiting area. Such "inappropriate items" ranged from baby formula and diapers to writing tablets, loose change and house keys. The visitor also is supposed to plan for exact change not to exceed $6.00 for the prison's over-priced vending machine beverages and snacks. The fact that these rules are not clearly explained to potential visitors beforehand adds more burden, stress and financial hardship to the forgotten victims in the criminal justice system: The women and children who are "left behind".

Since the Pennsylvania Department of Corrections often moves inmates hundreds of miles across state from where they live, the hardship on spouses is enormous. Usually women, whether they are mothers, wives or girlfriends of inmates, they are mostly very poor. Many are struggling to stretch food stamps or welfare checks or sometimes minimum-wage paychecks from month to month in order to get by. There usually isn't enough money to meet the rent, utilities, food and toiletries in any given month. They must make extremely difficult sacrifices in order to travel across state, especially with small children in tow, in order to maintain any family bond with their men behind bars. They have not only suffered the loss of the men they love and their family's breadwinner, but they must also suffer silently in shame for what he might have done to get incarcerated in the first place.

Many of these women lack their own car and must scrape together the cost of a bus ticket at the expense of either the rent or the utilities going unpaid that month, often the at risk of eviction. It's hard enough on women who have cars to travel long distances with young children, but having to do so by Greyhound is hell. After enduring such an arduous journey, these poor women then become the object of ridicule, scorn and harassment by prison guards. Many of these guards are high on power trips, taking delight in causing even further hardship for the wives, partners, and children of prisoners. The more anguish some of these guards can cause these women visitors, the more they seem to enjoy it. I watched as guards grinned and laughed with one another each time an inmate's wife or girlfriend was turned away and denied her visit, leaving in tears as she pleaded to be able to visit and telling these unsympathetic guards how it took all she had to be able to travel to the prison.

One guard in particular struck me as having a disposition not much different that the Nazi SS guards who enjoyed taunting and torturing Jews in the concentration camps. He grinned cruelly at the plight of a poor young mother whom he had reduced to tears by denying her and her infant their visit. She had been in line in front of me. This goose-stepping moron was laughing with another guard as he told her that with no locker and no car to lock up her forbidden belongings – spare diapers, anti-bacterial wipes and a bottle of baby formula – there would be no visit. He guffawed rudely and told her that he didn't care if she had come all the way from the moon to visit her man. The rules were the rules and that was all there was to it. It was up to her to find out from the prison before planning a visit what the rules were. The fact that these "rules" were not explicitly defined didn't matter.

Her name was Tanya. She was a tiny wisp of a girl with shoulder length red hair, only about twenty-two years old. She was turned away and denied her visit because she didn't have the required $10 in exact change to rent a locker. She had taken the Greyhound bus all the way from Philadelphia to Pittsburgh just to visit her husband so he could see their year old daughter who was born just after his conviction and incarceration. She just didn't have $10. She had less than a dollar to her name. She spent her last dime just paying for the bus fare. I offered to share my locker with her so she would have a place to store her contraband items: her house keys, diapers, a pacifier and baby formula. I told her I would be at my visit until 3:00 PM. That was fine with her. She couldn't stop thanking me enough.

There was no need for accolades. It was a simple matter of principle, a matter of what was right. The idea that this guard would abort her visit over her baby's diapers, formula and pacifier angered me. Did he actually think she was some modern day Bonnie Parker about to break her Clyde Barrow out of prison with *Enfamil*? And just what did this guard on a power trip expect her to feed her newborn infant? Pretzels or chips from the vending machine? The whole scenario was ludicrous. I was surprised and disheartened that none of the other women there seemed interested in helping her, given that they were all in similar straits. The guard who gave her a hard time gave me a dirty look, obviously angered by my humanitarianism. I looked directly back at him in defiance as if to say, *"You can't deny her visit now!"*

Prison visits are the only way for a lot of these women to hold their families together. For any woman who has already endured so much to have a visit with her man, it is unjust and cruel to turn her and the children away and deny the visit over a sweater being "too tight" or a dress being "too short". The insistence on renting a locker for items the baby would obviously need during the visit was uncalled for. The fact that the prison would make poor, desperate women pay ten dollars to rent a locker just to be able to get their visit in the first place is wrong. What justification can there possibly be for charging such an outrageous amount to people who are disproportionately poor and who are trying to do something good for someone else?

To be told after sacrificing so much already that they would not be able to have their visit unless they left to buy a different outfit if they lacked a change of "appropriate" clothing, or turned away over $10 to rent a locker for personal items needed by their infants is mean-spirited and inexcusable. It seems to me that the whole prison system is designed to punish the wives, girlfriends and babies of inmates, not just the inmates themselves. This aspect of our criminal justice system is not covered in any college textbooks. It is a hands-on educational experience.

My number was finally called. I was permitted to take a pen and a writing tablet once the guard at the last station realized I was having a "no-contact" visit with a capital prisoner. Ushered to another seating area, I waited until another guard inside the visiting room pointed me to the window where Rick Laird was seated behind bullet-proof glass. As I approached the window, I was shocked. My impressions from all the reports, trial testimony and even Rick's earlier letter to me had given me the impression that Rick was a sizeable man. I just stood there and stared for a minute, dumbfounded. I didn't realize he was so huge! This man towered over me! He wore a bright orange prison-issued jumpsuit, indicating his death row inmate status.

We stared at each other for a moment frozen in time, like strange wolf cubs from alien packs meeting for the first time. I instinctively placed my hand on the window. He did the same. My own hand was half the size of his. For a moment, I thought of just how helpless I would be if he ever managed to put a stranglehold on me in anger. I weighed almost the same as the victim, Anthony Milano and was the same height. I was 5' 7" - tall for a woman, but a dwarf next to Richard Laird. He was not fat. He was solid muscle and was very well built. His massive stature made me feel fragile, small and helpless. He would have been a formidable adversary for Arnold Schwarzenegger's character in *The Terminator*.

His massive arms had more tattoos than skin. His chestnut hair just reached his jumpsuit collar. His beard and mustache were trimmed close and framed his face in a flattering stylish look. In a three piece suit and tie, he could have passed for a lawyer or a stockbroker, or even a movie star. He was strikingly handsome, far more so than his brother Mark. But he was a colossal figure; huge. He was definitely not someone I would want to have angry at me.

Trying not to let him see how intimidated I was, I picked up the phone next to the ledge of the glass and sat down. As I was doing so, Rick suddenly thrust his huge grinning face right up against the glass as if to see me close up. I instinctively recoiled, jumping backwards in high heels and all, the phone receiver flying out of my hand swinging into the wall beneath the window ledge with a bang. Rick leaned his head back, laughing heartily and but good naturedly at me.

His brown eyes twinkled and sparkled and shone in amusement. He was enjoying himself immensely. He started talking. He told me how long he had looked forward to seeing me. He was bouncing with energy and excitement like a little kid on Christmas morning. I was the first visitor he had in months except for volunteers from Lighthouse Ministries, a Christian outreach group that conducts bible studies once a month with inmates.

Throughout the visit, every little thing distracted him. The clock on the wall, the children of other visitors and sounds from the vending machines seemed to break his concentration. He jumped from topic to topic while I tried to talk with him and he constantly shifted in his chair on the other side of the glass: He was the classic textbook case of extreme and untreated ADHD. As we talked, I grew convinced that he could not have met the criteria for premeditated murder. He couldn't premeditate a trip to the bathroom to save his life – no pun intended.

He talked about everything, except for the crime. He told me I reminded him a lot of an old girlfriend named Kim. Laughing, he reminisced how she got out of bed butt naked and cold-cocked him one time, sending him sprawling over the bed onto the floor after some of his biker buddies came into their bedroom and asked him about some other girl. He told me how Kim, like me, had long dishwater blonde hair and a gorgeous body. He said I looked a lot like her, except I had bigger breasts. He admired and respected Kim a lot. I couldn't help thinking how brave, or crazy, she must have been to punch Rick's lights out. I don't know too many *men* who would want to chance a physical encounter with someone the size of Rick!

It turned out that Kim wasn't the only woman who had punched him out. His ex-wife JoAnn had smacked him around on occasion, too. Especially after he had been out all night partying with the boys while she was at home with their kids, Ricky and Rachel. He told me that JoAnn had smacked him when he tried to sneak in the apartment through the bedroom window after getting into mischief. He'd hidden in the kids' closet under a pile of toys, but she found him and clocked him. Rick lived a colorful life and had been with a lot of wild women. His most recent woman, Barbara Anne Parr, was Kim's sister. And it was Barbara Anne whom he loved more deeply than all the others.

He told me how he was absolutely crushed inside when he lost her after getting sent to death row. At first, Barbara Anne had vowed to stand by Rick. She even married him while he was on death row after the trial. But the pressures of having her husband incarcerated and unable to be there for her and baby Nicholas had proven to be much more than she could handle. Even though she was collecting welfare, attending community college, and had aspirations to become a psychologist, she simply couldn't make it on her own while Rick sat behind bars unable to be the provider, the husband, and the father that she needed for her family. When another man was willing to marry her, accept her kids (a rare find for a woman in her situation) and help support her, she had to make a difficult choice: Remain true to Rick, the man she loved with all her heart, or divorce Rick in order to build a life with someone who was able to be there for her and take care of her. While Rick understood Barbara Anne's perfectly rational choice, it did not lessen the pain for him. Gradually, the flow of letters between them trickled down to occasional short notes and her visits ceased entirely. For her sake and that of baby Nicholas, she had to move on with her life. Her children needed a father on the outside who was willing to support them and accept them as his own more than they needed a father who would never leave his prison cell, except in a coffin.

He told me how he'd always bailed his younger brother Mark out of jams since they were teenagers, right up until he got convicted and sentenced for murder. He also spoke of a deeply rooted and long festering sibling rivalry between Mark and himself. Mark always wanted what Rick had: motorcycle gang status, drugs and women. According to Rick, Mark had even ratted him and some fellow bikers out to the police one time in order to get off with a lighter sentence on some drug charges. This was interesting information, albeit a bit confusing. Mark was concerned enough to get me to help Rick with this current legal mess, yet Mark had previously betrayed him like a modern day Judas Iscariot. If their sibling rivalry was the Cain and Abel situation Rick described, it didn't make sense to me that Mark would now want to save his brother. Unlike Cain, Mark had the perfect means to be rid of his rival: let the state execute him.

Rick told me how his appellate lawyer, Michael Goodwin, was basically ignoring him. Goodwin had not responded to any of Rick's letters or phone calls inquiring about the diminished capacity issue. There were more issues, in addition to what he had already written me about. A tipstaff or sheriff had inadvertently made a remark to one of the jurors during the deliberation phase hinting that Rick Laird should be found guilty as charged and punished accordingly. Discussing any aspect of the trial with a juror while that trial is in progress is forbidden: It is normally considered sufficient grounds in itself for a mistrial to be declared.

Rick also told me he had dropped out of high school in the 10th grade because he "just couldn't get it". The academics were simply too difficult for him to master and teachers didn't take the extra time with him that he would have needed in order to be successful in school. He had a history of learning difficulties. I believed that despite his intelligence, his ADHD would cause problems in the processing and retention of information. I asked him if Ron Elgart, the trial lawyer who had represented him, had understood the ramifications of his cognitive impairments and his extremely low frustration tolerance level. Rick told me no, nothing at all like that was brought up. Instead, Elgart had simply tried to paint Rick as a hard worker and family man who was the son of a Marine officer.

Four hours into the visit, Rick giggled like a school girl and motioned for me to turn around and look behind me. Two men were kissing and holding hands. This other inmate apparently was getting a visit from his boyfriend. Rick snickered to me, saying, "Fuckin' homos. Crack me up!" His voice and demeanor was not vicious, but he clearly indicated that he thought homosexuals were abnormal.

I solemnly told Rick that I was never phased one way or the other by gays. Having grown up in Philly I had seen a lot of things. What did I care who played kissy-face with whom? It was none of my business if they weren't bothering me. My best friend in high school, one of the very few kids who didn't pick on me for having a learning disability, was gay. His name was Frankie and he sang in the choir. He was damn good at it, too. He had a voice like Bonnie Tyler and he could sing her number one single hit *Total Eclipse of the Heart* better than she did.

When I was without a date for my senior prom, the most important event in a young woman's life other than her wedding day, it was Frankie who offered to accompany me so that I would be able to go. Although he would probably have preferred spending that evening meeting his lover for a tryst at a gay nightclub in New Jersey, he knew how much going to the prom meant to a girl like me. And he was willing to make that kind of sacrifice for me because that's the kind of friend he was. Had I not been too poor to afford even so much as a used formal gown for the occasion, I would have accepted his kind and generous offer.

Frankie's sensitivity to my feelings and my plight regarding the prom meant more to me than you can fathom. As the poorest girl in my high school, I wasn't one of the sought-after girls regularly asked out on dates by the nice, cute boys from "normal" families. I wasn't one of the popular girls from a nice neighborhood of spacious homes with neatly manicured lawns and a smooth orderly life with two successful parents. I didn't have the luxury of being able to think about joining clubs, cheerleading, majorettes, or participating in any typical middle class teen extracurricular activities. I didn't have a typical childhood after my grandmother died.

I was a poor woman without family, totally on my own and having to support myself in a man's world – a world that is anything but kind or fair to orphaned girls, a world that condones exploiting those who are a little "slow" all in the name of "merit". While all the other kids shopped for prom outfits and chose prom dates, while they navigated full schedules of activities mapped out by coddling parents, and while they were making full time jobs of preparing for SAT's, every penny of my full-time minimum wage job at the local McDonalds went toward the rent for a cramped, ratty, roach-infested apartment in the ghetto. I dwelt where all the homes were row homes sandwiched tightly on dirty, litter-filled noisy streets; tenement buildings decorated with boarded up windows from drive-by shootings bullet holes.

When you are extremely underprivileged, you are confronted daily by people who cannot imagine your world and who don't care about you. They drive the point home every day in every way they treat you. The happiness, dignity, and respect they feel *they* are entitled to are luxuries that you simply don't deserve – even though you didn't do anything wrong. You are a social inconvenience, a nuisance just for being born and existing in *their* world. You simply just don't count. Frankie was one of the few, perhaps the only, friend I had in high school who *did* care and that meant the world to me. When people are intolerant and judgmental of others because of things like sexual orientation, race, religion, ethnicity, disability or age, they miss out on having some of the best people in the world as friends. And true friends like Frankie are very hard to find.

Rick realized I was offended by his homophobia and he clumsily apologized to me "for coming off the wrong way." I finally asked as diplomatically as I could: "Did you kill Anthony Milano?" Rick replied in a subdued tone, "What do you think?" *What did I think*? I didn't know what to think, which is why I asked the question in the first place! He never really answered me. Wanting to see only the good in Rick, I began making excuses to myself: I thought it might be that it was because he was so incapacitated the night of the murder that he honestly didn't remember exactly what happened. Anything was possible. I was willing to give him the benefit of the doubt. I also believed that even murderers deserve a fair trial. This is one of the most important of those inalienable rights outlined in the Constitution that is supposed to be guaranteed to all US citizens, not just reserved for wealthy, privileged and beautiful people.

Recovering quickly from the tense and awkward moment of his anti-gay remark, Rick became the loveable charmer again. He chatted away amicably, telling me how exquisitely beautiful I was in person, far more so than in a photograph. I was eating it up. A burly guard came over and tapped me on the shoulder. The visit was over: it was 3:00 PM, time for all visitors to leave. The inmates having contact visits clung to their women and children as they said tearful goodbyes until the next visit. I got up to leave, turning around once to get a last look at Rick Laird. He also looked over his shoulder to get one last glimpse of me, too. I wondered how things might have been had he never been involved in a murder and never gone to prison, let alone death row. I wondered if we had met under different circumstances and he was not a convicted felon, how things might have been if our paths crossed. I wondered what it might feel like to be held in his strong arms at night, cherished and reassured in knowing I was loved. I left "the Wall" and headed east with the sun setting in the western sky.

Chapter 16

"***Recompense injury with justice and recompense kindness with kindness.***" ~ Confucious

My visit with Rick left me feeling uplifted. He'd said all the things I needed to hear at that point in time in my life. No one else had ever bothered to say those things to me. I really wanted so badly to believe he was wholly innocent.

That Monday at work Mark asked me over lunch how help for Rick's case was going; whether I'd gotten the confirmation of the ADHD, found other mitigating circumstances, or was getting appointments with lawyers to go over Rick's new evidence as grounds for appeal. As Andrea and Amy, two gossipy maids, finished their lunch and got up to leave, Mark leaned across the table toward me. Looking over his shoulder toward the lunchroom door to make sure no one else was listening, he whispered, "Is Rick gonna get his sentence commuted? Is he gonna be able to come home?"

I chose my words carefully: "Mark, this isn't as simple or as easy as you think it is. There are grounds for appeal. Your brother definitely did not get a fair trial. Personally, I think his trial lawyer was just another idiot from a rich family who got to go to law school because he had enough money, even if he lacked gray matter. But it's not that easy to get a new attorney to take up his appeal free of charge – especially when most lawyers are afraid to touch a case like this because of the stigma attached to defending anyone convicted of a "hate-crime." Inwardly I simmered and stewed. Mark came across as inferring that I wasn't doing enough, quickly enough, to help his brother while he was doing absolutely nothing.

I had not forgotten about his little stunt two months before when he complained to Rick behind my back that I'd asked him to help with the trial transcript copying fees! Now he wanted to jeopardize my job by bringing up my involvement in his brother's appeal at work where he could have been overheard by anyone. Back-stabbing employees were in abundance at the Hilton and I didn't need any attention drawn to myself for my extracurricular activity of helping a convicted hate-crime murderer on death row win a new trial.

Just the simple fact of being the only female maintenance mechanic was enough to earn the ire of the entire housekeeping department. The housekeeping department was overwhelmingly female, full of gossips and embittered women who were jealous of my position because of the whopping two dollars an hour more in pay I received as a maintenance mechanic. Most of the maids also felt that the entire maintenance department were screw-offs who got paid more for doing less work than they did. They were always quick to complain to Stumpy – our boss and Chief Engineer – if a maintenance mechanic didn't jump to their beck and call at the snap of a finger. Of course Stumpy wrote them off, but that wasn't the point.

Some of the maids had their eye on Mark because they thought he was cute and would be a great catch. He wasn't bad looking, and he could even be very funny and entertaining. Sometimes he was downright comical. Like the time when he radioed me to ask me to bring his wallet on my way from the maintenance shop up to the 7th floor. Expecting that it would be me coming out of the elevator when it opened on the 7th floor, he pulled out his cordless drill in a Jesse James style stick-up maneuver only to find that he had just "held up" Mr. Bill O'Boyle, the hotel's general manager! The maids resented that I was getting more attention from this tall, suave and debonair man and they were not, and they resented that. What they did not know was that the attention Mark paid to me was not the sort they imagined. It had everything to do with Rick's death sentence appeal and absolutely nothing to do with any workplace romance. What they also apparently didn't know was that Mark's romantic interests were mainly focused on Ginger DeLorenzo, the Assistant Human Resources Manager.

Ginger DeLorenzo was an exceedingly overweight with very short dark hair, and a rather plain face. She had a college degree and an impressive title, and as a white collar professional she enjoyed a higher career status and a far better salary than anyone in the maintenance department, even Stumpy. Ginger ate up all the flirtatious attention Mark paid to her. Unfortunately, we live in a society that worships youth and thinness. It is the Lindsey Lohans, the Angelina Jolies, the Paris Hiltons and the Ashley Judds who are idolized and adored by our superficial society, not the double or triple X's, not the Roseanne Barrs or the masses of average-looking working-class people that Roseanne Barr represents. The book is judged by its cover, regardless of any intelligence, talent or other inner qualities. We women may have come a long way, but we still have a long way to go.

Ginger had her own office. Her name and title was engraved on a little desk plaque prominently displayed on the front edge of her desk. She got to dress up in fashionable business attire and never had to look at – never mind scrub – a soiled bathtub or un-flushed toilet. She didn't have to push heavy carts around with clean linens in a thankless, back-breaking, minimum wage job of stripping down beds and scrubbing bathrooms, beholden to management's break-neck pace. If anyone should have been the recipient of the housekeepers' envy, it should have been Ginger DeLorenzo.

I always suspected that Mark's designs on Ginger had more to do with trying to win favors in employment rather than genuine romantic interest; not because Ginger was somehow undeserving of his attentions or beneath him, but because Mark was too superficial a guy to express interest in any woman unless it suited his agenda. Wooing someone in management would certainly be to his advantage. It certainly got him some expensive designer clothes as presents.

Although Ginger was a single mother, she owned her own home and was able to afford the trappings of a middle class lifestyle. But being part of the middle class isn't only the fine things that a middle class income can buy: it's also about status and complex social networks which open doors for you that are closed to the lower social classes. I wondered why it wasn't Ginger whom he entreated to help him with his brother's case. She certainly had access to office equipment: copying Rick's transcripts wouldn't have cost her a cent. Perhaps it was because having a family member on death row was unacceptable by members of middle class society – members like Ginger DeLorenzo.

I came home to find a surprise in the mail from Rick. Anticipating good news from him regarding possibly getting tested by Dr. Moran or one of the other multitude of psychology professionals specializing in dealing with adults with learning disabilities, I rushed to open his letter. He apparently was trying to conserve his postage allowance, for he had enclosed two letters in the same envelope: one letter was dated April 6th and the other April 8th. Unfortunately, the rain must have soaked through the envelope and the first paragraph of the longer letter - the one dated April 8th - was no longer legible. The ink had run, leaving only trails of black drool on the canary legal tablet paper. Disappointed, I began reading the shorter letter, the one dated April 6th:

Jacqueline April 6th, 1996

Hello! I just finished hours of legal work and am beat, so this will only be a short note. It was so good seeing you today. The time we had together went by too fast, though.

I have your mail here and will get to it in tomorrow's letter. For tonight, I lay here thinking of you and listening to the Flyers play. I will enclose a few lines of love, okay?

Do you like the sound of the rain? Ever sit on a porch andjust listen to the rain at night, with someone ya' care about? It's raining tonight. This is why I ask. Laying here wishing you & I were together at home, sitting together, listening to the rain. Do you like to stargaze? Would you like to lay out in a field, on a blanket, on a summer night w/ me and look at the stars? Just little things that cost nothing to do, that we could do, if you like? There are other things to do also. Like if you could go anywhere, anywhere at all, where would you like to go & visit and why? Have you ever been to the Smithsonian? I told you of a couple of things I'd like to do, if I have the chance, now you tell me, where would you like to go, if you could? Of course, I also much enjoy nice evenings at home. I look forward to cooking for you, and I look forward to eating your cooking. Hope I'm not boring you...

Love You Jacqueline,

Rick

Jacqueline, April 8th, 1996

Hello. I have learned a couple of things since I have been here. Namely, Frank Chester wants to work together to get this entire situation overturned. Furthermore, according to what

Goodwin told me at the Evidentiary hearing, Chester now has a new attorney, one of the attorneys from the O.J. Simpson team. Apparently they are telling his family that they intend to have him home soon. My thoughts are anything that would affect him would also affect me....Food for thought here. Also, one of the prosecution witnesses is dead. Pete Carpinona, hit by a train or something like that.

I am a bit leery of allowing Frank Chester to work so close w/ me on all of this. I get the feeling (gut feeling) that something isn't quite right there. Something else Chester passed along. The television show "Dateline" was supposed to do a piece on the case sometime this week. I wanted to see if it was a one-sided piece or what. You see, I was never contacted by them for an interview, so I am thinking one-sided piece possibly...

Here is some more interesting info. Apparently Chester's attorneys have Alan Rubenstein under investigation for something rather serious. He would not write this info down in the note he sent to me. Claimed it to be too sensitive (the guard was reading the notes he sent me).

BTW, did I ever tell you how much I really appreciated you being at my evidentiary hearing and how great you look? I just wish we could have had Asteak representing me for that hearing, but there wouldn't have been enough time for him to prepare, or the court to remove Goodwin first, etc.

Let's see, what else....I am sort of stuck in neutral here. Can do nothing but sit and wait.........

Love,

Rick

Rick's short April 6th letter spoke to the innermost secrets of my heart. Where would I like to go if money was no object? I had never even thought about it before. I'd never had the luxury of being able to plan for anything lofty like going on a far away vacation or traveling to visit new places I had only seen in pictures. I never had enough economic security to do so. And no man had ever cared enough about me to offer to take me some place far away. No man had ever asked me what I wanted, what I liked and what I might enjoy. At almost twenty-nine years of age, I didn't know *what* I liked. I never got the chance to find out because all my life up to that time had been spent in a struggle just to survive. Here was a man on death row telling me in a letter that he would love to enjoy the simple pleasures of a simple life with me and that if he had money; he would love to take me somewhere special.

The two years prior to my accident was the only time in my life that I ever had a decent income and actually had money left over after paying for the basics of survival: a roof over my head, utilities, food and the occasional thrift store outfit. Having had several harrowing experiences with periodic homelessness since I had been suddenly thrust out on my own at the tender age of thirteen, I was frugal to a fault. I did without cable television; my furniture was curbside special, my humble furnishings included several milk crates which did double duty as handy book shelves and end tables. I rarely ate out, if at all. The few times when I did indulge in a meal out, it was at a local diner where the most expensive entree was a very tasty portion of broiled stuffed flounder which cost $7.95 and included a salad bar. I never went to bars. I didn't drink or gamble. My only vice, my only comfort, was cigarettes. And I didn't buy the expensive name brands: I bought roll-your-own tobacco in a tin. My innate frugality was the only thing that saved me from ending up homeless with nowhere to go after my accident.

Of course, after the accident my income fell from $19 an hour down to zero, I had no choice but to continue living that way. I found solace in the simple things. I loved being able to simply relax quietly and listen to the rain and think about nothing in particular. Still, I often wished I had someone special to share such moments with. Someone who would appreciate and cherish every second with me would have been a welcome addition in my life. No man I had ever met was as poetic and sentimental about sharing and appreciating quiet intimate moments as Rick seemed.

Then again, since my accident, I'd really had no opportunity to go out and meet single men because I didn't have any money to go out. The only places I could afford to go were the public parks and the free public library, and neither of those places were hopping singles scenes. You can't talk in the library and most people there go, look for a book and hurry about their business: they are not there trying to meet a potential date. Public parks weren't full of people either, except the occasional bag lady feeding pigeons or a homeless old man sleeping on a park bench. I was at least twelve years older than everyone else at college, except for the professors who already had serious relationships with women who were set up and rolling in their own decent careers. The only other men I interacted with were the other maintenance mechanics at work. None of the options available to me for meeting people were conducive to dating.

Stumpy, my boss, was married and not very appealing. He was an entire head shorter than me. He was also a hothead who sent solid oak floor tiles whizzing across the maintenance shop when angry, without looking to see if any of them accidently hit anyone. Rich was twenty years older than me and married. There was blonde haired and blue-eyed Joe who was divorced and made no secret of the fact that he was a player: a fast moving smooth talker who viewed women merely as sexual conquests for his own gratification and nothing more. He wore so much cologne he smelled like a brothel and sported enough gold jewelry to pass as a pimp. The only other man was Mark Laird, who was single - and who I didn't trust. He was my age, but like most men in my age group, he wasn't interested in a commitment. And there was always something about him that spelled sneak with a capital "S". Availability and marital status aside, none of these men impressed me as the type who would love to spend time with me gazing at the stars or listening to the rain. And none of them were the kind of man I would be attracted to.

I thought about Rick. Underneath the rough exterior, I saw the child inside the man. I didn't see a monster. I saw redemption. I was starting to fall for Rick. I reached out, desperate for the love and warmth that I had never been shown, and out of six billion people in the entire world, he was the only one who reached back. This was all the more why I wanted to help him. He had no one else in his corner who he could really count on. I knew how that felt, even though I had never been in prison, let alone on death row. But I definitely knew what it was like to be taken advantage of by people whom I thought cared about me.

One such "friend" was Corky Fenstermacher. Feeling sorry for Corky because he was unemployed and out on the streets back in early 1986 - a year before I got in with the plasterers' union, I let him stay at my old apartment. I came home from my job one day to find my stereo stolen. Some rare silver dollars - Morgan dollars in mint condition - that my grammy had given me many years ago as a child were also missing. I cried until I got a migraine because I couldn't afford another stereo on my $5/hr job and that stereo had been a present from my Grammy before she died. Nor could I ever replace those rare silver dollars with their sentimental value.

Corky, whom I later discovered to be the culprit, had the nerve to sit there on my sofa pretending to be my friend, trying to console me for my loss while knowing all along he had ripped me off and sold my stereo for drugs. Being very gullible and far too trusting, I had no idea that Corky did drugs when he showed up at my door begging for a place to crash. I thought I was merely helping a friend down on his luck.

I didn't connect with the harsh reality of the situation until a police informant told me - for a fee of $20 - where my stereo was and who had stolen it. Accompanied by several Allentown policemen, I went to the house where my stereo was and got it back. It had been damaged beyond repair, except for the tape cassette deck. One speaker was ruined and the turntable was trashed.

Corky was a heartless sneak, a liar and a thief. My act of kindness had been repaid with insult and injury. Corky had the nerve to tell Detective Paul Snyder of the Allentown Police Department that I had given him the stereo and later tried to take it back out of spite because I was a jealous ex-girlfriend! Some friend! With friends like that, who needs enemies?

It seemed to me that Frank Chester was such a "friend." He enjoyed and admittedly benefited from Rick's friendship and the various male bonding rituals that they shared: whether it was picking up women at the bar or getting tattoos together. He willingly went along for the ride with Rick Laird and Anthony Milano, and then went back to Rick's apartment after the murder. Yet he claimed in his testimony that he was so terrified of Rick that he was too afraid to go to the police immediately. When he did go to the police, he told them that Rick - and solely Rick - was responsible for killing Milano. Then at the trial in 1988, he tried to put the crime squarely on Rick. Now they were both on death row fighting for their lives. What does this turncoat do after implicating his best friend and pointing the finger at him in court, which served to backfire horribly? He tells Rick some fantastic story about one of the O.J. Simpson “dream team” lawyers representing him and also some crazy stuff about keeping their appeals joined for their mutual benefit. At least that was what Rick told me. His depiction of his turn-coat pal left me with the opinion it was Frank Chester. According to Rick, Frank Chester was not only a psychopathic liar, but he was too stupid to even get his story straight.

I was very suspicious of Frank Chester's motives for wanting to work together with Rick on an appeal. Frank had been the one to go to the police and turn against Rick, according to the testimony in the trial transcripts. Now all of a sudden he wanted to collaborate with Rick on their appeals! Why would Chester have the need to ride Rick's shirttails all the way through the appeals process if he really did have one of the O.J. "Dream Team" lawyers working on his behalf? I didn't buy that story for a New York minute! It all sounded like a load of hooey to me. Perhaps it was merely jailhouse bragging rights or an attempt to pick Rick's brain to find the weak spots in Rick's appeal tactics so Frank could twist them and somehow use them to his advantage. Maybe he thought if he could find the chink in the proverbial armor, he could get one over on Rick.

Rick’s letters also included a transcript with his letters from *The Sally Jesse Raphael Show* featuring DA Alan Rubenstein. At that time, the “Sally” show was the most watched daytime talk show across America. Oprah Winfrey had not yet climbed the ladder to the pinnacle of daytime television limelight with her own talk show. Everyone with a television and cable/satellite dish connections had heard of Sally Jesse Raphael, or watched her show.

The episode was called *"They Got Me 'Cause I'm Gay"*. The topic was hate crimes against gays. According to the transcript, two guests were victims of near-fatal attacks for being gay. One of the guests was a girl named Claudia who saw her lover, Rebecca, die a slow, agonizing, terror-filled death after getting shot in the head by a crazed woodsman who had been stalking them all day during an outing. He followed them as they hiked in the mountains before they stopped to make love by a stream…and then he gunned down Claudia's lover.

After this harrowing tale, it was the Bucks County District Attorney's turn to talk, and he summarized the murder of Anthony Milano on national television. Rubenstein said that Rick Laird and Frank Chester specifically targeted Anthony Milano because he was gay and for no other reason and that they intended to kill him because of that. The end of the show featured various people from the audience questioning the speakers. Several said that homosexuality was not normal. One audience participant raised the issue of little kids who are molested by homosexuals as a justification of attacks on gays. Several other participants sympathized with the victims of gay-bashing. One fact remained unchallenged: after Rubenstein recounted the murder of Anthony Milano, Rick Laird and Frank Chester were painted in the worst possible light: as cold-hearted killers who were undeserving of having their lives spared.

Of course, the show did not feature an interview with either Chester or Laird. Daytime television-watching America did not see the side of Rick Laird that I had seen. They did not read the sweet nothings he wrote me or experience the warmth in his letters. They did not see how appreciative he was of the simple things in life that he wanted to share with a special woman. They did not see the unfairness of his inadequate legal representation and they did not realize that he could have been set up by a devious friend to take the fall. They simply saw a cold-blooded killer with no remorse.

But what truly separates those of us who kill from those who do not? How many murderers - with the possible exception of serial killers - actually wake up in the morning and decide while shaving and brushing their teeth that this will be the day they are going to kill somebody they may not even know? What causes someone to snap without warning? What really can deter that? How many killers think beforehand, “Gee I better not do this or I’ll get caught and executed?”

I was caught up in my college homework and had the next three days off from school, which gave me plenty of time to think about everything that Rick had sent me to read. Taking a break after reading the *Sally Jesse Raphael Show* transcripts and before responding to Rick’s letters, I opened up a can of comfort food: a can of Chef Boyardee Beefaroni. It was cheap and had been a special treat for me ever since I was a little kid. Of course Mini-Stain, with her feline charm and striking Calico good looks, was an incurable mooch. She would not be satisfied until she succeeded in badgering me into letting her swipe some out of my bowl. However I had discovered a way to prevent her from putting her paws into my dish of food: I dished out some in a bowl for her and ate the rest out of the pot. The bowl apparently faked her out into thinking she was eating from my dish.

After eating, I decided to take some “me time” for a long-deserved nap. My calculus book lay abandoned at the foot of my bed. I didn’t even bother to get undressed. I rolled up in my Holly Hobbie quilt with my boots on and was out like a light. I’d had that quilt since I was 8 years old. It had been patched over patches over patches. I didn’t care. It was my favorite “blankie” and I was going to keep it and use it until it disintegrated. The last thing I was conscious of was Mini-Stain nestling in next to me purring loudly in my ear with content.

After my nap, I fired up the coffee pot to make some strong brew for clearing the cobwebs from my head and wrote up a list of issues that I had questions about. This list was mainly for my own benefit so I could refer to it later when writing to Rick or talking with him. I also had to call Harriet, a very easy-going middle-aged lady who, together with her husband, volunteered with Lighthouse Ministries, a non-profit organization formed to help prisoners. She was photocopying more documents for Rick and was planning to mail them to me as per Rick's instructions. However Rick had asked me during his most recent phone call to drive to her house to pick them up and thus save mail time. Rick was out of patience with Goodwin and felt there was a reasonably good chance the Defenders Association would take up his case on appeal.

In between making calls to various professionals in the legal and medical community on Rick's behalf, I had to read through his lengthy letters so I could respond appropriately. Reciprocation of written contact is of the utmost importance to someone shut up in a solitary prison cell for 23 hours each day with no other means for maintaining any connection to the outside world. Every resounding bang of the mail slot in my front door meant another letter from Rick.

Jacqueline, *April 10th, 1996*

Just able to settle back for a few and start one to you. Tried all day, from 9:00 AM until 1:00 PM to call Goodwin. His secretary told me he would be in the afternoon. Yet each time I called he wasn't in. So all the notes I had to go over w/ him that I copied, sealed in an envelope and they will be off. I expressed my displeasure w/ him, said that I have lost any confidence I may have had in him, etc. So much more. Five pages of notes I had to review with him, told his secretary this, said I urgently needed to speak with him, yet he continues to pull this nonsense. I am tired of it, wish I had a new attorney. One who will truly act on my best interest.

Last night I laid here tossing and turning for hours in total frustration over all of this. I do this quite a lot. Lay awake thinking. Oh, well.

The mail has caught up w/ me. Got a couple of letters from you. Good to hear from you......

Now listen up young lady! When I say something to you like "Are you wearin' panties under that skirt", know this: I would never be so crude as to blurt that out in front of others. When I say something like this I do so in a good humored fashion. Do not think I am some kind of lout that would embarrass a lady in this way. Got it? Good.

Yes, I hope to be able to hold you and kiss you many times over. I shall continue to hope and pray. I hope to see you this evening in my dreams. Then one day begin to wake and see your beautiful blue eyes, see your smile, for real....God Bless.

Love,

Rick

I called Lighthouse Ministries and told Harriet Liddington who I was. Apparently, Rick had already called her and told her to expect me. She gave me directions to her house in Selinsgrove which is on the outskirts of Harrisburg. It was a two hour drive one way from my house in Allentown. Managing the winding stretch of Routes 11 & 15 northbound required some navigational effort. US 11 & 15 follow the Susquehanna River and are poorly lit. The exits and cross roads were not clearly marked and it is easy to miss a turn. I finally found her home; a classic clapboard-style farmhouse nestled among trees with the nearest neighbors, a quiet Mennonite couple, a quarter of a mile up the road.

When I finally arrived, Harriet had a pot of coffee freshly made. I couldn't tell how old she was. She had gray hair which she wore long, but she did not have a single wrinkle and she looked very youthful in her simple T-shirt and Levi jeans. She handed me the voluminous pile of record copies and invited me to join her for coffee. I needed the caffeine boost after my long drive and was grateful for the strong brew. Sitting down, I looked around at the tidy kitchen. The powder blue walls were accented by a stenciled border of geese that went around the perimeter of the kitchen. On the table was a matching napkin holder, salt & pepper set and sugar bowl all sporting the same goose theme as the wall border stencil. The coffee mugs and dishes also matched the goose design on the sugar bowl and salt & pepper shakers. One thing was for certain: Harriet loved geese and the color blue. Even the quaint, frilly curtains framing the kitchen windows were white and blue with geese on them! Everything matched and looked so picture perfect and homey.

Both Harriet and her husband were semi-retired and worked tirelessly on behalf of indigent prisoners because they believed it was the Christian thing to do. Harriet felt the death penalty really didn't provide justice and shared my belief that it was capricious. She and her husband devoted much of their time trying to bring God into the lives of the lowest of the low: prisoners on Pennsylvania's death row. At least the most despised among mankind would receive the salvation of Jesus Christ and not be condemned to an eternal inferno of hell. She was also the only born-again Christian with anti-abortion beliefs (except to save the mother's life) that I had ever met who was equally anti-death penalty. Although our beliefs about abortion and God differed, I definitely respected this Harriet because she was no hypocrite: She was pro-life across the board.

She told me of her experience in corresponding with Keith Zettlemoyer, a death row inmate convicted of the October 13th, 1980 shooting death of his best friend, Charles VeVetsco. VeVetsco apparently agreed to testify against Zettlemoyer about his role in robbing the Susquehanna Valley Mall Radio Shack where he had worked as a security guard. Zettlemoyer retaliated by killing his friend in a moment of irrational thought. Harriet had taken Zettlemoyer's execution particularly hard. You don't spend ten years faithfully sharing bible studies, correspondences and prayer visits with someone who gradually embraces God without becoming emotionally attached. Keith Zettlemoyer was executed on May 2nd, 1995. He had written Harriet a letter of goodbye on the eve of his execution and she received that letter the day after he was given the lethal injection. She showed me his last letter. She also gave me a copy of a letter she wrote to the local newspaper after Zettlemoyer's execution in which she chastised those who harshly judged him even after he paid his debt to society in the execution chamber.

Unlike many death row inmates, Keith Zettlemoyer openly took responsibility for his crime and acknowledged he owed a debt to society for what he did. He asked for God's forgiveness and he asked the prison ministry to pray for the other men on death row who did not have God in their lives. Tears welled in Harriet's eyes as she recounted Keith Zettlemoyer's final days and the insensitive remarks so many people made regarding his execution with no thought whatsoever for the feelings of the family he had left behind. Yes, Keith Zettlemoyer took a life and was condemned to pay for that murder by forfeiture of his own life; but was it really necessary for his parents and grandparents to have to hear others bad-mouthing him after his execution?

It was Harriet's firm belief that all people have some good inside of them and that all will stand equal in the sight of God. She believed that everyone, including Keith Zettlemoyer, Rick Laird, and Frank Chester can be redeemed. Judaism also teaches that we all have a spark of God in us. We all have something to offer. Harriet and I talked about Rick and his case. I asked her what she thought of the possibility that Rick was framed. She was unsure about that herself, but one thing she was certain of: Rick Laird spent all of his allotted monthly postage one month to help the ministry with postage to mail out flyers. Harriet was convinced Rick was a sincere God-fearing Christian. I don't know how God-fearing he was, but I knew how selfless he was when he gave away his TV set to another inmate whose own TV had blown up. Harriet gave me a copy of the prison ministry newsletter featuring an update on Rick Laird's legal situation. The article concluded with a request to everyone to keep Rick in their prayers because his attorney wasn't doing anything to help him despite new and powerful evidence.

Harriet told me she thought Rick would have made a fine husband and father for some woman out there, if given the chance. I told her about the occasionally passionate romantic letters he wrote to me. I also told her how no other man ever made me feel loved the way Rick Laird did with his words and his writings. I confessed to Harriet that I had very strong feelings for Rick after so many intimate letters. I told her of my visits with him.

I admitted to her that I tried to see this monster that a court judged to be evil incarnate, one whose crime was heinous enough to deserve execution. But he seemed anything but a monster. He seemed like an ordinary average man who laughed and cried; a man who loved and needed to be loved. He was human just like all the rest of us. I recounted to Harriet how his brown eyes sparkled with joy during my visit with him and how his long brown locks of hair danced like imps on his shoulders and framed his face. I personally was outraged at learning that the prison forced inmates to cut their hair short once it grew past their shoulders. It smacked of fascism, not too different from the Nazis who forced Jewish death camp prisoners to have their hair shorn. Leaving Harriet's to return home, I admitted to myself that I indeed found many qualities in Rick that would be difficult not to love.

I wrote Rick, keeping him abreast of the document situation, and told him that I had visited Harriet. I told him that I had the documents all packed up and ready to take with me when I met with Dr. Raymond Bell and Delores Miller from the state chapter of LDA in case they would be willing to help with his appeal. Dr. Bell was a psychiatrist whose practice was strictly limited to working with those who have learning disabilities. Delores Miller was the president of the LDA state chapter. I thought that if we could somehow make the public aware of the serious injustices that put the learning disabled at high risk in the criminal justice system, the public might just start demanding better treatment for children, teens and adults with learning disabilities.

I told Delores Miller on the phone, "Even if John Q. Public views this strictly from a dollars and cents standpoint, how much money could we have saved on Rick Laird had there been the proper social supports in place from his childhood through young adulthood, including the ability for him to succeed in a skilled trade, as opposed to him having no means to fit in with society and end up where he is at as a result. Now multiply that by the thousands of others incarcerated in Pennsylvania's prison system at $40,000 a year per inmate in taxpayer costs. And remember, it is more than that for prisoners on death row because of the cumbersome appeals process. We are letting society use the criminal justice system as a human garbage disposal for those in poverty, and those with disabilities. We are wasting the potential and talent they have to offer, if given a chance. I believe Rick Laird is the poster boy for that."

Delores agreed and referred me to Dr. Raymond Bell to see about getting Rick tested and getting the record of his brain injuries entered as new evidence on appeal. I made an appointment with Dr. Bell, who was located in western Pennsylvania. I would be driving across state with a milk crate full of Rick's documents for the appointment. A few days after calling Dr. Bell, I got another letter in the mail from Rick. In this letter, I learned how difficult it was for a death row inmate to use a telephone when needed to confer with attorneys, regardless of the importance of upcoming court hearings.

Being able to confer with your lawyer — hence receive counsel — for a legal proceeding is part of the due process rights American citizens are entitled to. I found it shocking and hard to believe that the prison system could legally deny telephone calls with lawyers, especially to those on death row. The ability to confer with one's attorney when time is of the essence is paramount to due process being a reality instead of abstract legal theory. I had asked Rick if it was possible for condemned inmates to sue the prison system for their interfering with the inmate's due process. He responded with the following letter:

Jacqueline: *April 12th, 1996*

Hello, how are you doing? I'm doing okay. Been another fairly busy day for me. Lots of writing, etc. Would you like to hear a bit of my day? Wtll, I'll tell ya anyway. Went out to the yard this morning, got a little exercize in & and a good sweat. Came in & had a shower, couldn't quite reach a certain spot on my back & wished I had someone to reach it for me...

A little later I went to the law library. Helped one of the guys I usually help out. Wrote a letter to the State Supreme Court for him, then one to his attorney. He can neither read nor write. After that I had a little time & put it to good use. Hit the books and gathered a little info on the Disciplinary Board of the PA State Supreme Court. I now have a focal point on that. I will bring Rubenstein up on charges. I am doing this for a couple of reasons:.

1) Apply pressure to him

2)He sees things my way, I drop charges.......Who knows? It's all in the battle strategy...

Wrote up a letter for Gary Asteak. Received a letter from Goodwin. He really didn't say much. I wrote him back & informed him to see to it that the PCRA's are consolidated. Hear me out. After what I have learned over the last couple of weeks I am of the mind that a Laird-Chester joint attack on the capital conviction stand a better chance of obtaining relief than a singular attack.

Also, Goodwin's daughter's class is doing a project on the death penalty & asked if I would answer some questions. So there was another 4 pages! I am writing way too much lately.

The state LDA chapter president Delores Miller knows of my case! Way to go Jacqueline! We must get a move on if we are to get this incorporated into the post-PCRA appeals. Do not worry about whether Goodwin thinks it is anything. If and when we get the evidence together I will insist that it be incorporated. He is obligated to do so. Again we will talk more on our up-coming visit.

However, I must express here how very much I appreciate all of your efforts. It means so very much to me Jacqueline.........

Civil suit against the prison system - Yes! Not only will this aid me, but also the others who suffer. You know, since you have made me aware of certain types of learning disabilities I have noticed the symptoms in others. I would very much like to get involved in the civil suit you mentioned. Not to mention apply it to my criminal case!...........We fight on, my Lady General! I say give me freedom or give me death!

I am flattered at the way you introduced me to Delores Miller. Woman, you're too good to be true. I am afraid I will wake up any minute and all of this will have been only a dream and I will be left to face this battle all alone.

Dr. Raymond Bell, got it. Sounds great! Hope you are able to make contact with him. Will discuss more on visit. Which reminds me, will you be able to write off the expense of travel & lodging for the visits off come income tax time? Assisting w/ ADD, being a L.D. Advocate of mine? Do you need official documentation of any kind?

Agree 100% - what you have come up with can do nothing but help. If we get Dr. Bell we have our "expert". And woman, experts are our "big guns". They shoot holes through the prosecution. We go in w/ guns blazing, no holds barred, taking no prisoners!

I am very sorry to hear that you sat by the phone waiting for my call. I tried twice and it would not go through. I very much wanted to talk to you. You are more special to me than you realize. If things work out, I fully intend to show you just how special you truly are to me. That is, if you wish for such......

Now the message I received from you while I was in Bucks County was this:

Counselor: "Do you know a Jacqueline Beckel?"

Me: "Yes"

Counselor: "She wants you to call her. Something about a witness."

Me: "OK. Thank you."

You are 100% correct. Guards and staff will attempt to sabotage anyone assisting a prisoner with their case. Not all staff, but you will run into "the wall". This is not a nice place. A lot of assholes work here, Jacqueline. Don't let such discourage you. When dealing with anyone, always get their name, note the time. I have noticed that this tends to have a positive effect on some.

You think it's infuriating to only get one 10 minute call per week? Take a guess at what the official policy for this place is for us? Two telephone calls per month! Sometimes this can be manipulated, though. When I was at Huntingdon, it was one 10 minute phone call per month! Disgusting treatment.

Your point on not allowing the prison system to interfere w/ due process is a good one. I agree w/ it. No one should be denied due process. It is a fundamental right guaranteed by the US Constitution. However, I will take it one step further and say that no one, whether prison employee, Joe Shmoe, or powerful district attorney, should interfere w/ a person's due process. Every American is entitled to "Equal Protection Under the Law" ~ 14th Amendment. No one should be allowed to subvert those rights....

Told Harriet you have grown to love me, did you? I am well aware that you are my Lady General, my LD Advocate. And as such, I respect and admire you. Those are only two of your many good qualities. I am also well aware that you are a woman. You possess warmth, a caring spirit, a heart that beats love. Your beauty is like that of the sun rising over a field of wild flowers moistened w/ the morning dew. I am well aware of your femininity and long o reach out to you, my Love......I pray for a change, I pray for a chance. For I know that given the chance I will see you smile evermore. I know, I know, just call me Mr. Cornball. But I tell you true, my love runs deep.....We have grown, Jacqueline. It is good to hear you saying all of this. It is very good.....

Before I came to prison and saw how the capital punishment system truly worked, I too favored the death penalty. But the system is so abused and twisted, not to mention my now spiritual and moral convictions, that I can no longer support capital punishment.

Hey, it is getting late and we should be seeing one another tomorrow. I will wrap this one up for now. You are good people, Jacqueline. I thank God that I know you. Thank you for caring, for being there. I love you, Jacqueline S. Beckel.

Rick

PS. I look like crap without my clothes on. Want to help me get into shape? 'Nite, woman!

R.

PPS. Where are the pics you spoke of?

R.

Regardless of what you might think of the inmates in our prison system, there is an inconvenient truth: many who were convicted of a crime and sent to prison were denied a fair trial.

Many have been effectively denied their US Constitutional right to due process and representation. Our system is made up of people, and it is flawed because it was derived by people and run by people. And people, however unintentionally, screw up. To balance this, it is particularly important that prisoners – especially those on death row who have active appeals – should be able to maintain timely communication with their legal advocates, families, and friends whose assistance with producing appeals information and documents is vital. This is compelling in cases like that of Karl Chambers, the illiterate inmate that Rick – in spite of his own limited education – was trying to help. It is a sad state of affairs when an illiterate and destitute prisoner on death row has only a fellow death row inmate with limited education to rely on for help in filing complicated legal motions in the appellate courts.

That illiterate inmate Rick referred to in his letter was Karl Chambers of York County, PA. He had no family to help him and he could not read or write, not even his own name. A handicapped and indigent man who is on death row should not have his only means of communicating with his court-appointed appellate lawyer restricted by denial of reasonable use of the telephone to facilitate his ability to participate in his defense. For someone who is totally illiterate, talking is their *only* means of communication with others. In restricting access to a prison telephone beyond what anyone would deem reasonable, an illiterate in prison possibly facing execution is effectively being denied equal protection and due process under the law. This is clearly discrimination based upon literacy skills and, as a guaranteed right under the 14th Amendment of the US Constitution, it is not a privilege reserved for a chosen few.

Karl Chambers was convicted and sentenced to die for the beating death of a 70 year old woman on a railroad bridge in 1987. Four years later, the PA Supreme Court threw out his death sentence because the District Attorney, H. Stanley Rebert, quoted the bible in his summation to the jury: "Karl Chambers has taken a life. As the bible says, *'And the murderer shall be put to death'.* " The higher court ruled that the biblical comments suggested that an independent source of law exists for imposing the death penalty. However, a new jury re-convicted and re-sentenced Karl Chambers to death again in 1994. While Karl Chambers was convicted of a terrible and inexcusable crime, the fact remains that he is illiterate and poor enough to cause one to think "but what if he was innocent?". Lack of ability to communicate properly with legal counsel would leave a wrongfully imprisoned person with almost no hope whatsoever that such an error would be corrected before it was too late and they were executed. This sort of thing raises even more questions about capital punishment. Such as the thought that perhaps Bruno Richard Hauptmann was wrongfully convicted and executed despite possibly being innocent.

Bruno Richard Hauptmann was convicted in what historians call the "crime of the century", the kidnapping of the Lindbergh baby. Charles Lindbergh was the golden boy, the adventurer and idol of 1920's Americana for his solo flight across the Atlantic. The young aviator married Anne Morrow, an heiress with unimaginable wealth, and the nation rejoiced. Then on the night of March 1st, 1932 their twenty month old son, Charles Augustus Lindbergh, Jr. was kidnapped and later found dead and hastily buried in a shallow grave near the Lindbergh's estate in Hopewell, New Jersey. In a trial that generated a whirlwind of national media publicity, Hauptmann was convicted amidst much fanfare.

The evidence against Hauptmann was circumstantial and justice scholars today would cringe at a death sentence handed down under similar trial conditions. There were a number of more likely candidates as plausible culprits than Hauptmann. But

Hauptmann, a working-class German immigrant who had little education, who struggled with mastering the skill of reading and writing basic English, made a convenient scapegoat. To illustrate the pervasiveness of unearned social privilege in shaping American jurisprudence is the fact that the Lindbergh baby kidnapping propelled the reclassification of kidnapping from a misdemeanor to a felony.

An unintentional homicide committed during the course of another felony is automatic grounds for the death penalty in states that uphold capital punishment. For example, if you hold up a convenience store without actually intending to shoot the clerk but the gun accidentally goes off and kills the clerk anyway, the death penalty applies because the killing occurred during the commission of another felony: armed robbery. The felony of armed robbery is the aggravating factor in determining whether the death sentence gets applied in such a killing, however unintentional that killing might have been.

In the Lindbergh baby tragedy, the infant was thought to have been dropped accidentally by the kidnapper as the kidnapper climbed down the ladder from the second story nursery window to the ground below. Had the child victim of this atrocity not been the son of a wealthy and powerful couple deemed as American royalty, it is doubtful that the kidnapping would have prompted an abrupt change in the criminal code raising kidnapping from a misdemeanor to a felony.

Hauptmann maintained his innocence up to the end, even to the very last moment as he was being strapped into the electric chair. He believed that the truth would prevail because he was innocent. The sad truth is that despite the supposed strengths and safeguards of the American legal system, you are only innocent until proven poor. Like so many other condemned prisoners on death row across the nation, Bruno Richard Hauptmann had very little education and was functionally illiterate. He was also from the bottom class of society: a poor German immigrant and an unemployed carpenter who was a renter, not a homeowner. His poor command of the English language in written form may have sealed his fate.

An error in writing words ending in "d" or "t" like the word "boat" was common among many German immigrants just like Hauptmann. Consequently, "boat" was often written as "boad" because of the differences in how the consonants "t" and "d" are treated in German as opposed to English. The ransom note allegedly written by the Lindbergh baby kidnapper said that the baby would be found "on the boad Nelly" – a boat in a nearby dock. When Hauptmann was directed by the investigation to write the word "boat" without further explanation from the police, he wrote "boad" instead. It was a common error any German immigrant that lacked formal schooling could easily make. Hauptmann was executed on April 3rd, 1936.

I cannot help but wonder if the lives of convicted killers like Karl Chambers and Bruno Richard Hauptmann would have turned out better and had different outcomes if they had received the resources and help to overcome their illiteracy and learning problems. Their lives and untimely deaths forced me to look at the unearned social privileges I had, few as they were, that really do make a difference. I did have critical advantages that determined whether or not I could overcome illiteracy and graduate from college. Without them, my life would have been very different.

For starters, at age 22, I had gotten into a skilled trades union and was paid a middle-class wage. Being in the union also ensured fair treatment: I was no longer paid less for doing the same job held by men because I was female. I enjoyed decent pay and after seven years I would have been vested and thus, had the benefit of a retirement pension. Now getting in with the plasterers' union is an unearned social privilege because, simply put, I was at the right place at the right time and the construction trades unions were under fire for not having any women in their ranks at the time. So when Adam Konopka, the business agent for Local #1269 of District Council #71 happened to meander into the historic Americus Hotel in Allentown where I was working on doing restorative plaster work on their ornate ballroom ceiling and solicited me to join the union, it was my lucky day. I had hit pay-dirt.

While I did have to pay the union initiation fee of $400 to get into the union before I could be put to work on union jobs, I had the benefit of having $400 to begin with to enable me to join. Most poor working-class girls who are single and totally on their own don't make enough money in "pink collar" jobs to come up with that kind of capital. Even as a non-union plasterer, I made more money than your garden variety waitress.

Unfortunately I only enjoyed that advantage briefly as my career was abruptly ended due to my car accident. But those two years of earning upwards of $38,000 per year enabled me to buy a modest multi-unit building on the poor side of town with cash on the barrel and no outstanding mortgage debt. So when I became disabled two years later at age 24 and began the long, arduous path toward retraining and an education to hopefully reenter the workforce in a new field, I didn't have to worry about a roof over my head, at least for a while. This meant I had the luxury of time to devote to becoming literate and eventually better educated than most working class people who might have met with similar misfortunes.

The second and extremely most important privilege I had was the benefit of a teacher, a mentor, and a friend in the person of Doc Weiler. Unlike the majority of education professionals who crossed my path in life, Doc Weiler didn't write me off as a stupid loser unworthy of an education because of my dyslexia. He took the extra time to help me succeed academically if and when I needed it...which was quite often. When you have no family and no other means of social support, friends like Doc Weiler are more priceless than all the rubies from all the mines of Madagascar.

The third unearned privilege I had was that I was born intelligent enough to be successful in college in spite of my handicap, albeit with some extra help from Doc. In sum, it was the benefit of having a friend and mentor, and being born with enough mental capacity to be able to learn and think, and having at least a brief although abruptly truncated stint in a high paying blue-collar union job that made the difference in the future path of my life. While I may not have had it great, things certainly could have been far worse. I could have ended up a poor single mother trapped in a cycle of poverty and despair in the welfare system, living in the crime-ridden housing projects with the children's father either skipping state or otherwise being recalcitrant in paying child support, or in prison, or simply shot dead in a drug deal gone sour in an impoverished neighborhood.

There is much to be said for unearned social privileges and luck. Privilege means that the beneficiaries need not explain why society works just fine for them while it fails for others not in the favored group. Privilege of being a member of the favored group confers another meta-privilege: one's philosophy of life need not account for the lives of those not in the favored group. The privileged can be (and usually are) cavalier in their judgments about those less fortunate.

They dismiss the underprivileged as "not working hard enough" or having made "poor choices." Criminals, welfare mothers and some unemployed people have indeed made poor choices and lacked the effort to work hard. But these same bad choices and lack of effort were also made by some "haves" and "have-mores", e.g. privileged people, but without the same consequences. The difference is that for the privileged, any poor choices made do not usually constitute lifelong punishment. In the cases of O.J. Simpson, Robert Blake, and the DuPont heir the "alleged" poor choice of committing murder was not met with the death penalty. Women with means can discreetly terminate an unplanned pregnancy. Criminal charges get tossed out, criminal records get expunged, and even abortions can be obtained so your future is not permanently ruined by poor choices you might have made; but this only holds true when you are one of the privileged, one of those who has plenty of money.

Unfortunately, those who have the most privileges and good fortune often fail to recognize the unfair advantages that they have over others. They don't realize that their winnings and social prizes come at a price: the losses suffered by others. The privileged like to believe they earned their wealth, their material comforts and their success. And to a certain degree, some may have. Not all affluent people were handed an Ivy League degree, a trust fund and an estate home. Some, albeit very few, came up through the ranks. However, they usually hailed from the middle-class, rarely from the working-class, and almost definitely not from the very bottom.

Henry Ford took a leap of faith and a lot of risk with revolutionizing the mass-produced automobile. But he also had luck on his side. The same could be said for Bill Gates and Colonel Sanders. But many other industrious and enterprising people never see any monetary reward or credit for their innovations and hard work. They come up with brilliant ideas, but because they don't have tens of thousands of dollars, no patent lawyer gives them the time of day. So they turn to the only other option available to them: they go to firms that promise patent protection for inventions and aid in getting money from manufacturers for their ideas. Instead, many of these firms rip them off with extraneous "fees" without securing a patent while simultaneously giving their ideas away to the big guns at trade shows and international manufacturers' symposiums. Huge manufacturing corporations wield enough weight and wealth to get patents which cost upwards of $12,000 or more and often take years to obtain, even with knowing the right people – the tinkerer of modest means and humble social standing operating out of his basement or garage does not have this luxury.

The ones who get filthy rich because they repeatedly steal and unjustly benefit from others' ideas and efforts are almost never seen among the ranks of prison populations. But the low-income woman who passes a bad check so she doesn't get evicted and the frustrated poor man who robs a convenience store are the ones that end up doing hard time. What about those not fortunate enough to have the IQ to succeed in school or in getting a decent job in our new high tech and global economy? Is it their fault that they couldn't make their own way in a world where labor laws rarely protect them from inhumane working conditions? Are they really undeserving of the civil rights which are supposed to level the playing field? Doesn't their hard work merit at least a minimum wage that would allow a person to live a decent life?

There is a big difference between starting out on third base than from hitting a triple when called up to bat. According to the Pennsylvania Prison Society and Amnesty International, the percentage of people incarcerated at any given time is 3.2% of the US population, and 98% of them are from the bottom socioeconomic rungs of society: the working-class and the poor, those with the least resources and least amount of hope for ever getting a chance because of the lack of unearned privileges so many middle and upper class people take for granted as being instrumental in one's life chances.

I thought about the various facets and factors in my own life and about earned vs. unearned privileges while driving west on I-76 across state to Pittsburgh for my second visit with Rick. This time I would be staying at a guest house belonging to one of the prisoner aid societies. A very caring and decent man, Michael Clate, owned the home and was a volunteer with the prisoners' aid society. It was a huge Victorian brick home nestled in one of Pittsburgh's more affluent neighborhoods, Point Breeze. The fee was a very affordable $10 per night. During my entire seven hour drive to Pittsburgh, the entire state of PA was deluged with heavy rainfall. The only reprieve from the driving rain that beat on my windshield was when the winding Interstate went through the series of tunnels in the Allegheny Mountains. By the time I reached the guest house – Friends House I believe it was called – I was dead tired and fell asleep over the plate of food his live-in partner placed before me at the table. It had been a long drive through relentless rain under endlessly dark and stormy skies.

I was awakened by the gentle nudge of a woman dressed in similar garb to that worn by the Old Order Amish. She asked me if I was okay and if I would like some tea or coffee. She said she and her husband often came down from the Canadian Bruderhof community to help Michael Clate and his friend run the guest house for those visiting their friends and loved ones incarcerated at SCI-Pitt. Instead of a white or black prayer cap, she sported a bright blue headscarf.

Like the Amish, the Bruderhof embrace the plain lifestyle of an agricultural commune. Like the Amish and Mennonites, the Bruderhof are pacifists who are opposed to war and the death penalty. My awakener and her husband were fascinating and interesting people who told me about their Bruderhof community and how they lived. One thing that really sticks out in my memory is that the Bruderhof also are very openly welcoming to black members! That sets them apart from the Amish and Mennonites.

The woman told me her husband would be driving a shuttle for any guests needing transportation to and from the prison. I didn't need the shuttle as I had my own car but I was so interested in these new and strange people whom I had previously known nothing about that I was quite tempted to say yes just so I could get to know them and learn more about them. But I could not do so in clear conscience because I had a car and it would be unfair for me to take up a seat on the shuttle that some poor prisoner's wife without a car might need. I told this kind Christian woman about the prison environment for visitors, about desperately poor single mothers being denied their visits over the selectively enforced dress code and the lack of $10 to rent a locker at the prison.

The Bruderhof woman nodded and told me how she herself had been humiliated by male prison guards during one of her volunteer prison outreach activities. She chalked it up as the guards just needing to get right with God. I opined that they needed to get right with a good shrink and get put on some ass-kicking medication to readjust their serotonin levels, as well as their attitudes. She hardly fit the stereotype of the sort of female whose deportment would invite any sort of improper harassment from these male prison guards. The fact that she had been subjected to the indignity of a full body cavity search angered me. There truly was no justice. Yet she was so forgiving of the pompous jerks who subjected her to that humiliating treatment, just because they could. I could never be as forgiving of such degradation. Forgive and forget are two f-words that are alien to my working vocabulary.

The next morning, I drove to the prison and began the long processing ritual once more. While waiting for my number to be called, my mind wandered. I watched the guards as they went about their routine job of treating the visitors like cattle. How could they possibly find any real fulfillment in doing their jobs? My thoughts drifted towards the guards who work on the prison's death row. I wondered which one injected the poison cocktail into doomed men's arms on the execution gurney. Or was it a member of the medical community, that humanitarian society of healers of the sick? I wondered if it was a doctor or nurse who administered the lethal injection as Susan Sarandon asked when playing Sister Helen Prejean in the movie *"Dead Man Walking"*.

What kind of people does the state hire to end the lives of others? Where do these people hail from who aspire to be executioners for hire? Are they like the Nazi guards of Hitler's death camps, average working men of middle-class origin who view their task as nothing more than a job with a better-than-average paycheck, the security of health benefits and a pension from the state? Are they like the Klaus Barbies and Adolph Eichmanns who justify doing what they do by rationalizing it as ridding society of its *Untermenchen*, its sub-humans, its lives unworthy of life? Do they mollify their consciences with the creature comforts their wages buy while telling themselves they are only doing their job and ridding society of vermin, of monsters?

And what about the guards assigned to the "strap-down team" - the crew whose duty it is to immobilize and secure the doomed prisoner to the state's sanctioned instrument of death? Where do such people come from and how similar are they mentally to those whom they execute? In exchange for what? A paycheck? Are they any better than the convicted murderers they execute? Many murderers in prison are disenfranchised men who have lashed out in frustration at society and have killed. While some coldly calculated their deeds like the Zodiac, Jeffery Dahmer and Ted Bundy, the majority of murderers have not; they snapped in a moment of rage, passion or irrationality killing one person in the space of an unrecoverable moment.

Some feel remorse for their deeds and others do not. Their crimes are terrible and they end up on death row. But prison employees who willingly participate in executing condemned death row inmates are making a conscious and rational choice to be instruments of the state in ending human lives. In fact, they are worse than many whom they execute because they take human lives repeatedly, for a paycheck.

America definitely has a culture of killing. It is glorified in our media and to some extent, by the fact that we kill in our justice system: capital punishment. Not surprisingly, European countries have refused to cooperate with extradition requests from the United States for that reason: they no longer have the death penalty and view the practice as a universal human rights violation. It is America's undesirable image of a barbaric nation due to having the death penalty that allowed hippie-turned-killer Ira Einhorn to evade justice for over 20 years, aided by a lack of European extradition cooperation.

Ira Einhorn had a history of being abusive towards women. Several years before his notorious murder of girlfriend Holly Maddux, he had strangled two former female associates and had smashed a Coke bottle over the head of one of those women. Ira Einhorn, an anti-war and environmentalist guru from Philadelphia, murdered his estranged lover Holly Maddux on September 9th, 1977. He stuffed her body in a steamer trunk which he kept padlocked in a closet in his Powelton Village apartment in the University City area of Philadelphia. He was granted bail which some of his wealthy supporters raised for him. He fled to Europe while free on bail and eventually settled into a life of comfort and leisure in France under the alias Eugene Mallon with his new flame and wife Anika Flodin. He lived a relatively privileged life while on the lam for 20 years in Europe. It was only upon a guarantee from the US Government that Einhorn would not be tried for capital murder that the French government agreed to cooperate with the extradition and send Ira Einhorn back to the United States. Ira Einhorn was retried by Philadelphia DA Lynne Abraham in 2002 and sentenced to life without parole. He is currently serving his sentence in Houtzdale Prison.

Excluding the serial murderer, the only difference between those participating in carrying out executions - state sanctioned murder - and the convicted killers condemned by law to die, is that executioners and the guards on the "strap-down team" make careers out of taking human lives, committing murder. No matter how you sugar coat it, taking someone's life -self-defense excepted - is murder. Robert G. Elliott, the executioner who pulled the switch of the electric chair in the execution of prisoners such as Ruth Snyder and Richard Bruno Hauptmann, was not too troubled by how he made his living: he did it for over thirty years.

What a bunch of monsters, I thought to myself as I watched the guards from SCI-Pitt's death row escort Rick to an empty seat behind the bullet-proof glass window. I would even take it a step further and compare them to Mafia hit men - button men or soldiers - who murder at the command of their superiors in the underworld, their *Caporegimes* like Pete Clemenza and Salvatore Tessio in Mario Puzo's famed book *The Godfather*. Unlike the majority of prison guards, at least Clemenza and Tessio were actually likeable.

My thoughts and opinions of executioners and death row guards retreated back into my subconscious and were replaced with thoughts on this visit with Rick Laird. Escorted to the window by another guard, I sat down and looked at Rick through the glass. I was discouraged at what I saw: his shoulder-length chestnut locks were gone! The prison barber, a trustee, had cut his hair short.

Rick beamed upon seeing me. He excitedly told me about three letters he wrote that he asked me to type for him and remail since they were of a formal nature. They were en route to me via US Mail. I would probably come home to find them on the floor in the pile of mail delivered through my mail slot. The first one he'd sent was a copy of one he wanted me to type and mail to Judge Beister who would hear the appeal at the superior court level. I thought this was a conflict of interest given that Judge Beister was the very same trial judge who presided over the original trial in 1988 in the county court of common pleas of Bucks County. I didn't want to deflate Rick's hopes, so I kept my suspicions to myself and agreed to type the handwritten letter to Judge Beister for him. The second letter was to Attorney Robert Dunham, begging for help in taking up his case on appeal. The third was to Dr. Silverman. I told Rick that it would be no problem for me to type all three letters for him and mail them. It seemed like such a small favor to do for someone with limited postage allotments and no computer or typewriter, and sometimes not even any paper.

The rest of the visit was small talk. He told me how before he ended up in jail for the very first time for drug possession charges that he constantly was cheated by out of wages by employers for small carpentry jobs that he did. He would put in an honest day's work only to get stiffed, and every dollar he got cheated out of was a dollar he didn't have to keep the electric from being shut off, or for the mandatory auto insurance he needed to drive his car to work. Public transportation was not an option for him because he worked in construction and handyman jobs. His early experiences of being ripped off and cheated out of wages reminded me of my own experiences with that same sort of thing.

Before I got into the union at age 22, I often had to chase down the non-union contractors who hired me in order to get my paychecks. I'd had to do this while also having to worry about coming home to my ghetto apartment to find an eviction notice on my door for nonpayment of rent because I didn't get paid and thus couldn't pay the landlord. Being gypped out of earned and justly deserved wages was something I experienced since my very first job of delivering newspapers…and what recourse does some poor kid have who is not covered by any labor laws when they are hired as an "independent contractor?" Adding insult to injury, whenever a customer failed to pay their newspaper bills, the carrier's sub-minimum wage pay was docked by the news company.

I told Rick that when I had a paper route at age thirteen, the newspaper docked the carrier's pay whenever unscrupulous customers on the paper route failed to pay the bill for their delivered papers. Not to mention that I, as the carrier, had to get up at 4:00 AM in all sorts of weather and lug around a heavy satchel of newspapers for the course of the assigned route. Paper carriers get paid as independent contractors, meaning they are not covered under workers comp and are not eligible for any sort of unemployment benefits. No credits are paid into social security for future old age benefits, either. If you are working as a paper carrier and you fall and break your leg on someone's icy walkway, too bad, you're screwed. Paper carriers were paid less than the minimum wage because in theory, we were supposed to get tips from the customers. But the number of customers who gave any tips at all could be counted on one hand. And I had one of the bigger routes in the more affluent part of the city, the side of town where the supposedly "nicer" people live. Doctors, lawyers, and large company executives comprised the majority of newspaper customers on my route.

It was a very early first-hand experience with economic injustice: doing a job that is unpleasant and thankless, and then not being paid fairly for my time and trouble. After all, I was just some poor dumb kid they could push around who probably didn't need the money anyway and if I didn't like working under those conditions, then it was all my own fault for "choosing to work" in that job. It didn't matter that I was only a thirteen year old kid and that I was on my own. It didn't matter that I desperately needed every nickel just to pay rent and eat. But even if I was only working for "pin money", it is hardly justifiable to stiff someone who works with the reasonable expectation of getting paid for doing their job. If those greedy adults wanted to teach the poor kid who delivered their newspapers a lesson, the only lesson I learned was resentment.

Ironically, it was always those who lived in huge houses in the nice part of town who were the worst when it came to tipping and when it came to simply paying for their newspapers. I remembered many a dark, dreary winter morning where I trudged through snow and traversed icy sidewalks with the risk of falling and getting hurt in order to get the papers delivered. I guess this "better class" of people who caused my pay to be docked when they didn't pay their bill and who never gave me one red cent in tips thought that the Good Newspaper Fairy provided this service for them out of kindness so they could leisurely come down from their warm beds in their slippers on cold snowy mornings to a nice dry newspaper inside their front door. Being one of the privileged people must be nice!

But let a poor person try to get out of paying a bill for anything and see what happens. I was no stranger to social and economic injustice. The very first pay I was docked for newspaper customers who decided not to pay their bill shaped my ideals about social justice. In sum, I do not need to draw it out in crayon why I take exception to those who are privileged and chant the mantra "anyone can make it in this country if they work hard enough." How many of them ever had to work in some thankless low-paying job under risk of on-the-job injury without even the benefit of workers comp, only to not get paid anything?

Apparently, being taken advantage of by unscrupulous employers and the inconsiderate public at large was something Rick Laird and I had in common. No wonder he turned to the more lucrative "job" of selling meth – "speed" – before he was eighteen years old! Of course, it was his chosen path to the criminal lifestyle that etched his future for him and ultimately led him down that path to death row. Regardless of the fact that turning to petty drug-selling was a poor choice, one cannot fail to see how slanted the system is against those who have the least power in society. Poor people who cannot pay their utilities and turn to pirating their utility services face the consequence of steep fines, court-ordered restitution and jail time. Yet it is not criminal for employers or the public at large to cheat the poor commissions-only paid salesperson, the newspaper carrier, the waitress or the beautician who give of their time providing a service. Why is robbing the poor of their wages earned and deserved for giving their time by working somehow perfectly acceptable while pirating electric or gas services is classified as "theft of services," a criminal offense? Stealing is stealing, right?

Apparently, when you're just a lowly newspaper carrier or handyman who gets exploited, someone who gets robbed by greedy people engaging in the theft of your services by not paying you after you've worked and provided them with a service, it doesn't matter. But if you are the CEO of a utility company, you can mold and shape the laws so that you can always be assured of getting yours – and you can count on the strong, heavy-handed arm of the law and the court system to make sure of it. The system, without a shadow of doubt, works just fine for you. If it does not work for the nameless, faceless and countless "others", it must somehow be entirely their own fault while all is fine in your over-privileged little world. In the words of Richard Bruno Hauptmann, *" Little men, little pieces of paper, little scraps of wood."*

Rick was fascinated by my wealth of knowledge of true crime cases. Prior to this visit, he had never heard about the Lindbergh baby kidnapping or Richard Bruno Hauptmann. Since I had two copies of the book about the Lindbergh baby, I offered to mail him a copy. He graciously declined my offer. Reading required the ability to keep his attention focused. Having extreme ADHD, this was a very difficult task which often left him fatigued. He needed to save his "focus reserve" for reading what mattered most: legal correspondence and books in the prison's law library for use in helping himself with his own case. I was not offended and this was completely understandable.

At roughly 2:30 PM, a burly, red-headed guard with chewing tobacco stains on his teeth came over to where I was seated. "Visit's up", he growled, leering at me. Trying not to be argumentative with this guard who obviously was on a power trip, I politely said, "I'm sorry. In the posted prison visitation rules, it states that visits are from 9:00 AM till 3:00 PM every day. Is something wrong?"

"Lady, are you givin' me a hard time?" the surly guard barked at me. He clearly wanted to pick a fight just to have an excuse to disrupt the visit and ultimately penalize Rick by depriving him of any potential future visits from me. I have since learned that this was a tactic often employed by guards on other prisoners' visitors, especially female visitors. Even without that knowledge I realized this was just a chauvinist ego power-play. Although I sucked it up and took it, every fiber of my soul wanted to put this macho egotistical mental midget in his place.

But I knew I would have to deal with this shmuck later. Now was not the time, nor the place. Since I was in no position to gain by making it obvious that I was looking for a badge and a name, I failed to get this guard's identity. I just meekly responded like a well-brought up lady with impeccable manners: "No sir. But I am a bit confused. Maybe you can help me". I continued, smiling, "You see, I do not understand why the prison would post something different in their visitation rules booklet because we visitors must make travel plans for coming to the facility based on this schedule." Completely disarmed by my meek, properly behaved lady-like routine, he softened. "It usually is, ma'am but today we have to do a routine cell search. I'm sorry for the confusion." I complied and said my goodbyes to Rick. The guard escorted me from the visitation area to the waiting area where the lockers were. He obviously felt the need to justify his behavior and began talking to me in a much more polite tone than he had taken a few minutes prior.

"I don't know who you are, but you seem like a nice lady. What are you doing visiting that scum? You know he's on death row, right? I mean, I know it's probably none of my business." he smiled sheepishly, showing rows of yellowish-brown teeth. I answered him politely but coolly, "You're right. It is none of your business. However, I will tell you anyway. I am with the Learning Disabilities Association of PA, the Lehigh Valley chapter. I am one of his advocates. Thank you for your concern, Mr.? I'm sorry, but I didn't get your name?"

"Mr. Johnson. My name is Mr. Johnson. Again, I apologize for the confusion, ma'am."

On my way out to the parking lot, I chuckled to myself. For my stellar performance of oh-so-proper decorum, I felt I should be nominated for an Academy Award. Everyone who knows me personally knows that I am not one to take any form of personal abuse, verbal or otherwise. I am nobody's doormat. But I won and I knew it. I got that guard's name and badge number and once home, I would be writing a strongly worded letter to my state representative over the behavior of employees of the PA Department of Corrections (PA DOC), although I seriously doubted that it would do any good. Nobody cares about the lowest of the low, or those who try to help them. They don't care about the women and children in these inmates' families, either. They aren't worth even a thought: guilt by association.

A few days after returning home, I got the letters Rick had mentioned during my visit. Along with these letters was the most beautiful card I had ever gotten from anyone. It was glossy-covered with a picture of one lone lovely huge pink rose on the front. It read "***Without you...***" on the front. Opening it up, it said "***...is a lonely place to be.***" Rick also wrote a message with it:

Jacqueline *April 18th, 1996*

Just a note to say hello. I have not heard from you since our visit. Received an old letter w/ today's mail dated 3/31/96 & 4/2/96. Hope you made it home okay? No, you're not plain looking. I think you are one very beautiful woman.

Also, you mentioned when we saw one another that you had a paper route when you were a girl. That just makes you all the more special to me. You have both inner and outer beauty and your strength, intestinal fortitude are to be admired. You're quite a woman, Jacqueline.

Love,

Rick

Out of six billion people on the planet, roughly 48% whom are male, no one – and I do mean no one – ever before told me once that I deserved to be admired for my inner strength and intestinal fortitude. All my life up until that point, I had been dismissed, ignored and rejected.

I was not one of the privileged, one of society's "winners", one of the "success stories." My needs, feelings, hopes and aspirations were always trivialized as somehow less important than everyone else's. One person, one man – a man slated to die for committing a murder – was the only human being who had ever given me this kind of recognition. He saw me as someone special, someone with admirable qualities that made me a worthy and deserving person.

Privileged males whose paths crossed mine in daily life looked at me and only saw poor white trash. Any effort I made to improve my lot in life despite having the whole deck stacked against my favor meant nothing. I was simply expected to try harder, work harder, make smarter choices. Although I have yet to meet anyone who can honestly tell me to my face that I have not tried hard enough, worked hard enough and made choices that were often choiceless choices – for lack of a better term since I often had no choices at all. Instead I was dismissed as a member of the lower class, as poor white trash from the ghetto: never really belonging, never quite fitting in, never good enough no matter how hard I tried. I could have discovered the cure for cancer and it would not have mattered. Someone else with more power, more money, and more social privilege would have stolen the credit for it anyway.

My white skin might not get me pulled over at random for traffic stops and might be preferred by elite university admissions boards, but if I can't afford the tuition it's a moot point. White privilege was definitely a bust for me. Class privilege enjoyed by "normal" whites (normal meaning upper-middle class, and usually male) had taken much more away from me than white privilege ever bestowed upon me. White privilege is not always a good deal. For me, it was hardly what you would consider a bargain.

Poor whites are vulnerable to class assumptions by everybody else. We are assumed to be lazy, emotionally demonstrative, uneducated, immoral, and sexually perverse. If you doubt this, consider that only in red-neck jokes is the topic of incest the flavor maxim of the "humor". We are criticized for being "unattractive, smokers, fat and missing teeth" because of being "too stupid" to take better care of themselves – not because of the real reason which is lack of access to good health and dental care, and the inability to afford the fees to join fitness clubs. In trying to improve ourselves with college educations obtained at unaffordable tuition prices on student loans, we find that when we graduate and try to get our slice of the pie to go from Poor White Trash to White Middle Class that we also better lose our accents and know which utensils to use in the right order at business luncheons if we are "serious" about getting the job or promotion.

But what about those of us poor whites who couldn't even begin to think about competing for the decent paying jobs which require a college degree just to enter the race in the first place? If we cannot go to college because we either can't afford it or if we simply can't handle the rigors of academia while working two or three low paying jobs, then our inability to get anyplace in life is somehow all our own fault for not being smart enough. We are an embarrassment to our fellow whites who are middle class and affluent. And if you are white and Jewish but poor, you simply don't exist except in the figment of some writer's imagination, in plays or movies like *Fiddler on the Roof.*

I could understand why poor white males like Richard Laird, Frank Chester, Martin Appel and Karl Chambers end up lashing out violently at society after years of being marginalized because they simply couldn't succeed academically and fit in anyplace. When you are put down often enough and rejected often enough, your life becomes a self-fulfilling prophesy because you were no good after all anyway. The rules are always clear as mud. And as soon as you think you've got a handle on the rules and know how to play the game, someone else with more status than you changes the rules in mid-stream…and it is never to your advantage.

Back then, I naively believed that with a college degree in a "real" discipline I would be marketable, even though I was in my thirties and lacked a stable work history. I would be worth something and the privileged ones with higher social status and power of choosing me for a job would judge me solely on my merits, on my talents, and on my proven track record of seeing difficult tasks through to completion. Boy did I call that one wrong! I just didn't know it yet.

Settling in at my computer desk, I proceeded to put some of my talent to work after reading Rick's April 20th & 23rd letters. Apparently, the guards or other employees of the prison system don't just screw over prisoners, their families and friends with sabotaged visits and inmate telephone calls, they also steal the inmates' mail after rifling through every letter…all justified by "security purposes." I discovered that part of a letter pack I sent via overnight mail to Rick never made it to his cell when Rick mentioned during a phone call that he did not get some of the documents that were in the letter pack I had sent. I began typing, editing and proof-reading Rick's letters to the judge, the prosecution's psychiatrist Dr. Silverman, and Attorney Dunham from the Defenders Association. All letters were sent back to Rick and mailed out by Rick from SCI-Pitt. Copies of those letters follow on the next several pages.

Jacqueline: *April 20th, 1996*

Hello. Relaxing and watching the sequel to one of your favorite movies. Mannequin 2 is on. Wish you and I were watching it together.

Received an overnight piece of mail from you yesterday. On the envelope you listed as enclosed two 7 page letters, 8 photos and two re-done legal typed letters. However there were no 7 page letters. Did you enclose them or did you forget? I received the typed legal letters but no other letters.

I tried to call you today. I asked this unit's lieutenant. No go. Sucks 'cause I really wanted to talk with you.

Thank you for typing those letters. My photocopy of Issue # 5 of my pro-se brief is still not back yet. When it does come in, I will file the charges against DA Rubenstein.

News items from this place: One of the guys had a visit today. When he came back, he informed us that we are now only permitted 1 visit every 7 days. There has been no official notice on this yet. But this is an assinine procedure the prison is instituting and from now on we must arrange our visits well in advance, and you be sure to call this place first each time before you leave to come out here for a visit to make sure all is well, all is OK. Suppose Harriet just stops in one day, you stop out for a visit a few days later. They will turn you away, see? I will try to notify all the appropriate parties to this new procedure. I also intend to file an official grievance over this new policy.

Oh, and also something is going on with the telephone policy. I don't know what it is yet. I heard something about how they are going to crack down and hold us to two 15 minute phone calls per month. There's a bunch of new rules being enacted. The atmosphere is becoming more and more oppressive. I do not say this to complain. I am saying this to keep you up to date on the situation from my end.

Thank you very much for the photos, the one of you and the ones of Centralia and the Blue Mountains, the Poconos. You look gorgeous in a dress! Pure feminine beauty from your head to your shoe-covered toes. Very beautiful, very sexy, very desirable. Jacqueline my love, I am such a lucky man to have you in my life. I love you, very deeply..........Shame you never responded to that one letter I sent. The one where I was writing ya' about all those intimate things. I wouldn't mind writing ya' now and then, getting a little hot & kinky, but if it does nothing for ya'........I'm going to wrap this one up . Before I close, how was your day? What's news? Make an appointment to get those teeth taken care of? If not, please do so.

Rick

Jacqueline: *April 23rd, 1996*

Hello. I received an interesting letter from Dr. Silverman today. I believe it is in response to my official request of Goodwin to help me with the ADHD situation, although Silverman did not say so.

Anyway, find enclosed my response. You will note that I left the door wide open for you to step in and break it all down for Silverman. Here is his telephone: (814) 943-5219.

Silverman may step in and officially document my ADHD. He may also be able to get me on Ritalin. This is all your department and I am confident that you will go into an in depth discussion on all of this w/ him. Other than that, no more news from my end, on the case anyway...........

What's new on your end? Oh, I will be speaking w/ my counselor on Thursday and checking into this visit procedure. Will let you know what I find out. Hope work is going well. Everything OK? Hope to hear from you soon, my love.

Rick

The copies of the letters Rick had asked me to re-type and edit for him are on the next couple of pages here. His originals were somewhat less polite and refined, so I took some liberty in polishing them up, although I must honestly say that I don't know how polite I would be to the judge who sentenced me to death row, regardless if I was guilty or innocent. We all tend to be at our worst under bad circumstances and bad circumstances can't get much worse than being in prison on death row.

To The Honorable Edward Beister, Jr.	*Richard Laird*
Bucks County Courthouse	*#AT-0811*
Doylestown, PA 18901	*PO Box 99901*
	Pittsburgh, PA 15233

RE: Commonwealth v. Laird 746/1988 *April 14th, 1996*

Your Honor:

I am writing to inform the court and to express my grave concern and immense displeasure regarding the representation by my court appointed counsel, Michael S. Goodwin, Esq.

Thus far, Attorney Goodwin has failed to effectively litigate meritous issues pertaining to my capital case. Mr. Goodwin has failed, or refused, to investigate several areas of my capital case by which I believe I am able to prove and show just cause for relief at the appellate level. Mr. Goodwin has refused to assist me and an official advocate of mine in obtaining and producing evidence of a medical nature directly relating to me and my case. Such evidence is meritous and must be gathered and incorporated into my PCRA motions.

Mr. Goodwin has refused to accept the lawful and valid assistance and testimony from this advocate and her organization. She is willing to come forth in court and testify to such evidence pertaining to me and has repeatedly assured Mr. Goodwin of her willingness to do so. Her name is Jacqueline S. Beckel.

Your Honor, I further note that on 04/01/1996 t the Evidentiary Hearing, Mr. Goodwin failed to call a witness to testify who was available and this testimony is crucial. I don't know why he would do this and not afford me advanced and reasonable explanation.

Your Honor, I am indigent. I am not an attorney. I have a learning-disability. I only have a 10th grade education. I am being denied the wherewithal to substantiate and argue my case accordingly and my life is at stake. I had to have my original draft to you regarding these valid concerns proof-read and typed by my

LD Advocate in order to present the aforesaid concerns to you in a logical and appropriate manner.

These statements are true and correct to the best of my knowledge and meets my approval for submission to the court for your review. I close in saying that due to my lack of education, legal expertise and resources, I should not be forced to act as my own litigator.

Yet apparently it seems this is the position Mr. Goodwin has put me in by his lack of action on my behalf, including lack of cooperation with those willing to take the stand.

Please respond at your immediate convenience, for as a fair and impartial adjudicator of the law, I pray you to respond and assist accordingly.

Humbly and Respectfully Submitted,

Richard R. Laird

Robert B. Dunham, Esq

437 Chestnut Street

Philadelphia, PA 19106

Richard R. Laird

#AT-0811

PO Box 99901

Pittsburgh, PA 15223

April 15th, 1996

Dear Attorney Dunham,

I am Rick Laird. I am writing you concerning a grave matter at hand. I am an indigent capital prisoner currently housed at SCI Pittsburgh. It is my understanding that my LD Advocate,

Jacqueline Beckel, has been in touch with you concerning problems we are having with my present court-appointed counsel. This attorney, Michael S. Goodwin, has failed to litigate meritous issues on my behalf.

Additionally, Mr. Goodwin has not researched and/or investigated my case as to come up with additional possible issues for my appeal. He has also failed to investigate any aspects of my legal case, past or present. Counsel is also well aware of the fact that I suffer from a medical condition known as Attention Deficit Hyperactivity Disorder (ADHD). Evidence of this medical problem was not gathered by my trial attorney and used at my capital trial.

My advocate, Miss Jacqueline Beckel, has tried very hard to stress to my present court-appointed counsel the importance and relevance of this medical evidence with regard to my appeal. I wanted said evidence incorporated into my appeal, my PCRA - IneffectiveTrial Counsel, Failure to Gather and Marshal Evidence, et al. All to no avail. Present court-appointed counsel, Mr. Goodwin, also in impromptu notice, dismissed a credible and available witness for the defense at my April 1st Evidentiary Hearing. The witness was present, waiting to be called. Toward the end of said hearing, Mr. Goodwin announced he would not be calling this witness. He did so without informing me in advance or give me a valid compelling reason as to why. I was not afforded the opportunity to ask the witness any questions. My advocate, Jacqueline Beckel, was present and can attest to this.

Finally, Jacqueline has informed me that she was in contact with you and that you have expressed an interest regarding this matter at hand. I know of your reputation and expertise. I ask you to aid me, an indigent capital prisoner. As further note, I have only a 10th grade education. I have a learning disability affecting my ability to speak and write to express myself effectively and in an appropriate manner. This in and of itself has been equally impairing to me as an indifferent court-appointed attorney. My life is at stake. I am not an attorney. I should not be placed in the position of having to represent myself. My LD Advocate, Jacqueline, has been of more help to me than my present court-appointed counsel. I ask for your assistance in these matters I have set forth.

In closing, Jacqueline has assisted with the writing of this letter so I could set forth my aforesaid concerns to you. Again, I appreciate any assistance from you in this matter and I thank you in advance for your time and consideration with the same. Please do respond. My PCRA Hearing is coming up in a couple of months and I am in dire need of the assistance a capital case should have. Again, I thank you for looking into this. I can be contacted at the above address or feel free to contact me through my advocate Jacqueline Beckel at her address and telephone number:

Jacqueline S. Beckel
235 N. Church St.
Allentown, PA 18102 (610)776-1521

I tried once again to get through to someone at the Capital Defenders Association in Philadelphia. They are a stalwart group of dedicated lawyers operating on a shoestring budget. They cannot return calls as quickly as they would often like to, a circumstance which is frustrating for the prisoner on death row who has no idea what's going on, not knowing whether or not they are even going to take his case.

Prisoners tend to lean too much on what little outside support they may have and tend to come off as if they think everyone on the outside can just drop everything to make a full time job out of chasing down attorneys, investigators, medical professionals and everyone else involved in their cases. The problem for those in prisons has only worsened with slashed defense funds and a shrinking pie of help for an increasing population in dire need. Since Ronald Reagan cut legal aid for the poor, even when lives are at stake in death penalty cases, the situation for those in need has gotten even worse. But greed is good and whoever dies with the most toys wins, right? If some of the "ugly, poor people" - to quote hotel heiress Paris Hilton - get stepped on and sacrificed along the way, oh well, too bad for them.

Around my own schedule of trying to handle a college course schedule and a part-time job, my own plate was more than full. I could not always hop right on some task for Rick, whether it was answering all of his letters immediately so he would not think he was being neglected or spending hours on hold on the phone trying to get through to the appropriate people who were better equipped to help him than I was. There was really only so much that I as one person could do, and Rick's impatience and demands on my time were starting to wear my patience to a frazzle. I tried to be sensitive to his feelings as a condemned man on death row where even hope is dead beyond resurrection. I let him know that I had my limitations. I could only do so much and that I had plenty of problems of my own. The worst of it was that while Rick leaned on me, I myself had no one to lean on.

Jacqueline: *April 25th, 1996*

Hello again, Love. Yes, I know you have been working very hard on your end. I do greatly appreciate that, too. You are working harder than anyone else ever has, and as I said before, seeing you so involved and working so hard has motivated me to pick up the pace on my end. I cannot thank you enough.

Your friend Roger Mohr, the intellectual born-again Christian, would change his tune if it was himself in prison, having to endure the conditions. Where is the room for repentance & salvation if one is executed? Roger, as a Christian, should realize that death outside of salvation means eternal punishment. Not one or two lifetimes of punishment, but <u>forever</u>. No true Christian would wish that on a fellow soul. Joe Shmoe is executed tomorrow, the following day a preacher intended to visit & tell him of Jesus & how he too could find salvation. Unfortunately Joe Shmoe never got to hear that. What Christian would deny anyone that? Jesus did not come to heal the well of spirit, but the sick. He hung out with criminals and hookers.

Hold on - mail call, legal. OK, a letter from Goodwin came in. He was not at all happy with the letters I sent. I must call him tomorrow and speak w/ him some more about this. I will say this, apparently my letters got him off his ass & checking into the notes I took. However, I detect all he did was call dear Arthur (Chester's attorney) and ask a bunch of questions.

Now a piece of interesting info: Chester, according to Goodwin, is "seeking two witnesses who allegedly saw me in the act of cutting Milano at the time of the killing." Goodwin also states that Chester has no investigator working on the case. Well now, I have a question: If there is no investigator, then who is looking for these alleged witnesses? The killing was alleged to have happened after 2 AM, in a wooded area (I take it these witnesses, phantoms, had star-light night sight equipment or something), never mind, it is ridiculous. I'll tell ya' this, I am pretty pissed off right now.

Goodwin failed to address my complaints of him, though. Like I am supposed to just forget about why I have lost any confidence I may have had in him. This piece of news about

Chester's trying to dig up 2 witnesses has me giving serious thought to objecting to the consolidation......

I just received my copy of the grievance form back. I am sending out another tonight over the visit policy. Anyway, we are leaving a paper trail over all of this.

Spoke at a public function, "Dead Man Walking". You have been a very busy person! Do you know that in just 14 months, Gov. Tom Ridge has signed 42 death warrants? Wow!

I will try to go to the law library tomorrow to research case law on possible new issues. Have trouble getting time in the law library due to the fact that (1) The Sgt on my unit is an asshole, and; (2) Many guys go to the library, whether they do work is another thing, but if too many sign up, you get the idea. Will let you know how it goes.....

Love,

Rick

Joseph S. Silverman, M.D.

Blair Medical Center, Building B, Suite 203

501 Howard Avenue

Altoona, PA 16601-4888 *April 23rd, 1996*

RE: Commonwealth v. Laird 749/1988

Dr. Silverman:

Received your letter of 4-18-96, thank you. As far as my intentionally withholding information from you during our

September 1994 interview, I do not believe I did anything of the sort. I answered every question posed to me to the best of my ability. However, since our September 1994 interview I have uncovered information pertaining to me which should have been brought up at my capital trial.

I was fortunate enough to meet a person who is a board member with the Lehigh Valley Chapter and non-profit organization known as Learning Disabilities Association. After my initial visit with the aforementioned person I was sent literature on ADD/ADHD. I then proceeded to telephone my mother. I asked my mother if I was a hyperactive child. My mother informed me that yes I was a hyper child.

In fact, when I was in the fourth grade my teacher had called her in for a conference and suggested that I be placed on Ritalin. I then proceeded to review your report and noted where you wrote: "Possible Attention Deficit during childhood and, in fact, during adulthood to some extent as well."

Regards,

Richard R. Laird

A few days after I received Rick's April 25th letter, Rob Dunham from the Defenders Association returned my call. I was elated! He wanted me to come at once and bring every document I had in my possession relating to Rick's case. He gave me driving directions from Allentown to his office in downtown Philadelphia. I checked the clock. It was already 5PM and Philly rush hour traffic was atrocious. It could take as long as 2 hours just to get from one side of Philadelphia to the other in rush hour on the Schuylkill Expressway. The traffic mess extended well up onto the "Blue Route" (I-476), and Allentown was about an hour north of Philly. Rob Dunham assured me he would be in his office most of the night. He was working on an emergency appeal for another capital prisoner and he would probably be at the office until midnight, so if I didn't make it in until 8:00 PM, that would be fine. Packing up the copies of transcripts, the correspondences to Judge Beister, Dr. Silverman and everything else I had into a milk crate, I shot out my front door like a bolt of lightning, jumped in my '87 Hyundai and was off.

It was almost 8 PM by the time I pulled up in front of the Defenders Association's office at 437 Chestnut Street. Bob Dunham's office was on the top floor. Smiling, he greeted me warmly as I got off the elevator, assisting me with my crate of papers. He was a young and very studious-looking sincere man who definitely believed in what he was doing in helping indigent prisoners on death row. He told me he spent many nights sleeping on the couch in his office because he was up until the wee hours of the morning working on cases while having to be in the federal courthouse bright and early, so his night's sleep often consisted of little more than a power nap. His office looked like a paper blizzard had hit it: files from other cases that he and his fellow litigators were working on lay open on the huge cherry conference table.

He showed me some of the work he was doing and we talked about the capriciousness of the death penalty. I told him that although I was not sure whether Rick Laird was guilty as sin or innocent as a baby, I firmly believed he had been denied a fair trial. At this time ADHD and other learning disabilities in general were not considered handicaps, thus not falling under the realm of protection of laws regarding those with disabilities. People had a very hard time understanding how someone who "looks normal" could really be having a serious problem beyond their control. Attorney Dunham, trying to play devil's advocate, grilled me on the merits of diminished capacity claims by reason of ADHD.

In full advocate mode, I stated my premise and conclusion regarding Rick's case. When someone is unaware that they have a learning disability, ADHD and organic brain damage, they do not know what the problem is. They may not even know that they have a problem. They don't know why small amounts of methamphetamine help them to concentrate and remain focused enough to function normally the way most people can without such "aid". Unfortunately, anyone who uses any type of illicit drug is usually automatically judged as having an unforgivable character flaw. Thus, the self-medicating ADHD sufferer often bears the awful burden of struggling in silent shame. They don't know why they can't control their impulsiveness. When lawyers and court psychologists, the educated "experts", know better but fail; it is hardly the handicapped person's fault. One of those who failed Rick miserably was his own trial attorney: by failing to thoroughly investigate his client's background and pursue a diminished capacity claim. Although diminished capacity does not let someone off the hook entirely, it can clearly mean the difference between a sentence of life in prison without the possibility of parole and a sentence of death.

Due to the chemical nature of ADHD's effect on the brain, its sufferers cannot think clearly and connect cause and effect as other people do. If we as a society do not hold guilty the diabetic who, in a state of sugar shock, lashes out against the paramedics trying to help him or her, how then is it reasonable to hold the ADHD person fully responsible for his actions when he lashes out at others without planning to? How can the ADHD sufferer be any less handicapped by his condition than the diabetic, or than the bipolar schizophrenic? The very nature of ADHD makes it next to impossible for its sufferers to handle the same level of frustration that a normal person can because so much effort is required by the ADHD sufferer just to function around the condition in daily life activities. By the time I was done with my presentation, Rob Dunham smiled at me, saying, "Sold!" He liked what I had said and he would take Rick's case!

He asked me if I had eaten before making the drive to Philadelphia. I sheepishly confessed that I had not. I had forgotten in my excitement over hearing from him and learning that he was interested in the case: remembering to eat sort of went out the window. Welcoming me to help him organize and compile all of Rick's case documents, he invited me to share some Chinese take-out that he would call and have delivered.

Rob Dunham and I poured over Rick's trial transcripts between mouthfuls of General Tsao's Chicken, vegetable Mei Fun, egg rolls, and iced tea. He pulled the DSM IV from his book shelf and looked up ADHD and then showed me the comparison of ADHD symptoms with those of Antisocial Personality Disorder. They were similar, yet very different. He told me that while I, as an advocate for those with learning disabilities knew my stuff about ADHD and learning disabilities inside out and backwards, psychologists and psychiatrists who did not receive special training in this field could easily mistake Rick's ADHD for Antisocial Personality Disorder. Rick Laird was written off as a psychopath by Dr. Silverman who examined Rick as a formality for the original trial. So the defense was faced with no possibility for a diminished capacity claim because the inability to feel remorse - which is by definition what a psychopath is - does not count as diminished mental capacity because there is not an inherent lack of intelligence preventing the comprehension of the difference between right and wrong. Psychopaths know the difference between right and wrong but they don't care. I was stunned. I thought these experts with their fancy PhD's would know better!

Before getting involved with this case I never gave the death penalty much thought. Like most Americans, I assumed that extra care was taken to ensure a fair trial when a person's life was at stake. Even if one is guilty of a heinous crime, one is still entitled to a fair trial. And that means one is deserving of adequate representation. It means investigating the defendant's background and it means that if there is cause to argue a case based on diminished capacity, then that avenue must be pursued.

Dunham told me something else that really shocked me. The mentally retarded, even juveniles, have been sentenced to death in this country! He told me that it is next to impossible to get commutation of sentence in a case where a defendant is mentally retarded, even if his IQ is just one stinking point above what the law considers for diminished culpability under the McNaughten Rule – the mental capacity for being able to differentiate between right and wrong. While we must draw the line at some point, it begs the question of the reliability of using an IQ digit in determining definitively that a person has the ability to differentiate between right and wrong. How much more comprehension does someone with an IQ of 56 have versus someone with an IQ of 55? Perhaps we need to re-examine the standards based upon the drawing of that line. When it involves murdering a human being, pursuing a death penalty appeal based on diminished capacity by reason of ADHD was an uphill battle. But it was a battle such as this that Dunham and the others at the Defenders Association were committed to fighting.

Not all lawyers are spoiled rich brats with arrogant condescending attitudes. Some, like Robert Dunham and the rest of his team at the Defenders Association, care about fairness. They care about having a justice system we can believe in: one that works for *everyone* in this nation, not just for the privileged. And they have devoted their entire lives to making a difference for the better, making society better for the least among us; even if it means foregoing higher incomes from more lucrative areas of law practice. They not only make the personal sacrifice of declining the opportunity to earn more money, they are also often the targets of threats from outraged citizens who think those sentenced to death should simply fry – no appeals – nothing. Sometimes a pedestal is the loneliest place in the world: it can be just as lonely at the top as at the bottom.

Chapter 17

"I should have known what fruit would spring from such a seed." ~ Lord Byron

Now that I knew that Rick's case was safely in the hands of the Defenders Association, I had to tell Rick. After getting home, I wrote Rick a very short letter, telling him that Rob Dunham from the Defenders Association took his case and that Rick would be hearing from them. Having been let down repeatedly by others in my life, there were not many people I believed in or trusted. But I trusted Rob Dunham. I trusted him because he was sincere.

The rest of the summer flew by. I had finished with college and would not have to worry about classes until the fall, which meant I had one less thing on my plate. It was starting to get hot and the next thing on the agenda before anything else was getting my air conditioner put in the window. It was too heavy for me to lift by myself and with back problems I couldn't lift it even with help. I had to find someone to do it for me that wouldn't charge me because I had no money to pay. Meanwhile, letters from Rick kept coming. The next thing he wanted was for me to fill out and mail the forms for him to get copies of his birth certificate and social security card. He also enclosed a signed Power of Attorney form granting me the power to get them on his behalf. Why he wanted or needed these items when he was in a 9' x 9' concrete cell for 23 hours each day, I'll never know.

Jacqueline: *May 6th, 1996*

Hello Love. I have a few minutes to write before they come and get me for yard, exercise time. I have been very busy all

morning. Trying to catch up on my correspondences. I was so far behind.

First off, I tried calling Dunham this morning. He was not in but Carol took a message and will relay it to him. I relayed how I will need official notice, how Dunham must move to make appearance on my behalf, etc. She said not to worry, if Dunham said he would take the case he is on it. She was real nice. In case I have not said it, Thank You my Love. You are a true God-send to me. Oh damn! Before I forget. Here is the information for the birth certificate and social security card:

Mother's Maiden Name: Doris Joyce Spielman

Father's name: Richard Roland Laird

My name: Richard Roland Laird, Jr.

Place of birth: Beaufort, South Carolina

My Social Security Number: 209-58-5226

Okay. Let me know how it goes. And again, please do not over-do it. I realize you are one person doing so much as it is and I ask you to relax a bit, ease up a bit so ya' don't stress out or nothing. The only reason I say all of this is because I love you and care. And believe me, I know what it's like to try & over-do it & stress out on all of this stuff............

Got 3 letters ready to go, too. One to the President of the Pittsburgh Paralegal Association asking if there's a course or if she knows of a place that will let an indigent capital prisoner take a paralegal course. One to Duquesne U. & one to Muhlenburg College. All inquiring after paralegal courses for an indigent capital prisoner. I did mention that I am an indigent capital prisoner. Who knows, maybe I'll get lucky and someone will take pity on a poor man and show some charity. Will let you know of the responses, if any.

Me, I want something sweet and juicy to eat. Any suggestions? Since you're not here and I have an orange, I guess that will have to do.

Well, how is work? Anything new happen? How are you feeling, everything OK? Okay I'm going to have to wrap this one up. Hope to hear from you soon.

Love,

Rick

Less than a week later, I was resting with the air conditioner running full blast. I was prone to heat sickness so I rarely left home in the summer, except when I absolutely had to. I was jarred from a sound sleep by the phone ringing. Since I had an unlisted number, I thought it was either Rick calling from prison or the hotel calling to ask me to come in on my day off because of an emergency of some kind. I was not prepared for the angry, screeching woman's voice that came out of the other end of the phone, threatening me and telling me to stay away from Rick! I demanded to know who she thought she was to call and threaten me on my unlisted phone when I did not even know here. She told me her name was JoAnn, that Rick would always be her man and that I should never forget that and just back off or she'd have to come up and kick my ass. *Back off?* I was floored. I left her have it, both barrels. I won't tolerate *anyone* calling me and harassing me, especially if I didn't give them my private number. And I don't take threats against my life and personal safety lightly.

"Let me get this straight. The guy's on death row that you're insanely jealous about. He had a baby and a relationship with another woman at the time he went to prison. His brother gets me involved in helping him with the appeal of his death sentence, then balks at helping me cover any costs, and *you're* gonna call me and threaten me because you think I am somehow having an affair with your man — who hasn't been your man since before he went to prison? I don't fuckin' think so! You come within 50 feet of my house and you'll be picking your teeth out of your shit for a month! Got it? And I don't take a stick to a gunfight!" JoAnn immediately began apologizing.

She told me she was Rick's first wife and had his first two kids. She began crying. Then she abruptly says to someone on her end of the phone that she would be with them to ring up their sale of a puppy in a minute. This was getting good! This woman (and I use that term loosely) not only called me without knowing me and threatened me for no reason, but she did so from her job at some pet store down in Levittown. She explained she was the assistant manager at the pet shop and had to wait on a customer. While doing so, she continued the conversation, "Maybe you are the right one for Rick." She really didn't get it. Either she was on drugs, or crazy, or stupid, or all three.

"Look, I don't know where you're coming up with this crazy stuff about me being 'the right woman for Rick.' I am only involved as an advocate who is helping him with his death sentence appeal. Nothing more. You might be a little grateful and show a little appreciation. No one else stepped up to the plate, not even Mark. The only other people I know of that helped Rick were Harriet Liddington and her husband from the Lighthouse Prison Ministry. Did you call Harriet and threaten her, too? And how the fuck did you get my phone number anyway? Don't call here again. Just go back to whatever hole you crawled out of and leave me alone." I hung up on JoAnn.

Although she never told me how she got my number, I had a pretty good idea who gave it to her. This was before almost everybody had a PC with Internet access in their homes, so getting unlisted phone numbers was not possible unless someone who already had it gave it out. There were only two people on the entire planet who could have given it to JoAnn: Rick Laird or his brother Mark. I doubted that Rick was the one who gave it to her, but anything was possible. Mark on the other hand, worked with me. He also was having a fling with Ginger DeLorenzo that no one else at work was supposed to know about due to the Hilton Hotel's company policy against fraternizing, although their mutual flirting was not very discreet.

Of course while such a rule might be enforced between two non-management employees, there was always a double standard for those in management. Ginger was the assistant human resources manager, she had access to all Hilton employee files, hence had access to personal contact information in my personnel file. Mark getting my number from Ginger was the most likely source. Mark was also in contact with his family, including this former sister-in-law JoAnn. He was not restricted to two phone calls per month, locked up in isolation clear across the state. I stewed over the matter. Some nerve! Of course, I knew that if I confronted Mark about invasively obtaining my phone number and giving it out, he would just deny it. I could not rule Rick out completely, but it was highly unlikely. He had a death sentence to worry about. Why would he, knowing that his ex-wife was unstable, sabotage the only support network on the outside that he had by causing a problem?

I wrote to Rick, mentioning the call from JoAnn but without directly accusing him of giving her my number. I also enclosed with my letter a book on ADHD and how it affects adults if it is left untreated from childhood as well as a newspaper clipping of yet another murder trial where Rick's trial attorney, Ron Elgart, was representing the defendant. Making the same mistakes he made with Rick's case back in 1988, he was reportedly shocked at the outcome of the trial, which went unfavorably for his client. Rick responded with a phone call telling me he would write more on the matter about JoAnn in a follow up letter. He also thanked me for the book and told me that he had given little Ricky, his son, my number. He wanted to let Ricky get some questions answered on ADHD because he might have it too since it tends to be hereditary. That solved the mystery of JoAnn getting my number. If Rick gave my number to his son Ricky, that was how JoAnn got it. Rick also asked me to look into some back disability checks from when he worked at Rogalas' Auto Body Shop in Bensalem. He believed that he was still owed some past monies from work-related injury. The checks would help defray the costs for all the photocopying I did.

While it was admirable that Rick wanted to see about some help for his son, he should never have given out my unlisted home telephone number to an unstable ex-wife. He must have known how she might react. You don't marry someone, father two kids by them, live with them and not know them. Rick also could have given the main contact number for the LDA group which is listed in the Human Services section of the telephone book if his intent really was to see about getting help for Ricky. Part of me wondered if it was simply to stir up trouble for his personal amusement.

Jacqueline: *May 14th, 1996*

Received the package of material you sent. Thank you. Will read book on ADHD and return it as you have requested. In fact, I intend to start reading it this evening.

I read the newspaper clippings that you sent. Clearly Ron Elgart was as shocked as the prosecutor at the jury's decision in that case. Elgart has no business taking on a case of that magnitude. Read the letter, transcript, of your call w/ JoAnn. I appreciate your letting me know of the call & its contents. I truly cannot stand it when things of this nature are kept from me. Anyway, as I noted on our telephone call on 5-13-96, JoAnn is a spaz. It's as simple as that. She is also quite immature as well as insecure w/ herself. Enough of all that.

From your letter and our call you sounded quite ill. I do hope and pray you are feeling much better by the time this letter reaches you.........

I spent a couple of hours this morning working on a couple of issues that have come to mind. First off, I drew a floor plan of Apt# E-4 Ambassador Arms. See, G. Gardner testified that when I came in the apartment early that morning she saw blood on my pants. Well, (1) It was dark in the apartment except for the light of the television, the TV was pointed in her direction - away from me. (2) I was wearing blue jeans.

(3) It was raining out & I just got off a bike.

So I drew up a diagram of the apt. Will probably go over it w/ Dunham when I see him, see if he finds it useful.

Second thing I did was make up a seating chart for the jury. I have no idea why Goodwin didn't do this in the courtroom during the April 1st hearing. Anyway, I drew it up. Had to go through the transcripts to get the exact seating arrangement. What I uncovered was this: Maurizzo had a conversation w/ a fellow juror, a sheriff or tipstaff decided to add their 2 cents worth which is not permissible. Guess who sat next to Maurizzo in the jury box? The one <u>dead</u> juror who could not testify at the hearing. Now, when the *jury was issued their rooms at the hotel, they were issued out in order: Juror # 1 take the first room, juror # 2 etc. If so, then Maurizzo was next door to that dead male juror. Do you see what I'm getting at? Chances are very good that Maurizzo did in fact have the conversation w/ the then alive, now dead juror! Fully intend to go over all this with Dunham when I see him. Will wait until then to do so because of the visual aids I have drawn up.*

Well, let's see. Tonight I intend to watch the Flyers game. They must win or they are out of the play-offs. So I will be watching/listening to the game while I start the book you sent on ADHD. Other than that I have no plans. Wonder what you're up to this evening? Would be real nice if I had an attractive female to join me. Any ideas on who would like to join me in the shower? Well, I guess I will wrap this one up. I miss you terribly.

Love,

Rick

PS. What's the news on the teeth?

<u>R.</u>

I drove down to the auto body shop in Bensalem that Rick had mentioned during our telephone conversation. It was a small family owned business, a real mom & pop shop. I spoke to the proprietor and his reaction was not what I expected! The owner tersely replied that Rick never worked there. His mother had worked there as a bookkeeper back in the early 1980's and was fired for stealing money. While this gentleman, presumably Mr. Rogalas, ranted about Joyce stealing him blind and about her good-for-nothing sons, I remembered the part about Rick's mother having had a criminal record for embezzlement which was mentioned in Lisa DePaulo's article, "*Killing Anthony*" in the

Philadelphia Magazine that Rick had sent me many months ago. This must have been the employer! What kind of a hornet's nest did Rick send me into, here? I had never felt so embarrassed in my entire life. I thought I was helping an indigent death row prisoner get some past workers comp monies that he was legally entitled to! All I could do was apologize profusely to the owner and make a gracious exit.

I fumed the during the entire drive home to Allentown. It is one thing to have made bad choices during a period of youthful indiscretion. It is one thing to steal once, on an impulse, and then own up to the mistake. But to try and get away with it again knowing it is wrong – there is no excuse for that. I was angry that Rick would want me to be a party to what amounted to theft. It was situations like that which makes it hard, if not almost impossible, for those legally entitled to such benefits to be able to collect them. I was angry because he collected workers comp disability checks when he did not deserve them or earn them, and also that he expected me to put myself at risk in helping him fraudulently collect some of these back checks. What really irked me was that Rick did not think about what would happen to his appeal and the outside support he was getting from me had I chosen to help him commit fraud and been caught. Defrauding workers comp is insurance fraud which is a felony in the Commonwealth of Pennsylvania. There was also the matter of principle involved. Workers genuinely in need of workers comp have almost an extraordinarily difficult time collecting.

I remembered when a friend of mine, Blair Lamb, was sent to Lehigh County Prison for failure to make child support payments because he had to wait over six weeks for his first workers comp check for a *legitimate* on-the-job injury. He had fallen off of a roof he was working on and sustained a compound fracture of his right arm. He worked for a non-union roofing contractor for very low pay. After Domestic Relations Court garnished his pay for child support, he had barely enough to afford his rent and food. He got hurt while working, yet he had to fight for the workers comp that was rightfully his.

I wrote Rick and told him of the reception I got at Rogalas's. He responded in a lengthy 8-page letter. I began to regret ever getting involved with this case. I had done what I promised his brother Mark I would do. I had gone the third mile. I did so because I knew how it felt to be an underdog. I did so because I wanted to make a difference for the better, to see some fairness and social justice brought back into the legal system. Thus far, I had been threatened by Rick's hostile ex-wife JoAnn, intimidated during my initial investigation down at the Edgely Inn, harassed by prison guards with the IQ's of houseplants – and all at my own personal expense!

I felt bad that Rick was on death row. I felt bad that he didn't get a fair trial because his trial counsel was ineffective. And I felt bad for Rick's kids. God only knew what they had to endure through all of this! Even though the kids couldn't help it that their father messed up, adults can be downright ignorant and cruel. Other kids can be even worse. I remembered how I was treated as a child being raised by a grandmother instead of a mother and father like everybody else, and the way many adults looked down on me for that and wouldn't let their kids associate with me. I could not begin to imagine how Rick's kids were treated after his arrest and conviction. But when I said I would help, when I made the commitment to do so, aiding and abetting in a fraud scheme was not part of the deal!

I had done what I had promised Mark I would do: I helped Rick get the proper representation on appeal. I had done all the leg-work involved with getting the right people with the power to do something involved. I had photocopied thousands of documents – at my own expense of time and money. I had investigated Mark's claims of Rick being railroaded by an unscrupulous pal, Frank Chester. What I then found was that Rick was not so scrupulous himself. Plus he never, ever, answered my question to him during that very first visit: "Did you kill Anthony Milano?"

The truth was I felt used. I felt humiliated. I felt like I had been made the butt of an ongoing horrible joke that wasn't funny at all. Why, the whole damn family was a bunch of criminals! And I was just a patsy with "sucker" written all over my face. I had gotten a brilliant hardworking legal team at the Defenders Association to take his case, replacing an indifferent court-appointed appellate counsel. I did so because I wanted him to have a fair trial. Most of all, I wanted the truth to come out as to what really happened in the woods that night in 1987.

I wrote Rick a very short and pointed letter simply telling him the disability checks could not be obtained. I was not emotionally up for any debate about it. I apologized to him for not being able to help him along those lines, and told him I understood he was anxious due to his situation. I did not need to draw it out for him in crayon as to why those back-disability checks were a no-go.

I was struggling, living hand-to-mouth because of having to start all over after becoming permanently injured, and doing so with absolutely no support at all except for some occasional tutoring from Doc Weiler. I was trying to better myself and improve my lot in life the right way: trying to get an education that would get me a good job so I wouldn't be desperately poor. I was going to turn twenty-nine in a matter of days. I had community college to finish. Getting my Associates Degree was a milestone, but also just a stepping stone. From there I had to transfer to a state university and work toward my Bachelors Degree. I wanted to have a life, or at least a fair fighting chance to have a life; not a reservation for a cell at Camp Cupcake. Rick was shrewd enough to know without my going into detail that I was disappointed in him for what he asked of me regarding the disability checks. His 8-page letter of May 17th was an attempt to smooth everything over.

Jacqueline: *May 17th, 1996*

Good morning. You have mentioned that this is a very scary time for me. I'll tell you what kind of time it truly is for me. It is a very depressing time, a very frustrating time. The reason for this is that everything is so disorganized. I still haven't made contact w/ Dunham. I have no idea what Goodwin is up to. I hear all sorts of good things that may happen with my case, yet I actually see nothing. It is all very disorganized and that to me is very frustrating & depressing. I now know that I am ADD/ADHD. I am disorganized enough in my own ways. I try very hard to keep everything as organized as possible so that my life runs much smoother. When things outside of my control that affect me & my life are in disorder it makes my life a mess. Do you understand? Lunch is here........

Not to worry. I will not come off like a nut when I finally do get to speak w/ Dunham. I am going to try and call him again today around 1:00, if permitted to do so. I hope to speak w/ him then. Will not let my nerves go to shit, will hang in there. And Jacqueline, thanks for being there for me...

What do you mean by saying, "Got the teeth under control?" Explain yourself better. You're not letting some dentist talk you into those root canals, are you?! Have the problem fixed & fixed correctly!

Now about Rogalas Auto Body shop. This is how it goes. I was not working there. Someone I know was, she had me "on the books" as working there. I got paychecks, etc. When I hurt my ankle, she asked me if I wanted to collect disability checks also. I said yes. So she hooked it all up & I started to receive a check in the mail from disability. Now, I only received a few of those checks because we moved out of the area shortly thereafter & I did not bother to keep up w/ it.

Now contacting Rogalas would get you nowhere! You would have to go through the "disability office". Also, as you have noted, what I was doing was not exactly above board. Disability does not know that, though.

Yes, I was very immature in my relationship with JoAnn. Rest assured, I am much more mature now, was with Kimberly as well as Barbara Anne. It's not much of an excuse, but JoAnn and I were just kids and if she wants to lay 100% of the blame on me, well I will allow her to do so, knowing full & well the truth to that situation.

One thing I will note here, in case I failed to. She brought up how I used to abuse her, physically. This was way back, when we were like 16, 17 yrs old and we fought like cats and dogs, the both of us. I wish for you to know that after that period I no longer physically fought w/ a female, verbally yes, mentally yes, but <u>not</u> physically. Since then I have been slapped, punched, kicked by females. Some in fun and some in anger, but I did not physically retaliate. JoAnn is a basket case, stuck in the past somewhere, I guess. You can take what I said for what it's worth.

OK. I have the copy of the letter and the photocopies of the legal material you sent Dunham. Good job, my Lady General, and thank you again....

<u>Same Day:</u>

Power went out here. I am writing by the light of the window. Power was out for about an hour. Maybe something blew.

Got mail from Goodwin's office. His secretary wrote & sent a copy of the April 1st hearing transcripts. That's it.

Dude who I lent the book on ADHD to sent it back to me already. Said it would take him longer to read it than the time I allotted. He is ordering a copy of his own next month.

I tried to call Dunham at 1:00, 1:45 and 2:00. No go, got an answering machine.

Oh, I also received mail from South Carolina! Dept. of Health & Environmental Control. They sent a form to fill out for a copy of my birth certificate. These guys want $8.00 to search the records; if they find it I will receive one copy. They also have additional services, wallet size birth certificate - $8.00, etc. However I will need to get on the telephone my mother. Need to make certain of her maiden name spelling, etc. Any news on the social security card situation? Anyway my plans are to get 1 certified copy of the birth certificate, my social security card, & 1 copy of the wallet-sized I.D. that I believe will be $16.00.

You know, it would really mean something to me to get all of this together. I don't know, it's hard to explain, I need "order", you see? As I told you once on a visit I would very much like to obtain a valid driver's license. You cannot imagine how very much that would mean to me. May sound a bit silly to you, but it would mean a lot to me. The last time I had a valid driver's license I was 16 yrs old. Back then they issued driver's licenses without photos on them. (Dinosaur days)

I would very much like to talk w/ you. I have no intelligent conversation here, very little....Is all well on your end? Hope to hear from you soon.

Love,

Rick

I couldn't believe it! Rick Laird was on death row in a cell the size of a broom closet. Even if he was successful in getting his sentence reduced to life in prison, there isn't any place he would be able to drive to. Yet he wanted a valid driver's license. This man was unbelievable! In my response I told him (for the third time) that he would have to apply to the US Dept. of Health & Human Services to get his duplicate SSN card and they require a valid photo ID such as a state-issued ID (excluding prison mugshots) or a valid US Passport as proof that you are who you say you are. These rules and procedures exist for a reason: namely to ensure that you - and only you - can get a copy of your social security card. Unless the prison gave out day passes for good behavior (which they do not in PA), I didn't see Rick being able to go in person to the local Social Security Office with a state-issued photo ID to get a duplicate Social Security card, and then travel to the nearest Penn DOT driver licensing center for a road test and license. He was unable to walk unshackled and unattended by a retinue of armed guards from his cell to the shower yet he wanted to make sure he had a driver's license, with nowhere to go and no opportunity to drive! He sure had style.

I wrote that everything else was pretty much the same with me. Final exams, scheduling my Fall '96 & Spring '97 courses around my work schedule at the Hilton, then transferring to a university in Fall '97 and then hopefully I would get my Bachelors Degree eventually. I didn't bother Rick with the details of applying to Drexel for a scholarship, or my time-wasting meetings with my OVR counselor. Why bother? Besides, now that I had done all I could do on my end as a non-lawyer, the rest of his case was in the hands of the attorneys from the Defenders Association.

Rick's reply to my letter came two days later. He came up with a hare-brained idea that was so crazy, it just might work. The idea was to go for a sentence commutation from death to life in prison based on something known as "Deliberate Indifference". I had never heard of such a thing and did not know if it really existed. He sure was highly creative. What a shame he didn't put any of his creativity to a good use before that fateful night way back in 1987 when he participated in a murder.

Jacqueline: *May 20th, 1996*

Sittin' here after my shower, listening to the radio & thinking of you. I am trying to think of who does this song I really like. Maybe you could help me out. I believe the song's title is "The Rooster". Goes something like: "They come to snuff the rooster, oh yeah, but he ain't gonna die...." Rea tough song, like it a lot, know the one I'm talkin' about? Know who does it? And what's this crap going on w/ Metallica? They really rocked a few years ago. I turn on the radio this AM & all I hear is how they sold out. A station out this way is polling listeners & asking if they want to hear Metallica anymore. Most people are calling in & saying no.

Well, I have law library at 11:00. Then I'll go outside for a few minutes. Get some fresh air & stretch the legs a bit. Did you get the packet w/ the book on ADHD, etc? Room service is here w/ lunch. Back at ya in a bit....Okay, got a letter from ya! Good to hear all is going rather smoothly. I'll tell ya' I was feeling really bummed until I read your letter. Saved it for last reading. Got a couple of other pieces of mail too! Saved the best for last.

Anyway, I got a note from JoAnn. She tells me that neither she nor my kids never want anything to do w/ me ever again. Well I was like, okay psycho bitch, was really bummed out about it because of the kids, will probably continue to feel that. But what can I do? Fuck it & them if they want to be like that. I do not need that kind of shit now. Anyway, apparently she went psycho over you. Again, fuck her, who is she to do or say anything like this. She has been using the kids like this against me for years. So fuck them all. I am too tired for any of that, ya' know? I mean I love the kids, always will, but fuck that noise. I hope you can understand all of that. I know I didn't express myself very well there.

Anyway, I sit & think about psycho bitch & the kids for awhile. Read the next letter from a pen-pal of mine, then read yours. Your letter did cheer me up.

New issues found: #1 During the penalty phase of the trial the prosecutor used the term "guilt trip", etc when addressing the jury. This is not permissible. Elgart raised this issue. The court ruled against saying that he, Elgart, "opened the door". Well, clearly by Elgart opening the door that allowed the prosecution to do something that is normally impermissible. Hence, Elgart was ineffective for doing so.

#2 Elgart was ineffective for failing to object to improper instructions given by the court to the jury. This is the possible issue I mentioned. The Supreme Court has already ruled that the aforementioned instructions were proper. However, this issue has been raised as Improper Instructions & will be addressed by the federal courts, should we need to go there. Now, Elgart should be held ineffective for failing to object to the improper instructions.

A) The issue should be raised because it is an issue w/ merit. The fed courts may rule differently than the state court on said issue.

B) It is another issue to sweat Elgart over when he is on the stand at the PCRA hearing.

Water is on. Dinner was truly horrible & I refused to eat any of it. Thank God I have a couple of soups & some rice left. I will make my own dinner. While we are on a roll here I will tell you of my thoughts on how I may be able to attack capital punishment on a grand scheme, at least state wide, if so it will go national.

Now, in a nutshell: Deliberate Indifference". The courts have ruled that by showing Deliberate Indifference (D.I.) to a party, it violates the party's constitutional rights to the 8th & 14th Amendments. I ran across this and the other night it hit me like a thunderbolt:

<u>Question: "Is the state of Pennsylvania and the US Gov't being D.I. towards my family, kids, mother, etc by sentencing me to death and seeking my execution?"</u> I discussed this in great detail w/ Al today. He & I went back & forth, covered every area of this. New attack on the death penalty & we concluded that if nothing else, it should be raised & the courts should be forced to rule on it because it is an issue which holds merit. If PA and/or the US Gov't are in fact showing D.I. towards my family by seeking & eventually carrying out my execution, that violates the 8th, 9th & 14th Amendments to the US Constitution. There is the possibility that the courts will be forced to rule in a very positive fashion here...

I have briefly explained this D.I. issue to you. If done in better depth I know you will "see" it, if you don't already? Anyway I fully intend to run it by Dunham when& if he shows up the week of the 25th. Will let you know how meeting goes. Want to hear a real bite in the ass about this issue? I don't know if I have any real family support to present if need be for this issue! I may need family members to join in the said suit. Ha Ha {sarcasm}. Doubt very much if I could name the kids in the suit now...See? Psycho bitch would not permit it. Mom & Mark may not want to "get involved".

Well I guess I will wrap this one up. It's getting late, guess I'll take my pants off & get in between the sheets naked, alone...sigh...

Miss you. God Bless

Love,

Rick

I didn't know about the validity of the deliberate indifference issue. I honestly did not think the lawyers handling Rick's case would want to go there. The courts would probably take the view that Rick himself showed "deliberate indifference" to the family & loved ones of Anthony Milano by being a party to his murder. Unless some sympathetic judge held the personal view that a living father behind prison bars was better than an executed father as far as Rick's kids were concerned, I did not see Rick's death sentence being thrown out on the grounds of deliberate indifference. I would have to wait until after I was through final exams before I could afford to take any time to research that. At the moment, my priority was just getting through those difficult final exams.

Final exam week was the same week as my 29th birthday. But it didn't matter because I didn't have the means to go out and celebrate. I was certainly not expecting the two birthday cards Rick sent me in the mail. They were the same kind of glossy covered cards with high quality pictures on the front as the first card he sent me, the one he sent just to say he missed me and thought I was special. One of the birthday cards had a picture of a yellow rose on the front cover underneath the caption *"Wishing you a birthday full of loveliness.."* When I opened it to read the inside, a lock of chestnut brown hair fell out. It was bound at one end with a rubber band. A Polaroid instant photo of Rick after his most recent prison haircut was tucked inside. The inside read:

"Like a pocket full of sunshine,

Like the gold at rainbows end,

Like an unexpected greeting

For a dear and cherished friend –

Like the sweet and haunting fragrance

Of a rosebud wet with dew,

Like all these lovely things and more,

May this day be for you!"

Hope your day is special – because you are.

Love, Rick

The second card had a picture of lace with pink day lilies and a pink ribbon strewn over them, nestled next to one of those antique silver hair brush, comb and mirror sets – like the kind you might find in your great-grandmother's special hope chest. It was beautiful in its elegant simplicity. The caption simply said, *"Happy Birthday"*. Rick had written on the inside of the card:

J.

Wish I were able to take you out to dinner, a nice restaurant, soft lights, light music, good food, you & I, maybe even a slow dance or two. You know there is still much I do not know about you. I feel as if you know very much about me, yet I only know a little about you. For instance, your favorite flower? I want for you to have a dozen of them on your birthday, if I could, I would have them there for you. Maybe the future will hold better birthdays. Want to take you to dinner, dance once or twice, see you smile at my two left feet..Want to see you smile all the time...I have never seen you smile.

R.

They were the only birthday cards I had gotten from anyone since my grandmother died. I do not know how difficult it is to buy nice cards from a prison cell. I didn't even know if the prison commissary had such things. Actually, prisoners on death row are not permitted prison jobs and instead receive "idle pay" – a stipend of $14.00 per month for incidentals such as toothpaste, shampoo, stationary, postage and envelopes. Inmates are not automatically provided with these essentials. I am certain that Rick spent a significant portion of his income to get those cards. That touched me and saddened me at the same time. I thought about all the people whom I thought were my friends who had forgotten about me after my accident. I thought about how only two men had asked me to go out for dinner since my accident. I remembered how they bitched when their sexual advances were rebuffed because they thought they were entitled to getting laid in exchange for buying me a meal. I was sour on the dating scene even before my injuries. I had already begun living as a recluse even then in my early twenties, with my only companions being a few cats. As for my favorite flower, it is the rose. He was the only man who had ever asked me about that.

The only time I had ever gotten any roses was when I had the money to spring for a few rose bushes to plant out back in the small yard behind my building. I never told Rick that my favorite flower was the rose. I wasn't used to anybody thinking of me or caring whether or not I was happy, or even whether I had anything nice that I wanted. In fact, I couldn't remember any guy ever doing anything nice for me without some ulterior motive. Most guys my age that were single were too selfish, too stuck on themselves, too concerned about getting their own way. They were too self-absorbed to suit me and I was quite content to live out the remainder of my life as "the cat lady of Church Street" – until my path crossed that of Rick Laird.

Rick made me think about what it would be like to have someone special, a life mate. It was something I had given up on long ago. The few men I had dated soured me on the idea of living any other way than as a recluse.

My favorite flower – roses. Lots of roses, and preferably still attached to the bush so they would live and bloom each year, full petaled fragrant blossoms to greet me every morning as I would step outside. Here is a man on death row wishing he had the means to send me flowers, while no man who had enjoyed the benefit of my company, who was not in prison and took such things for granted, had ever cared enough to buy me roses. When I am dead and can no longer enjoy beautiful, fragrant roses, that is when "friends" will come out of the woodwork to see to it that there are plenty of roses at my funeral, but nobody could give a damn to send me any while I'm alive, I thought bitterly. My birthday came and went.

Other than my Ripperology meetings with Doc, the summer was hot and uneventful. I went to work, minded my own business, didn't talk to anyone and just did my job. I came home to letters from Rick, many which were the same ups and downs of prison life. Some were rather steamy and on the romantic side. Others were fraught with impatience because he thought the lawyers at the Defenders Association had forgotten about his case – which they had not. I reassured Rick several times in my letters that Attorney Dunham had not forgotten about his appeal. I chided Rick, telling him that just because Dunham wasn't in his office every time he called, that didn't mean he had forgotten about his case. Lawyers do actually have to be in court once in awhile after all.

Prisoners can be a real pain in the ass. I suppose that being locked up with nothing else to do they forget that those on the outside have to cope with everyday life. Daily routines of going to work, dealing with unaffordable car repair bills, rent or mortgage payments, over-due utility bills, hoping there's enough money for food after an unexpected emergency arises that eats up half of an entire month's income and praying not to get sick because of being one paycheck away from destitution. One thing prisoners do not have to worry about is eviction. Mortgage and rent payments are not real high on their priority list.

While I may not have had a mortgage payment to worry about, I did have property taxes and utilities to pay on a very low income. I was still also three months away from being eligible for medical and dental benefits at the Hilton. But rotting teeth don't wait until you have money, or qualify for employer benefits and can afford proper treatment. I was trying to build up a meager savings on a very low income in order to get my most severe dental problems addressed because abscesses don't wait. Rick's calls from prison were not exactly what I would consider affordable, either. They ate up a princely sum of what money I did have in my budget for regular bills.

Although a prisoner must call collect in order to call outside of the prison, the long distance charges that would be incurred for such calls under normal conditions would not normally be a budget-buster. However, the Pennsylvania inmate telephone system does not go through the regular telephone company. Inmate calls to the outside go through a company called T-Netix. Their rates are quadruple what a normal collect call through Verizon would be. My first telephone bill after Rick first began calling had hit me like a right cross with the sticker shock. Now bear in mind, Rick could only call twice a month, if that. My telephone bill for two 15- minute collect calls from Rick in prison amounted to over $100!

Inmates in the prison's general population were not under the same restrictions of telephone privilege as those housed in the Restricted Housing Unit (RHU), i.e. those on death row. I could only imagine how financially crushing inmate calls were for low-income women struggling to hold their families together while their men were behind bars. Many prisoners only had elderly mothers to visit them because their girlfriends or wives ended the relationships due to the financial strain. Prison telephone charges that were nothing short of highway robbery didn't help matters. I could see why so many women ended up breaking up with their men after their men went to prison.

The pressure and constant demands that prisoners make on their loved ones' time and lives plus the financial strain on those left behind who were often poor to begin with are enough to break even the strongest of bonds. Then there is the whole issue of prison guards on a power trip who make it miserably difficult for the women to visit their men in prison, especially those with children.

There is only so much strain a relationship can withstand. In fact, money and financial strain is the number one cause for divorce in this country. I know couldn't afford to maintain a close relationship with someone in prison, and I don't even have little ones to support. I felt bad telling Rick to only call in the event of a dire emergency, such as needing me to hand deliver more legal documents for a potential hearing on short notice. Rick kept his phone calls to me at a minimum because he understood my financial constraints.

One telephone conversation in particular struck a chord when Rick mentioned briefly that he loaned the book on ADHD that I had sent him to a fellow "row man". The fellow inmate read the book and realized his own two kids had ADHD and other learning difficulties as well. He now knew to tell his ex-wife where to go to get some help for their sons. He wrote her a long explanatory letter all about learning disabilities and ADHD, and included the number to the local LDA chapter in his home county. His ex-wife acted on it immediately, getting help and support for the two boys. If I have done any good in my involvement with Rick Laird's death penalty appeal, it was that. It was getting the message out to those who could be helped, for whom it wasn't too late for their lives to be turned around. It was getting the information into the hands of those in most need of it: those who couldn't afford the costs of sending their children to a Sylvan Learning Center or hiring private tutors.

No one should have to end up on death row before learning what was wrong with them, and why they weren't successful in society. The information on learning disabilities and ADHD is not hard to find. Every municipality has a local library, free and open to the public. While many parents may not have much education beyond a high school diploma or know what to do when their child is struggling, organizations like LDA are listed in the Human

Services Guide section of most telephone books. Once pointed in the right direction and given some support and advocacy, even the least educated parent is armed with enough knowledge to know how to seek more knowledge from books at the library. Knowledge is power. The educated professionals in whose care we leave our young should certainly know better. After all, they are the ones in the education business.

There will always be an element in society that will choose to break the laws in order to get what they want no matter what. But the fact remains that an ounce of prevention is worth far more than a pound of cure.

One way to prevent that level of frustration is to intercept problems when they are small, taking the extra time to aid the child for whom learning is difficult, helping someone who doesn't quite fit in. We need to reinstate the funding for jobs programs for the disadvantaged. We need to build on strengths instead of crushing people because of their weaknesses. Of course, those ideals are best implemented in a fair or shared society rather than a strictly competitive one. One need not be as brilliant as renowned mathematician Dr. John Nash, who's groundbreaking Theory of Governing Dynamics changed the world, to see the advantage of that.

When the least among us wins, we all win. Unfortunately, in our society it's "Me first", "I don't care if my neighbor is poor and not making it – I don't care if my co-worker lost her job – I've got mine", "it's a dog-eat-dog world", and "it's survival of the fittest". Being considerate of others' needs or being cooperative and a real team player is seen as a weakness. Getting ahead at all costs, even at others' expense, is all that matters. We see it in the workplace, especially in the white-collar world of office politics. We see it in factories and union construction jobs. Children learn from their parents' examples. The same child who throws a fit when they are told by the teacher to assist their learning disabled classmate because doing so will "slow them down" is the same spoiled child who grows up to be the greedy, ruthless, grasping adult. They grow up to become the climber who does not get ahead by fair play. Rather than seeking to get ahead by merit, skill and talent, they stab co-workers in the back, steal credit for others' work, and step on everyone along the way – just so they get theirs. Yet they are the first to cry foul and scream hypocritically that their "hard-earned" wealth should not be taxed in order to help others who are less fortunate who didn't "earn" it.

I was seeing back-stabbing in my own job at the Hilton. Even minimum-wage maids in the housekeeping department were quick to bite a newly hired maid in the back with the intent of causing her to lose her job. It helped ensure the security of their positions. Because of this atmosphere I preferred, if possible, to simply avoid any situation that would give anyone an excuse to target me. I rarely spoke to anyone and when I did, I didn't tell them anything about myself. The most benign things can be used against you on the job by an insecure co-worker. No one except the Human Resources Department and Mark Laird knew I was even attending college. And the only reason Mark knew was because I studied homework assignments during my lunch hour.

One day at work, about a month before my benefits were due to kick in, Mark and I were assigned to change out all the bathroom plumbing fixtures and lights in the guest rooms on the penthouse floor of the hotel. He took the rooms on one side of the hall and I took the other. While I was busy installing new lighting fixtures by the guestroom beds, Mark wandered into the room I was working in. He shut the door, presumably to prevent any busybody housekeepers from listening to what he had to say.

“Things are getting really bad. I don’t know what the fuck I’m going to do.” He sat down on an ottoman shaking his head, “My mom called me last night and told me I had to be prepared to step into my brother’s shoes and be a father to his kids when he gets executed.” He started to cry. His entire upper body heaved with sobs. I had never seen a grown man, especially a macho male like him, break down in tears. I didn’t know what to do. I felt so sorry for him. I sat down next to him, putting my arm around his shoulders trying to calm him and console him. I tried my best to be genuinely reassuring. “Mark, your brother is not dead yet, he’s still alive. The Capital Defenders Association took the case. The new evidence about your brother’s ADHD and brain damage is pretty solid material for them to go on. As long as your brother is alive, there is hope.” I had heard enough empty clichés throughout my own life. I had seen and heard a lot of insincerity from others who really didn’t care, who just wanted to spout off like know-it-all gas bags and feel good about themselves for saying the right things. I had never liked it when others had done it to me. Spouting insincere platitudes was the last thing I wanted to do to the tortured soul sitting next to me whose tears were soaking my shirt.

Mark recoiled violently and suddenly, and yelled at me, “You don’t give a damn! You don’t understand anything! It’s not *your* brother on death row!” Any shred of sympathy I might have felt for Mark was gone that very instant. He remained seated. Not wishing to have any further discourse with him, I decided to collect my tools and leave. I could find another room to work in. That was the last straw.

Mark followed me down the hall apologizing. I didn’t want to hear anything he had to say. I thought about the time he whined in a letter to Rick claiming that I was harassing him about money for defraying the costs of obtaining the trial transcripts. I thought about the harassment and abuse I had taken from JoAnn just for helping Rick when no one else was willing to step up to the plate. I thought about the crap I was subjected to by prison guards when I went to visit Rick. I thought of how my involvement in helping Rick at Mark's behest strained my friendship with Doc Weiler, who felt I shouldn't be helping someone who was a monster – fair trial or no fair trial. I thought about the precarious situation I put myself in on the evening I went to investigate the crime scene and question Jimmy Phillips at the establishment where it all began. I thought about the peril I put myself in driving an old car 400 miles across state to visit Rick, and the additional miles entailed driving to Selinsgrove to pick up Rick's photocopied court documents from Harriet, and trucking everything to Rob Dunham in Philadelphia. I thought about all I had done in trying to help this ingrate and his brother. And this bastard acted as if I had done nothing while accusing me of not caring!

No, there was nothing Mark had to say that I cared to hear. I refused to acknowledge his half-assed apologies. He had shown his true colors. He was a manipulative, conniving creep who had played me for a fool to get me involved in helping his brother while he refused to contribute one red cent towards defraying the costs. I kept walking down the hall towards the service elevator, refusing to look at him. It was the end of my shift. I just wanted to punch out, go home and not have to deal with him.

He persisted, following me to the service elevator, still trying to apologize. I would hear none of it. Positioning himself between me and the elevator doors once inside the elevator, forcing me to look at him, he continued to say he was sorry. I merely fixed him with a frozen stare. When the elevator finally reached the kitchen on the first floor, the doors automatically opened before the elevator went to the lower level where the maintenance shop was. When the doors opened at the kitchen, Mark jumped out and yelled, "You're just jealous because I won't let you kiss me!" He yelled it loud enough for the kitchen supervisor to hear from within her office. I went from angry to confused. Kiss him? Was he nuts? When the elevator reached the lower level, I got out. I just wanted to put my tools away and go home. I had more important things to do in my life than think about some unappreciative creep who was a criminal and a liar.

The next morning when I reported to work, Stumpy told me to finish working where I left off the day before. Mark came in and tried to say hello to me as if nothing had happened. I just nodded at him and headed out of the shop with my tools and the cart full of replacement lighting fixtures. I resumed working where I had left off the day before. Around 11:30, Stumpy called me on my walkie-talkie, telling me I needed to report to the Human Resources Office at 11:45. Since I was coming up for being eligible for health and dental on the hotel benefit plan, I thought that was what it was about. I thought I would have to go over enrollment forms and sign stuff for my health and dental benefits, which I desperately needed. But when I got there and saw Stumpy, Mark, Ginger DeLorenzo and some guy named Tim from Human Resources and saw the solemn expressions on their faces, I got a bad feeling.

Tim shoved a paper in front of me, ordering me to sign it as acknowledgement that I had been given my third and final written warning for sexually harassing Mark Laird. This was too unreal! I denounced it for the bold-faced lie that it was. I called Mark, who couldn't look me in the face, a good-for-nothing ex-convict and a liar. I said I wasn't signing anything without legal counsel first. I didn't sexually harass anybody, least of all Mark. I got up to leave and look up labor lawyers in the yellow pages when Stumpy yelled after me that if I called an attorney, I would definitely be fired and that if I didn't want to lose my job I better get my ass back to the conference table and sit down. I returned unwillingly because I knew I was right, but I refused to sign the paper.

Mark said nothing while Tim, the human resources lackey, did all the talking, basically paraphrasing all the accusations and the formal charge of sexual harassment on the paper, which was signed by Ginger DeLorenzo acting on the behalf of Mark Laird – because he "feared retaliation." The charge claimed that I entered into the room Mark was working in, shut the door and attempted to forcibly kiss and hug him. My face flushed hot with rage. When Tim finished, he asked, "OK Jackie, now what do you have to say?"

I had plenty to say. I didn't hold back. I spilled the whole story, beginning from January of 1996 when Mark approached me on the job, begging me to help his brother Rick with a death sentence appeal because Rick was supposedly framed. I told them that having a conscience and a penchant for pursuing social justice, I had agreed to help Mark and Rick. I told them about Mark balking at my reasonable request to help defray some of the costs of obtaining the trial transcripts. I told them how Mark whined behind my back to Rick that I was "harassing him for money" to cover some of the costs involved. I even offered to produce Rick's letter to me on the matter as proof. I deliberately looked Tim, Ginger, and Stumpy directly in the eye and reminded them that it was Mark who had solicited my help in the first place. Ginger looked quizzically at Mark as if to say, *'Uh...this isn't what you told me!'* Stumpy and Tim sat there in silence. Stumpy broke away from my gaze first, looked down at the table and nervously began mangling a paper clip that had previously lain forgotten on the table among the papers.

I concluded with the truth as to what had transpired in that guest room up on the 11th floor where I was working when Mark came in, closed the door and began sobbing hysterically. I told them that due to Mark's outburst and actions, I was refusing to speak to him outside of what was required of me to do so in the course of my job at the hotel. Glaring at Mark, who was nervously staring down at his shoes, I concluded my side of the story, "And that is what this really is all about. It's not about sexual harassment because there never was any sexual harassment. It's not about inappropriate behavior on the job." I continued, pointing at Mark emphatically, "It's about that liar getting in the last word, even though he is as wrong as the original sin and he knows it! And now you all know it, too."

Stumpy told me to leave the room and wait in the lobby while they made their decision on whether or not I should be disciplined. Mark was also asked to leave. He avoided looking at me as he passed me on his way back to the maintenance shop. About twenty minutes went by. I strained to hear what was being said about me behind the closed doors. They finally emerged and Stumpy told me they had not reached a decision yet. I was told to remain waiting where I was.

However, three hours later I was still sitting in the lobby when it was time to punch out, Stumpy asked me for my hotel-issued master guest room key. He told me I would not need to report in to work the next day. I was fired. Mark however, got to keep his job. So much for trying to do the right thing: No good deed goes unpunished. Apparently, there was one thing my grandmother had been wrong about: Honesty is not the best policy. It certainly hadn't paid off very well for me.

Chapter 18

"They have as king over them the angel of the bottomless pit; his name in Hebrew is Abaddon, and in Greek he is called Apollyon." ~ The Bible (Revelations 9:11)

I went down to the Unemployment Office the very next morning to file for unemployment benefits. I had not earned very much, so there was a chance I would be denied on the grounds of not having enough earnings in the last two quarters to be able to collect. After waiting in line for over three hours, I was finally seen by an Intake Interviewer. I had earned enough to be able to collect but I would have to wait during one full week of being unemployed before I could file for my very first check. After that, my checks would come in the mail. I would be lucky to be able to keep the gas and electric turned on with what I would get.

I didn't know how I was going to break the news to Rick. I didn't want to burden him with a guilt trip about money problems because of the loss of my job, even though it was Mark's fault. I knew he would have to be told why I might not be able to afford to make any more trips across state for visits or be able to afford to accept any collect calls from the prison in the future. I wrote him a short letter briefly explaining what had happened. If he wanted to know why I was now more limited in helping him in any real and meaningful way, he needed to ask Mark why he had deliberately brought up false sexual harassment charges against me.

Rick wrote back a brief letter expressing disappointment in his brother. He didn't understand why Mark would do such a thing when he knew full well that in sabotaging me he was actually sabotaging Rick's best outside support system. But that was not the worst of it. The worst of it was that I had done *nothing* to deserve the loss of my job which I desperately needed – a point obviously lost on Rick. I wrote back and told Rick I would try to make one last visit after Gary Hendrix from the Defenders Association went out to interview him. Gary Hendrix was the primary investigator into the background of Rick's case.

From my own end, there was really nothing more I could do. I had gone above and beyond the third mile with keeping my word. In my letter to Rick I wrote that his appeal was in the best hands possible because the Defenders Association does only death penalty appeals, and nothing else. They are specialists. They would thoroughly investigate everything starting with Rick's childhood and adult untreated ADHD and other issues as well. I also told Rick I would see him in a couple of weeks after he was finished with his visits from Attorney Dunham and Gary Hendrix.

Meanwhile, the prison had enacted a new rule restricting the frequency of prisoners' visits within any given week. Only two visits per week were allowed under this new rule. I did not want to go all the way out to Pittsburgh only to be turned away when I did not know when I would ever be able to afford to go back out there again. A part of me did not want to be involved even as a pen-pal, much less as a visitor or an advocate on any level because of all the aggravation it had caused me.

Although it was not Rick's fault that I had lost my job at the Hilton, that didn't belie the fact that it was his brother who had deliberately gotten me fired. It was a lousy way of thanking someone for their help if you ask me. No good deed goes unpunished.

After hearing from Rick about the dates when the guys from the Defenders Association were going to be visiting him, I planned my last visit accordingly. I would be getting my first unemployment check three days before the date I had told Rick I would visit one final time. However, I was in for yet one more unpleasant surprise. On my appointed date for going into the Unemployment Office in person to sign up for my first check, I was apprised that the Hilton was fighting my claim for unemployment benefits. Therefore my unemployment benefits were not going to begin unless I was ruled eligible after an "impartial" administrator at the Unemployment Office reviewed the employer's appeal, my rebuttal, and then rendered a final decision as to whether I was wrongfully terminated or not.

Apparently, the Hilton claimed that I had been fired for "just cause" under their zero tolerance policy on sexual harassment. I would be able to respond with my rebuttal the week after the Hilton had their say as to what happened. Nonetheless, I made up my mind that I had had it up to here with everything. I would keep my word to Rick about the visit, but I would no longer be involved further. I had to worry about how I was going to just be able to live! Getting another job isn't easy when one is constrained by college schedules and a disability. Plus there was also the fact that I would not be able to use the Hilton as a reference because I had been fired, even though I was wrongfully discharged. When you are fired for just cause, especially for something as bad as sexual harassment, you are damaged goods in the eyes of any future potential employer. You have a black mark in your employee record that follows you for life, ruining any hopes of ever getting another job. At least, a good job with benefits anyway. I also faced the possibility of being unable to get any unemployment benefits as a result.

It would be their word against mine. After the way management had ganged up on me in the conference room in the Human Resources Office that final day, it was obvious to me that they would stick together with the lie all the way to the

Unemployment Office. Ginger DeLorenzo, Tim and Stumpy would not risk their positions by admitting they screwed up when Mark made the false accusation against me to begin with. But I suspected there was something more to it than that.

Mark was an ex-convict in transition between prison and parole while residing in a halfway center. Employers in Pennsylvania are given generous financial and tax incentives for hiring ex-offenders. Maintaining employment is a condition for being able to leave the halfway center and move to full parole. An employee who is an ex-convict has a lot of incentive to use workplace politics to his advantage if it means securing his position. Mark possibly feared management would learn that he had a brother on death row due to my involvement in Rick's case (at Mark's behest) and that this would be used against him, which could mess up his parole plan. This could also explain why Mark did nothing to discourage a relationship with Ginger. He gladly accepted expensive designer clothing as Christmas gifts from her that she had given him at work in the maintenance office quite openly in front of other Hilton employees. If Mark would stoop to selling drugs to get easy money to enjoy the good life and then rat on his "associates" (including the mother of his kids) in exchange for a lenient prison sentence, he would play on Ginger's feelings to get expensive gifts and favoritism on the job out of the deal.

Either way, I was wrongly accused of something that I didn't do. I was fired for something that never happened and I ended up with a permanent blemish on my work record because of it while the convict got to keep *his* job. I would never trust anyone ever again and think twice before being helpful. I was jaded in my views of the system and had no faith that there was any justice before getting involved with the case of Richard Laird. This unimaginable betrayal had served only to cement my pessimism about people.

People are devious, selfish and cruel. It seemed safer to befriend a rattlesnake than another human being. Most people could care less if they destroy someone else's life. All they care about are their own petty agendas, getting their own way at everyone else's expense. Doc Weiler had the right idea: animals make much better companions than most people. I would keep my word and visit Rick one last time. After that, no more phone calls, no more contact, nothing. I had enough problems of my own and now, thanks to Rick's brother Mark, I had even more serious problems on my plate.

When I had to go back to the Unemployment Office to counter the Hilton's attempt to deny me my unemployment, all I could do was tell the truth. Whether or not it would matter was another story. I recounted everything that happened to the arbitrator as it had happened. When I got to the part about Mark bawling like a baby and then accusing me of not caring after I extended myself to try and help, the arbitrator rolled his eyes and told me that is why I should never help anyone because it doesn't pay. Good guys – or good women in this case – finish last.

Before the words were out of his mouth, his facial expression said it all: his hands were tied. The arbitrator was honest and leveled with me. He began explaining: "I believe every word you have told me. Anytime you're dealing with ex-convicts as co-workers or employees, they prove to be the least trustworthy of all people. But unfortunately, the employer is not obligated to pay unemployment claims when an employee is fired with cause. Any sort of civil rights violation such as sexual harassment is automatic grounds for an employer to deny the payment of unemployment benefits. All I can do is present your rebuttal to the employer in this case. If the Hilton still denies your benefit, there's nothing more I can do."

I was disgusted. "What about MY civil rights as a disadvantaged woman with a disability? What about the fact that I was falsely accused?" His response was, "I'm sorry, but there's nothing I can do."

So I was not only out of a job before becoming eligible for my badly needed medical and dental benefits, I couldn't even collect unemployment. The undeserved black mark on my employee record would go against me if I tried to get a half decent job elsewhere. I would never be able to use the Hilton Hotel as a work reference. I felt terribly humiliated and my good name had been besmirched. Adding insult to injury, the Hilton also had a policy that stated any fired employee could never re-enter the hotel, neither as a guest nor as an invitee to a function held there. This meant that if I was invited to a social function and it was going to be held at the Allentown Hilton, I wouldn't be able to go.

With no money to get a lawyer, I had no recourse, no access to justice. It didn't matter that the Hilton was wrong and I was right. It didn't matter that I had an excellent employee record, worked hard at my job, did what I was told and kept my nose clean. It didn't matter that I wasn't a convicted criminal. It didn't matter that a co-worker lied. It didn't matter that I was honest. I was poor, so I was screwed: I couldn't afford legal help to appeal the unjust firing as well as the denial of my unemployment benefits. There really is no justice.

Three days later, after my meeting with the unemployment arbitrator, I drove out to SCI-Pitt for a last visit with Rick. I thought about the fact that during the entire time I was involved with his case, Rick had never answered my question about killing Anthony. He never once expressed any sympathy for the Milano family. He never expressed any sorrow that Anthony was murdered. Remembering the telephone conversations and my two prior visits, everything was always all about him and his appeal. Not once did he appear to be sad that someone else was murdered without good reason. For what helping Rick Laird was costing me, I hoped to find at least some vindication. I hoped that Dr. Silverman was wrong, that Rick wasn't a psychopath and that my helping him had been the right thing. It felt like the longest drive of my life.

Mike, the guy running Friends House, welcomed me again. The people from the Bruderhof were not there this time. They came down only on certain days to volunteer. They had always struck me as being really nice people. I tried to keep remembering that there are good people out there. They just are not always easy to find. I wondered to myself if any of the prisoners that the Bruderhof community had helped had turned their lives around. But I also wondered if I had a neon sign on my forehead that read "Sucker".

Although I was exhausted from my long drive across state, I had difficulty sleeping that night. I tossed and turned, torturing myself with questions as to whether or not I had made the biggest mistake of my life by getting involved and helping Rick. I finally fell asleep around 3:30 AM – less than four hours before I had to wake up to be at the prison.

I woke up energized and alert and got ready for my final visit. It was a bright sunny day. Driving past the neatly manicured lawns and flowerbeds along my way to the prison, I wondered if Rick remembered what roses in full bloom smelled like.

Arriving at the prison, I went through the ritual of visitor processing for the last time. This time, the processing didn't seem to take as long. Before long, I was seated at the window of bullet-proof glass facing Rick. He began chattering like a squirrel about the strategy that the legal team at the Defenders Association was planning to use. He rattled on incessantly about Gary Hendrix investigating his childhood and about everything that led up to the night in question when Anthony Milano was murdered.

It was an hour and a half before I was able to get a word in edgewise. I told Rick I was happy for him that things were going well for his appeal now that the Defenders Association had taken his case. I reassured him that Rob Dunham had my utmost confidence. He rambled on some more about how horribly the inmates on death row are treated and how the death penalty should be abolished entirely. He went on about how unfair it was that Pennsylvania prisoners could not have conjugal visits. He went on explaining that sex is a biological need, and that therefore being deprived of any physical intimacy including sex was a bona fide health hazard which violates prisoners' rights to healthy and humane prison conditions. All of this was unfair. Unbelievable! He finally had a chance for a reprieve from his death sentence and all he could talk about was getting laid! He went on to talk about how sorry he was for befriending Frank Chester because it was Frank Chester who got him into this mess to begin with (Note: not that Frank killed Anthony). If it wasn't for Frank running off at the mouth to the police, he (referring to himself) wouldn't be in the predicament he was.

Finally I put the cross-hairs on him: "Rick, I have done what I promised I would do, right?" He nodded as I continued…"I have gone the third mile to help you. I am happy for you that your case is now in the hands of Attorney Dunham. I have never asked anything of you thus far. Do you remember back in March in one of your letters to me, you stated that if there was anything you could do for me, you would do it if it were within your power to do so?" Rick looked at me warily and said, "Yeah."

I forged ahead with what I was burning to ask him, what I had to know, "Rick, I really need to know: don't you feel any sympathy for the Milano family? Don't you feel it is unfair that Anthony died? Don't you feel any sympathy at all for Anthony Milano?"

As soon as the words were out of my mouth, an angry scowl darkened Rick's face like a brewing storm. In that instant, all signs of humanity left the eyes that were fixed on me in an icy, dead-pan stare. I felt as if whatever was looking at me on the other side of that bullet-proof glass was no longer human, if it ever truly had been human at all. He stood up slowly, fixing his unwavering steely glare on me the entire time. He did not blink, not even once. The expression on his face said that if he could have gotten his hands on me at that very moment, I would be joining Anthony Milano: I would be dead. His eyes were like black ice, completely soulless. I pulled backed from the window in a genuine feeling of utter terror. I felt like I had seen the eyes of Abaddon, the angel of the bottomless pit. I knew I was looking into the eyes of a monster.

They were the same soulless eyes of pure unadulterated evil that poor Anthony Milano must have seen as his throat was being slashed. I knew then at that instant, that monsters *do* exist: one of them is Richard Roland Laird, Jr.

As I dropped the phone receiver, and backed away from the window I accidentally bumped into a guard who asked if I was OK. I couldn't speak. I'd been chilled by what I had seen, chilled to the bone as if someone walked across my own grave. It was the most terrifying experience of my life. I fled the prison, running as fast as I could to get out into the warm sun. Shaking, I fumbled for my keys to unlock my car. I felt a crushing sensation on my chest and couldn't breathe. I felt the overwhelming need to put my head between my knees just to be able to breathe. An older guard hurried over to my car as I sat in the driver's seat; head down between my knees with the door wide open as I struggled to catch my breath between sobs.

"Miss! Are you OK? Do you need help? Do you need to go to the hospital?" he placed his hand gently on my shoulder. I shook my head 'No'. I didn't need to go to the hospital. I was having a major anxiety attack. It lasted only a few minutes. If I were an older lady, I might have thought I was having a heart attack and opted for the hospital. Once I was able to breathe again, I told the guard what had happened. I was still crying. He handed me some Kleenex tissues and tried to calm me down, "You're OK Miss. Nobody's going to hurt you now. You're going to be all right. You know, I hate to say it, but I see it every day. People like you who want to be do-gooders, who want to help these creeps in here. Let me tell you something. These men on the 'row' are like mad dogs. Putting them down is the best thing for 'em, really."

There are no words to adequately convey what I felt that day. Everything I believed in, everything I thought was right, everything I believed about redemption, was shattered like a fragile crystal menagerie. Everything was suddenly upside down and inside out. It was as if my entire world, every principle I had ever believed in, everything…just came crashing in on me and everything was no longer real. I felt sick to my stomach. Although it was a hot summer day, I was freezing. I couldn't stop shivering the entire 7 hour drive home. It was a chill that just would not subside. I had never felt anything like that before in my entire life.

I knew when I looked into those eyes – the eyes of a monster – that Rick Laird had murdered Anthony Milano in cold blood. Suddenly, the picture of what had happened that night in 1987 became so vivid and clear: Anthony pleading and begging for his life while huge, vicious and demented Rick Laird hauled him out of the car and into that field, his massive fists slamming into Anthony's head and face with the first blow, then the second knocking Anthony senseless to the ground, and then the knife coming down and hacking away…And I knew that if he had not been bound by shackles and leg irons and if there had been no bullet-proof glass between us, he would have just as quickly and easily snuffed the life right out of me with his bare hands without giving it a second thought. He had no remorse. He had no compassion. He had no conscience.

The same man who could write all of the things I needed to hear to encourage me and make me feel like I was somebody and who boosted my self-confidence when others had put me down, was the very same man who did not have any qualm about snuffing out the life of another and would do it again if he could. The same man who seemed to know all the right things to say in the beautiful cards that he sent me for my birthday when no one else noticed or cared that I existed, that was the same man who had no heart at all for the untold pain and suffering he caused Anthony Milano and the Milano family.

How could I have been so easily misled? How could I have been so naïve? I truly wanted to believe – I needed to believe – that I had helped someone who had been the victim of injustice. A part of me wanted to take a stand for social justice for others because of all the injustices I had suffered in my own life. I needed to believe that the man I had helped had remorse and compassion for his role in the savage murder of an innocent man. I desperately wanted and needed to believe all these things because I wanted to make a difference in a case where someone with a disability, someone who was poor, someone who had been a victim, had been egregiously wronged by society. I wanted to know that I had helped someone who had been unfairly ensnared in the criminal justice system that

I believed was biased against those at the bottom just because they were powerless.

Reality hit me like ice water. I had not helped a victim of injustice. I had not helped right a wrong and make a difference for the better in our system. I had unwittingly helped a monster, a manipulative calculating fiend who was evil incarnate. The eyes which are the mirror of the conscience had shown me what Rick Laird's true nature really was. Rick Laird might have had brain damage, and he might have been handicapped by learning disabilities and ADHD, but that did not alter the fact that he was a cold and calculating monster bereft of any sympathy for his fellow man. With or without his handicap, Rick Laird was still a monster without remorse.

Alan Rubenstein was right in his assessment of Richard Laird. Rubenstein's closing argument from the 1988 trial played over and over in my head: *With a coldness of heart that we cannot comprehend and ice-water running through their veins, they treated him [Milano] like a cheap piece of tenderloin and carved him up.*

When I got home, I packed up all correspondence from Rick, every document spare copy I had retained, and locked it all in a file cabinet buried in my basement. I crawled into bed under a pile of heavy blankets and cried myself to sleep and slept for a very, very, very long time. My world, everything I thought I knew was the right thing to believe in, had been torn asunder. I would never be the same person again.

Chapter 19

"Blood, though it sleeps a time, yet never dies." ~ George Chapman

I had buried the experience of getting involved in Rick Laird's appeal and tried to put everything connected to that experience out of my mind as I moved on with my own life. I finally graduated from Kutztown University on May 19th, 2001. Immediately following graduation, I was recruited by a brokerage firm to work as a stockbroker/financial planner. I got my NASD Series 7 & 66 licenses plus my PA insurance license and began a bright future as a certified financial planner and stockbroker. However, what was supposed to be a promising new career and a new life for me ended abruptly.

Without warning on the morning of September 11th, 2001 life as we all knew it came to a screeching halt when terrorists hijacked four airplanes. Two crashed into the World Trade Center towers and a third into the Pentagon. A fourth plane which was also hijacked by the terrorists is thought to have been headed to the White House. Instead it was commandeered by several brave passengers led by Todd Beemer who immortalized the phrase "Let's roll", and crashed the plane into a field in western Pennsylvania.

The economy came to a standstill. The financial services industry beyond all others had been hit the worst. Commerce and industry was devastated as everyone was frozen with fear. It was, for my generation and those younger than me just starting out, our day which would live in infamy.

After a year of fruitless job searching, the savings and investment account I'd built up during my abbreviated career at the brokerage firm dwindled. I was back to square one again. Due to the high costs of living in the Lehigh Valley and the lack of business activity, I headed west to Erie, Pennsylvania where housing costs were a quarter of those in the Allentown-Philly region. I hoped to be able to find employment with my degree and licenses because Erie was the same size as Allentown and was far enough away from ground zero that my chances might be better there. I bought a modest house in the central/east side of Erie on December 27th 2002, dropped back and punted.

I did not know at that time that Rick's appeal had made it all the way to the federal court in Philadelphia where Judge Jan DuBois ordered Laird's death sentence vacated, awarding Laird relief in the form of a new trial. The Bucks County Court of Common Pleas, Criminal Division, would have to retry the case all over again. Apparently I was not the only one having to start all over again.

I was unable to get another job. One factor I had not counted on when I moved was that I would be viewed as an "outsider" in Erie. The other factor I had not anticipated was the age discrimination factor I would face as I still pounded the pavements seeking employment in 2004. I was far from being a candidate for the local geriatric ward, but at age 37 I was no longer the svelte, pretty young woman that I once was. I was considered "too fat" and "over the hill" by prospective employers. Success in the dating scene grew more elusive for me. I was not one of society's "winners", despite having done "all the right things." I was rejected as being "overqualified" for the entry level jobs, but on the plus side I did manage to find a husband, Donnie E. Homan, Sr.

Donnie was a disabled widower. After we married on July 3rd 2003, we pooled our resources. He supported me in my efforts to be successful in starting my own small independent property & casualty insurance agency, selling auto, dwelling and flood insurance to the non-standard market. I sold my house and we made our home together in a large brick Victorian house in the light commercial area of east/central Erie. The memories of my bad experience at the Hilton and the case of Rick Laird were long forgotten, buried deep within the coiled labyrinths of my sub-conscious. I had not told Donnie about the crime, the case, the appeal, or my naïve involvement. I was ashamed and scarred by the experience. He was on a need-to-know basis, and at the time I felt he did not need to know.

I was unsure if I should tell Donnie, or anyone else for that matter. After years of being desperately poor, I had barely climbed out of poverty to join the ranks of the educated middle-class. My hold was tenuous at best. I was trying to find social acceptance by those academic and professional peers who had always been middle-class, who had never experienced the level of social ostracism, marginalization, extreme economic insecurity and deprivation that I had suffered.

I always felt unsure of myself: never quite belonging and never quite fitting in. The last thing I wanted anyone to know was that I had been stupid enough to waste the last years of my youth by allowing myself to get suckered into helping a vicious fiend. Helping someone on death row who was convicted of a savage killing is not socially acceptable to most people, especially those in the middle-class who tend to be less skeptical of the justice system than those who are working class or poor. I felt ashamed of my own shortcomings, of failing to "know better" when I got involved over a decade ago.

One morning in 2005 when business was painfully slow, Donnie suggested bringing the old file cabinet up from the basement to help organize my modest home office during the "down time". I remembered that all of my files containing the letters, cards and copies of legal documents relating to Richard Laird were there and Donnie would surely see them. Now I had no choice but to tell him everything, which was painfully hard for me. I didn't know where to begin. So I began by downloading the federal court decision from an online database. That is one perk of self-employment: I could take as many Internet breaks as I wanted.

Although Donnie really didn't understand me in many ways, he was not judgmental of me for my prior involvement with the Laird case. He did not inundate me with a bunch of useless "why didn't you's" so typical of others who had never walked a mile in my shoes, yet who always seemed to have an answer for everything like they it all. He understood how vulnerable I was all those years ago when I was all alone, didn't have anybody, and wasn't even able to support myself — getting nothing but put down instead of helped. He told me, "You should write a book about this, about all of it. Then maybe other people would understand why you are the way you are." I wasn't quite ready for that yet. It was too much of a personal risk that I wasn't prepared to take yet.

It was difficult enough trying to start a business with nothing but my licenses and a computer operating from my house. My position was too fragile: word-of-mouth could make or break me. I didn't think anyone from the local synagogue, my colleagues in the property & casualty field, or even my neighbors would understand. I mean, what would everybody else think of me? I was not willing to allow myself to be made vulnerable to every cheap shot imaginable. My life experiences taught me just how cruel, thoughtless, and downright ignorant other people can be when they are confronted by situations and people whom they do not understand. Would anyone else *really* understand what I had been through?

I suspected that I already knew the answer to that question. I'd had more than my fair share of experience in the past with being looked down on and judged by the "haves" for simply being one of the "have-nots". Donnie chided me, "Don't be so negative." What he failed to see was that it was not a matter of being negative. It was the fact that I had been there, done that. It was as simple as that.

However, I began thinking about what Donnie said. Maybe if I *did* write this book, others who are vulnerable, others who are all alone with no one to understand them, maybe they would read it and gain the knowledge and insight I could provide from my experience. Experience is the best teacher. If I actually was able to get a book about this case and my involvement in it published, it would educate a lot of people who don't know why our criminal justice system works the way it does, why a convicted killer can spend twenty years on death row while their appeals drag through the PCRA process, and why someone can be easily beguiled into helping a ruthless criminal. Nothing about our justice system is as simple as we think it is.

In the case of Rick Laird and Frank Chester, their direct appeals pursuant to the PCRA after their conviction and sentence first had to go before the very same judge, Judge Beister, and in the same courthouse in which they were initially tried. From there, the appeals went through the Pennsylvania State Supreme Court, which usually does not issue a ruling that contradicts that of the lower courts. Even in a case where someone is innocent and wrongfully convicted, it is almost impossible to obtain relief on appeal. In the case where someone is guilty but denied their constitutional right to a fair trial, it is even more impossible.

One of the reasons I believe getting a favorable outcome on appeal is nearly impossible is the fact that such a ruling means the trial court screwed up. The district attorney, who is an elected official, would be judged to have fouled the ball. Lastly, the defense counsel would be judged at fault – possibly risking a hefty lawsuit, severe discipline and sanctions that include being disbarred, thus losing their license to practice law. Just as in the corporate world, it's cover your ass and pass the buck. The system is anything but fair. It is comprised of people, and people are responsible for the unfairness in it – just as they are responsible for the unfairness in other aspects of life. Anyone who has ever been discriminated against for a job or unjustly fired and then subsequently denied remedy of back pay or unemployment compensation can attest to just how unfair life is. Our legal system is no less flawed. It is for this reason that the defendant seems to have more rights than the victim. It would be too easy for a flawed system to convict and execute the innocent otherwise, and such incidents *have* happened more often than we would like to admit. But since the dead cannot come back to tell their side of it, people tend to believe – because they need to believe – that justice eventually prevails and that those wronged will somehow be made whole because "the justice system" won't fail. But in reality it *does* fail...often.

It certainly failed in the infamous case of Rueben "Hurricane" Carter, a young black prize fighter from Paterson, NJ who was wrongfully arrested, convicted, and imprisoned for nearly twenty years for shooting and killing three people at the Lafayette Bar & Grill. Racism, classism, and concealment of evidence had everything to do with it. The prosecutor's failure to seek the truth and using the false testimony of another convicted criminal, Alfred Bello, played a huge role.

Bello, the prosecution's "eye witness", was allegedly committing a burglary in the vicinity at the time of the Lafyaette Bar & Grill shooting. None of the patrons at the Lafayette Bar identified Rueben Carter and his friend Johnny Artis as the killers. But Carter and Artis made convenient scapegoats because they were both black and had been driving a white car, similar to the white car the shooter was seen in when fleeing the scene. To make matters worse, "the Hurricane" did have a prior criminal record. He was no angel. And because he was no angel, he was the perfect scapegoat. Folk singer Bob Dylan immortalized the saga of injustice suffered by Rueben Carter and Johnny Artis in his classic hit song *"The Hurricane"*.

Amidst mounting political pressure from civil rights activists, the NJ State Supreme Court begrudgingly agreed to give "the Hurricane" and Johnny Artis a new trial in 1976 on the grounds that the prosecution withheld material facts from the defense during the first trial in 1967. Such facts were primarily the "backroom deals" it made with felons Alfred Bello and Arthur Dexter Bradley: they testified against Carter for the prosecution in exchange for leniency in their own prison sentences for crimes. Hurricane Carter's supporters pressured Bello into recanting the false testimony he gave at the original 1967 trial. But during the second trial in 1976, Bello recanted his recantation and so Carter and Artis were once again convicted and sentenced to life in prison. In the meantime, the US Supreme Court ordered a nationwide moratorium on the death penalty based on the constitutional violations grounds cited in Furman v. Georgia. If not for this abrupt halt to the death penalty, Carter and Artis could have easily found themselves sentenced to death by the state of New Jersey.

Even though the state of New Jersey refused to admit its role in the wrongful conviction and concealment of evidence (which could have proved Carter's innocence), "the Hurricane" was eventually and begrudgingly set free in 1985 after Carter's attorneys filed a Writ of Habeas Corpus in federal court resulting in an order for a new trial. The State of New Jersey declined to prosecute in a new trial because of international political pressure. Carter's innocence didn't matter to the court; public scrutiny was the end motivator.

Rueben "Hurricane" Carter got no monetary recompense for all those years he rotted in a New Jersey state prison cell for a murder he didn't commit. After twenty years into his three consecutive life sentences, he couldn't simply resume his life, his dissolved marriage and his career as a prize fighter and pick up where his life was abruptly derailed. He was set free, but that in and of itself will never make him whole for the injustice he and his family suffered.

Unfortunately, there is no adequate remedy for that in most states. No amount of money can truly compensate for missing out on your children's first Little League game, your children's lead role in a school play, or their senior prom, plus all your wedding anniversaries. But an adequate amount of money to make up for a destroyed life and lost earnings is a damn good start. It is better than nothing but a proverbial pat on the head, a bunch of useless "we're sorrys", and being told "you are free to be on about your life now", as if nothing happened.

Suing the state is next to impossible because of something known as sovereign immunity. Sovereign immunity is why state agencies, including those like PA OVR, are beyond reproach. They are unaccountable if they, by and through their agents and/or employees, cause harm by negligence, malice, or indifference to any of us. And there is nothing we can do about it unless we pressure our elected officials to change the status quo through enactment of legislation. Even that possibility does not lead us out of the woods. Lawmakers are by and large, lawyers. Reading any type of legal document in all of its mysterious "legalese" is a daunting prospect for average Americans.

I read over the 120 page legal memorandum followed by the order setting aside Rick's death sentence signed by Judge DuBois. It was not an easy read. Simply put, Laird's appeals process went as follows:

1) New counsel [Atty. Dunham/Defenders Assoc.] entered an appearance for Laird on July 19th 1997. Additional testimony in support of Laird's petition for relief was heard at the PCRA hearing held in Bucks County from January 21st through January 28th in 1997. That court rendered its decision, denying PCRA relief on September 2nd 1997.The PA Supreme Court affirmed the lower court's order. <u>*Commonwealth v. Laird*</u>, 555 Pa.629, 726 A.2d 346 (1999).

2) Petitioner [Laird] filed a *pro se* Petition for Writ of Habeas Corpus under 28 U.S.C. § 2254 on May 5th 1999. Counsel was appointed by the court.

3) A counseled petition – a petition filed by the court-appointed counsel – for a Petition for Writ of Habeas Corpus was subsequently filed on Laird's behalf.

4) A supporting Memorandum of Law was filed on December 17th 1999.

5) Respondents [Bucks County Court] filed their answer to Laird's petition on February 18th 2000.

6) Rick Laird [through his counsel] filed a reply on March 23rd 2000.

7) Order for Habeas Corpus relief was granted on September 5th, 2001, pursuant to the Antiterrorism and Effective Death Penalty Act (AEDPA), 28 U.S.C. § 2254.

Several issues Rick raised on appeal were reviewed by the 3rd Circuit Federal Court in the eastern district. But the ones that resulted in Rick Laird being granted *habeas corpus* relief were based on four issues previously ruled on by the United States Supreme Court. These were *Bronshtein v. Horn*, *Mills v. Maryland*, *Holbrook v. Flynn* and *Strickland v. Washington* respectively where Laird's rights under the 8th & 14th Amendments of the US Constitution had been violated by errors on the part of the trial court, the prosecutor, and defense counsel.

Citing *Bronshtein*, the federal court ruled that the trial court had erred in allowing the jury to be instructed erroneously insofar as to absolve the prosecution of its burden of proof beyond reasonable doubt that Laird harbored "specific intent" to kill Milano. The reason intent plays such a vital part here is because of its key role in defining the varying degrees of homicide. Murder in the first degree requires that the prosecution meet its burden of proof beyond a reasonable doubt that a defendant had formed specific intent to kill. In order to determine intent, the defendant's state of mind must be examined. *"To determine the kind of homicide which the accomplice [defendant] is guilty, it is necessary to look into his state of mind; the requisite mental state must be proved beyond a reasonable doubt to be one which the accomplice harbored and cannot depend upon proof of intent to kill only in principle.....in the Petitioner's case, the jury was not specifically instructed that it needed to find that both defendants harbored a specific intent to kill in order to convict them both of first degree murder..."* Bronshtein v. Horn, __F.Supp.2d__, 2001 WL 767593. On this basis, the federal court granted Laird *habeas* relief.

Citing *Mills* on page 68 of the *habeas* ruling, the federal court cited US Supreme Court ruling: *"The 8th Amendment requires that the jury be able to consider and give effect to all relevant mitigating evidence offered by a defendant."* Boyde v. California, 494 U.S. 370, 377-78 (1990).

"The US Supreme Court made clear in Mills v. Maryland, 486 U.S. 367 (1988), *that if jurors were improperly led to believe that they could not each individually consider certain mitigating circumstances because they failed to agree unanimously as to the existence of that circumstance, then "some jurors were prevented from considering factors which may call for a less severe penalty". If a juror is thus prevented from considering the factors that call for a less severe penalty, the death sentence cannot stand.......Because the state court applied the incorrect rule to Petitioner's case, the Court concludes that the PA Supreme Court's determination on this issue is contrary to federal law as determined by the US Supreme Court...Laird's petition for habeas corpus relief will be granted on this claim."* (page 77 of the *habeas* ruling for Laird)

Now in plain English some examples of those mitigating factors the federal court referred to include Rick Laird's ADHD and his brain damage and learning disabilities stemming from a fractured skull as a result of beatings from his father. Sexual molestation by his father when he was only 9 years old could explain some of the unreasonable and intense hatred he expressed for homosexuals when he brutally slashed Anthony Milano's throat. A jury would not be obligated to let Laird off the hook entirely because of that, but they must be presented with the opportunity to consider it. And they must be instructed clearly by the trial court that their consideration of it does not have to be unanimous.

A single juror might vote for a lesser penalty than death because of that. If that occurs, then the sentence of death cannot be imposed by the trial court. Life in prison without the possibility of parole is imposed instead. In sum, Rick Laird was granted *habeas* relief because the trial court gave ambiguous and/or improper instructions to the jury with regard to weighing mitigating circumstances during the penalty phase of the trial. This violated Laird's rights under the 8th Amendment of the US Constitution.

In citing Holbrook, the federal court opined on Laird's appeal and recited the prior US Supreme Court ruling as follows: *"Petitioner claims that his right to a fair and reliable capital sentencing was violated when he was forced to wear visible shackles and handcuffs in front of the jury and that his trial counsel was ineffective for failing to object to the error....On direct appeal, the PA Supreme Court concluded that this claim did not entitle Petitioner to relief........The US Supreme Court has written that practices such as shackling and other overt displays of security are inherently prejudicial.....and* ***"should only be permitted where justified by an essential state interest specific to each trial."*** Holbrook v. Flynn, 475 U.S. 560, 568-69 (1986).

In plain English, the federal court, based on US Supreme Court ruling, held that Laird's appearance of being shackled gave the image of someone who was too dangerous to move about freely, even in the highly secure and regulated environs of a courtroom. That image could very well have influenced the jury into a death sentence instead of life in prison without the possibility of parole. On the surface, this may sound silly. However, upon digging below the surface, I can see the reasoning for such a ruling. Whether or not I can agree fully with it as being a violation of US Constitutional rights is a different story.

The power of suggestive reasoning is also referred to as "subliminal advertising" as it pertains to sub-conscious subtle advertising of products within movies and TV shows. It is a powerful thing that should never be underestimated. The best way to explain this concept of the *Holbrook* ruling in plain English would be to cite an example which everyone can relate to. Take the example of the negative public opinion against smoking.

The act of smoking and even the smokers themselves have come under voracious public attack within the last twenty years. Smoking and those who smoke have been made unpopular to the majority. The tobacco control movement, armed with generous funding (made possible through the "Master Settlement Agreement" – which is collusion between "Big Tobacco" and an arguably unconstitutional compact of state attorney generals), uses a significant portion of these funds for advertising. Even beyond overt advertising the "Tobacco Control" groups have pressured filmmakers to "de-normalize" smoking by restricting its occurrence to deeply faulted or outright evil characters. In order to "de-normalize" smoking, filmmakers no longer portray any characters smoking unless it is the villain, the bad guy. A classic example of this can be seen in the movie *"The Core"*.

The character of Dr. Zimsky – an evil scientist, depicted as a smoker was a plagiarist who stole credit for another scientist's work. He exceeded the authority granted by the US Dept. of Defense by doing an unauthorized experiment with a seismic weapon. This experiment ended up stalling the rotation of the Earth's core, resulting in the disintegration of Earth's magnetosphere – the magnetic field shielding Earth from solar winds and cosmic radiation. Without that shield our planet would be burned to a cinder, destroying all life as we know it. The connection of the smoking habit to his despicable character serves as subliminal advertising/suggestive reasoning that smokers are responsible for all of the world's ills, and hence are all evil selfish addicts who would destroy the entire planet.

Meanwhile, the movie's heroes are portrayed as non-smokers. One scene shows two of them socializing in a bar where none of the bar patrons are smoking. This gives the subconscious message that all smokers are criminals while all good and "normal" people are non-smokers. The power of suggestive reasoning should not be underestimated.

The primary reason that suggestive reasoning is so powerful is because people are visually oriented by nature. Most of the information we process comes to us visually. What we see affects what we think, how we behave, and what we learn. When a jury sees a defendant shackled like a wild animal, it serves to subliminally dehumanize him and gives the subconscious suggestion that out of two possible sentences, life in prison without parole, or death, the extreme sentence of execution is the only appropriate one. Applying this logic to the *Holbrook* ruling, I think we can more fully understand the US Supreme Court's logic behind this ruling. It is not small matter – especially in a capital trial during the penalty phase.

But the meat and potatoes of the appeal for Rick Laird's petition for *habeas* relief in the federal court is found beginning on page 81 and ending on page 94 of the federal court's ruling. The mitigating factors previously described in brief detail are treated and addressed more fully in this part insofar as how they relate to grounds for *habeas* relief pursuant to case precedent and US Supreme Court interpretation of the law in the treatment of "Ineffectiveness of Trial Counsel."

The way Ineffectiveness of Counsel should be treated is cited using the "Strickland Test." Under *Strickland v. Washington*, 466 U.S. 668 (1984), in order to establish a claim for ineffective assistance of counsel at trial or at a death penalty sentencing hearing, a convicted defendant must demonstrate that his counsel's performance:

(1) Fell below an objective standard of reasonableness, and;

(2) That counsel's deficient performance prejudiced the defense.

Both prongs of *Strickland* must hold and be satisfied in order for *habeas* relief to be granted on the claim of Ineffectiveness of Counsel. If a defendant's claim fails to meet either condition, his claim will not hold. On page 93 of the federal court's *habeas* ruling for Laird, the court's analysis reads: *"This Court concludes that the fact trial counsel presented some mitigating evidence does not warrant the conclusion that his failure to investigate other potential sources of mitigating evidence was reasonable..... "Presentation of some mitigating evidence does not excuse the failure to provide evidence of different mitigating circumstances"* *Jermyn v. Horn*, 1998 WL 754567 at *17 (M.D. Pa. Oct 27, 1998)..........*As there is no strategic explanation for trial counsel's failure to investigate the wealth of mitigating evidence available in this case, the Court concludes that trial counsel's performance was objectively unreasonable* [1st condition of Strickland]......*The Court further concluded that Petitioner suffered substantial prejudice as a result of trial counsel's deficient performance, resulting in a questionable penalty phase outcome.....Given the overwhelming mitigating evidence that would have been available in this case had trial counsel conducted even a cursory investigation into Petitioner's background, the Court concludes that, absent trial counsel's* *egregious errors, there is reasonable probability that the sentencing jury would have concluded the mitigating circumstances in this case substantially outweigh the aggravating circumstances. "In the context of a death penalty hearing, the second prong [of Strickland]is satisfied if there was a reasonable probability that at least one juror would be sufficiently influenced by mitigating evidence to vote against the imposition of the death penalty."* United States ex rel Emerson .v Gramley, 883 F. Supp.225,242 (N.D. Ill. 1995) - [2nd condition of Strickland].

In sum, defense Attorney Ron Elgart's failure to present readily and easily available mitigating evidence could have made a difference in the penalty phase outcome. Since death penalty cases are bifurcated into two parts, the guilt phase and the penalty phase, the mitigating evidence would not have had to be used in both. But when considering the sentence, it certainly should have been used. Not so much as to excuse Rick Laird for committing murder, but to demonstrate the idea that without those circumstances, Laird might not have violently lashed out to the extremes which he did when he killed Anthony Milano. Mitigating circumstances do not completely excuse or abrogate someone of criminal liability, but they do determine the degree and depth of punishment for that criminal liability.

The weighty mitigating factors in the case of Richard Laird were: untreated ADHD, organic brain damage caused by a skull fracture from beatings at the hands of his father, lack of intervention by the appropriate juvenile authorities when Rick Laird began getting into legal scrapes, sexual molestation by his father, a history of mental and emotional problems attested to by Laird's friend Kimberly Kessler, his ex-fiancée Barbara Parr (now Barbara Sylvia), his co-defendant Frank Chester, his mother Joyce Kessler, and his ex-wife JoAnne Samsel.

Barbara Sylvia stated in the sworn affidavit she submitted in support of Laird's petition for *habeas* relief that *"[she] was instructed by Mr. Elgart to plead for Rick's life and to show the jury our newborn son. Mr. Elgart never visited my home and never asked me any questions about Rick's background or his personality. I did not know that Rick's mental problems, head injuries or what he had gone through were important."*

Joyce Kessler stated in her submitted declaration that Rick Laird's father, Richard Laird, Sr., was an alcoholic who regularly abused her and often forced Rick to watch that abuse as a child. She stated that Rick was beaten frequently and severely, often without provocation. She further gave testament to the extreme difficulty of Rick's birth: he had been delivered with a forceps which is known to sometimes cause brain damage. The following statement given by Joyce Kessler was particularly heartbreaking:

"[Rick's father] never showed Ricky love or affection of any kind. He called him names all the time. He beat young Ricky constantly, for no reason at all. He would punch young Ricky. He would kick him all over his body, and would kick him on the groin. He would punch him in the face and head, and kick him there also. He hit him with boards and belts and wire hangers, all over Ricky's body. He seemed to especially enjoy striking Ricky on the groin and the head. Ricky's crying only made the beatings last longer, until Mr. Laird, Sr. was out of breath. Mr. Laird treated Ricky horribly. He choked young Ricky several times with his large hands, as he did with me. Mr. Laird also acted very inappropriately in his abuse of Ricky, forcing Ricky to engage in acts that no child should do and no one should be forced to do."

One need not be a rocket scientist to understand what "acts" Rick Laird was forced by his father to perform as a child. Examples of those acts were elaborated in greater detail in the following statements given by Kimberly Kessler – the former girlfriend of Rick's who had cold-cocked him.

Kimberly Kessler stated, in full agreement with and supported by the other two women's declarations, that: *"Rick confided in me that he had been sexually abused by his father. Rick told me that when he was a child, Mr. Laird would come naked into his bedroom and force Rick to perform oral sex on him. After Mr. Laird was done, he would beat Rick up, call him a 'nasty son-of-a-bitch' and tell him to go wash his mouth out or brush his teeth. Rick hated talking about this."*

Frank Chester, along with JoAnn Samsel and Barbara Sylvia, testified that the drug known as speed (methamphetamine) calmed Rick Laird down, helped him to focus, and even helped him to sleep.

In support of those sworn declarations were Laird's school records, medical records dealing with his skull fracture, his drug and alcohol addiction, and his arrests for his usage of methamphetamine as a self-medication for his undiagnosed ADHD. Finally, after his conviction during the PCRA process and after I entered the scene, Rick Laird was formally diagnosed with ADHD and organic brain injury by neuropsychologist Dr. Henry Dee and psychiatrist Dr. Robert Fox respectively. These experts were procured by the legal team at the Capital Defenders Association and they gave testimony during the state PCRA hearings.

In reference to Rick's drug and alcohol abuse Dr. Dee explained that since Rick suffered from ADHD, "You frequently find [abuse of] stimulant medications in patients that are Attention Deficit Disorder patients because they sort of accidently discover that that medication helps them focus, behave more productively."

That observation by Dr. Dee was corroborated and supported by other witnesses' statements given about Rick, saying that "speed calmed him down and helped him sleep".

Dr. Dee also affirmed at the PCRA hearing on January 21st 1997 that *"mental health problems can result from childhood physical and sexual abuse."* Recalling previous mention of Phineas Gage and how tissue damage to the brain caused Gage to become psychotic and unable to function in a socially acceptable manner, the evidence of Rick's brain damage certainly should have served as a mitigating circumstance. It was mitigating evidence the jury didn't have the chance to consider because it was never introduced by Attorney Elgart at the 1988 trial during the penalty phase after the guilt phase commenced. It was mitigating evidence that any reasonably competent attorney certainly should have introduced.

Dr. Dee's testimony about Rick's tendency to use speed and his reaction to that usewas reinforced by the testimony of Dr. Robert Fox – the psychiatrist who conducted an assessment of Rick at the request of Rick's lawyers from the Capital Defenders Association during the PCRA hearing. According to Dr. Fox: *"Individuals suffering from Attention Deficit, whether they be children or adults, they have what is described as a paradoxical, in other words, an opposite response to stimulating substances. So if you give somebody who is hyperactive a drug that would make a normal individual hyperactive, rather than making them more hyperactive it, in fact, slows them down."*

Dr. Silverman's report and his evaluation of Rick Laird during the original trial and on direct appeal corroborate the conclusions of Dr. Dee and Dr. Fox. There was no excuse for the defense counsel to not know of its significance in 1988. Silverman's report included the professional opinion that Laird's homophobia may have been caused by the fact that *"at about age 9 he had been required to perform fellatio on an adult male relative on a few separate occasions."* Therefore Elgart was derelict in his duty to Rick by failing to use that information during the penalty phase of the trial. Elgart held the position that his neglecting to investigate and present these factors was based on strategy. Elgart held that Rick had refused to plead anything other than not guilty and such mitigating factors would have meant changing to a guilty plea because the only way any diminished criminal liability factors can be used is under a diminished capacity claim. However, the US Supreme Court said in its ruling on *Strickland*: *"Counsel has a duty to make reasonable investigations or to make a reasonable decision that makes particular investigations unnecessary."* Clearly, the duties outlined by this include an attorney's duty to investigate and introduce a defendant's school and medical records as mitigating evidence.

The way appeals are handled within the justice system is very complicated. Interpretation of the law is often subjective. As demonstrated here, two courts can rule very differently on the exact same case law. If someone is found guilty of murder and sentenced to death, and new evidence that was not previously used surfaces, the condemned cannot simply enter it on their first appeal during the PCRA process. The rules and guidelines for filing appeals are very stringent. It is the rules of court which determine the grounds and guidelines on which an appeal may be filed, and then either granted or denied. It is not as simple as merely submitting proof that you are innocent or proof that you were denied your constitutional rights.

This is why it takes so long for those sentenced to death to have the courts rule on their appeals. The rules of procedure in the appellate courts differ from those of the trial court. Every aspect of the trial court and counsel is scrutinized for procedural error. For every appeal a prisoner files, the trial courts also have the right to counter-file and the appellate courts have the right to drag their feet. The system is not a series of black and white issues. Everything is subject to interpretation.

Chapter 20

"Justice renders unto everyone his due." ~ Cicero

The order signed by Judge Jan DuBois of the 3rd Circuit Federal Court granting Rick Laird *habeas corpus* relief was issued on September 5th 2001. The prosecution from the trial court had the right to appeal that order. That is the way our justice system works. Both sides have the right to appeal a ruling of the court, all the way to the US Supreme Court if necessary. As of 2005, Rick Laird still hadn't had his new trial. I had signed up for the news alerts on Google specifically to keep watch for that item. Donnie asked me why I never wrote to Frank Chester and got his side of the story. I had not previously thought to do so. The truth of the matter is that I was too ashamed.

I felt ashamed because I realized on a fateful bright sunny August day back in 1996, I had chosen to champion the cause of someone I mistakenly viewed as a victim when in fact he was a monster. He was diabolical to the core – regardless of the mitigating evidence. The fact was that he had not even once expressed any remorse for the slaying of Anthony Milano. I felt ashamed of my own piss poor judgment call to help a monster when I should have instead sought out and extended a helping hand to the Milano family. Did I really want to repeat the mistake of my naïve younger days? But Donnie made a good point: If I was ever to write this book, it would not be complete without something from Frank Chester. And so I began to write to him early in 2006, nineteen years after that horrific night that changed his life, Rick Laird's life, and ended Anthony Milano's life altogether.

I Googled his name online and found that a man named Jim Jenkins set up a webpage about Frank and the Milano murder. This site depicted Frank as being guilty of being a stupid teenager at the time of the murder and nothing more. An old picture of Frank from when he was a misguided younger man was posted on the page. He was really cute when he was younger. What a pity, I thought. He looked like he had so much going for him at one time – what a waste. Jim Jenkins painted Frank in a more favorable light than the mainstream news media had ever done. At the bottom of the webpage there was an address for sending donations to help pay for a good lawyer and the experts needed for Frank's appeals. Jim Jenkins firmly believed that Frank Chester was innocent and was wrongfully convicted for something he did not do.

Writing Frank was very awkward for me at first. Frank was initially surprised that I would write to him. He knew that I had previously helped his former buddy, his co-defendant, Rick Laird. Frank knew that Rick had maintained to me and his attorneys that he (Frank) was the killer. Frank's letters were always brief, but very cordial. He kept his letters very low key, nothing beyond civil pleasantries. One thing was certain; Frank Robert Chester was not going to do any talking about the case, not even about Laird's appeal. Frank Chester had only one thing to say about the Milano murder: He didn't do it, end of story.

When I asked Frank how he felt about all of it, expecting him to not reply, he surprised me. He stated that if he could change one thing, it would be that Anthony Milano would be alive and well today. Frank said that it [the murder] was stupid and should have never happened to begin with. Anthony should not have died. He felt bad for the Milanos. That was all he had to say about the crime and his case. He told me he was under strict orders from his attorneys to keep his mouth shut about the case, especially his appeal, and he couldn't discuss anything about it.

Frank also was very level-headed in the few letters we had exchanged. He was not into playing "convict-on-the-make" games. And that was a good thing. But he did have a sense of humor. When I wrote him I told him about finding Jim Jenkins' website about him and that based on his picture from when he was much younger, he was really cute. Frank wrote back to me, saying "Whaddya mean 'used to be really cute'! I still *am* cute!" Frank Chester sure had style.

Frank wrote about his Italian heritage, about memories of his childhood. He reminisced over the homemade spaghetti sauce his grandparents made from the vine-ripened tomatoes that they grew in their backyard. He inquired about my Jewish heritage and was interested but confused about *kashrut*, the set of Jewish kosher dietary laws enumerated in the Torah. He wrote about his love for classic cars. He told me of the time his ex-fiancée Colleen had hit him over the head with a cast iron fry pan because "he had called her the c-word" and then hastily admitted that he totally deserved the cast iron attitude adjustment for disrespecting her.

I began to have second thoughts about the narrow and harsh view I had previously harbored about Frank Chester. He was not out for pity and the nature of his letters bespoke a man who did not attempt to make excuses for himself and who was willing to take responsibility for his own actions – a quality that is rare among convicted felons, especially those on death row. But I had learned from my previous mistake of opening myself up to being manipulated, used and conned by Rick Laird when I was still young enough to be naïve and idealistic. I was not only conned by Rick, but also conned and then betrayed by Rick's brother Mark. I will never forget how badly I let Rick manipulate my thoughts and feelings all those years ago when I was naïvely misled into believing that Rick Laird was the victim. It was a mistake I vowed I would never repeat, ever. My confidence in my ability to trust my own judgment and make the right choices in trusting other people had been shaken to the core forever. I had come to realize that Rick was a monster with no remorse for anything. I was not going to allow myself to get conned again. As likeable and congenial as Frank Chester might be, I would maintain an "arm's length" correspondence with him. I simply did not trust myself to refrain from turning into a complete sap all over again. I remained emotionally detached. Our letters were about interesting trivia instead.

He wrote about an interest in pictures of our galaxy from the Hubble telescope. I sent him an artist's rendition of the most recently discovered new planet Sedna, named after the Arctic Ocean goddess of Inuit lore. I explained to him that Sedna was in the outermost region of our solar system, in the Oort cloud which is way beyond the Kuiper Belt where Pluto and Halley's Comet hails from. He seemed to enjoy that, especially when I explained that it took Sedna 10,500 years to make one complete orbit around the Sun and hence 1 Sedna year = 10,500 Earth years. He was fascinated to learn from me that the temperature on Sedna was roughly absolute zero: -460 °F = -273 °C = 0 °Kelvin and that absolute zero is defined as the temperature at which all known molecular movement ceases to occur.

When Frank asked me how I was able to get all this information, I explained that NASA had a very in-depth website on the Internet. This concept of an "information superhighway" really confused Frank. He had been in prison since December 30th, 1987. The Internet was in its infancy in 1987. Back then, if you said you could link to NASA from your home computer or that you had a "computer friend", people would call the men in the white coats for you (*too bad they missed Al Gore*). It was an overwhelming concept for him to grasp. His only concept of state of the art technology was the Holly four-barrel carburetor! He asked me if we were now living like the Jetsons or something. He reminded me that he had been in a 9 ft by 9 ft concrete cell for 23 hours a day these past nineteen years and that prisons did not have this new thing called the Internet. At least, inmates in the Restricted Housing Unit (RHU) on death row do not have access to it. He was totally lost when it came to things like email, computer viruses or the use of search engines like Google to access an infinite amount of information. I felt like I was trying to explain the concept of human life basics to an alien visitor from a faraway distant galaxy coming to Earth for the very first time.

Every day I faithfully read the Google alerts that arrived in my daily email, looking for news about Rick Laird's tentative new trial. Since the crime and original trial nineteen years ago generated national publicity, I knew that the online news from the suburban Philadelphia region in lower Bucks County would have coverage about the new trial date. On June 30th 2006, I got a Google alert with a link to the online newspaper Phillyburbs.com with news about Laird's new trial.

The Bucks County judge who would be presiding set a tentative trial date for sometime in October 2006. The judge had appointed Attorney John Kerrigan, former president of the Pennsylvania Criminal Defense Lawyers Association, to take over from Laird's previous attorneys who had withdrawn from the case. Kerrigan asked the judge to set bail for Rick Laird. That motion was opposed by the prosecution and the judge sided with the prosecutor. Meanwhile, Kerrigan said he would look into a parole bid for Laird and ask the judge to revisit the bail issue if parole is granted. Even though capital murder suspects no longer get bail in Pennsylvania, the laws in 1987 did allow for bail to be granted in such cases. Rick Laird's case would fall under the old rules. However, the chances of winning either a parole bid or bail were extremely slim. This was a high profile case which had helped to spark anti-hate crime legislation.

Kerrigan was asked how much he would be paid for representing Laird and declined to comment. However, it is well known that court-appointed attorneys in Pennsylvania are typically paid about $155,000 a year to represent indigent defendants. Sometimes exceptions to this norm are made in murder cases where some lawyers do get paid an hourly fee instead and are given extra money for the purpose of paying for expert testimonies. Not a bad paycheck for representing indigent defendants! That sum is over and above what they are simultaneously making from legal fees paid by their private practice clients who are not indigent and who have paid retainer fees. The average hourly fee charged by attorneys to represent someone in a criminal case is around $200 an hour.

During the "down" times when I had no insurance customers in my office, I went over all the letters I had received from Rick Laird. If I was going to write a book, I needed to catalogue and organize everything. Many evenings were spent falling asleep fully clothed on the comfortable old couch in my living room-turned-insurance office. That couch was too comfortable for me to part with: it may not have looked very professional, but I was running a very small business (that I started literally with nothing) from my home, so utility trumped image. I spent many late nights organizing everything I had filed about the Laird case while memories from my distant and buried past resurfaced as my mind reached back across the sands of time. I was uncertain whether I was emotionally ready to write this story, even though almost twelve years had passed. Time does not heal all wounds.

I felt torn up inside. I felt immensely inadequate for not seeing Rick Laird for what he was back in 1996. I also blamed myself for being blinded by my resentment of the smug and affluent "haves" for their cavalier and condescending attitudes towards the poor. I felt that had I not stepped in and helped, I would simply be part of the problem instead of part of the solution where social justice is concerned. On the other hand, I also felt that victims of crimes and their families, particularly like Anthony Milano's family, are inadequately served and are too often ignored. Victims cannot ever truly be made completely whole. The closest we can come to that is through enforcing our laws and making criminals pay their debts to society.

Too often, the rights of the victims are ignored while almost everyone focuses on the rights of the criminals. A good case in point was that of Larry Singleton.

Larry Singleton was a 51 year old retired merchant marine. On September 30th, 1978, Singleton picked up Mary Bell Vincent – a 15 year old run-away who was hitchhiking from Las Vegas to California to go live with her grandfather. When Singleton failed to take the correct exit off of I-5, Mary Vincent sensed something was terribly wrong and she got scared. Singleton pulled off to the side of the road on a deserted part of I-5, telling young Mary that he needed to relieve himself. She got out of the van, planning to make a run for it. The moment she bent down to tie her sneaker Larry Singleton hit her over the head, knocking her senseless. He tied her wrists together and repeatedly raped and sodomized her. During the whole ordeal, she cried and pleaded with her attacker to let her go. After several hours of hell, Singleton got an axe out of the back of his van and hacked off both of Mary Vincent's arms right below the elbow, snarling at the poor terrified girl as he hacked away, "You wanna be free? There – now you're free." It took a total of five blows to sever her arms – while she screamed in pain and despair, feeling every blow of the axe. She was found by tourists while she was wandering bloody and naked along the road, with the stumps of her arms held up to slow the bleeding. She was wrapped in towels and rushed to the nearest hospital.

Larry Singleton had taken her innocence, both of her arms, and ruined her entire life. For his monstrous crime, he was sentenced to a mere 14 years in prison. From his prison cell in San Quentin, he wrote threatening letters to Mary Singleton's family vowing to hunt her down to "finish the job" because she had testified against him in court. After serving only 8 years of his sentence, he was released on parole for good behavior – despite the fact that he had threatened his victim and her family and obviously had no remorse for the pain and suffering he caused this poor girl. He was not even compelled to pay his victim any restitution for her medical bills or for the two prosthetic hooks she now wore – thanks to him. In fact, her family would not have been able to afford the prosthetic arms she got in 1978 if it were not for the good will and sympathy of other citizens in the community who set up a donation fund for her to get the prosthetic arms she needed.

Meanwhile, Larry Singleton manipulated countless prisoners' rights groups into believing that *he* was the victim because the citizens of California refused to accept him back into the community upon his release! Singleton ended up moving to Florida where ex-offenders' advocate groups and Singleton's family helped set him up with a home of his own and a job. The media portrayed Singleton as a victim of social injustice who had paid his debt to society and deserved a second chance. Like so many hard-core criminals, Singleton swore up and down that he was innocent, that he had been framed. The state of California had been lenient in releasing him on parole without forcing him to pay any restitution. His story got nationwide attention while his victim, Mary Vincent, was all but forgotten and relegated to eking out a subsistence on welfare and SSI combined payments totaling a mere $600 per month. To add insult to injury, Medicaid refused to cover the new prosthetic arms she needed after her original ones wore out. But this same system helps dangerous men like Larry Singleton, giving them everything they need from housing assistance to job placement and free counseling in order to re-enter society. There was no state-funded counseling or much other help for poor Mary Vincent. She was denied justice forever while he was set free for good behavior.

Then in February 1997, 69 year old Singleton bludgeoned and stabbed 31 year old Roxanne Hayes to death. Roxanne Hayes was a poor single mother who resorted to prostitution in order to keep her three children fed, clothed and housed. Her acquaintances told police that Roxanne would not normally go to a john's house, but in the case of Larry Singleton, she didn't think that this grandfatherly looking 69 year old man was dangerous. She was wrong. And she paid for her mistake with her life. The prosecution for the state of Florida knew of Singleton's past and flew 39 year old Mary Vincent in from across the country to testify. After the jury saw the two claw-like prosthetics in place of arms and heard her testimony, they sentenced Singleton to death. Singleton died of cancer in prison in January of 2002. If the judicial system in California had not been lenient on Singleton by releasing him on parole after he had served only half of his sentence; if Singleton had originally been sentenced to life without parole for what he did to Mary Vincent, he would not have been able to harm or kill anyone else.

But for all the vicious fiends like Larry Singleton and Rick Laird who are justly imprisoned and sentenced to death, there are many who truly are innocent and who have been wrongfully convicted by over-zealous prosecutors who are willing to win at all costs – even if that means sacrificing those from the bottom social rungs of society. There have been one hundred and twenty-three men released from death row who were wrongfully convicted. They were released *only* because DNA proved their innocence beyond a reasonable doubt. For every Rick Laird, there's a Ray Krone, a Nick Yarris, a Dennis Counterman, and a Kerry Max Cook; innocents who had years of their lives stolen from them by a faulted judicial system.

Because they are poor, because they aren't "smart" and "successful", and because they don't enjoy any social prestige, nobody cares about such people. The poor are good enough to fight and die in this nation's military. The poor are good enough to provide paychecks for government agency employees by being welfare "case files", and good enough to ensure a comfortable living for probation officers. But they are not good enough for society to give a damn about. I was at war with my own confused conscience over all of it.

However, I was not the only one in turmoil: Frank Chester's stepfather passed away and his mother was inconsolable. The week before Thanksgiving 2006, I received a handwritten letter from Frank Chester. A handwritten letter was completely out of character for him: all the rest of his letters were typed on an electric typewriter with spell-checking capability. Frank informed me that Governor Ed Rendell had just signed his death warrant. He was taken to a special cell near the lethal injection chamber and put under suicide watch. He could not take his typewriter with him so he drafted this letter by hand. He was trying to be strong for his mother. He seemed more concerned about how his mother was bearing up than he was about his own fate. The toll this exerted on his mother was unfathomable. I did not even know how to begin to respond. Before Frank could write me with an update, the news via Google Alert informed me that his execution had been stayed because of an appeal that is still in process as I write this book. I wrote Frank to let him know I that I got his letter and the Google Alert and that I understood what happened.

Although Frank Chester did not divulge any information as to the basis for his appeal or anything about its status in any of his letters to me, it is what his letters did *not* say that spoke volumes of his character. He did not seek feedback from me on ways to help him beat the death penalty. He did not lean on me and make unreasonable demands on my time the way Rick Laird had done. He did not lay guilt trips on me or pressure me into putting my life on hold in order to help him. He did not attempt to play the "lost-kitten-in-the-rain" game with me. In the face of his possible execution, his concern was for others instead of himself. He would have been fully justified in being self-centered in his situation, but he was not.

I began thinking that the low opinion I once had of him were poorly founded because of how much I had let Rick manipulate my thoughts and feelings all those years ago when I was a naïve younger woman and thought Rick Laird was the victim. Maybe I had been wrong in my feelings about Frank altogether and owed him an apology for having concentrated all my efforts on helping Rick while ignoring him completely.

After Frank's brief scare with his near-execution, I received another Google Alert in my email. Rick Laird's new trial was finally going to begin shortly after the New Year sometime in January 2007. Diane Gibbons, District Attorney for Bucks County, expressed moral indignation at having to retry the twenty year old murder case. Her anger was fully justifiable. Her office would have to re-do the job that someone else had screwed up with seemingly hair-splitting technicalities. And these errors had not occurred under her watch.

Her deputy district attorney Michelle Henry, a top shelf and well-respected prosecutor, was assigned to prosecute the case for the Commonwealth. She would be seeking the death penalty against Richard Laird. This case would not be an easy one because retrials never are. The prosecution always has the greatest burden. Ten or twenty years after the fact that burden seem almost as difficult and heavy as the task entailing the rock of Sisyphus. If Michelle Henry failed to successfully prosecute this case, she would never live it down. Even if she was successful in making her case before the jury, her *modus operandi* would be scrutinized by anti-death penalty groups who would undoubtedly cry foul. Michelle Henry was stuck walking a tightrope and her position was decidedly unenviable. She had very little time to prepare her case and time is of the essence in any formal legal proceeding.

Since the case was nearly twenty years old, tracking down witnesses for the prosecution was a daunting prospect. A lot happens over twenty years. People die, people become old and ill, and people move out of state and cannot be easily located. One witness for the prosecution, Gale Gardner, had moved to Florida and would have to be formally subpoenaed. Another, Pete Carpinona, had died several years ago. His testimony was crucial to the case, but dead witnesses cannot re-testify, for obvious reasons. However, there was a lot more at stake than the professionalism and reputation of the district attorney's office: the new trial for this twenty year old homicide would also rip open old wounds that had never healed for the families involved.

Rose Milano had died several years ago, going to her grave grief-stricken over the loss of her only son. Vito Milano, the victim's father, was now seventy-eight years old and had a heart condition. He stated to a news reporter for *The Trentonian*, "They should have killed him [Laird] 18 years ago when he was convicted. It's ridiculous….My wife Rose died 12 years ago of grief over the death of our son. This has destroyed our whole family……They [Chester and Laird] tricked my son and forced him to go into the woods."

The stress and ordeal of this new trial would be colossal for everyone involved. Annamarie, Anthony's sister, had never quite gotten over her brother's murder. Every Christmas for the past twenty years, the memories of her brother's murder had haunted her. Emotionally scarred and traumatized for life, she had been through years upon years of psychological counseling in her attempt to cope. Now she and her father would have to relive the nightmare all over again, because the killer had not been properly brought to justice and made to pay his debt to society - all because of technical errors from the first trial, and because of my error in helping him get a new one.

But the Milanos were not the only victims. The families of both Rick Laird and Frank Chester were peripheral victims, forgotten victims who would suffer, too. Once more, they would be thrust into the limelight of the media and the press. Once more they would be put in the awkward position of being subjected to silent, judgmental stares for a crime that they themselves had nothing to do with. Rick's children, Ricky and Rachel by his ex-wife JoAnn, were in grade school when the murder happened. They were now young adults. They would see their father's name splattered all over the front page news because he committed a grisly murder. Their lives would be torn asunder once more with the publicized account of how a member of their family utterly destroyed another family out of inexplicable hatred and malice. They would be confronted with every last gory detail – again.

Barbara (Parr) Sylvia, who was pregnant with Rick's child at the time of the murder and his subsequent arrest, would have to relive the moment that she realized that the love of her life was involved in a murder. The painful memories would come flooding back to haunt her.

Could anyone understand how she must have felt, enduring the travails of childbirth alone, facing the daunting prospect of single motherhood while the baby's father was in prison facing a death penalty trial? How it felt knowing that the man who had sired the life within her womb during an act of love was the same man who snuffed out the life of another human being, another mother's child? Or how it felt not knowing what to tell that child about his father while he grows up? This must have been an inescapable and ongoing nightmare for her.

Their son Nicholas was only a newborn when Rick Laird was convicted and sentenced to death at the original trial on May 19th, 1988. And how well did poor Nicholas cope growing up, wondering what had happened to his father – and why it happened? Knowing your father is on death row for first degree murder would be enough to break the spirit of even the most resilient of children. Nicholas was eighteen or nineteen years old now. He would be a senior in high school, or maybe even a freshman in college.

The retrial for Richard Laird reopened bad memories and old wounds for many. There are some things that the passage of time does not fix. The new trial, set to begin on January 31st 2007, was to be presided over by Judge Rea Boylan. Judge Boylan was taking every conceivable precaution so that no one would be able to come back and point the finger at her for failing to ensure Richard Laird's right to a fair trial under her watch. She issued a gag order that was to remain in effect until the trial was over. No one was permitted to talk to anyone about the case until the trial ended. That order applied to the media and to the public at large. She made it perfectly clear that anyone –including the DA – who violated the gag order would be subject to a contempt of court charge and possible jail time. Judge Rea Boylan was not fooling around. While gathering the final details for this book I found that I would have to wait until the gag order was lifted before I could even talk with the defense counsel, much less any witnesses, the police, or the prosecutor about the new trial.

The gag order prevented me from doing any interviews over the phone from Erie, Pennsylvania where I live. That meant I would have to travel all the way across state and attend the trial if I was going to be able to completely and accurately write about this case. Luckily for me, I had a very good friend in Philadelphia who offered to put me up on a spare cot in his living room. I would commute from his home in Philadelphia to the Bucks County Courthouse in Doylestown to observe the trial and hopefully speak with witnesses afterward. My friend was intrigued by the case.

That friend – Michael Joseph Francis McFadden – is a brilliant writer, social activist, and Wharton scholar who, during his college days in the 1970's, became heavily involved with the peace movement. Coming of age during an insanely expensive arms race during the Cold War, world peace was of paramount importance to Michael and countless others of his generation. His work as a peace activist was recognized internationally, even by persons as notable as Her Majesty Queen Elizabeth II of England! He is a published author in his own right: his book, *"Dissecting Antismokers Brains"* is highly controversial due to the subject matter involving the debates over second hand smoke and smoking bans. We found a common bond in our mutual tendencies to champion the causes of underdogs and take a stand for social justice even when such a stand might be politically unpopular.

Like many intelligent and talented people, he is an eccentric by any standard. A recluse by nature, he is too modest about his accomplishments and happiest when surrounded with the company of a library full of good books, an endless supply of chocolates, recorded episodes of *Monk*, and his Burmese cat, Buster. When a wayward bat accidently flew into his house through an open window, he was more concerned for the bat's happiness and well-being than anything else. He is vehemently opposed to the notion of harming any animal – even those that most people would consider vermin – although he does draw the line at mosquitoes.

A youthful, almost boyish, even at 55, his long brownish-gray hair reaches all the way down his back, usually worn in a ponytail. As a child of the sixties, he has never quite lost the idealism of his youth. He is still a hippie peacenik. Never one to be fashion conscious, he doesn't pay too much attention to color-coordination. He's got a lot of style. And that's what I love about him. His blue-gray eyes shine like opals when he is happy and his smile would melt your heart. He is as likeable and charming as he is intelligent. Understanding him however, was another story. Complex, brilliant people are not always the easiest to understand – but nice ones like Michael can be a treat and a rare privilege to know. He is a friend who has enriched my life enormously.

It was the gentle reassurance of acceptance from Michael which was the deciding factor for me to follow through with writing this book. I left for Philadelphia with my Mapquested driving directions to Michael's house.

Before leaving Erie, my husband Donnie who has been enormously supportive of my efforts in writing this book, made a large batch of homemade spaghetti sauce for me to take with me to share with Michael in gratitude for his hospitality while I would be covering Laird's new trial. I called Michael to let him know approximately what time I would be arriving. It would be close to an eight hour drive, including fuel stops. I would be arriving long after dark, close to midnight. Michael described his house to me because he wanted to make sure I didn't miss it on a dark, unfamiliar street. He described it to me as looking abandoned, and of course I thought he was speaking metaphorically. However, when I finally arrived in Philly and found his street, I saw that he was indeed quite serious. His house is an eerie looking 3-story row home reminiscent of the house belonging to the Once-ler, the fictitious villain who turned remorseful for his ruining of the environment in Dr. Suess's *The Lorax*. After parking the truck and walking up the creaking front porch steps, I almost expected a long hand to appear from the top story window and drop a truffula seed down for me to catch.

But the house was not abandoned and the Once-ler did not live there. Michael answered the door beaming with happiness that I finally made it to Philadelphia safe and sound. He was wearing a long camouflage colored wool hat. Exchange it for one with red and white stripes and he would have looked exactly like one of the Dr. Suess characters. It was "to keep his brain warm", he explained smiling at me while pointing to his hat. He actually looked very cute wearing it and reminded me of an elf, a very cute elf. Michael J. McFadden definitely has a unique style.

Since January was usually a dead month for any insurance customers, Donnie would be able to hold down the fort while I was in Philadelphia at Michael's to cover the trial. The trial was scheduled to begin on January 31st, 2007. However, as I soon found out, courts can reschedule at the last minute without advance notice to the public. On January 31st, I drove from Michael's house in Philadelphia to Doylestown, the county seat of Bucks County where the trial was to be held. I was in for a shock. Expecting to hear both John Kerrigan and Michelle Henry make their opening arguments, I found upon arriving that the court had not yet finished with the *voir dire* process of jury selection! Arguments would begin on the following Monday, February 5th 2007.

I had to call Donnie. I was afraid he would go absolutely nuclear at hearing of the delay. Donnie was very uncomfortable with computers. He was not computer savvy and was afraid of accidently hitting the wrong key or clicking on the wrong icon by mistake and wiping out something of critical importance. The learning curve for computer use and literacy is very steep for many people –especially those who were not riding the technology wave from the beginning when computers started to become commonplace. Donnie is a retired and disabled former foundry worker in his early sixties. Even if we could have afforded classes for Donnie to learn the basics, at his age it was mission impossible to overcome the learning curve of this technology because of all the intricate details involved. And there are always things that can – and often do – go wrong when using a computer. A basic task such as uploading customers' premium payments was a nerve-racking experience for him because the insurance carriers' websites are often not very user-friendly.

Being a micro-enterprise business owner who began without any start-up capital or even access to business credit, I didn't have the money to hire a temp – much less a temp who had a PA property & casualty insurance producer's license. Any potential new customers coming in requesting quotes and buying new policies would have to speak with me as is required under state law: only licensed agents may give quotes and discuss coverage options. But I was nearly 500 miles away from home, across the state in Philadelphia until after the end of the trial. And even after the trial I would have to stay in Philadelphia to interview those with whom I could not speak to while the gag order was in effect. Donnie was not going to be thrilled at having to suffer my absence an extra week or two. And we could not afford to shut down my small insurance agency until the trial was over when I would be returning home to Erie. All we could do was try our best and hope nothing went wrong during the three weeks I would be gone.

I had computer and Internet access at Michael's house so I was able to handle some of the agency stuff that Donnie was not licensed to do. But handling any potential new business from across state would be tricky. As noted earlier, under state law, only a licensed agent may give quotes and upload new policies. Donnie would not be legally allowed to do this in my absence, even if he knew how to. In order to sell a policy, the customer would have to talk to me, and that had to be done on my cell phone after I got out of the courthouse. I had to leave my cell phone in the truck because cell phones were not permitted to be turned on and serve as a potential disruption inside Judge Boylan's courtroom.

If a new customer came in needing a quote and auto insurance instantly because he or she was buying a car, they would have to wait to contact me until court was adjourned at the end of each day and I could turn the cell phone back on. Then they would have to wait two hours for me to fight suburban Philadelphia rush hour traffic to get from Doylestown back to Michael's where I would be able to get online, log on to AIG's site to do a quote to process the policy. Covering this new trial was fraught with hurdles and difficulties. It was difficult for someone with limited resources who was simultaneously trying to run a small business. But there was something bigger than that which weighed on my mind: It was something that weighed on my soul like a battleship chain. There was nothing that either Donnie or Michael could say or do to console me.

If for any reason Rick Laird was found guilty of a lesser degree of murder, given credit for time served and walked out of prison a free man, the release of a remorseless psychopathic monster would ultimately be all my fault. It would be my fault because I was the one who helped him get his new trial initially by bringing his ADHD and learning disabilities to the forefront. It would be my fault because I was the one who sold Rick Laird to Attorney Robert Dunham at the Defenders Association. Attorney Dunham was initially uncomfortable with taking over Rick's appeal because Rick was not completely innocent. The Defenders Association had sparse resources and wrongfully convicted inmates with proof of innocence were more compelling cases to undertake. But I sold Dunham on championing Laird's cause on the basis of failure of trial counsel to pursue the diminished capacity claim, as well as failure to bring up the mitigating circumstances during the penalty phase. It was I who had convinced Dunham that undertaking Rick Laird's appeal was the right thing to do.

But now my conscience was gnawing at me constantly over my involvement in Rick Laird's appeals ten years in the past. The implications for the Milanos devastated me: they could be denied justice by the very same system that they had supported, lived within and believed in. The Milanos had been crushed once by the senseless loss of Anthony, a son and a brother. Then their world was torn asunder once again when a new trial was granted for one of the men convicted as being responsible for their loss. If Rick Laird walked out of the Bucks County Courthouse a free man and returned to their small community, it would utterly destroy them.

Not only would the injustice of a murderer going free destroy the Milanos, it would also mean that a psychopath who had already tasted blood with no remorse would be released back into civilized society. If he could kill once and not feel a shred of sorrow for what he had done, he could very easily kill again without a qualm of conscience. He had a taste for it now, and the brutalities of life within the Pennsylvania prison system's death row certainly were not exactly conducive to his rehabilitation and normal functioning once he was released back into society.

Regardless of what anyone else tried to tell me in an attempt to comfort me, I firmly believed it would be my entire fault if this monster walked. Nothing could lift that burden from my soul. It is easy to sanctimoniously stand on a pedestal of principles and pound the pulpit when the real lives at stake and the communities involved are not your own. But it's different if you're the one looking down the barrel of the gun.

Opening arguments began on Monday, February 5th 2007. It was one of the coldest and most brutal late winter snaps in southeastern Pennsylvania history. Temperatures hovered in the single digits during the day. The icy winds that whipped me from every direction sliced through my clothes like a knife as I shivered during the walk from the courthouse parking lot. It was so bitter cold that the short walk seemed like a marathon mile. It was even too cold to snow.

Upon entering the courthouse, I went through the metal detectors and had my attaché case put on the X-ray conveyor belt to be scanned for any contraband. The Bucks County Courthouse was small, but modern-looking in its architecture that was Frank Lloyd Wright inspired. It was a rotund building with an open floor plan and spiral stairs that hugged the curved wall. The courtroom where the trial was to be held was in the lower level of the rotund shaped courthouse building. A bronze framed legend hung on the wall next to an elevator listing the room numbers and offices within the courthouse. Clerks busily scurried about wheeling huge carts containing Rubbermaid bins filled with files. Uniformed police and sheriffs milled around chatting excitedly in nervous anticipation of the impending re-trial of Richard Laird. The sheriffs smiled and greeted each courthouse visitor politely as they directed them to place their hand bags or briefcases on the X-ray conveyor belt and stepped through the metal detector. At the doorway to the courtroom there was another metal detector manned by another sheriff. Once again I had to empty my change, keys and contents of my briefcase into a plastic tray.

The courtroom had a high domed ceiling and walls that were all painted a bright white. The maroon upholstered seats for spectators were similar to seats in movie theaters. Richard Laird was seated at a large table flanked by two very imposing and distinguished looking attorneys opposite the district attorney's table. It had been twelve years since I had last seen Richard Laird. The ageing process had been far kinder to him than it had been to me. Perimenopausal weight gain was my nemesis and it left me feeling extremely self-conscious about going out in public. Meanwhile the only noticeable difference about Rick Laird was his hair and eyeglasses. His hair was cropped stylishly short, and had turned a very distinguished looking salt and pepper gray. His black-rimmed eyeglasses were of the latest fashionable style. Instead of a bright orange prison jumpsuit, he wore casual dress pants and a cream colored Cardigan sweater over a pressed white dress shirt. He did not look like the drug-crazed, bearded and tattooed thug who had brutally murdered someone 19 years ago. Instead, he looked like he could have been a bank vice president or a mainstream CEO. The table of three, Rick Laird and his two attorneys, looked like a trio of power brokers about to make a corporate acquisition.

I snuck into the back row in the spectators' section behind other trial observers, mostly newspaper journalists covering the trial, hoping that Rick wouldn't notice my presence. I didn't want him to see me. Not so much because of my personal self-consciousness, but because of the parting of ways that we had on that dreadful day 12 years ago when I last saw him in prison: that day when his soulless eyes seared through me with hatred for my audacity in asking him if he felt any sorrow for poor Anthony Milano: a day I will never forget. He was not tucked safely away behind bullet-proof glass this time and constrained by shackles and leg irons. Despite the fact that I was among plenty of guards and armed sheriffs, I was afraid of Rick. I knew what he was, diminished capacity or no diminished capacity. I had looked into the eyes of a monster. I knew what degree of evil, what depth of depravity, dwelt there…and I was afraid.

Seated in the front row closest to the jury box were Vito Milano, his daughter Annamarie, and their legal advocate, a woman about my age who was accompanying the Milanos for moral support.

Annamarie was a couple years older than me. Twenty years after the murder, she was a plump but pretty woman with dark brown eyes and jet black shoulder length hair. She and her father held each other's hands for support.

On the opposite end in the front row, seated directly behind Richard Laird and his lawyers, was a very tiny and petite young blonde. Her name was Nicole Knox and she was Richard Laird's niece. A friendly young reporter, Tim Cwiek, from the Philadelphia Gay News sat next to me. Although he was obviously affiliated with an organization supportive of gays and sympathetic to the abuse gays often endure, he told me he didn't want to see Rick Laird get the death penalty. Other journalists from other newspapers were not quite as sympathetic to Laird's situation. While they refrained from voicing their opinions, their general mood was clearly reserved.

The district attorney, Michelle Henry, looked to be younger than I. She was smaller in stature and height, with shoulder length straight brown hair. Wearing no make-up or jewelry except for a string of pearls that accentuated her navy dress suit, she looked very austere. She was the picture of a highly educated and accomplished patrician WASP woman of the east coast. Seated next to Michelle Henry was another deputy district attorney, Robin Twombly. Robin was visibly pregnant and dressed fashionably and professionally in a tailored maternity suit. A laptop computer and a screen for viewing Power Point slide presentations were located close to the judge.

After the jurors filed into the jury box, the court was brought formally into session. John Kerrigan's opening statement to the jury was well presented. He chose his words with care as he spoke: "Richard Laird admits he is guilty of murder. We submit that it's not first degree murder. He spent the last 19 years of his life in prison and will spend the rest of his life in prison. He was impaired, his brain is damaged, and he had diminished capacity and underwent serious alcohol consumption that night." Kerrigan was confident that he could prevail, but he would soon find out that Deputy District Attorney Michelle Henry was a tenacious adversary.

Deputy District Attorney Michelle Henry's strategy was very different from Alan Rubenstein's. She would not use emotionally charged statements or the aggressive type of litigation favored by John Kerrigan. Instead of being a high-energy dynamo, she was reserved. Her approach was to give the defense counsel enough rope and let them hang themselves. Her opening statement to the jury was simple and spoken in a quiet gracious manner. That was *her* style. She quietly stood and faced the jury, and spoke in a calm level-headed manner.

"He's saying, *'I'm a killer, but excuse me. Excuse me for the savage brutality I did, because I drank too much.'* " Michelle Henry let the jury meditate on the thought that personal responsibility on the part of Richard Laird should not simply be ignored.

Her first witness was Vito Milano, the victim's father. She asked Vito about the last time he saw his son alive. With tears welling up in his eyes, Vito painfully recalled the last night he and his now deceased wife had seen Anthony alive. Anthony stopped home to drop off his Bible study class notes and then went to go get a beer and a sandwich and was planning to return home early. "And then I never see my son no more," Vito said, choking back tears.

John Kerrigan launched into a harsh cross-examination of Vito Milano regarding the $50,000 he and his late wife had received from the settlement of their *dram shop* liability suit against the Edgely Inn. I believe I was not the only one to perceive Kerrigan's approach as a low-ball attempt to imply that Rose and Vito Milano had somehow been made whole by their *dram shop* suit for the killing of their son and that Vito simply wanted to use the court system to exact revenge rather than to pursue justice. It was a defense tactic that was in very poor taste; however, defense attorneys are often put in the distasteful position of trying to make silk purses from sows' ears.

Since Kerrigan and his co-counsel Attorney Keith Williams together with Laird agreed that admitting criminal liability under a diminished capacity claim was in Laird's best interest, the subject of intoxication as well as bar owner liability would have to be mentioned. However, the tactic of mercilessly attacking the victim's now octogenarian father was not well received. Brief mention of *dram shop* and how it tied in with this case was one thing – launching into the victim's family was quite a different matter.

Dram shop is a legal term that refers to bars, pubs, taverns and the like which serve alcoholic beverages. Originally, it literally meant a shop where spirits are sold by the *dram*, a unit of small measurement of liquid. Generally, the dram shop laws establish the liability of businesses arising out of the sale of alcohol to visibly intoxicated patrons and/or minors who subsequently cause injury or death to third parties as a result of car accidents and other sorts of injuries and deaths directly resulting from alcohol-induced impaired judgment. These laws are intended to protect the public from the hazards caused by irresponsibly serving alcohol to minors and intoxicated patrons. They seek to define the balance, the line, between personal responsibility borne by alcohol consumers and the comparative negligence liability of those serving them.

As soon as Kerrigan became antagonistic in his questioning of Vito Milano leading into the dram shop settlement, Judge Boylan sternly scolded him from the bench: "I am not going to allow you, Mr. Kerrigan, to cross-examine this witness on this because the only information he might have would be third party hearsay."

Judge Boylan quickly called for a short recess and addressed both Michelle Henry and John Kerrigan without calling them to approach the bench. Kerrigan was insistent about the relevance of the dram shop issue and the money received by the Milanos. However, Judge Boylan was not about to be moved from her firm position on the matter. And this was *her* courtroom. She was conscientiously taking every conceivable precaution to prevent this case from boomeranging back to her from an appellate court for procedural error and failure to ensure the defendant a fair trial. She was not about to have *that* jeopardized by any rash decisions as to what would be permissible for the defense to introduce and what would not.

"If I allow you to cross-examine this witness along these lines, I am then going to have to be fair to the prosecution and allow Ms. Henry to produce evidence and witnesses that will substantiate the claim that your client was a homicidal psychopath regardless of the alcohol liability issue. I am sure you do not want *that*, Mr. Kerrigan." The message was clear to Kerrigan that the dram shop issue was one sleeping dog that would be best left undisturbed. Kerrigan looked frustrated and disappointed as he returned to the defense table and the judge directed the tipstaff to bring the jurors back into the courtroom.

The next witness for the Commonwealth was Orpah Newswanger. She had been the Bible study teacher with whom Anthony Milano had met before going out for that fateful sandwich and beer. Ms. Newswanger testified that she lived in Morrisville, PA for the past 10 years and worked as an Activities Aide at Penn Village, an assisted living community for the elderly and disabled. She recalled in a very meek voice that the polite, mild-mannered victim left her home after the Bible study class at roughly 10:40 PM on the evening of December 14th 1987. After Ms. Newswanger stepped down from the witness stand, the district attorney called Lt. Charles McGuigan to the stand. He was a very distinguished-looking older gentleman in his crisp charcoal suit. He reminded me of a slimmer and younger version of Clint Eastwood, although with softer facial features.

Lt. McGuigan had been on the Bristol Police force for 20 years. He was a young patrolman when the murder happened. He was now a lieutenant with a distinguished career, free from any disciplinary actions or complaints. McGuigan recalled for the court the specifics of the night in question so long ago. He received a call from dispatch at 11:17 PM regarding a suspicious car fire off of US Rte 13 at 1324 Ashby Avenue. Upon arriving at the scene he found a black 1976 Chevy Nova fully engulfed in flames and the fire department in the process of getting the blaze under control.

"I got the tag, the license plate information from the car. EKF-822, Pennsylvania, belonging to a Rose Milano," McGuigan testified. The young district attorney politely asked him what he did next after obtaining the registration information from the car. He answered, "Around 1:35 AM, accompanied by Officer Newsinski, I walked 20-25 yards into the woods and then I came upon the victim, Anthony Milano."

The petite soft-spoken DA responded by asking, "Can you describe any weeds or grass in the area at that time?" McGuigan replied that the area had 4 ft tall weeds and field grass. Michelle Henry then politely requested the court's permission to set up the Power Point slide presentation of the crime scene photos. Judge Boylan granted permission to do so with the agreement of John Kerrigan.

The lights were dimmed and the laptop computer with the Power Point slide presentation was quickly set up. Pictures of the crime scene were projected larger than life onto the screen near the front of the courtroom close to the judge where it was clearly visible to the judge, jury and all court spectators within the courtroom. Some of the shots taken were from a bird's eye view of the scene, others were shots taken from eye level with respect to the ground. Each slide was listed in alpha-numeric order. The most disturbing picture of them all was Exhibit C-19. It was the picture of Anthony Milano exactly as Officer McGuigan had found him.

For the very first time since my initial involvement with Rick Laird's appeal, I saw the full depth and depravity of the carnage he had exacted on a smaller and innocent man who never had a chance. Anthony Milano, cut down in what should have been the best years of his life, lay lifeless and crumpled in a semi-fetal position among the weeds and tall grass. An expression of fear was frozen on his young face. Where his throat had been viciously hacked to shreds with a utility knife, he looked more like the victim of a Great White shark attack than a homicide. His neck had been so violently and repeatedly slashed that there was nothing but a jagged and gaping hole where his throat had been. This was definitely the work of a monster.

It took every ounce of inner strength to remain properly composed and to refrain from letting my emotions get the best of me, causing me to break down in tears while observing the solemn and formal proceedings of the trial. I was not the only one present who was visibly shaken. The jurors seemed to be in shock as the gravity of the situation came crashing down on them like a ton of bricks. Even Judge Boylan was struggling to maintain her composure as she fought to hold back the tears that had welled up in her eyes. Michelle Henry remained steady and graciously composed. But her cool gaze belied a righteous anger and indignation on behalf of the victim, the victim's family, and the entire community which had been torn asunder by the actions of the monster who committed this savage brutality.

I have never felt more ashamed of myself in my entire life than I did at that moment. I blamed myself for my degree of involvement that was instrumental in Rick Laird's retrial – and for the pain this obviously caused all parties concerned. I was disgusted with myself at the thought that I had helped a monster. I was also saddened for the immeasurable anguish this whole thing was causing the Milanos. If there was nothing else I could do, I could do one thing: I would approach the Milanos and give them all my moral support throughout the remainder of the proceedings.

I also vowed to myself to be a voice for them, and for Anthony, when writing this book.

The other journalists reporting for various newspapers were visibly shaken as well. Even John Kerrigan and Keith Williams, the defense team, could not avoid being perturbed by what they had seen. It was their duty to provide Richard Laird with adequate representation, but it was not part of their job description to approve of what he had done. The only person present in the courtroom that seemed completely un-phased by the pictures was Rick Laird. It seemed to me that he simply looked at the slides of the crime scene with no more emotion than if he were watching a re-run of Oprah Winfrey.

After Michelle Henry showed the photos of the crime scene, including the ones taken by the pathologist, the lights were turned up and the laptop was shut off. But the pictures will remain engraved upon my memory forever. The pictures of Anthony Milano's destroyed body would eternally serve to remind me that there are indeed monsters that walk among us, monsters who should never have another opportunity to harm another living soul. The silence and the somber mood in the courtroom became oppressively heavy. Judge Boylan decided to call a short recess to let the jury get up and stretch their legs. She also wanted to give the smokers on the jury a chance to go outside for a cigarette break. I needed a smoke break myself, and apparently so did Annamarie Milano.

In the lobby outside of the courtroom, I approached Annamarie and her father and introduced myself. I explained my previous involvement with the case and profusely apologized to the both of them. I told them that I could not find words strong enough to convey just how deeply I regretted helping a monster whom I had mistakenly thought of as a victim when the true victim in all of this was Anthony Milano. They were very warm and forgiving and grateful for my support. They also admonished me not be so hard on myself because I didn't know the truth twelve years ago. Vito Milano put a fatherly hand on my arm, and told me that I was being too harsh of a critic of myself. He knew I hadn't known the full reality and had misguidedly thought I was doing the right thing. He looked at me through sad but forgiving eyes and continued, "You must be strong. I am strong. Rosa, my wife, was not strong and that's what killed her. But I will live to see justice prevail."

I sincerely hoped justice would prevail in his lifetime, for his sake. However, if Rick Laird sat for another 19 years on death row with appeals going on, it would be highly unlikely that Vito Milano would still be alive to see it happen, to get his justice. Even if Rick Laird was swiftly brought to an execution chamber within Vito's lifetime, there was also another possible end result: Vito and Annamarie might feel only marginally better that justice had been served. Many families of murder victims never get the emotional closure they desperately need, not even after they have witnessed the execution of those responsible for the murder of a loved one.

When you lose a loved one to a senseless murder it leaves a gaping wound in your heart that is never filled: it takes away part of your soul. There is no prosthetic for an amputated spirit. There are certain wrongs, certain deeds, so vile that there is no way to truly make the victims whole afterwards. To judge aggrieved murder victims' surviving families as being out for revenge instead of justice is sanctimonious and shallow.

Richard Laird enjoyed nineteen years of life that Anthony Milano did not get to enjoy. Even though those nineteen years on Pennsylvania's death row could hardly be considered enjoyable, Laird was able to communicate with supporters and loved ones and have visits. The Milanos could never visit Anthony – except for visiting his grave. While we strive to remain a civilized society that does not bring us to the same level of low as that of murderers, we also need to keep in mind that the victims and their families deserve a justice system that they can believe in, too: a justice system that will not mock them by coddling fiends whose vicious deeds have proved them unfit to roam freely in society.

During the courtroom break, I noticed that several journalists had crowded around the petite thin young blonde who was seated directly behind the defendant's table. Annamarie told me she thought the girl was Richard Laird's niece but she wasn't sure. "Are you going to go over there and talk to her?" Annamarie asked me. I told her that while I felt I should, I also felt very uncomfortable about doing so. The truth was that I felt that the Milanos were being unjustly ignored by the press. Everyone seemed to be so eager to pay attention to the defendant and those in his corner: apparently that was more exciting than talking with the victim's family.

However there was also the possibility that the reporters were avoiding the Milanos for a more compelling reason. Vito and Annamarie were witnesses. Judge Boylan had issued a standing gag order that was binding on all parties and witnesses to the case. Anyone who violated that gag order would be dealt with severely and harshly. Judge Boylan may have been a good-natured judge with a light sense of humor whose statuesque figure, perfectly coiffed blonde hair, and good looks would have easily awarded her a lead part on "*Law & Order*", but she was a no-nonsense judge. When she gave an order, she meant that it would be upheld, or else. While this gag order prevented anyone from talking about the case with jurors, witnesses, attorneys and law enforcement officers; it did not preclude interviewing someone who was a non-witness or a spectator.

Still, I did not feel quite right about approaching anyone from Laird's corner without first getting some sort of approval from the Milanos. They had clearly been through so much already that they deserved to have their feelings respected. I felt that they deserved deference. However, Annamarie indicated she didn't mind if I spoke to this girl.

I cautiously approached her, trying to think of what to say. I awkwardly introduced myself, told her that I was writing a book about the case, and had previously been involved with helping Rick with his appeal. She told me her name was Nicole Knox and that she was Richard Laird's niece through his former marriage to JoAnne Samsel (neé Walters). JoAnne Samsel was her mother's sister, an aunt. JoAnne's kids, Ricky and Rachel who were now grown, were her cousins. Nicole was very open and willing to talk to me. She knew that her uncle Rick had done an awfully bad thing, but she believed that redemption was possible for everyone and that Rick had learned from his mistake. She did not want to see him get the death penalty.

At that point, we were interrupted as the tipstaff announced to everyone in the lobby that court was about to resume. After the short recess was over, everyone filed back inside the courtroom. Once the court was brought back into sessions, Lt. McGuigan was called back to the witness stand to be cross-examined by Kerrigan. While no one was sure what John Kerrigan would say, or could say, that would be of any material value for the defense of his client, everyone was astounded by what he *did* say.

Launching into McGuigan, Kerrigan blasted away like a sanctimonious gas bag with questions in rapid-fire succession without giving the police officer a chance to respond. He bellowed loudly at the Commonwealth's witness: "Are you a medical doctor? You *assumed* Anthony Milano was dead! Why didn't you check to see if he was still alive? Does Bristol Township have doctors?"

Before Lt. McGuigan could regain his composure, Kerrigan swooped in again. He sarcastically demanded to know if Bristol Township had medical personnel back in 1987, insinuating that sloppy police response – not the actions of his client – could have been the reason Anthony Milano died.

"You didn't even call a doctor?" Kerrigan fired at the hapless officer. Judge Boylan was growing visibly annoyed. A reporter seated next to me sucked in his breath, shocked at the limits Kerrigan was testing. Kerrigan opened his mouth, but before more words tumbled out, the judge cut him off sharply: "Counselor!"

Kerrigan managed to get the last word in, "Why didn't you do *that*?"

"Objection, Your Honor!" DA Henry barked.

"Sustained," came the firm reply as Judge Boylan glared at Kerrigan from the bench. Her patience was wearing thin.

Lt. McGuigan sat there in the witness box, flustered, not really knowing how to respond, or if he should. Things were getting ugly. "He was obviously dead, sir!" he replied from the witness stand.

In less than 10 minutes into his cross-examination of this distinguished career police officer, John Kerrigan had alienated the judge, the district attorney, the jury, and the spectators – including members of the press. Judge Boylan excused the witness, "You may step down."

For a moment frozen in eternity, the courtroom was so quiet you could hear a pin drop. One of the reporters seated behind me whispered to his colleague that it didn't take rocket science to tell if the victim was dead when he had been laying out in the elements for two hours with over half of his throat gone. Anyone with an IQ above a houseplant could tell that Anthony Milano wasn't simply lying down taking a nap!

Now any decent criminal defense attorney knows that cross-examining highly respected police officers is a tricky business. Verbally bullying them on the witness stand typically does not go over well with largely middle class juries. The middle class is generally very supportive of police officers. Part of that is due to the fact that civil service jobs are mostly held by members of the middle class. Police officer and fire fighter are very common career paths for middle class sons and daughters to take if they are not academically inclined for college. Therefore, attacking someone who jurors might see as one of their own, someone they can easily relate to, is not usually the best tactic. It comes across as arrogant and sanctimonious. If an attorney alienates the jury that way, chances are very high that the jury will react negatively towards the attorney's client by returning an unfavorable verdict. It was clear that this was not one of John Kerrigan's most shining moments.

Kerrigan's position was not an easy one, however. As appointed counsel for a client who was admittedly guilty of a murder, a grisly and barbaric slashing, he was already given the impossible task of trying to paint a huge deranged killer as a victim. In order to show diminished capacity due to alcohol consumption and existing organic brain damage, his avenues were limited. The judge forbade him from bringing up the dram shop laws as relevant to the case. Kerrigan wanted to raise the possibility that Milano's death was caused by a number of factors

– not all due to his client's premeditation. He wanted to show the jury that an honest mistake in the judgment call of the responding police officer could have made a difference in Anthony Milano getting medical attention and possibly being saved. But the way he went about presenting this argument went over like a lead balloon.

Kerrigan also had a formidable adversary in Michelle Henry, the petite and soft-spoken DA who was cleverly establishing her case for the Commonwealth against his client. She was showing the court that no evidence existed that could substantiate Kerrigan's argument that Rick Laird had diminished capacity from having had too much to drink. Contrary to claims set forth by the defense, Rick Laird was in sufficient control of his mental and physical faculties on the night in question to be a coldly rational and merciless killer when he murdered Anthony Milano.

The next witness called by the prosecution was Yolanda Thompson, who had been at the Edgely Inn early on the evening of December 14th, 1987 while Richard Laird and Frank Chester were there. She was at the bar and was someone of reputable character who was not intoxicated when she observed Frank Chester and Rick Laird there that night.

Yolanda Thompson gave her current residence as Berlin, NJ and her occupation as working with disabled kids. In 1987, she worked at the De Grande Diner with Frank Chester. She knew Frank and Frank's mother Elaine Holley very well. She had often been Frank's confidante regarding matters the young man was too embarrassed to discuss with his own mom. She had spoken with Frank earlier that day and told the court how Frank Chester was despondent over his break-up with Colleen, who apparently had had an abortion. When Frank came into the Edgely Inn with Rick Laird, Yolanda recalled how he introduced her to Rick and tried to get her to come over from her side of the bar to where he, Rick,

Barbara Anne and Gale were gathered. Yolanda declined, explaining to the court that "Rick Laird gave me the creeps." She didn't care for his loud, boisterous manner and stated that Rick made her very uncomfortable.

Yolanda Thompson recounted how the defendant was shooting pool with Frank Chester and a few other patrons in the bar. This was the first of a series of examples the prosecution would use to disprove the defense claim of diminished capacity. Shooting pool requires a significant amount of hand-eye coordination. Someone too impaired to form the intent to commit murder would logically be too impaired to shoot pool.

Michelle Henry proceeded: "Did you observe the defendant to slur his speech?" Yolanda Thompson answered that she did not observe Rick Laird to have done that.

Michelle Henry continued, "Did he stagger or did he sway?" Again, Yolanda Thompson answered that she did not observe Laird to do that, either. Yolanda Thompson was only on the stand for a very short time. Kerrigan declined cross examination. Ms. Thompson's testimony was simple and clear: Rick Laird did not exhibit any obvious signs of diminished capacity on that fateful night.

After Yolanda Thompson stepped down, the Commonwealth called Jimmy Phillips, Jr. – owner of the Edgely Inn – to the witness stand and he was sworn in. He stated he was 44 years old. Back in 1987, his parents owned the Edgely Inn and he worked there as a 22 year old bartender along with another part-time employee. He now owned the bar and had worked there for a total of 26 years. Jurors watched him intensely as he told the court that he was not in the bar when Laird and Chester initially arrived because he had ducked out to go to another bar about 50 feet away to fill in on short notice for a fellow shuffleboard team member who had been unable to make it for an important league match that evening. Shuffleboard leagues operate similarly to bowling leagues: An absence of one team member could cause the team to forfeit the rest of their games in that particular season and lose money.

Jimmy also explained that December 14th 1987 was a Monday evening, a night when bars are typically dead because it is a work night at the beginning of the work week. He felt confident that the part-time bartender his family had hired would not have too much trouble holding down the fort until he returned from the shuffleboard match. Jimmy Phillips then stated that he returned immediately after the shuffleboard game to find Rick Laird and Frank Chester and another male dressed in a karate uniform at the bar, drinking and getting loud and nasty over by the pool tables. His testimony was pretty much the same now as it was back in 1988.

Jimmy Phillips recalled when Anthony came into the bar and how he quietly sat down at the bar opposite the side where Laird and Chester and the pool tables were, and politely ordered a cheesesteak and a beer. Just as he had testified 19 years ago, he reiterated that Laird and Chester approached Anthony Milano, each man taking seats on bar stools on either side of Anthony. When Anthony got up to go to the bathroom Rick Laird said loudly, "I hate fuckin' faggots!" When Anthony returned from the restroom, Rick demanded that Anthony buy them all shots. Phillips testified that Anthony said he didn't want any and so did Frank Chester. But Laird insisted – forcefully.

Michelle Henry next directed Jimmy Phillips' attention to how much alcohol he served the defendant.

"I refilled a pitcher of beer twice for the defendant and Frank Chester. Plus the two rounds of shots." A pitcher of beer holds 64 ounces.

"Did you observe the defendant to stagger or sway? Did he slur his speech?" Michelle Henry asked. Phillips answered that he did not.

Next, Michelle Henry questioned the witness about the police coming in to the Edgely Inn to investigate a stolen car complaint. Jimmy once again told the same story as he did in 1987: Laird got loud and abusive towards the police and told Officer McGuigan to "go fuck himself" when he was asked to show his ID while Chester tried to placate him and be the peacemaker.

Jimmy recalled trying to get Anthony to leave when Laird and Chester got up and began slow dancing with each other by the jukebox. He recounted how Laird coerced a promise of a ride from Anthony that Frank Chester said they did not need. Jimmy recalled that Anthony was afraid of angering the two men and thought it would be best if he just sucked it up and gave them a ride and got it over with, since he wouldn't have to drive them very far as Laird lived just across the street and down the road apiece.

Jimmy repeated his testimony given in 1988: Upon closing up the bar, Frank Chester purchased a six-pack of beer to go and walked out first, followed by Anthony Milano and then Richard Laird. He recalled seeing Frank approach McGuigan's patrol car in the parking lot to speak briefly with the police officer and then getting into the back seat of Anthony's Chevy Nova while Rick Laird piled into the front passenger seat. He stated he saw the car carrying the three men pull out of the parking lot.

Jimmy then testified that while he was cleaning up, a female called the bar and he answered the phone. The female caller wanted to know if Rick was still at the bar. Jimmy told her he was not; he had left with two other men. The call came in at roughly 2:45 AM. He did not connect the voice of the caller with that of Barbara Anne Parr at the time. It was 4:30 AM when Jimmy Phillips finished cleaning up, restocked the coolers and was able to lock up and go home.

When it was the defense's turn to cross-examine, Kerrigan launched into Jimmy Phillips. First, he asked if Phillips noticed whether or not Laird had any alcoholic beverages when he returned to the Edgely Inn and first observed Laird already there. Jimmy responded that he recalled observing that Laird and Chester were already sharing a pitcher of beer when he returned to the bar. Then Kerrigan went for the jugular: "So Mr. Chester and Mr. Laird had at least three pitchers of beer and two rounds of shots, right?"

"Yes sir."

Kerrigan then blasted the bartender sarcastically trying to make Jimmy Phillips look stupid and irresponsible.

"Did you ever *think* of flagging Mr. Laird? He was nasty, right? He was nasty to the other patrons, right? Are you concerned about serving people who have had too much, right? You say you were *so* concerned for Anthony Milano, why didn't you call the cops?"

Jimmy Phillips was in shock and at a loss for words. He was just a simple bartender – not a super sleuth. Regaining his composure, he replied: "I really don't know what you think I should do, sir. The cops *were* there!"

Kerrigan stated that he had no more questions and the flustered and shaken bartender was allowed to step down. The next witness called by the prosecution was Christine Bogarde. Her husband, Pete Carpinona, had died when he was run over by a train many years ago and she had since resumed her maiden name of Bogarde.

Michelle Henry directed the witness to her recollection of Laird's behavior immediately after the murder when he and Frank Chester came to the apartment that she had shared with her husband and his buddy Rich Griscavage.

Christine testified, "He told me to *'get the f out of here; this ain't no place for a woman.'* I did not know who he was and thought he had a lot of nerve to come into my apartment and talk to me that way."

"Did you observe Mr. Laird to stagger or sway?"

"No."

"Did he slur his speech?"

"No."

"Do you remember smelling alcohol on the defendant?"

"No."

"Is it fair to say that the defendant didn't appear to be drunk?"

Christine Bogarde replied that to the best of her knowledge and recollection at that time, Laird was not drunk – just rude, disrespectful, and nasty.

It was already after four in the afternoon and Judge Boylan wanted to let the jury take their dinner break. Court would reconvene at 9:00 AM the next day.

A younger reporter from the Philadelphia Gay News (PGN) who was seated next to me asked me if he might catch a ride back to the city with me. It was bitter cold, far too cold for anyone to walk to the train station in Doylestown to wait for the train back into the city. The record-breaking cold snap that gripped Pennsylvania was dangerous, so dangerous that elderly people, disabled persons and people with circulatory trouble were advised against going outdoors, period. In fact, normally healthy people were even being advised that being outdoors for any length of time would be dangerous. I didn't want to see this reporter get frostbite or any other cold weather malady from having to stand on an open train platform.

I told him that I was going to the University City area of Philly, near the 46th Street station and offered to take him there if that was all right with him. I also told him that I could bring him home from the courthouse every day of the trial, if need be.

He was very open and friendly, and very much opposed to capital punishment. He was also a die-hard vegan and did not hesitate to inform me that eating honey on my French toast was terrible. It was cruel to the baby chickens that never got a chance to hatch and grow up as well as to the poor bees whose young were being robbed of vital nutrition because of humans taking their honey, their food. He was definitely a unique character; there was no getting around that!

I reassured him that the unborn chicken embryos he expressed concern for were actually unfertilized eggs and thus it was OK to eat them. I told him that chickens laying eggs are sort of like human women menstruating after ovulation: if the egg is unfertilized, it is expelled. With chickens, once an egg is laid, if it is not fertilized by a rooster, the egg never develops into a chicken embryo, a potential future chicken. I philosophized that the claim that eating eggs is killing chickens is like saying that women have abortions and are killing babies with each menstrual period. No baby chickens were aborted in order for me to enjoy breakfast. He admitted he hadn't thought of it that way before. To be honest, neither had I. But then again, it isn't every day that someone tries to make me feel guilty for simply eating breakfast. I wonder what he would have said had I told him that my diet consists mostly of beef, rib-eye steaks in particular!

He didn't preach the religion of veganism at me any more for the entire commute back into the heart of Philadelphia. The "City of Brotherly Love" is definitely inhabited by a diverse group of people. My native Philadelphia definitely has a lot of style.

I finally arrived back at Michael's around 8:00 PM. Philadelphia rush hour traffic on the Schuylkill Expressway is brutal. What should be a forty-five minute drive from the Bucks County Courthouse in Doylestown takes two hours or even longer when there's an accident or a lane closure.

Michael was sitting on his haunches on the couch, busy tapping away on his computer, and working intently on a journal article regarding smoking bans when I came in. Buster, his adorable black Burmese cat, sat perched next to the laptop screen. He asked me how the first day of the trial testimony went. I told him all about John Kerrigan's attempt to make minced meat out of the police officer, Lt. McGuigan, who had been the one to discover Anthony Milano's body. Michael stared at me wide-eyed blinking in disbelief, "Is he nuts? I bet *that* went over well with the jury."

I told him about my interesting ride back to the city with the vegan reporter from Philadelphia gay News (PGN) and Michael laughed good-naturedly, "Yep. Vegans are a little extreme. But I have to admit, I do feel guilty about animals dying just so I can enjoy a deviled ham sandwich or bacon with my eggs."

I told Michael that I, on the other hand, do *not* feel guilty about such things. *Kashrut*, the kosher dietary laws, provides for the humane treatment and slaughtering of animals raised for food. I enjoy beef with impunity, especially since that was something I could not afford when I was younger and much poorer. The only time I feel guilty about food is if I slip up and eat some tasty, tempting *treif* – foods forbidden to Jews according to *kashrut* – like a piece of maple-cured ham steak.

Speaking of food, Michael offered to treat me to a nice filet dinner at a university type pub called "The Mill Creek" while he engaged in what he calls "Irish politicking" with his smoking ban activism. I was excited about it but I was also hesitant because I didn't want to have to wear a skirt and sheer pantyhose and high heels in freezing weather to a place where long johns and overalls might not be the thing to wear. But his sweet offer to treat me to a wonderful meal was more compelling than the bitter cold.

The cold snap would normally have kept Michael indoors to some extent. He is a die-hard bicyclist, opposed enough to cars that he's never bothered to get a driver's license although he never pushed his beliefs on his friends. There is ample subway and bus service in Brooklyn, NY where Michael grew up and even in Philadelphia. A car has never been a necessity for Michael. But this was not a night safe for bicycling anywhere. Michael generally loathed automobiles, but he was quite inclined to ride in a warm one on a freezing cold night in order to go out to socialize for a bit at the local pub –and he used his most polished Irish diplomacy to get me to take him in my truck. That's what you have to love about Michael Joseph Francis McFadden: he's got style.

When we got to the Mill Creek, I noticed that there was only one other patron in the place. Michael told me that I should not be surprised. It was two below zero and the icy winds whipped relentlessly. The wind chill factor made it feel more like minus twenty rather than minus two. Ever since Philadelphia had passed a city-wide smoking ban, smokers have been going out much less often. Many bars had begun closing early. Those offering live bands cut back on their shows. On cold nights like this, smokers were not about to go out and have to stand outside just to be able to have a cigarette while having to leave their drinks, food and friends unattended.

Michael introduced me to the manager and bartender, a likeable Irish fellow named Ken. Over dinner, I asked Ken how much business was affected by the smoking ban. He shook his head and said that the year before the ban was enacted the place was always busy. It was well known for its reasonably priced top quality food. But the smoking ban had killed business on nights like this one. It was simply too cold. Consequently, Jack Gillespie – the Mill Creek's owner and a proud retired Philadelphia police officer – was forced to take a pay cut.

Michael told Ken and Jack that I was staying in Philadelphia for a few weeks for this trial, that I was writing a book about this case and that I was from Erie – a small blue collar town in the heart of America's Rust Belt in the northwestern-most part of Pennsylvania. Jack and Ken seemed impressed. I wondered if there was a chance that Rick Laird's smoking status at the time of the crime would be raised. Michael certainly had a point about the extremes that the vilification of smokers has taken. Smokers were being reviled by society as if they were brutal psychopathic killers.

I forgot about Rick Laird and his trial when a steaming hot plate heaped with a generous portion of filet mignon arrived, complete with the chef's vegetables. The sauce and seasonings were out of this world. I told Michael that if I ever won the Powerball jackpot, I was going to kidnap the chef and abscond back to Erie with him by hiring him to be my personal chef at home, doubling his current salary if need be. I had been to a lot of steak houses all across Pennsylvania and had never tasted a filet this good!

After I finished my delicious meal and Michael finished his drinks – his Irish sustenance as he called it – we left and headed back to the house. I had to get up early to beat morning rush hour commuter traffic back to the courthouse in Doylestown. I checked in with my husband to make sure everything was OK back home and to make sure that there were no computer nightmares spelling imminent doom for him while he processed customer's premium payments. All was well, but he missed me terribly.

It was our first experience with being apart for any length of time. He chatted briefly with Michael too and thanked him for taking care of me by seeing to it that I had a good meal since I was obviously worn out from a long day and too tired to cook. Donnie told me that a freak snow storm had swept across Lake Erie from the Canadian side and dumped several feet of snow causing a 50 car pile-up on I-90. The entire eastbound lane from Erie PA to upstate NY had been shut down and all traffic was now being re-routed via US 20, East 26th Street in Erie – where my home and office was. But the freak storm meant an extended stay in Philadelphia.

The next morning, Barbara Anne (Parr) Sylvia was called by the prosecution to the witness stand. Everyone was riveted on the petite, thin woman who had given birth to Rick's baby 19 years ago while he sat in prison awaiting trial. The soft curves of her face captured by a photographer from Philadelphia Magazine as she clasped her newborn infant back in 1988 were replaced by the harsher lines and angles of age. She had obviously had a very hard life these past 19 years. Dressed in a flattering black pinstripe skirt suit with black pantyhose and matching shoes, she approached the stand and was sworn in.

All eyes in the courtroom were riveted on Barbara Anne as she opened a small window into the realities and life of what life was like for a poor pregnant woman whose boyfriend had faced arrest for murder. Her painful story led everyone in the courtroom across the sands of time back to December 1987. She gave sequential testimony as to the events immediately before and after the murder of Anthony Milano. District Attorney Henry began by asking her what happened during the day of December 14th, 1987.

According to Barbara Anne the day of December 14th 1987 began with Rick blowing off work due to a shoulder injury incurred in his job as handyman for the Ambassador Arms apartment complex where he and Barbara Anne had lived at the time. Later that same afternoon, Barbara Anne's cousin Frankie (Frank Chester) called and asked Rick to come over to see his new apartment. Barbara recalled that she didn't feel like going because she didn't feel well. She was suffering from complications due to a very difficult pregnancy and was forced to give up her job cleaning wealthy people's homes because she was supposed to be on complete bed rest for the remainder of her pregnancy. But Rick wore the pants in the family and whatever Rick wanted to do, they always ended up doing – regardless of whether Barbara and her 9 year old son from a prior relationship, "little David", wanted to or not.

After hanging out at Frank's for awhile, they went to the Edgely Inn with Gale Gardner; a young lady friend of Frank's who was also at the apartment. Gale was pregnant and her boyfriend was in jail at the time. Barbara told the jury she "had a bit of an argument with Rick over his drinking and Rick's ordering shots of Wild Turkey for little David, who was only 9 years old at the time."

Establishing that the brand of cigarettes Barbara Anne bought for Rick a few hours before the murder as being the same brand found underneath the victim's body helped cement the case against Rick. It also verified that Barbara Anne had a very clear memory of that evening even though it was 20 years ago.

Michelle Henry asked, "I believe you purchased cigarettes for Rick. What brand were they?"

"I believe they were Kools." Barbara Anne replied.

Michelle Henry then asked Barbara Anne what happened after she, little David, and Gale Gardner returned to the Edgely Inn with Rick's pack of cigarettes. Barbara Anne replied that they left Frank Chester and Rick Laird at the bar and went across the street to Barbara and Rick's apartment where they remained for the rest of the evening watching television until Barbara Anne went to bed, leaving Gale sleep on the couch. Barbara Anne woke up in the middle of the night and noticed that Rick had still not come home even though it was after closing time. She called the bar and asked for Rick and was told by the bartender that he had already left. Barbara Anne then recounted the events after Rick returned home. As with all the other witnesses, Michelle Henry led Barbara Anne through the same line of questioning so as to establish that Rick was not too drunk and under a state of diminished capacity when he murdered Anthony Milano.

"Did he stagger and did he sway?"

"Not that I recall."

"Did he slur his speech?"

"Not that I recall."

"Is it fair to say he was in full control of his actions at that time?"

"Yes."

Barbara Anne reiterated the same thing she told the court 19 years earlier about how she scrubbed the mud off Rick's boots. She recounted how the next morning she woke up to Rick stuffing his boots and leather jacket into a trash bag and saw that there was blood on Rick's keychain: the Father's Day present given to him by little David. She also mentioned noticing a small crystal prism in the shape of an orb, similar to a disco ball, that she knew didn't belong to Rick. She told the jury how distressed she was that Rick was discarding his boots and jacket. When Michelle Henry asked Barbara Anne why this distressed her, she replied, lowering her eyes because she was somewhat embarrassed and ashamed, "Back then, we were very, very poor and just starting out. We didn't have the money to replace them." She also stated that she had not yet realized or fully grasped the seriousness of the situation: that Rick had been involved in a horrific murder.

Barbara Anne thought Rick had merely been in a bad fight at the bar. She was pregnant and poor and their electricity had been shut off because they fell behind on the bill and couldn't pay. They were behind on their rent, too. Barbara Anne really couldn't afford to buy even a few cheap toys and K-Mart T-shirts for her little boy so he would have presents to open on Christmas morning. Extra money for replacing an expensive leather jacket and a pair of biker boots simply did not exist in her world.

While the concept and reality of poverty was not alien to me, it apparently was to the reporters and journalists who sat around me. A twittering of sharp judgmental hisses of disapproval made under their breath was not lost on my ears: *'Can you believe it? Someone is murdered and all she's worried about is some clothes! Maybe if they didn't smoke and drink she would have had money to buy more clothes! Such irresponsible people – having more kids they can't afford!'* The clucking disapproval swirled around me. But the full reality of the chasm between the "haves" and "have-nots" hit me full force when Judge Boylan called for a lunch recess for about an hour.

My vegan reporter friend from PGN asked to join me for lunch. He wanted to go to the local Starbucks for some hot gourmet coffee. The Starbucks was about a mile down the road from the courthouse. He exclaimed incredulously as I drove: "Can you believe that Barbara woman?" he gasped. "Her boyfriend did this crime and she only thought about the cost of replacing his clothes! And then she married him while he was in prison after he had been found guilty!"

I was stunned. I thought of all people, reporters and journalists would have seen enough of the world outside of their immediate comfort zone to understand how differently others lived. I especially thought that this very liberal-minded professional writer, a defender of an oppressed group himself, could understand where Barbara Anne was coming from, even if many of the others did not.

Most middle class people, especially yuppie types, tend to live in isolated suburban enclaves surrounded by others of their same socio-economic status group and normally do not have to interact with those from the lower classes. They tend to live sheltered lives where the ramifications and sensations of poverty are incomprehensible to them. But reporters, journalists and other news media professionals do not have jobs that insulate them from the other America, the poor America. The very nature of their jobs takes them into many places where they are made privy to the lives and realities of others whose lives are far different from their own.

Surely, in the wake of Hurricane Katrina and the bungled rescue effort, even the most sheltered of people had to know that there was poverty among them in the land of plenty. Had my lunch companion been unconscious during the searing coverage of the aftermath of Hurricane Katrina which rudely exposed to the entire world the harsh reality of the other America? Had people forgotten so soon that there are millions mired so deeply in poverty, bound to a hand-to-mouth existence, that the ability to leave and escape the wrath of a deadly storm is simply too far beyond their reach? The desperate people "looting" clothing and other basic necessities were doing so because they had absolutely no means whatsoever to obtain a change of clothes, food, diapers, medicines and baby formula – basic human necessities that the non-poor take for granted. Did this educated and intelligent writer think that such poverty was strictly a Black problem, a southern problem or a New Orleans problem? Living and working in the heart of Philadelphia, surely he had seen or at least knew that there were slums, entire neighborhoods ruled by despair and apathy. I was floored!

This reporter, Tim Cwiek, who was so sympathetic to prisoners on death row, to mistreatment of terrorist suspects at Abu Ghraib, to hate crime victims, and to unfertilized chicken eggs and bees was judgmental of Barbara Anne (Parr) Sylvia: a woman who was extremely poor and pregnant in 1987, a woman who didn't have an opportunity for a good job who lacked the income to keep her rent current and the utilities on, and who couldn't afford to replace her boyfriend's destroyed or discarded clothing. How could he not understand this? Did he need this to be drawn out in crayon for him in order to connect the dots? Maybe he had overdosed on the Calvinist indoctrination that had permeated all facets of American culture: that the poor are all "undeserving" because their poverty was divine punishment for failing to live right, hence the poor lack virtue, morals and principles.

While the middle and upper classes in general tend to be sanctimonious, arrogant, narrow-minded and condescending, this journalist had not struck me as being that way before Barbara Anne's painful testimony. He had impressed me as being very intellectually and politically liberal. I was taken so aback by his reaction. Some of the others who had been sitting near us did not surprise me with their classist attitudes, but *this* man did. I can only surmise that it was because he had not spent a lot of time during the course of his career covering issues that pertain to poverty, the reality of the other America. Poverty, inequality and classism are taboo subjects. Classism is the elephant in the living room that everyone tries to pretend isn't there.

I explained to my well-meaning companion why the concern for material needs takes precedence in the lives of poor people. When it takes 70% or more of your total monthly income to cover things like rent, electric and gas – not including the costs connected with basic transportation – there is very little money left to apportion for food, personal hygiene products, toiletries, and school supplies for your child: there often isn't enough money to afford even just *those* things. There isn't any wiggle room in poor people's budgets for replacing expensive boots and a leather jacket that might have been bought as an indulgence during better times.

When you have money for tomorrow instead of only today, you can afford to be sanctimonious and primarily concern yourself with principles. For those who are poor, any meager savings that you might be able to cobble together is inadequate and does not last long: that "rainy day" is every day when you are poor. Being poor is living in a constant static state: your past, present and future converge on the present – and remain there. Too often, the only helping hand many poor people get is the hand at the end of their own arm.

He thought quietly about what I tried to share with him. He responded that he thought it was terrible that anyone should have to live that way in America. We finished our lunch and quickly scrambled to find a parking spot in the courthouse parking lot. Court was about to reconvene.

Upon re-entering the lobby right outside the courtroom, I noticed that the judge and jury were still out. Nicole Knox, who had been sitting behind Rick Laird in the courtroom, was seated alone on a bench in the lobby next to the spiral stairs. She looked forlorn. She was a struggling single mother battling cervical cancer and her entire family had turned their backs on her because she was in support of her Uncle Rick. She told me how her Aunt JoAnne (Rick's first wife – JoAnne Samsel) kept calling her and leaving threats on her answering machine for simply attending the trial. She was only 12 years old when Rick Laird was tried, convicted, and subsequently sentenced to death back in 1988. She didn't know much about what had happened. She had early childhood memories of her Uncle Rick. He had been her favorite uncle because he had always been nice to her, nicer than anyone else in her immediate family.

She told me how she kept every newspaper article she found about the case and had begun writing Rick after she had moved out and away from her severely dysfunctional family in Levittown. She now lived in Philadelphia and was just trying to survive with her three kids and remain in good health, hoping that her cervical cancer would remain in remission and not come back. She seemed so eager for me to see the good in her uncle and not see him as a monster. She explained, "When my TV died, my kids didn't have a TV anymore. I couldn't afford one and my Uncle Rick sent me his TV from death row just so my kids would have something. He can't be all bad, right?" Hmm…where had I heard about him generously giving away a TV to someone else before? Memory of a letter from Rick in my distant past from 1996 was suddenly clear: he told me about giving his TV to "fellow row man" Alan Pursell, the same inmate who read the book on ADHD that I had sent Rick.

Not wanting to cause this poor young woman any unnecessary emotional distress I tried to be as gentle as possible. But at the same time I was overwhelmed with an urgency to let her know how dangerous her uncle really was, to warn her that she did not want him inside her head – favorite uncle or not. She had enough on her plate just dealing with the threat of cancer recurrence and scraping by in poverty to raise three small kids on her own. A manipulative psychopath playing her emotions, getting her to over-extend herself financially, was something she really didn't need. Her kids didn't need that, either. I felt genuinely bad for this frail girl who really got dealt a rotten hand in life.

"Nicole. Please. I need you to understand something. First, I am no fan of the death penalty. If we all believed in executing people, we would all be in your Uncle Rick's seat right now. But I need to share something with you. Twelve years ago, Rick's brother – your Uncle Mark – approached me on the job and basically conned me into helping your Uncle Rick fight for a new trial, relief from death row." Memories came pouring back from across the sands of time, painfully opening a floodgate of memories and bringing them to the surface as I continued to explain:

"I too, was young, naïve, lonely and very poor. I had no family because I was orphaned at age 13. I had bad luck with men and nobody cared about me at all. What was worse is that I was disabled and had no one. I was vulnerable. I kept every letter your Uncle Rick had ever sent me, including the most beautiful and heart-warming birthday cards I had ever gotten from anybody in my entire life. In one of his letters to me, he told me how he gave his TV to a fellow inmate on death row, a man named Alan Pursell, because Al's TV had blown up. Your Uncle Rick wanted me to think he was a good guy. But he had an ulterior motive: when he wrote to me he wanted someone to jump to his beck and call and do his bidding on the outside for him. I lost my job, the only job since my accident that had health benefits, because of getting involved with the Lairds. When I couldn't afford to simply have my life revolve around him and his appeal anymore, he got very cold towards me. On the last day I visited him, I asked him if he had any sympathy for Anthony Milano. Had there not been a bullet-proof plate glass wall separating us, I felt that he would have killed me. I saw it in his eyes, Nicole. I saw the eyes of a monster. The same eyes that Anthony Milano saw when he realized he was a dead man."

I knew from my own prior dealings with Rick that the instant his poor niece was unable to do something for him, he would turn on her just as he had done with me. I felt sorry for the girl. I knew she desperately needed to believe in redemption. I also knew that she desperately needed people in her corner that weren't just out for themselves.

As with me all those years ago, he probably told her all the things she needed to hear – so she would be inclined to overextend herself in helping him. She admitted that she was giving him $25 a month to put on his books. This poor girl could barely support herself and her kids, and Rick knew it. On top of that, she was battling a cancer which could come back, rearing its ugly head at any time without warning. Yet he had no trouble whatsoever taking money from her and her kids when they needed it a lot more than he did! I wanted her to see this and understand. I wanted her to pull back before she got hurt.

The tipstaff emerged from the courtroom. Court was now in session again and we filed back in. The next witness called by the district attorney was 38 year old Richard Griscavage. He was a short, stocky, clean-shaven man with chestnut brown hair and a quiet demeanor. He seemed timid and embarrassed to be the center of attention on a witness stand in a courtroom. He stated that he worked as an electrician.

Griscavage's testimony was essentially the same as it was 19 years ago in 1988: He was sleeping on Pete Carpinona's sofa in the living room of Christine Bogarde and Pete Carpinona's apartment when he was startled from a sound sleep by Frank Chester pounding on the door, begging to be let in. He stated that Frank told him to "hurry up and open the door and quickly lock the door behind him" because Rick Laird was on his heels and he didn't want his buddy to let Laird into the apartment. But Griscavage wasn't fully awake and before he got the chance to lock the door behind Chester, Laird was already shoving his way in. The commotion roused Pete and Christine from their bed and disturbed their sleeping baby as well, much to Pete Carpinona's annoyance who demanded that Griscavage get Chester and Laird the hell out of the apartment. Griscavage testified that Laird said, "Yeah, gimme a ride home."

Michelle Henry asked Griscavage what sort of transportation he had to give Laird a ride home with and Richard Griscavage replied he had a Kawasaki GPZ. The district attorney then asked him to describe for the jury what kind of motorcycle that was and Griscavage answered that it was a small motorcycle, classified as a sports bike.

"Mr. Griscavage, recalling the early morning hours of December 15th 1987 when you gave Mr. Laird a ride home on the back of your motorcycle, did you observe Mr. Laird to be drunk?" Griscavage answered that he did not and further said that he didn't recall smelling any alcohol on Laird.

"Mr. Laird had to walk down two flights of stairs from your apartment, is that correct?"

"Yes."

"Did he stagger or did he sway?"

"Uh..no."

"Was he able to walk down those stairs without assistance?"

"Uh..yeah – I mean yes."

"Did Mr. Laird put on a helmet?"

"Yes."

"Did you help him put the helmet on?"

"No."

"Was he able to get onto the back of the motorcycle without help; was he able to maintain his balance?"

"Yes."

"Is it fair to say that Mr. Laird was not too drunk to do this?"

"Yes."

"It was pouring rain when you drove Mr. Laird home on your motorcycle, correct?"

"Yes."

"Is it fair to say that controlling a motorcycle in the rain is more difficult than when it is not raining and a passenger must be able to keep their balance?"

"Yes."

"And was Mr. Laird able to keep his balance on the back of your motorcycle?"

"Yes."

Michelle Henry skillfully and tactfully established through this witness's answers that Rick Laird was not impaired enough to warrant a valid diminished capacity claim. Laird was able to engage in activities or conversations that required at least a minimum degree of control of his mental faculties. Kerrigan's case was being blown to smithereens.

Under circumstances that would require both operator and passenger of a motorcycle to have complete control of their actions in a combined and coordinated effort to keep control of the bike, Richard Laird rode home in the dark and in pouring rain without a problem. Had Laird been impaired sufficiently to the degree the defense claimed regarding his state of mind, emotional and physical self control or lack thereof, in the murder of Anthony

Milano, he would not have been able to ride home on the back of a small sports bike without losing his balance and causing Rich Griscavage and himself to fall and dump the bike - particularly given the poor visibility of dark unlit back roads and a torrential rain. The amount of self-awareness and coordination needed to ride successfully as a passenger under such circumstances is exceptional. I don't know if anyone on that jury had ever driven or ridden on the back of a motorcycle, but even if they had not, Michelle Henry left them with a clear enough picture of what it entailed.

After Griscavage's testimony, the judge asked Michelle Henry and Robin Twombly how many more witnesses they planned to call before the end of the day. The prosecution was planning to call at least three more witnesses, all law enforcement officers, before court adjourned for the afternoon. This would be one of the longest days of the trial.

Michelle Henry called Detective Frank Dykes to the stand at 3:00 PM and he was sworn in. The tall, auburn-haired and clean-shaven detective was the chief detective for all of Bucks County, and he worked in the office of the district attorney. He had a distinguished and impressive career, and during the entire tenure of that career he said that he had never seen a homicide so visceral, barbaric and stupid.

He stated that he was present when Anthony Milano's body was removed from the crime scene. He noted the victim's personal effects, including $10.50 in cash and a pack of Salem cigarettes in the victim's pocket. He told the court about setting up the appointment with Chester for the wiretapped phone call to Richard Laird and that he had advised Frank Chester to otherwise have no contact whatsoever with Laird or anyone else connected with the case. The wiretapped call took place on December 20th 1987.

On December 22nd 1987, Dykes recounted accompanying the Falls Township police to the Falls Motel and arresting Rick Laird. He described Laird's demeanor as very nonchalant. Detective Dykes also emphasized that Frank Chester, Laird's co-defendant, had changed his story several times regarding the role he played in the murder. He recapped what Rick Laird said while in custody: "Are two rats better than one?" Effectively, Dykes' testimony further cemented the fact that Laird willfully and knowingly attempted to conceal information relating to the crime he committed.

Next witness was the lab director and crime scene investigator from New Jersey, now retired, who had been brought in to aid the Bucks County detectives in solving the crime. His name was Mr. McConnell. He described what was entailed in his processing of the pack of Kools for latent fingerprints. This was the same pack of Kools that had been found underneath Anthony Milano's body at the crime scene. Latent fingerprints are those which are not visible to the naked eye; a special light and lab equipment is required.

The technique he used in 1987 to look for latent fingerprints entailed use of an argon laser. He described that it was next to impossible to obtain fingerprints from any object that had come into contact with water or water soluble/water based solution. Fingerprints are 99% water to begin with. Fingerprints belonging to the killer that were on the pack of Kools were washed away from the rain.

After a short recess, Detective Bob Potts was sworn in. He was slender and distinguished, a tall bespectacled and clean-shaven man with silver hair. He was actually quite handsome. In his navy blue tailored suit, he looked more like a bank president than a detective. I would have guessed him at being no older than his late forties. It was only when he began enumerating his work history and credentials that I realized he was much older than he looked.

Detective Potts works with the Bucks County DA's office. He began his career in law enforcement with the Bensalem Police Department in 1972. Michelle Henry set up the laptop and projector screen once more to have Detective Potts identify the crime scene. Potts had overseen the wiretapped phone call between Frank Chester and Rick Laird in the presence of Detective Frank Dykes back in 1987.

Detective Potts held a Class A Electronic Surveillance license. Describing the legal technicalities involved with police wiretapping, he told the court that a "soft wire" – such as the one used in this case – required approval from the district attorney as well as consent of the party making the phone call. His testimony was brief and merely was introduced to show that based on the telephone conversation between Chester and Laird, Rick Laird certainly was not too mentally incompetent to discuss plans for beating polygraphs and splitting the state for seven years until the homicide went into a "dead case file". After Detective Potts' brief testimony, court was adjourned and scheduled to resume the next morning.

On Wednesday February 7th 2007, the first witness brought in was Frank Chester. He was a hostile witness, which means he refused to cooperate along any lines and he pled the 5th on everything the district attorney tried to ask him. Frank Chester simply replied politely but firmly that he was "sorry but he was invoking his Constitutional rights under the 5th Amendment". He was simply not going to answer any of Michelle Henry's questions. The Judge excused Frank Chester from the stand once it became obvious that he was not willing to testify to anything that might dually incriminate him and jeopardize his own appeal. It was probably a waste of time even bringing him in from Graterford State Prison to testify, but it was worth a shot.

The next witness sworn in was Gale Gardner. She had to be flown in from Florida to testify for the Commonwealth. She had light blonde hair and looked younger than her 38 years would have suggested. Michelle Henry directed her to focus on the events immediately before and after the murder. Ms. Gardner testified that Mark Laird, the defendant's brother, had called Barbara Anne's looking for Rick on December 14th 1987. While she wasn't privy to the entire phone call, she did remember that whatever was said had upset Barbara Anne. As to what happened after Rich Griscavage brought Rick Laird home, she remembered asking Rick where Frank was and that Rick had simply answered tersely, "He's OK."

She testified that when Rich Griscavage returned a few minutes later with Frank Chester and dropped him off at Barbara Anne's apartment, Barbara Anne had asked Frank what happened and that Frank responded, "Go get Rick up and get him to tell you." Gale Gardner also corroborated Barbara Anne's testimony about Rick putting his clothes into a trash bag. When Michelle Henry asked her if she recalled how much Rick Laird had to drink at Frank Chester's apartment before going to the bar and before the murder, Gale replied that she couldn't remember exactly. The incident had happened almost 20 years ago. Next, Michelle Henry asked the witness if she recalled Laird being drunk.

"When Mr. Laird entered the apartment, did he stagger or did he sway?"

"No."

"Did he slur his speech?"

“No.”

When Kerrigan cross-examined Gale Gardner, he questioned her sarcastically, “You don’t recall how much beer Mr. Laird drank 20 years ago, but you recall other significant details about that evening?”

“Ok. I would say maybe at least two cases of beer between the two of them”, Gale Gardner answered.

When she was asked why she, Rich Griscavage and the others went to look for Anthony Milano’s car, she replied that it was “out of morbid curiosity”. She stated that she and Frank Chester’s other friends were in a state of disbelief, and wanted to see if this had really happened.

After Gale Gardner stepped down, Judge Boylan called for the usual lunch time recess. My vegan acquaintance was joining me for lunch again. I noticed two shabbily dressed older women huddled on the bench next to the elevator in the lobby outside of the courtroom. Annamarie discreetly pointed towards one of the women and told me that she was Elaine Holley, the mother of Frank Chester.

“Are you going to try to talk to her? See what she says?” Annamarie asked me. “You know she’s going to insist that Frank is innocent. But he’s a psychopathic liar. So is Rick Laird.” I agreed. Annamarie asked me if I had ever communicated with Frank Chester while he was in prison and if I ever visited him. I told her that I did visit him once, but he wasn’t willing to talk to me about anything concerning the case. All he would say was that he didn’t do it: Laird did it. I shrugged, and Annamarie knew that I was not convinced of his innocence. “He *says* he’s innocent. But the operative word here is he *says* – and I am sure he would say anything if it would help him get his death sentence overturned,” I told Annamarie. But I was no longer the gullible young woman who had agreed to help Rick Laird.

I confessed to Annamarie that Chester did come off as somewhat believable, because he *did* show remorse for failing to stop the crime from occurring in the first place. That was a lot more than Rick Laird ever had done. I told Annamarie what Chester told me during that one visit I had with him: if he could change just one thing, he would do whatever he could to undo the murder, and that if he had one wish it would be that Anthony Milano would still be alive today.

Annamarie seemed to think Chester was merely blowing rose petals up my arse. That thought had also crossed my own mind more than once. After the experience of getting involved with Laird's appeals 12 years ago, I no longer believe anyone in prison is as innocent as they say they are. And of course, with all the publicity around this new trial for Laird, Chester would say anything to make himself look good.

I would like to believe Frank Chester was innocent because of the fact that even having just one monster is too much of an unpleasant reality to have to think about. But I was reconciled to the fact that innocent men do not behave the way Frank Chester did immediately after such a crime, and subsequently try to aid in the concealment of the crime. The fact that he referred to Anthony Milano as a "dead deer" when trying to borrow his buddy's car the next day to get rid of the *corpus delecti* was sufficient proof to me that Annamarie was right: Both men were cold-blooded psychopaths; both were monsters.

Annamarie told me, "Do you know that my brother would probably have died just from the beating alone had Laird not cut his throat? He was beaten up so badly, he would have been a vegetable, comatose. And Chester was the martial artist – and you heard the testimony about the injuries, the blows to his head? Frank Chester killed my brother just as much as Rick Laird did."

My stomach turned sour as I thought about what Annamarie shared with me because nobody deserved to experience what happened to her brother Anthony. To beat somebody up so badly that they would be better off dead is unconscionable. I didn't know which was worse: being a vegetable and so severely permanently disabled that one requires permanent nursing home care, or being dead. Still, I wanted to try to talk with Elaine Holley to get her story. In order to write about this case as accurately as humanly possible, I was obligated to give her the opportunity to tell things from her viewpoint as to what happened.

I approached her and she looked up at me suspiciously. When I asked her if she was Elaine Holley, Frank Chester's mom, she denied it. I carefully asked if she and her friend were here to observe the retrial of Rick Laird like I was. She answered, "No. We just happened to be in town and decided to stop by here because we were bored and wanted to see if anything interesting was going on here." It was the worst line of crap I ever heard in my life. She knew that *I* knew that she was lying through her teeth – although I couldn't prove it.

Neither she nor her friend looked to be well-off enough to simply go tooling around a stuffy "old money" town like Doylestown. Doylestown is not exactly the friendliest place in Pennsylvania to poor people or "outsiders". In fact, all you have to do is *look* poor and you will be treated rudely and denied service at businesses that are supposedly open to the general public.

I had found this out first hand. On the first day of the trial before I had unloaded all my gear at Michael's house in

Philadelphia, I had stopped for gas at a Gulf station. It was one of the full-service gas stations in the heart of Doylestown. I waited at the pump for service. While I waited, I noticed other cars and SUV's, mostly new luxury models that typically cost $40,000 or more, pull in at the pumps next to me where they were promptly served – while I sat there in my 12 year old Ford F-150 completely ignored. The attendant had seen me waiting there. He looked right at me as he walked past my truck to pump the gas for the other customers. There was no way he could have possibly not seen me waiting there. After about twenty minutes of waiting patiently to be served so I could get my empty dual gas tanks filled, I gave the horn a light tap. I was rudely ordered by the young attendant to take my business elsewhere. He snapped, "Go back where you belong. We don't need *your* kind in our town."

The message was clear: if you look like you're poor, even if you are white and well-behaved, you're not welcome in Doylestown – not even to buy gas. I drove off hoping to make it to the next gas station on my empty dual tanks. It was a bitter irony that the only time any of the poorer of Bucks County's citizens was welcome in Doylestown was if they had to go to the Bucks County courthouse to face a judge.

For the remainder of the trial, I made a very conscious effort to avoid buying even so much as one single lunch in Doylestown. As a matter of principle, I would rather go all day on nothing but a coffee –no matter how low my blood sugar dropped – before buying one morsel of food (or anything else for that matter) in Doylestown. Whenever I am staying in the Philadelphia region for any reason, I make it a point to patronize establishments that are anywhere *except* within the town limits of Doylestown. If I couldn't buy gas for my truck there, I surely don't want to buy a meal. With such blatant classism hanging so heavily in the air, I am sure Mrs. Holley would not have enjoyed visiting Doylestown "just for something to do."

A part of me could understand where Elaine Holley was coming from. She loved her youngest son. No mother wants to believe their son is a monster. No mother wants to spend the last part of her life being scrutinized and judged by society for being the mother of a homicidal maniac. Frank was her youngest child, the baby of the family. It was only this past Thanksgiving that she had almost lost her baby to the executioner's needle and poison cocktail. And that was right after her husband had died. I felt sorry for her. She had a story and it needed to be told, but if she wouldn't talk to me, I couldn't tell it for her.

Maybe she didn't want her story told. Maybe she was simply too embarrassed. Maybe she had just grown apathetic over the years. If I was treated shabbily in Doylestown as a friendly visitor who had just traveled several hundred miles across state to cover a trial when all I needed to do was refuel my truck, I can only imagine how Mrs. Holley, the mother of a convicted killer, would have been received by the people there.

After lunch and after court reconvened, the prosecution called Dr. Rafat Ahmad to the witness stand. Dr. Ahmad had a long and distinguished career in forensic pathology that spanned more than 30 years. She had even worked with the FBI labs in Quantico, Washington DC, and the Armed Forces. In 1987, Dr. Ahmad was a forensic pathologist with St. Mary's Hospital in Langhorne, a small community near Bristol in Bucks County.

Michelle Henry asked Dr. Ahmad to describe the injuries and cause of death of Anthony Milano to the jury. Her testimony was the same as it had been at the original trial in May of 1988. Anthony Milano had been beaten up badly before his throat was slashed. His skull was fractured and his brain had begun to swell in his head prior to his death. His head suffered blunt trauma damage, caused by some very powerful punches or kicks – coincident with the lethal force of a karate kick. She testified that Anthony Milano aspirated in his own blood and that had been the cause of death – when his throat was slashed and blood filled his trachea and entered his lungs. He drowned in his own blood. Dr. Ahmad also stated that Anthony Milano's death was such that he never had a chance and couldn't get away from his attacker. The first blow to his head would have knocked him senseless and the second could have knocked him unconscious. The two blows to Anthony's head were consistent with Rick Laird's ability to deliver hard punches. She also stated that it was very possible for all of this damage to be inflicted by one man, not necessarily two. Thus, it was very possible that Rick Laird – and no other – committed this assault and murder.

Rick Laird admitted he killed Anthony Milano, but was trying for a lesser sentence under a diminished capacity claim. But the jury wasn't buying it. Based on Dr. Ahmad's testimony alone, it was obvious that the man who attacked Anthony Milano wanted to hurt him, wanted to make him suffer before he died. And suffer he did. One of the pathology photos projected with the laptop Power Point slides showed a picture of a gauge measuring the depth of the wounds to the victim's throat. The victim, Dr. Ahmad explained, had been struck very forcefully and then slashed and slashed and slashed.

A box cutter or utility knife has a very short retractable blade, one that extends only about an inch from the shaft. To achieve the depth of such wounds with such a short blade, the attack had to go on for several minutes.

After Dr. Ahmad finished testifying, the judge explained to the jury that in light of Frank Chester being a hostile witness, she was going to allow the prosecutors, Michelle Henry and Robin Twombly, and an unidentified male district attorney, to read from the 1988 trial transcripts. Before allowing the prosecution to proceed, Judge Boylan instructed the jury: "You are to regard the following testimony of an accomplice as polluted as it came from a corrupted source."

Polluted as it was, it shed a lot of light on the character of Frank Chester – and on the calculating capabilities of a man who claimed diminished capacity 19 years later. Chester testified in 1988 that "the bartender [Jimmy Phillips, Jr.] knew me and knew Anthony Milano pretty well." Further testimony by Frank Chester stated that he "saw Rick Laird wash his hands at Richard Griscavage's apartment" immediately after the murder. Chester also answered DA Rubenstein when he said under oath in 1988 that the reason he went back to Laird's apartment after the murder was because "I wanted to find out what was going to happen, what to do."

Why would Chester need to turn to a man for guidance that was supposedly mentally incapable of premeditating a murder, a man whose thinking was too disorganized to have full control over his mental faculties? That doesn't make much sense. Why would Laird be in a position of deciding what the pair of them should do next? Unless, one can infer, that it was because Rick Laird's mental capacity was not as diminished as he was trying to claim.

After court adjourned, I waited for my vegan friend Tim to join me for a ride back to Philly. He was delightful and interesting company during long rush hour traffic jams and his thought-provoking conversation helped make the time pass faster. But he threw me for a loop when he began chatting about Frank Chester's brief appearance in court earlier that day.

He gushed like a teenage schoolgirl, "Oh my God! Did you get a good look at Chester? He is so cute! He's absolutely handsome! And what a sexy body – even in prison clothes! He doesn't belong on death row. He doesn't belong in prison. They should let him out and rehabilitate him."

Laughing and shaking my head, I told him that given Frank's proven record of being involved in a horrific gay-bashing murder, Frank Robert Chester is hardly suitable for the ideal date – for either a gay man or a straight woman. "So you think Frank Chester is just a poor, misunderstood convict who needs hugs instead of handcuffs?" I laughed. Having a captive audience – since we were crawling along at a snail's pace on I-76 westbound – I gave Tim a well-meaning and obviously long overdue lecture on the realities of life.

"Ok. What if he was as homely as a mud fence? Would you want to see him set free then? It doesn't matter how cute he is! Do you know *what* he is? Well, I'll tell you what he is, OK? Gee, this guy's drop-dead gorgeous and I wanna get into his pants – even if it means I might get the shit kicked out of me and knocked to the ground while Mr. Loverboy with his cute face and sexy ass stands by watching while his Neanderthal buddy takes a bigger chomp out of my throat with a knife than a Great White shark would. And after my mutilated corpse is left in some deserted, desolate field among weeds and mud, Mr. Dream Date discusses concealing the evidence that my murder even happened, referring to me as a "dead deer" that he needs to dispose of. Yeah, some sweetheart *he'd* make all right! Such an ideal date – not! Look, my older sister told me before she died that no piece of ass was worth dying for. Now that advice does not only apply to girls, or even to straight people in general – it applies to everyone who is out there looking for Mr. Goodbar, got it?"

Tim pleaded, "Oh, Jacqueline! You can't be *that* cynical. Please tell me you're not that jaded. Don't you think he can be rehabilitated? Don't you think that he can be reformed and live a productive life? Please tell me you believe in trying to reform someone who makes a mistake."

Beating someone to a pulp and refraining from stopping a murder is hardly what I would call a mistake. This guy was unreal! "Yeah – and a Great White shark would make a cute pool pet, too. After all, he's only a poor misunderstood big dumb carnivorous garbage can with fins and razor sharp regenerating teeth! But we can reform him so he doesn't bite your legs off, right? Just a few behavioral modification and anger management classes should fix him right up, make him into the perfect pet. He just needs to go for counseling."

I may be jaded and cynical, but the idealistic gay man riding shotgun in my truck to Philly was way too trusting for his own good. He found my rapier wit and sharp opinionated tongue amusing. I just hope some of what I told him sunk in so he would never have to learn the hard way. Nobody deserved to suffer what Anthony Milano suffered. But reality is that there are evil people in the world who simply don't care about anyone or anything. Monsters don't have three eyes, purple hair and protruding fangs and hide under our beds – they look just like you and me. Some of America's most vicious killers looked so very ordinary and harmless – like Jeffery Dahmer. Some looked too grandfatherly to be dangerous. Others were strikingly handsome like Ted Bundy. Just because somebody is cute, doesn't mean they aren't dangerous.

Tim pressed on, "Jackie – may I call you Jackie? You can't compare humans to sharks. Gay men see getting lucky with a straight man as sort of the ultimate thing. It's the forbidden fruit. It's sort of like always wanting that illusive dream liaison that you can't have. I think Anthony Milano saw Frank Chester as a chance to score with the forbidden fruit. He just didn't expect Chester's friend Rick Laird to kill him. And even with Rick Laird, I don't think he's beyond redemption."

Shaking my head I said, "OK, you're right: sharks have gills and fins and live in the ocean. Humans have lungs and live on land. But a predator is a predator. Like a Great White shark, Richard Laird was an opportunistic predator. Frank Chester may have been, as well. I understand the allure of the forbidden fruit. But do you realize that you could possibly be murdered horribly like poor Anthony Milano if you make a fatal error in judgment? As for redemption, there's something you need to understand. Once someone kills, it becomes easier for them to do it again. Didn't you notice Laird's ambivalence when the crime scene photos were being shown? Rick Laird had no sympathy for his victim 12 years ago. He still has no remorse today. Just think: that could have been *you* instead of Anthony Milano that rainy December night in 1987. Laird and Chester didn't care who they attacked that night. They were looking to raise hell."

I was nearing our exit, W. Girard Ave. I continued my lecture as I took the ramp to get off the expressway: "If Rick Laird has no remorse for what he did, no sympathy for his victim, how can he truly be reformed to the point where the rest of society would be safe if he should be released back into the community? He doesn't even feel any shame about taking money from his niece – Nicole Knox – a poor single mother who is battling cancer who needs every dime she's got for herself and her kids. What does *that* tell you? That's not being a predator?"

Tim Cwiek, that idealistic PGN reporter, meditated on everything I had to say. But he was still very much against the death penalty. I am no fan of it personally. I think it's a shame that there is even a need for it to begin with. I dropped my friend off at the 46th Street station, two blocks away from Michael's house. I hoped he would still be up so I could share the day's events with him.

Michael was snoozing comfortably on the couch with his feline friend Buster nestled in his armpit. Buster's adorable black face was poking out from beneath the blanket. Michael has a weird sleeping schedule. He sleeps in spurts and shifts, with a tendency to be night owl like me. I tip-toed into the kitchen to make a fresh pot of coffee, careful not to wake him. I really needed someone to talk to at that moment. I called to check in with my husband Donnie, and using Michael's laptop was able to process some premium payments and upload a policy from a new customer. I turned in and slept through until the next morning.

Chapter 21

"For all guilt is avenged on Earth." ~ Johann Wolfgang von Göethe

The defense called its expert witnesses for the guilt phase in preparation for the penalty phase beginning next week. Each had essentially the same thing to say about Rick Laird: he had brain damage, ADHD and cognitive deficits that were exacerbated by his alcohol consumption the night of the murder. Their testimonies were short.

One defense expert, Dr. Spike, testified that from speaking with those who had been with Laird during the hours leading up to the murder he estimated Laird's blood alcohol content to be around 0.45. A blood alcohol content of 0.45 is five times the legal limit. Since there was no way to get an accurate measurement of Laird's blood alcohol content the night of the murder, Dr. Spike's educated guess was the best estimate available.

The defense was relying mostly on the expert testimony of Dr. Robert Fox who had reviewed Laird's medical records over his years in prison and who had observed Laird at length.

"It is notable that Mr. Laird is disorganized in his thinking and has memory impairments and had difficulty answering questions about his childhood. He has problems with the executive functions of his brain and people with these problems tend to be impulsive. They also tend to use alcohol to relieve anxieties over their lack of control. Mr. Laird has permanent problems with his memory and couldn't spell the word "world" backwards."

Assistant DA Robin Twombly politely asked Dr. Fox if he had ever read Laird's testimony from the original trial transcripts back in 1988 where he recalled significant details about the night of the crime. Rick Laird remembered leaving the bar with his co-defendant Frank Chester and the victim Anthony Milano. He remembered exact roads that they took during the car ride, and specifics about stops made along the way before finally arriving at the murder scene. Dr. Fox replied he had not read about those.

In his closing arguments to the jury, Kerrigan asked them to put aside their feelings towards the graphic crime scene photos and directed them to focus instead on the basic elements of the crime.

"This is not a first degree murder simply because of its horrible nature. That is an argument that may appeal in a court of emotion, but should not appeal in a court of law." Kerrigan emphatically stated that Rick Laird killed Anthony Milano in a drunken frenzy but did not form the specific intent to kill before the act.

In her own closing statement to the jury, Michelle Henry strongly disagreed with Kerrigan's definition of "specific intent." The Pennsylvania Crime Code defines "specific intent" as something that can be formed in an instant, literally seconds before killing someone. She directed the jury to recall that despite Laird's alcohol consumption and brain damage, he was capable of engaging in activities that required full and total control over his faculties. If his capacity had been as diminished as the defense was trying to say, if his intoxication from alcohol was that overpowering, Laird would not have had any control over his faculties. He would have been falling down drunk; he would have been unable to think clearly enough to immediately begin concealing his crime by telling his co-defendant to "Shut up" and to wash his hands. He would not have discarded his bloody shirt immediately after the murder. He would have been unable to walk unaided up and down the two flights of stairs at Griscavage's apartment and he would not have been able to get onto the back of a motorcycle and ride home.

Michelle Henry told the jury, "To Frank Chester and Richard Laird, Anthony Milano was easy prey. He was smaller, he was quiet and he was different. They saw him and they were gonna play." Paraphrasing former DA Alan Rubenstein, Michelle Henry said, "He butchered him like a cheap piece of meat and left him there."

Judge Boylan instructed the jury to begin their deliberation and told them that they could break for lunch and then take the rest of the afternoon to reach a decision. Court was adjourned for the guilt determination phase. The penalty phase would begin after the jurors decided whether the degree of murder should be first degree or manslaughter.

Everyone except the jurors milled about leisurely in the lobby. Tim and I sat with Nicole Knox. She was fearful of what the verdict would be. Then Nicole did the most remarkable thing, a thing which must have really taken a lot of courage on her part. She walked over to Annamarie and Vito Milano and apologized to them for what her uncle had done to Anthony. She agreed with them that her uncle should not get off the hook, but felt that life in prison without parole was sufficient punishment. Annamarie graciously told the girl that she was not responsible for what her Uncle Rick had done and that she and her father appreciated the acknowledgement and apology. However, Annamarie had a very strong opinion, which she shared with me once Nicole Knox was out of hearing range.

"I hate to say it but I still think the death penalty would be fair. If Rick Laird gets life without parole, he can still have visits with his family and special holiday visitation rights and meals that my brother didn't get these past 19 years and never will get. My brother will never get to hold my hand or my father's hand and sit at the table with us. Why should Laird get Thanksgiving and Christmas dinners and be able to hug his family? That's not right." I fully agreed with the Milanos on that point. It wasn't right that Rick Laird should have those privileges. He deserved to be held accountable for what he did. Cable TV, a prison job, contact visits and holiday meals were not suitable justice in this case.

But there was something else that bothered me about a "life without parole" sentence. A killer sentenced to life without parole is usually put in the general prison population. There is always a chance that a killer serving a life sentence will kill another inmate, prison medical staff, or a guard. Killers who have already killed have indeed killed again while they're in prison. This is not an uncommon occurrence. Such was the case of Robert "Mudman" Simon.

Robert "Mudman" Simon was a vicious member of a notorious outlaw motorcycle gang known as The Warlocks. He had murdered his girlfriend Beth Dusenberg when she refused to cooperate in allowing Simon's fellow biker gang members to "pull a train on her", e.g., take successive turns raping her. While serving time in Graterford Prison for the murder of his girlfriend, "Mudman" stabbed a fellow inmate to death in 1984. He claimed it was self-defense.

He was released on parole for "good behavior" on February 18th 1995, despite the fact that he had killed twice. One of his parole conditions was that he had to refrain from having any contact with members of the Warlocks. "Mudman" blatantly violated that stipulation by promptly moving to Gloucester County, NJ – an area known to be heavily populated by the Warlocks. On

May 6th 1995, eleven weeks after his release on parole, Robert "Mudman" Simon and a fellow Warlock, Charles "Shovel" Staples, were pulled over in a routine traffic stop by police officer Ippolito "Lee" Gonzales. While Sgt. Gonzales waited politely for the men to produce their drivers' licenses and proof of registration and insurance, "Mudman" shot him in the neck and then fired a second bullet into the back of his head killing him – executioner's style.

Robert "Mudman" Simon was eventually tried and convicted of capital murder by the state of New Jersey. However, before the executioner's needle could reach his vein, "Mudman" was beaten to death by fellow death row prisoner Ambrose Harris in 1999: poetic justice.

While a part of me still feels uneasy about the existence of the death penalty because of the risk of an innocent person getting executed, the other part of me sees the need to ensure that psychopathic killers do not have the chance to kill anyone else ever again.

If Laird was in general population instead of in the restricted housing unit on death row, he would be in a position to kill another inmate and possibly even a guard or other prison staff who worked there. Plus he would be in a part of the prison where escape would be more likely. Prison escapes have not been an uncommon occurrence. Laird would not be in handcuffs and leg irons if he was out in the prison's general population. Convicts with lesser sentences than life have escaped, robbed people to get money, cars, and clothing and then killed their victims so that there would be no identifying witness. I shared those thoughts and that sentiment with Annamarie and her father, but I did not say so to Nicole Knox. There was nothing to gain by saying anything more that would be hurtful to her.

Nicole told me that she truly believed her uncle did not mean to do what he did that night and that he was sorry. "I *know* he's remorseful. My Uncle Rick is like a father to me. I have no one else in my family that I can turn to for anything. I don't want to see him die. Why can't he just be made to spend the rest of his life in prison? Killing my uncle won't bring back that poor man that he killed." That was true, but if her uncle was to be sentenced to death once again, it would not be because of people wanting revenge. People want to be safe. They don't want convicted murderers to have the opportunity to harm or kill another innocent person ever again. There is only one way to ensure that is never a possibility: the death penalty. Executed killers have a zero recidivism rate.

Keith Williams, the defense attorney assisting John Kerrigan, stood next to me. He told me that diminished capacity cases have always been very hard to prove, but he was more optimistic about the verdict than Laird's niece. However, his optimism was short-lived: the jury returned with their verdict in less than two hours, right before lunch time. Deliberations in capital murder trials that end in less than two hours are usually a bad sign for the defense and the defendant.

Twelve solemn jurors filed somberly into the jury box. Judge Boylan called for the jury foreperson to read the verdict.

"On the charge of first degree murder, we find the defendant guilty."

Nicole Knox put her head down on her arms on the back of the row of seats in front of her and sobbed. Judge Boylan announced that the penalty phase would begin on Monday, February 12th at 2:00 PM at which time the jurors would be asked to determine the appropriate sentence based on mitigating factors as well as aggravating factors.

When the penalty phase began, Judge Boylan addressed everyone present in the courtroom. "I realize that this is the most emotional phase of this trial. However, if anyone is talking during this proceeding they will be asked to leave and will not be allowed to return." Turning to face the jury, the judge stated, "Members of the jury, the sentence will depend on mitigating circumstances."

Michelle Henry began by explaining the difference between mitigating circumstances and aggravating factors. Aggravating factors are acts or omissions of acts that directly pertain to the crime and how the crime was committed. Mitigating factors are situations or conditions that may have been a contributing factor to the crime being committed. Provocation of the defendant by the victim, diminished mental capacity, coercion forcing the defendant to act against his or her will to commit the crime, these are examples of mitigating factors. The prosecution has the greater burden of proof in establishing the aggravating factors. Aggravating factors must be proved absolutely whereas mitigating factors must be shown by the defendant by preponderance.

Addressing the jury, Michelle Henry began her opening statement: "Not every first degree murder is a capital case in Pennsylvania. Because Anthony Milano was taken against his will by Frank Chester and Rick Laird, there is the aggravating factor of kidnapping. Because of what Anthony Milano suffered, the second aggravating factor of torture applies. The defendant has been convicted of kidnapping by removing Anthony Milano a substantial distance with the intent to do bodily harm, from, in this case, the Edgely Inn. The second aggravating factor is this murder was committed by means of torture. They went beyond killing. His throat was cut over and over and over again."

Kerrigan sat quietly, letting his co-counsel, Keith Williams, address the jury. Pacing slowly back and forth in front of the jury, Attorney Williams spoke with intensity, "There is no excuse for what happened here – none. Mitigation is not an excuse. Anthony Milano did not deserve to die. We're not asking you to discount Anthony Milano's life. Richard Laird did not have a great childhood. You heard before about his alcohol abuse and his mental problems. He was sexually abused by his father. Richard Laird will spend the rest of his life in prison. It is for you to decide how long that will be."

One of the defense witnesses who had been called to give mitigating testimony was Mark Laird. He remembered me as he looked at me, and then quickly averted his gaze as he passed by me on his way to the witness stand. He told the jury that his parents met while they were in the Marine Corps in South Carolina and described his and Rick's childhood as "not normal." In a blunt manner laced with expletives, he recounted a childhood of beatings and abuse at the hands of Richard Laird, Sr. The Laird family history was a history of violence.

"When my father snapped his fingers like this," he said while demonstrating a sharp snap of his fingers for the jury, "you had better know what was expected of you or you got your ass beat and that's it. He hit us with either a military belt with holes in it, or he would thump you on the head with his large, gold Marine Corp ring. He hit Rick harder than he hit me." Mark also recounted how he and Rick were not allowed to make a lot of noise as children, and not allowed to run about and play normally. He also described seeing his mother beaten and raped by his father.

Describing the sexual molestation of Rick by their father, Mark recalled wanting to go into the bedroom he and Rick shared and where their toys were because he wanted to play with his brother. But he wasn't allowed in because their father was sexually assaulting Rick. "I remember crying. I know they were naked. I was not allowed in and I did not understand why."

"I remember my father would beat the shit out of our mother. I remember waking up to the noise, and me and Rick would go see and we would see him beating our mother violently. When the beatings got bad enough, she finally got the balls to leave." Mark continued, saying that Rick, his mother, and he moved to PA from the south when he was nine and Rick was thirteen. His testimony, peppered with slang and profanity, put several spectators in the courtroom off and probably the jury as well. He continued, however, describing how Rick suffered a blow to his head when he was hit with a 2X4 at a high school graduation party by the father of the kid throwing the party. In recalling how Rick never drank moderately, rather always in extremes, he described Rick as getting "shit-faced and passing out." If Mark's testimony of childhood abuse and head injuries was supposed to elicit sympathy from the jury, it did not appear to be working.

The defense called Deacon James Shield. The deacon was a member of The Ministry of Charity & Justice, a group of church volunteers that bring communion to inmates unable to attend the main service in general population because they are on death row. He told the jury that Rick Laird had converted to Catholicism while in prison and had received the sacraments.

"I would give him communion each week and we would talk about the scriptures of the Bible. He was able to bring faith into his life."

Kerrigan called Sgt. Martin Saunders, one of the prison guards who knew Rick Laird from working as a guard on death row. He testified that Laird had earned, by reason of his good behavior, a job on the death row cell block of mopping the floors.

"Not every inmate gets a job. Mr. Laird never had any disciplinary actions and only one or two minor write-ups."

Michelle Henry countered, "In the past 6 years you've been in contact with the defendant, there have been *no* misconducts, correct?"

Sgt. Saunders affirmed that was correct, no misconducts.

"Are you aware that he smoked where not permitted?"

"No."

"So you don't recall the 15 times items had to be taken out of his cell? Is it fair to say that?"

"You can get items confiscated for a number of reasons."

No criminal trial would be complete without mention of the act of smoking cigarettes being thrown into the mix. The case had been easily proven against Laird without having to add *that*.

The second prison guard called to testify on Laird's behalf about his good behavior was Capt. John Warner who stated that his job was the "care and custody and control of the inmates." He described Laird as a "very caring person, very respectful of others." The defense asked Capt. Warner how hard to was to get and keep a prison job.

"You are under scrutiny at all times. You have to be strong-willed and be able to take a lot of heat. It ain't something that's given to you – you have to earn that."

Michelle Henry countered, "Are you aware of what he did to Anthony Milano? Is it fair to say that *that* was not caring?"

In her closing statement to the jury, she reiterated what the aggravating factors were: torture and kidnapping. Kidnapping, according to the definition of the Pa Criminal Code, is where *the victim is removed a substantial distance to a place he or she does not want to be*. She asked the jury to consider Anthony Milano's final moments; how scared he must have been when Rick Laird forced him to drive to a desolate, secluded wooded lot, dragged him from the car, beat him up and then came after him with the box cutter.

"If, at that point, he could imagine what Richard Laird had in store for him, I am sure that it was a fear that I cannot describe."

Michelle Henry did not see the same evil that Anthony Milano saw, and that I subsequently saw. She did not have to. She knew from all accounts of this case that Rick Laird was a monster. In court, Rick Laird was well-behaved and carried himself like a banker or a CEO and refrained from displaying that look that could kill. But I knew the truth – I had seen the other Rick Laird, the monster, the killer who would probably kill again if the season was ripe and he had the chance. Of that truth I had no doubt. The jury obviously knew the truth, too.

The day before Valentine's Day 2007 dawned with a gray, stormy winter sky. A snow storm was moving in. The snow began falling steadily without showing signs of letting up as people arrived. Judge Boylan considered excusing the jury for the day so that they would not risk any difficulties with driving in a snow storm. But the jury returned after deliberating for just four hours: the verdict was death. They too, had seen the eyes of a monster in Rick Laird's visage.

Chapter 22

"Search for truth is the noblest occupation; its publication, a duty." ~ Madame de Stael

Vito Milano walked with his daughter silently through the falling snow. Justice had been served. Some of the jurors approached the Milanos to shake Vito's hand. With tears welling up in his eyes, Vito Milano hugged the jurors, thanking them for the justice they had given.

Now that the trial was finally over, the gag order was lifted. District Attorney Diane Gibbons and her husband, Detective Frank Dykes, were elated with the outcome. "I hope our system does not let this family down a second time and now actually executes the defendant." Detective Dykes agreed, stating "I was the one who pointed a gun at Richard Laird nineteen years ago when I arrested him. Now he is finally going back to death row where he belongs."

A courthouse secretary who asked that she not be named told me that she had observed the trial of Richard Laird and Frank Chester 19 years before. She told me that Richard Laird was purely evil then, just as he was purely evil that day when I looked into his eyes – the day I asked him if he had any sympathy for the victim. Laird is still evil today. No one and nothing can ever convince me otherwise.

Detective Dykes asked me how it was that I got conned into giving any of my time to investigate this case 12 years ago. I concisely recounted how Mark Laird told me that his brother had been railroaded.

I struggled to find the words to convey what I was feeling. "The problem is that all we ever hear about are the district attorneys who commit wrongdoing in order to win, of policemen who arrest the wrong guys, and of the wrongfully convicted whose rights were trampled on. But what people do *not* hear about are the monsters that are guilty as hell. That is something I found out the hard way. This experience has given me a lot more respect for what police and prosecutors have to do in order to protect society – me included – from monsters just like Richard Laird."

Diane Gibbons asked me how I felt about the death penalty now. I told her that I was not in favor of it – until the case of Robert "Mudman" Simon. The recidivism rate for homicidal maniacs who get the death penalty is zero. When there is no way to absolutely guarantee that admittedly guilty and remorseless killers cannot harm or kill again there isn't much of a choice. Michelle Henry was standing by listening silently. I told the group that Michelle Henry was an exemplary DA. She beamed with appreciation for the compliment. It's not too often prosecutors ever get praised or appreciated for the work they do. Usually, they are criticized and looked upon with suspicion and scrutiny.

I believe the public needs to know about the Michelle Henrys, the Robin Twomblys and the Diane Gibbonses instead of only hearing about the occasional bad apples and mistakes that the death penalty opponents hold up as reasons to overturn sentences and convictions.

I told Michelle Henry and Diane Gibbons that no higher court in this land can ever come back and point the finger at Judge Boylan or at them and cry foul that Richard Laird didn't get a fair trial this time around. No one in their right mind could ever say that. If that should ever occur again in *this* case, justice and all that is right would be mocked.

Laird was given every opportunity to present his case. No stone was left unturned. Michelle Henry was an exceptionally gracious district attorney who did not resort to hot-dog antics in court in order to win the case against Laird. No vital evidence was withheld from the defense or the jury. No inflammatory theatrics had been engaged in. It was not an easy case for her to prosecute considering the daunting task of tracking down witnesses after 19 years, but she did it and she did it with a civility and grace that was unparalleled. Michelle Henry played by the rules, went strictly by the book, and she won fair and square. We as a society, as law-abiding citizens, won as a result: for justice had been served. Richard Laird would be one less monster walking among us.

It was too cold to stand outside the courthouse and chat for too long. I had a long drive back to Philadelphia to Michael's where I would remain for another few days with the hope that I could interview Elaine Holley and a few of the other witnesses now that the gag order was lifted. However, I would wait a day or two until the winter storm let up.

On my way back to Philadelphia, traffic crawled along in a snow storm whose intensity had increased. I could not help but think that Laird's sentence was one hell of a Valentine – for *him*. I just hoped for the Milanos' sake that Rick Laird would not come back 20 years from now with another overturned sentence and an order for a *third* trial. It was bad enough that the Milanos might have to suffer through a retrial of Frank Chester after having just gone through this with Richard Laird. Chester has appeals in process.

Richard Laird is definitely a monster. He may have admitted to murdering Anthony Milano, but I sincerely doubt that he will ever feel remorse for it. He never has. How Laird's admission to murdering Milano will affect Frank Chester's appeal remains to be seen. As of the writing of this book, Frank Chester has not yet received a new trial, nor has he been exonerated from any of the charges connected with the murder of Anthony Milano. Chester still maintains that he is innocent. Maybe he is. I doubt, however, that his innocence is 100%. Only one man could tell us for sure if Frank Chester was innocent and unfortunately, he is the one man who will never be able to walk into a courtroom and tell anyone what really happened in the woods that night. Anthony Milano's voice had been silenced forever that fatal night in 1987.

When the snow finally let up over the weekend, I drove to Bristol, PA to visit Elaine Holley in Tullytown. It was a forty minute drive from Philadelphia, located along US Rte 13, right off of I-95, a stone's throw from New Jersey.

It was a crisp, cold, sunny winter Saturday morning. Tullytown is a quaint little hamlet between Levittown and Bristol. It looks exactly like one of those model toy towns that come with model train sets. The tiny streets seemed more like driveways than roads. The house where Frank Chester grew up and where his mother still lives is on Lovett Street. It's a frame split-level house with yellow-goldenrod colored siding. On the sidewalk in front of Elaine Holley's house there was an antique, very old fashioned, gas pump with its inner mechanisms removed. It had been re-fabricated into an unusual mail box. It was definitely one of a kind. The house appeared to have been split up into four tiny apartments, evidenced by the four separate electrical meters mounted on the side by the chain link fence. I nervously wondered what I should say if Mrs. Holley should answer the door.

After hearing the testimony read from the 1988 trial and after reading the trial transcript copy I had, I was still unsure as to the degree of Frank Chester's culpability. From all other accounts, I knew that Frank Chester's mother believed her youngest boy to be totally innocent. But there was a nagging hunch in the pit of my stomach that haunted me and forced me to conclude that Elaine Holley's boy was not totally innocent.

A totally innocent man, however young and immature, would not have accompanied a vicious, knife-wielding monster back to his apartment and slept there. He could have gotten Rich Griscavage to give him a ride straight to the Bristol Police Department instead. Fear of an out-of-control monster should have overridden any fear of a possible jail sentence, if Frank Chester was indeed caught between the devil and the deep blue sea. Was it fear? Was it teenage stupidity? Was it shock and denial? Nothing is ever as it appears.

But there was also the testimony from those present in Chester's apartment the day after the murder where Chester was more preoccupied with extricating himself from any involvement in the crime – even contemplating the destruction of evidence, including the victim's body – in asking to borrow a car to get rid of the "dead deer". Actions of an innocent man?

However, from the face-to-face visit I'd had with Chester at Graterford the week before Laird's retrial, I found some things pointing in Chester's favor. For one, he showed a genuine remorse that Anthony Milano had been killed and he had given me the impression that he wished with all sincerity that he could undo the events that culminated in Anthony Milano's murder.

For another, he also seemed secure enough about his own sexual identity that he was not uncomfortable with having friends who were gay. This makes him an unlikely candidate for engaging in a brutal anti-gay motivated murder. One such friend and supporter is a man named Jim Jenkins who gave an eloquent speech and said this about Frank Chester:

"Once Frank finished his story and I looked into eyes. I could see the 19 year old boy who was still lost in the woods and yet I also saw the eyes of a 27 year old man whose life has been senselessly taken away from him. I walked away from Frank believing him. If you had journeyed with me through the same hell Frank described, you would understand today how innocent he is. Because he was young, naive, poor and ignorant of his rights, he was offered up by the District Attorney as some sort of sacrificial lamb."

The speech in its entirety is available online at http://fishfoodministries.com/speech.html on behalf of Frank Chester at an anti-death penalty event in Philadelphia. Mr. Jenkins also maintains a website at http://www.kmf.org/chester/ which tells Frank Chester's version of the story from his viewpoint.

It turned out that I would never get Elaine Holley's side of the story. If she was home, she wasn't answering her door. Disappointed, I had no choice but to turn around and head back to Philly. I would be having another filet dinner with Michael at our favorite pub, the Mill Creek Tavern, and spend another evening enjoying political discussions with Michael and the Mill Creek's wonderfully opinionated owner, Jack Gillespie.

The Richard Laird case has forever changed my view on justice, on the trustworthiness of people and on life in general. I think of my eccentric but brilliant author friend and his smoking ban activism and his penchant for imbibing at late night bars. I worry about his safety – with good reason. Like Anthony Milano, my friend Michael is a very slender man and definitely not the brawling type. He is a gentle, soft-spoken and well-educated man who believes in verbally resolving differences and walking away from physical confrontations, avoiding them altogether. He would have no chance against a psychopath the size of Richard Laird.

I know from this case that there are monsters that walk among us. Monsters that could possibly hurt and kill someone I care about. Just as with the prejudice that homosexuals often face, smokers and those championing smokers' rights are publicly vilified. Like gay men such as Anthony Milano and Matthew Shepard, smokers and smokers' rights activists like Michael have been targeted for physical assaults and harassment. Recently, a pregnant 18 year old was shot in an Alabama supermarket parking lot. The gunman said shot her because he was enraged at the idea that she was smoking while pregnant. Smokers have been the target of "hate crimes." The only difference is that sexual orientation is defined as a protected class under the law, while being a smoker is not. Society still has a long way to go in the tolerance department.

After a delightful meal and discussion with Michael and Jack Gillespie about private property rights, I slept one last night on the cot in Michael's living room. The next morning I packed my laptop, all of my trial notes, my clothes, and my traveler's Starbucks coffee stash. It was time to drive across state back to my home in Erie, in the northwestern-most corner of the state. I had an 8 hour drive ahead of me, taking bathroom breaks and refueling stops into account.

During my long drive home, I examined my own position on the death penalty. The long drive gave me plenty of time to reflect. I am still not completely sure of where I stand. There are indeed monsters out there that should not have the slimmest chance of ever escaping prison and killing anyone else. If monsters like Rick Laird are executed, there is no chance that they will ever get out of prison and harm someone else, and no possibility that they will harm others inside of the prisons either. But problems with the death penalty persist and they are too compelling to be ignored.

For every Richard Laird, there are many innocent people wrongfully convicted and sentenced to death. For every Richard Laird, there are innocent people like Leo Frank, Dr. Jay C. Smith, Ray Krone, Nick Yarris, Kerry Max Cook, William Neives, and Dennis Counterman. In the cases of Nick Yarris and Ray Krone, DNA and other improved forensics science methods proved conclusively that these men were not guilty. But both Ray Krone and Nick Yarris lost irreplaceable time from their lives, languishing on death row until they finally were allowed to have the DNA tests that ultimately proved their innocence.

Ray Krone spent 10 years on Arizona's death row before being exonerated and freed in April 2002 after DNA proved that Kenneth Phillips, ironically a witness against Krone, was indeed the murderer of cocktail waitress Kim Ancona. Nick Yarris languished on Pennsylvania's death row for 22 years before he was finally permitted to have DNA testing which proved him innocent in the murder of 33 year old Linda Craig in 1981. Nick Yarris is married and living in Great Britain today with his wife and baby. Amazingly, after 22 years on death row he was able to get a new lease on life, finding love and having a family of his own. But DNA is only an appropriate tool in some capital cases – in others it has no bearing at all.

If someone stands accused of murder that lived in the same house as the victim, DNA would not be of much help – as in the case of Dennis Counterman. Dennis Counterman was convicted and sentenced to death in 1990 for setting fire to his house in Allentown, killing his three children and severely injuring his wife Janet Counterman. Both Counterman and his wife have very low IQ's and learning disabilities. During Counterman's appeal process, his attorneys found that former Lehigh County DA Richard Tomsho withheld vital evidence proving Counterman's innocence from the defense in 1990. Richard Tomsho now has a cushy job with the State Attorney General's Office. His reward for breaching the integrity of the justice system was a successful move up the career ladder where he now works with Attorney General Tom Corbett, presumably for a much higher salary than what he earned as a prosecutor in Lehigh County when he prosecuted Dennis Counterman.

One major piece of evidence showed that one of Counterman's children – who were also learning disabled – had a history of fire-setting. After spending over 16 years on death row, Counterman's appeal was picked up by Attorney Robert Dunham of the Defenders Association. After hearing the appeal, Judge Brenner of Lehigh County awarded Counterman a new trial, finding that Counterman had not received a fair trial in 1990. In 2006, the Lehigh County District Attorney's Office realized its precarious position and offered Counterman an Alford plea – a plea similar to a *nolo contendre* insofar as it does not admit guilt but concedes that the prosecution has enough evidence to possibly convict. Alford pleas, named for the precedent 1970 US Supreme Court case <u>*Alford v. North Carolina*</u>, allow defendants to enter such a plea when they do not want to admit guilt but are willing to accept this alternative because it is in their best interest. While this allowed for Dennis Counterman to be released immediately as a free man without having to go through another trial, an Alford plea does not clear his name. A condition of his release is that he is to have no contact whatsoever with his estranged wife. He will also have similar terms to abide by as other regular parolees: report for urine tests on a regular basis and notify the parole officer in the event of any change in employment or residence.

But parolees don't make out as badly as those who are completely exonerated. Exonerees face more problems than the guilty that end up released on parole. There is no help out there for exonerees in most states. Some states do not even provide for remuneration or recompense to those wrongfully convicted and wrongfully sentenced. There is no shortage of social services for ex-cons on parole. Generous tax credits and wage subsidies encourage employers to hire them, thus putting law-abiding job seekers or exonorees at a disadvantage. Parolees also get free counseling, temporary housing and job placement assistance.

Exonerees are lucky to get a change of clothes, a bus ticket, and an apology in Pennsylvania. After spending years – even decades – in prison, exonerees are unable to get jobs. Nobody wants to hire you when you have a gap in your work history spanning a year, much less ten or twenty years — regardless of the reason. With no means to support themselves, exonerees have to move in with relatives – if they have any — who are willing and able to financially support them. If they don't, they end up as homeless beggars and vagrants. Meanwhile, those responsible for prosecutorial misconduct and the wrongful convictions that ruined innocent people's lives go unpunished. When caught for misconduct, they are not even barred from the practice of law! There currently is no accountability.

The scope of prosecutorial misconduct is significant enough that the US Supreme Court is calling for change and more accountability on the part of prosecutors. In writing the opinion for the majority in the US Supreme Court ruling on the Delma Banks case which entailed prosecutorial concealment of vital evidence from the defense, US Supreme Court Justice Ruth Bader-Ginsburg stated, "A rule thus declaring 'prosecutor may hide, defendant must seek', is not tenable in a system constitutionally bound to accord defendants due process."

While Diane Gibbons, Michelle Henry and Robin Twombly are decent district attorneys with integrity and high regard for playing by the rules, there are many others that unfortunately are not. Those who suffer are not only those wrongly convicted, but also the victims and the victims' families who suffer as well because justice was denied.

We all suffer when innocent people are punished while the guilty go free. Monsters should not be able to roam freely, preying on the public seeking their next victim because of systemic flaws. If more district attorneys adhered to the standards of taking the higher ground as Michelle Henry did in the trial of Richard Laird, more people would have faith that the justice system was one that we can all believe in.

I thought about all of these things during my long drive. Heading west on I-80, the skies were starting to clear as the snow storm clouds lifted. Shades of orange and mauve splashed across the sky among the wispy clouds as I headed towards home where the sun was setting in the western sky.

Acknowledgements

I am indebted to many sources of information connected with my work for this book, especially the following:

NEWSPAPERS:

In Bucks County, PA, *The Courier Times, The Trentonian*

In Philadelphia, PA, *The Inquirer*

MAGAZINES:

"Killing Anthony" by Lisa DePaulo, *Philadelphia Magazine, 12/88, 01/89*

MISCELLANEOUS ARTICLES:

"Wrongly Convicted Walk Away With Scars" by Stephanie Armour, *USA Today*

"Emotional Problems in Adults With Learning Disabilities" by Dr. Sam Golstein, Ph.D.

INTERNET:

"Blind Privilege" by Jennifer Kesler, http://www.com/white-trash-blues-class-privilege-v-white-privilege/

"Blind Justice Report" by Richard C. Deiter, http://www.deathpenaltyinfo.org/BlindJusticeReport.pdf

"Treatment of ADHD" http://www.LDAAmerica.org

"Facts About the Death Penalty in Pennsylvania" http://www.cpadp.org/facts.html

RECORDS AND TRANSCRIPTS:

Transcripts of the trial proceedings and testimony, Commonwealth of Pennsylvania vs. Richard Laird & Frank Chester

Transcripts of the appellate court ruling and opinion, Richard Laird vs. Martin Horn

BOOKS:

Kidnap by George Waller, 1961

Principal Suspect by William Costopoulos, 1996

Engaged to Murder by Loretta Schwartz-Nobel, 1987

The Encyclopedia of Modern Murder by Colin Wilson & Donald Seaman, 1988

Murder in Greenwich by Mark Fuhrman, 1998,1999

Zodiac by Robert Graysmith, 1976

The Status Seekers by Vance Packard, 1959

The Leo Frank Case by Leonard Dinnerstein, 1987

CPSIA information can be obtained at www.ICGtesting.com
Printed in the USA
BVOW03*1655230514

354142BV00003B/345/P

9 780981 567921